Texas: New Perspectives

Texas:
New Perspectives

by June Rayfield Welch

University of Dallas

EDITORIAL CONSULTANT: Ann Fears Crawford

Steck-Vaughn Company Austin, Texas

An Intext Publisher

58254

JUNE RAYFIELD WELCH is chairman of the Department of
History at the University of Dallas. He is the author of
several books and of articles on law and history.

ANN FEARS CRAWFORD, former research associate at the Institute of Texan Cultures, is the author of numerous articles
in the field of Texas history. She is a graduate student in
American Studies at The University of Texas.

ISBN 0-8114-3917-8

Copyright © 1972 by Steck-Vaughn Company, Austin, Texas

Printed and bound in the United States of America

Preface

Texas: New Perspectives was written for a unique audience, the high school students of the last third of the twentieth century. The book tries to tell, for its time, the long, proud story of the Texas experience.

As the student of this era is different from his predecessors, so does this book differ from earlier Texas history texts. The emphasis is on the Texas of this century. The book is divided into two parts. The first, "Texas's Cultural Foundation," provides the background for the main story. It surveys those beautiful and colorful times of the conquistadores, the early Texians, the Indians, the longhorns, and the badmen. It treats of a Texas just being made inhabitable. The second part, "The Dynamic Century," tells how the Texans have lived in their state. It tries to show the economic, social, and political developments with which the student will have to contend during the balance of the century.

Throughout an attempt has been made to demonstrate that Texas was built by people from all over the world, that the Texas culture of today is really a blending of many cultures made richer by virtue of the diversity of origins of the Texans.

In addition an effort has been made to put Texas history into context, to show what was happening in Texas in relation to events occurring elsewhere in the nation and the world.

This approach was intended to give the student a view of history more attuned to his time. Hopefully he will find something of himself and his ancestors here, and it will enhance his pride in himself, in his state, and in his people.

The author is indebted to all those who made this book possible. The assistance of personnel at the Institute of Texan Cultures is especially appreciated.

JUNE RAYFIELD WELCH

Table of Contents

List of Maps

Part 1

TEXAS'S
CULTURAL FOUNDATION

1490 1495 1500 1505 1510 1515 1520 1525 1530 1535 1540 1545 1550 1555 1560 1565 1570 1575 1580 1585 1590 1595 1600 1605 1610 1615 1620 1625 1630 1635 1640 1645 1650 1655 1660 1665 1670 1675 1680 1685 1690 1695 1700 1705 1710 1715 1720

COLUMBUS DISCOVERS AMERICA

DE VACA ENTERS TEXAS

FRENCH FOUND FORT ST. LOUIS

SPANISH FOUND SAN ANTONIO

The University of Texas, Institute of Texan Cultures at San Antonio

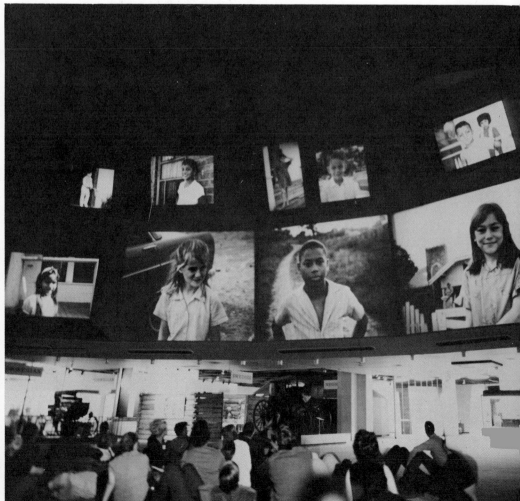

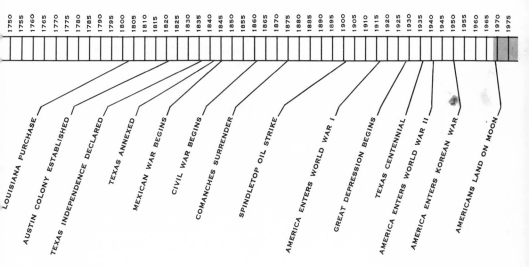

1750 1755 1760 1765 1770 1775 1780 1785 1790 1795 1800 1805 1810 1815 1820 1825 1830 1835 1840 1845 1850 1855 1860 1865 1870 1875 1880 1885 1890 1895 1900 1905 1910 1915 1920 1925 1930 1935 1940 1945 1950 1955 1960 1965 1970 1975

LOUISIANA PURCHASE

AUSTIN COLONY ESTABLISHED

TEXAS INDEPENDENCE DECLARED

TEXAS ANNEXED

MEXICAN WAR BEGINS

CIVIL WAR BEGINS

COMANCHES SURRENDER

SPINDLETOP OIL STRIKE

AMERICA ENTERS WORLD WAR I

GREAT DEPRESSION BEGINS

TEXAS CENTENNIAL

AMERICA ENTERS WORLD WAR II

AMERICA ENTERS KOREAN WAR

AMERICANS LAND ON MOON

CHAPTER 1

"The Land of Beginning Again"

From the start Texas was, as Judge Julien Hyer called it, "The Land of Beginning Again." Men from many countries came—one by one, in groups, and later in waves of immigrants. They came searching for many things—for gold, for adventure, for freedom from oppression. But mostly they came for the land, which was rich in promise. Some moved on, seeking Cíbola, Quivira, or just elbow room. Many stayed and adapted, changing the land and in turn being changed by it. They brought with them their cultural traditions, knowledge, and beliefs. They brought skills and arts, languages, and lore. They brought their customs, institutions, and attitudes. Each culture left an imprint on the state. Many times these cultures

1

Senator Barbara Jordan represents Houston in the state legislature.

were in conflict, and the Texas of today is shaped in part by the resolutions of those conflicts.

The Spaniards came as early as 1519, seeking first the treasures of the East and later the Seven Cities of Cíbola and the golden land of Quivira. To the Spanish conquistadores, we owe the horse culture of the Southwest. Before the Spanish conquest, North America knew no domestic animal except the dog. Horses, cattle, sheep, and goats came with, or after, the conquistadores. With the horse, the Indian became a formidable foe.

Brown-robed friars brought the Christian religion to the Indians of Mexico and Texas. The conquistador subjugated the land and the people. The padres of the missions brought civilization to New Spain. The Spanish influence in Texas survives today in religion, festivals, songs, dances, and especially in the names of places and landmarks. The Spanish love for grandeur and ornamentation is reflected in the lavish decoration and tracery windows of the missions of Texas.

The first Negro came to Texas with the Spaniards in 1528.

2

Esteban, a Moor from North Africa, was a member of the Narváez expedition and was shipwrecked on the Texas Gulf Coast. He learned to converse with the Indians and led Spanish explorers in search of the Seven Cities of Cíbola.

Other Negroes played important roles in the development of Texas. Hendrick Arnold settled in Texas in 1826 and fought at San Antonio and at the Battle of San Jacinto. Matt Gaines and G. T. Ruby were among those who served in the Texas legislature, and Norris Wright Cuney was for years the leader of the Republican party in Texas. Barbara Jordan of Houston is today a member of the Texas Senate. Negroes serve their state as educators, physicians, and merchants and businessmen. Not the least of the Negro influences in Texas has been his contribution to the field of music. Spirituals, folk songs, blues, and soul music reflect Negro attitudes toward religion, life, and society.

Negroes proved to be excellent horsemen and soldiers. On the frontier in Texas, cowmen said that a man was measured not by his color but by whether he could work cattle and handle horses. Al Jones and Daniel Webster Wallace were top cowhands in a state that produced the best.

Three English sailors visited Texas in 1568, and David Ingram's description of Texas's "Great and fayre Plains" stirred English interest in the area. Later colonization efforts were attempted, and the town of Hallettsville was named for the family of John Hallett, the son of an English nobleman who settled at Goliad in 1817. The settlers from the United States brought to Texas a system of government with English roots and laws and courts based on the English common law.

The British Isles sent other native sons. Irishmen died with James Fannin at Goliad, and more than one hundred Irishmen marched with Houston's forces at San Jacinto. The Irish contributed one of Texas's major artists, Henry A. McArdle, who painted many Texas heroes and scenes of the battles at the Alamo and at San Jacinto. A wealthy Scotsman, Robert Hamilton, signed the Texas Declaration of Independence and journeyed to Washington to help establish relations between the United States and the Republic of Texas. In 1839 Neil McLennan surveyed and settled in the county that bears his name.

Sword dancing is one of many traditional activities engaged in at the annual Scottish gathering in Austin.

The tartans of Scotland perform each year in Salado and Austin in token of the many Scottish immigrants who became Texans.

A love of adventure and desire for land characterized the German immigrants to Texas. A letter written by Frederick Ernst to his homeland in 1831 inspired hundreds of Germans to journey to Texas seeking new homes. Ernst named his German settlement Industry, and the name typifies the German settlers of such Texas towns as New Braunfels and Fredericksburg. Early travelers in Texas were impressed by the neatly kept German towns and homes and the friendliness of the people. German singing societies, bands, and chamber music ensembles were usually part of each town, and many well-educated German doctors and scientists, such as Dr. Ferdinand Herff and the paleontologist Ferdinand von Roemer, contributed to the scientific knowledge of early Texas.

Americans might never have been able to establish Texas colonies if it had not been for a native of Holland. The Baron de Bastrop, Felipe Neri, aided Moses Austin in his attempts to gain permission from the Spanish governor of Texas to bring settlers to the region, and he later served as commissioner of colonization for Austin's colony. Although the Dutch settled only one permanent town, Nederland, their contribution to Texas was substantial. Robert Onderdonk, his son Julian, and his daughter Eleanor were fine painters of landscapes and portraits.

New Sweden, East Sweden, Swedonia, Palm Valley, and Swenson were settled by Swedes. The University of Texas has profited from Swedish immigrant Sir Svante Palm's donation of his library of ten thousand books. Dr. Johan A. Udden's mineral survey of the university's lands served as a basis for oil exploration and production on these holdings. Svante Magnus Swenson founded the SMS Ranches.

Immigrants also came from other parts of Scandinavia. Norwegians came to Texas seeking religious freedom and economic security. They found it in scenic Bosque County with its woods, water, and rolling hills. Texas's Mildred ("Babe") Didriksen Zaharias, the greatest woman athlete of her time, claimed Norwegian ancestry. Danish settlers established Danevang in Wharton County, and have since moved into communities such as Hutto, Benchley, and Austin.

Immigrants came from all parts of Europe. The rich agricultural area of Central Texas is dotted with communities of Czech farmers who saw in Texas the land of opportunity. Praha, Dubina, Moravia, Smetana, and Tabor are all communities with a Czech flavor, and Fayetteville in Fayette County has been called the "Cradle of Czech Settlement in Texas." Texas owes the development of one of its largest industries to an Austrian naval officer and geologist, Captain Anthony F. Lucas. In 1899 Captain Lucas leased land near Beaumont and began drilling for oil. On January 10, 1901, the Lucas gusher came in at the Spindletop Field, beginning the great oil boom that was to revolutionize the economy of the state.

Oppression and poverty led many Poles to leave their native country. In 1854 the Poles settled Panna Maria in Karnes County, the oldest Polish settlement in Texas. An early Polish settler, Simon Wiess, became a leading merchant and riverman. His descendants have pioneered in the development of Texas's lumber and oil industries.

The Swiss who came to Texas were cultured and cosmopolitan additions to the frontier society. Texas philanthropists George H. Hermann and Henry Rosenberg claim Swiss ancestors, and industrious and prosperous Swiss settlers have made their homes in Bexar, Fayette, Travis, and Williamson counties. San Antonio claims many Belgians, who operate truck farms and whose ancestors walked San Antonio streets in wooden shoes.

Italian immigrants have enriched the cultural and business life of Texas. Central Texas businessmen advertised for settlers in the 1880s, and Italian farmers took up land near Bryan and Hearne. Frederick E. Ruffini, an Italian architect, designed the temporary capitol of the state and also buildings at The University of Texas. The present capitol building and grounds contain many works of the Italian sculptor Pompeo Coppini.

Many Lebanese immigrated to escape religious persecution and seek economic advancement. United States congressman Abraham Kazen, Jr., from Laredo is a member of a distinguished Lebanese family. Michel T. Halbouty, son of a Beaumont merchant, gained fame as a geologist and oilman. World famous heart surgeon Dr. Michael E. DeBakey is of Lebanese ancestry.

Many Greek immigrants came to Texas in the latter half of the nineteenth century to work as farmers, and many obtained employment in the meat-packing plants in Fort Worth. A Greek immigrant, Faithon P. Lucas, pioneered soil conservation methods on his farmland near Mesquite, and families of Greek immigrants celebrate Greek Independence Day each March 25th.

Just as the first Indians came from Asia, so have later immigrants. The Chinese New Year and the Spring and Moon festivals are celebrated in Texas by Chinese families. The first Chinese immigrants came to lay tracks for the railroads. They stayed to become businessmen. The thriving rice industry of the Texas Gulf Coast area owes much to Japanese immigrants who seeded their lands with Japanese rice, doubling rice production in the area. The early part of the twentieth century saw acute food shortages in Japan, and immigrants arrived in Texas looking for land on which to plant rice and to truck farm. Japanese farmers, many of whom worked the fields in their native costumes, settled near Webster.

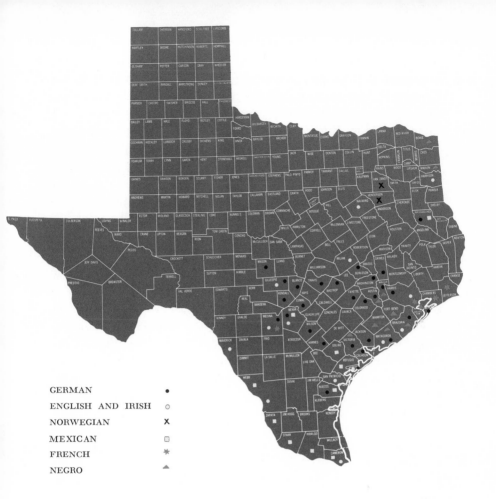

GERMAN   ●
ENGLISH AND IRISH   ○
NORWEGIAN   X
MEXICAN   □
FRENCH   ✳
NEGRO   ▲

LOCATION OF MAJOR ETHNIC GROUPS IN 1850

Plaza, bronco, mesa, lariat, rodeo, fiesta—the language of Texans reflects the influence of the land to the south, Mexico. Native Mexicans came to Texas as guides and interpreters for the Spanish conquistadores. Mexican Americans form the second largest population group in Texas.

Mexican immigrants brought their colorful art, music, and dances, and the influence of Mexican architecture is visible in patios, courtyards, and decorative tiled walls throughout the state. Texans quickly adopted the spicy chili and the rolled tamales of their Mexican friends, and the practical and picturesque costume of the Spanish charro became the working uniform of the Mexican vaquero and the Texas cowboy.

7

Names of Texas towns reflect the strong cultural ties between Texas and Mexico. Goliad is an anagram for Hidalgo, the name of a Mexican priest who led an attempt to free Mexico from Spanish rule in 1810, and Victoria is named in honor of another Mexican patriot, Guadalupe Victoria. DeLeon was named for Martín de León, a pioneer immigrant and rancher from Mexico, and Manchaca in Travis County bears a variation of the name of José Antonio Menchaca, who fought at San Jacinto. Erasmo Seguin, the first *alcalde* (mayor) of Bexar, and his son Juan, who commanded a company at San Jacinto, lent their family name to Seguin.

Of the fifty-nine men who signed the Texas Declaration of Independence, only two were native Texans. Both were of Mexican descent, and both were from San Antonio de Bexar. José Antonio Navarro and José Francisco Ruíz chose the cause of Texas independence and served in the congress of the Republic of Texas. A Mexican statesman, Lorenzo de Zavala, fled Santa Anna's dictatorship to join the cause of Texas independence and became the *ad interim* vice-president of the Republic of Texas. Texas contributed a hero to Mexico when Ignacio Zaragoza, born in Goliad, turned back French forces on Mexican soil on May 5, 1862—a victory commemorated by the annual *Cinco de Mayo* celebration in Mexico.

Texans of Mexican descent continue to play an important role in the state's political and cultural life. United States

Henry B. Gonzalez has built a record of distinguished service to his state and nation.

The University of Texas, Institute of Texan Cultures at San Antonio

8

congressmen Henry B. Gonzalez and Eligio de la Garza represent important Texas congressional districts. Vicente T. Ximenes, a native of Floresville, has served as chairman of the President's Cabinet Committee on Mexican-American Affairs. Dr. Hector P. Garcia, a resident of Corpus Christi, served as a member of the United States delegation to the United Nations, and Porfirio Salinas and Manuel Acosta, Texas artists, have received national recognition for their paintings.

Texas today is the product of the efforts of her people, past and present. They came from all over the world and for many purposes. Each of the Texans has added something of the culture he brought with him. The result is a richly diverse population and a culture with facets reminiscent of almost every inhabited part of the earth.

Discuss

1. "The confluence of cultures in Texas has been a never-ending process which began with the arrival of prehistoric man and which has as its end product the 11 million Texans of today." Explain what the author of this statement meant, giving examples from your reading.

2. Select one or two paragraphs from this chapter and tell how the material shows the contributions made to Texas by different ethnic groups.

3. Which of the contributions made by various people to the culture of Texas do you feel is the most significant?

Identify

Esteban	Anthony F. Lucas
Henry A. McArdle	Frederick E. Ruffini
Hendrick Arnold	Lorenzo de Zavala
Svante Palm	José Antonio Navarro
Mildred Didriksen Zaharias	Henry B. Gonzalez

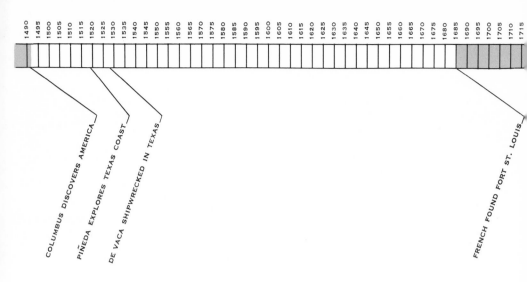

1490 | 1495 | 1500 | 1505 | 1510 | 1515 | 1520 | 1525 | 1530 | 1535 | 1540 | 1545 | 1550 | 1555 | 1560 | 1565 | 1570 | 1575 | 1580 | 1585 | 1590 | 1595 | 1600 | 1605 | 1610 | 1615 | 1620 | 1625 | 1630 | 1635 | 1640 | 1645 | 1650 | 1655 | 1660 | 1665 | 1670 | 1675 | 1680 | 1685 | 1690 | 1695 | 1700 | 1705 | 1710 | 1715

COLUMBUS DISCOVERS AMERICA

PIÑEDA EXPLORES TEXAS COAST

DE VACA SHIPWRECKED IN TEXAS

FRENCH FOUND FORT ST. LOUIS

CHAPTER 2

"The Great and Fayre Plains"

The early explorers of Texas found a vast land sparsely inhabited by Indians. During the next century and a half, however, the Spanish had little interest in Texas. Not until the presence of the French in Louisiana threatened Spain's hold on Texas did Spain begin to search for a way to maintain her claim. The solution—the civilization of the East Texas Indians by establishing missions among them—was destined to be a failure partly because of a lack of understanding of the land and the peoples of Texas.

The geography of Texas, with its variety in topography and climate, determined to a great extent the type of cultures the Indian tribes developed. The Indians domesticated many of

11

CORONADO SETS OUT FOR QUIVIRA IN THIS DRAWING
BY NORMAN PRICE.

the plants now a part of our everyday diet. Newcomers borrowed from these earlier residents techniques and wisdom the Indians had developed in their centuries of sustaining themselves upon the Texas earth.

The Land

Texas can be divided into four main regions, each a part of a major natural region of North America. The four natural regions of Texas are the Coastal Plains, the Great Plains, the North Central Plains, and the Mountains and Basins. The major landforms and the geological formations determine the various regions.

The Coastal Plains. The Coastal Plains are lowlands, extending from the Rio Grande to the Red River and bounded on the west by the Great Plains and North Central Plains. The land is low, level to gently rolling, and sometimes marshy near the coast. The Coastal Plains are divided into a number of geographic regions by differences in topography, soil, vegetation, and climate. The South Texas Plain is part prairie and part brush country. Although the Indians who roamed this section were hunters and gatherers, today this area is cattle country. Irrigation has helped the Lower Rio Grande Valley become one of the richest agricultural regions in the state.

The Indians who lived on the Coastal Prairies depended in part on oysters and fish for their existence. Marine resources today support an important industry in this grassland and water area. Plentiful rainfall in the northern section around Beaumont creates a climate that is conducive to rice farming, and the cultivation of rice and cattle ranching are important industries in this area today.

The Blackland Prairies grow tall grasses, and their soil is rich and deep. The Indians who inhabited this area were primarily hunters, although the area had great agricultural potential. Today the Blackland Prairies are one of the most important agricultural areas in the state.

The highest level of Indian agriculture was reached in the Pine Woods of East Texas. However, in recent years much of that farmland has been returned to timber, and this extension of the Southern Pine Forest of the United States constitutes virtually all of Texas's timber.

The North Central Plains. The North Central Plains are an extension of the large area that forms the central part of the United States. The western part of this region is composed of rolling plains and high mesas and plateaus. The grassy Grand Prairie of the North Central Plains lies sandwiched between two branches of the Cross Timbers. The Wichita Indians hunted the buffalo in this region, and today cattle ranching is an important industry. The Indians farmed in this region, and early settlers pursued an agricultural economy also. However, in the early part of the twentieth century the soil in some sections was overused, and major areas of the region were eroded. Cattle raising is an important industry in the region now.

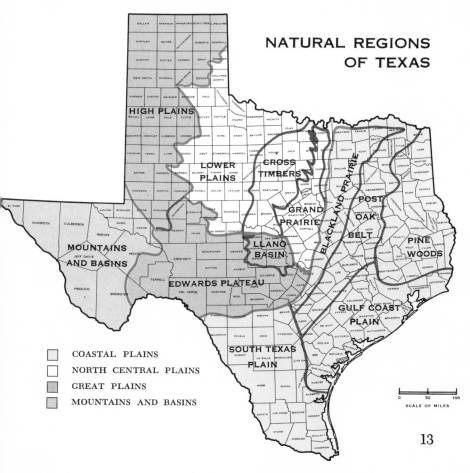

NATURAL REGIONS OF TEXAS

COASTAL PLAINS
NORTH CENTRAL PLAINS
GREAT PLAINS
MOUNTAINS AND BASINS

SCALE OF MILES

13

The Great Plains. The Great Plains are high plateau areas, bordered by the top of the Panhandle on the north, the Rio Grande on the south, the Cap Rock on the east, and the Pecos River on the west. The region the Spaniards called the Llano Estacado, or Staked Plain, is covered with short grass, and for centuries large herds of buffalo roamed the area, furnishing the livelihood of the Comanches and Kiowas. Extensive cattle ranching was done in the area for many years, but in recent years irrigation by means of groundwater has converted the area into one of Texas's largest agricultural regions. A depletion of the water supply may in the future cause the region to be utilized in some other way.

Grass, weeds, and small trees cover the southern part of the Great Plains, the Edwards Plateau. Thin, rocky soil in many places makes the area unsuitable for agriculture, but sheep and goats graze the plateau and constitute an important economic asset of the state. In the valleys where water is plentiful, agriculture is possible.

The following description of the Great Plains was written by Pedro de Castañeda, who accompanied the Coronado expedition.

Now we will speak of the plains. The country is spacious and level. . . .

In traversing 250 leagues . . . was not seen . . . a hill nor a hillock which was three times as high as a man. . . . The country is like a bowl, so that when a man sits down, the horizon surrounds him all around at the distance of a musket shot. There are no groves of trees except at the rivers. . . . [The] people follow the cows, [the buffalo] hunting them and tanning the skins to take to the settlements in the winter to sell. . . .

. . . The country [the buffalo] traveled over was so level and smooth that if one looked at them the sky could be seen between their legs. . . . if a man only lay down on his back he lost sight of the ground. . . . [1]

---

[1]George Parker Winship, "The Coronado Expedition, 1540-1542," *Fourteenth Annual Report of the Bureau of Ethnology* (2 pts.; Washington, 1896), I, 491-583. Reproduced in Wallace and Vigness, *Documents of Texas History* (Austin: Steck-Vaughn Company, 1963), 5-6.

The Mountains and Basins. The natural region designated as the Mountains and Basins consists of mountain ranges west of the Pecos River with the basins and plateaus between. The land is dry and arid, covered with grass and shrubs. The Indian population of the area was small except along the Rio Grande. The mountains can support cattle ranching, and irrigation with groundwater makes some agriculture possible.

The variety of landforms and climate meant that the Indians could cultivate only certain regions of Texas. The woodlands of East Texas, the river valleys and the Cross Timbers section of the North Central Plains, and other river valley areas throughout the state could support an agricultural economy, but many times the Indians had to resume a nomadic way of life when rainfall was scarce or streams dried up.

The People

During the Ice Age of the Pleistocene Era, when most of the northern extremity of the United States lay buried beneath glaciers and ice, men and women from Asia wandered from Siberia to America across a land bridge now covered by the waters of the Bering Strait. These early Paleo-Americans were erect, intelligent wanderers and hunters. They covered their bodies with animal skins, used fire, and could communicate with each other. They brought stone and bone tools with them to the new land. Herds of animals now extinct, such as mastodons, mammoths, camels, sloths, peccary pigs, and small horses, came to North America by the same route used by these early men. The bands of men wandered in search of the animals, killing the gigantic Columbian elephant and the giant bison, which was twice the size of the buffalo the Indian hunted on the plains of Texas. Paleo-American men met the elephant and the bison on foot and hurled their spears at the giant beasts with atlatls (throwing sticks).

Paleo-American man carried a culture, or way of life, across the Bering Strait to the new land. He possessed objects such as tools, and he had distinct patterns of behavior, customs, and rituals. Little is known about his beliefs and his knowledge, but his feelings and attitudes are reflected in three stone heads excavated from the Trinity River bed near Malakoff in Henderson County. Although crude, two of the heads depict human attitudes and facial characteristics. The other head might have been intended to represent an animal. One of the state's earliest known inhabitants was nicknamed Midland Minnie by archeologists who uncovered her fossilized remains on the Scharbauer Ranch near Midland in 1953. How old Minnie actually is has been difficult to determine, but she may have lived on the Llano Estacado as early as twelve thousand years ago when the plains area was cooler and wetter.

No one knows what happened to these ancient men. Perhaps they died out or wandered into other lands. Perhaps they evolved into other types of men. But they left a rich heritage of tools, patterns of behavior, customs, beliefs, and attitudes which links this Paleo-American man to the Indians of Texas in historic times.

Other distinct cultural groups began hunting the bison and gathering seeds and plants on the Texas plains by 5000 B.C. These people used many tools of bone and stone and had domesticated the dog. These groups of people gradually developed an agricultural economy cultivating crops of grains and cereals. Around 700 B.C. East Texas Indians had developed a sedentary way of life. These farming Indians built mound dwellings and temples for the worship of their sun gods. Their society was highly developed and well organized. Paleo-American man would have recognized many of his own ways of life in the culture of these early East Texas Indians.

The Indian utilized available plants and animals to sustain himself. The ways in which he used the land and the natural resources around him determined the cultural group to which he belonged. The Texas Indians can be divided into four general cultural groups, with several tribes forming each group. The four basic cultural groups are the Indians of the Western Gulf, the Caddoes of East Texas, the Indians of Southwestern Texas, and the Plains Indians.

The Western Gulf Culture. The Karankawas and the Coahuiltecans formed the Western Gulf group, centering along the Texas Gulf Coast and maintaining a nomadic existence. The Karankawas adapted to the coastal environment, living a

16

Karankawa warrior, painted
by Edna Collins

hunting, fishing, and gathering existence by following the sources of food supply. They used the bow and arrow to hunt and to fish with as they had no fishhooks. Many times they fished from dugout canoes. The physical appearance of the Karankawas was frightening to the explorers who encountered them, and they gained a reputation for cannibalism. Tall, well-built, and muscular, the men went naked except in war, when they wore breechclouts. They smeared their bodies with dirt and alligator grease as protection against mosquitoes, and painted and tattooed their bodies and faces. The men pierced their breasts and lower lips and inserted pieces of cane through them. They also wore ornaments of seashells and animal teeth.

The Karankawas migrated from offshore islands to the mainland when food became scarce. They lived off fish, shellfish, turtles, small animals, nuts, roots, and berries. The Karankawas erected crude homes of poles covered with skins and woven mats that could be easily moved. They built their homes on shell middens near water to be close to their food supply.

The life of the Coahuiltecans was harsh, as the South Texas Plain that they wandered formed one of the most desolate regions of Texas. They were nomadic hunters and gatherers who eked out an existence on buffalo, deer, javelina, small animals, birds, prickly pear tunas, and mesquite beans. They resorted to earth, rotten wood, snakes, lizards, and ant eggs in times of scarcity of other foods. They lived in low circular huts that were covered with hides and reed mats, and they hunted with bows and arrows, often capturing animals by encircling them.

The Caddo Culture. The Caddoes formed the largest cultural group that the Spanish and the French encountered. They were described as the "most productive, advanced, and populous peoples of Texas." The Caddo culture seems to have developed from the Mississippi River Valley and from Mexico. The Caddoes constructed temples and burial mounds and buried their dead with offerings of pottery and weapons. Their agricultural economy was based on corn, many varieties of beans, squash, cantaloupes, watermelons, sunflowers, and tobacco. They supplemented their diet with deer, buffalo, small animals, fish, nuts, and fruit. They cultivated their crops with hoes, ground corn with wooden mortars and pestles, and produced kiln-fired pottery. The Caddoes hunted with bows and arrows and fished with trotlines.

The Caddoes joined together in unions of tribes called confederacies. The largest of these was the Hasinai Confederacy, located in the Neches and Angelina River valleys. The Kadohadacho lived around the Great Bend of the Red River and in Arkansas, and the Natchitoches occupied the area around the Natchitoches River in Louisiana. The Adaes on the Red River and the Ais living near San Augustine, Texas, formed independent Caddo tribes.

The Caddoes usually located their villages near water. They built permanent houses, which were round, shaped like a beehive, and thatched with grass and leaves. Several families lived in each house, and a center hearth held a year-round fire. The Caddo culture was advanced to the point that many people could become specialists and did not need to work to produce food. Men worked together in kinship groups, and the society had different classes of people with a *xinesi* (headman) in command of a confederacy or tribe.

The early explorers were alarmed by the Caddo custom of greeting all visitors with weeping and wailing. However, in contrast to the savage Karankawas, their appearance was less frightening. They painted and tattooed their bodies for war or for ceremonial occasions, but they wore moccasins, leggings,

18

and deerskin or buffalo shirts, as well as breechclouts. Their garments were fringed and decorated with shell and bone ornaments, and they tanned the hides of buffalo and deer for clothing and coverings.

The Southwestern Culture. The Jumano Indians were probably related to the Pueblo Indians of New Mexico. By the time of the arrival of the first Spanish explorers in the trans-Pecos region, the territory inhabited by the Jumanos was contracting, probably due to drought and raids by the Apaches. Of all the Indians of Texas, the Jumanos are the least known, because their way of life began to decline a century before the Spaniards arrived and was almost completely gone by the end of the eighteenth century.

The Jumanos were divided into two groups. One group depended mostly on agriculture, but the buffalo was hunted to some extent. Their agriculture was centered in the river valleys, and the Jumanos located the fields so that overflow or underground moisture from streams would water the crops. Beans,

From Marcy: EXPLORATION OF THE RED RIVER

A Wichita village as sketched in 1852, showing the influence of geography on the Wichita culture

19

squash, and corn were the main crops, and in dry years they gathered prickly pear tunas and mesquite beans. Their houses were quite impressive, averaging almost thirty feet square. Part of the house was sunk into the ground, with the upper walls being made of adobe. The other group of Jumanos were a nomadic people who built no permanent homes. They hunted the buffalo on the plains in the warm season and returned to the river valleys for the winter.

The Plains Culture. Buffalo molded the culture of the Plains Indians. The Indians hunted them for food and made their clothing and shelter from the hides. Until the Indian obtained the horse from the Spaniard, he hunted the buffalo on foot, carrying his possessions with him by means of dog travois. When the Plains Indian had the horse, he met the white man as an equal. The warlike Plains Indian and his culture died when the buffalo were exterminated.

The Tonkawas of Central Texas lived in temporary camps east of the Balcones Escarpment between the Brazos and the Colorado rivers. They were hunters, pursuing the buffalo until the Comanches cut them off from the herds. They lived a nomadic life, following the herds and living in tepees of buffalo hide. They were forced to change to small coneshaped grass huts similar to those of the Wichita when they could no longer reach the buffalo.

The Wichitas originally ranged the Great Plains in Kansas but were pushed southward by other tribes. Thus they share the characteristics of the plains culture and of their agricultural neighbors, the Caddoes. The men tattooed their eyelids and pierced their ears. They recorded their accomplishments in war in tattooed designs on their chests. They lived in circular thatched houses from fifteen to thirty feet in diameter. Open arbors served as work areas and places to dry and store food. However, they used the buffalo-hide tepee while hunting buffalo on the plains. The Wichitas left a great many cultural artifacts, including well-made dishes of pottery, wood, and stone, and elbow pipes of pottery used for smoking the tobacco they cultivated.

The Indians we know as Apaches were actually several distinct tribes; among them were the Lipans, the Mescaleros, and the Kiowas. Only the Lipans were present in Texas in substantial numbers during the nineteenth century.

The Lipan Apaches hunted the buffalo on the Great Plains, using their horse travois to carry their household goods. When the Comanches drove them from Texas into Mexico, they resorted to living on plants and stolen cattle. However, during their days as buffalo hunters they were fierce warriors and cruel opponents. They carried shields of buffalo hides and used bows, arrows, and tomahawks. On the march they carried water in bags made of the stomachs of buffalo or cattle. In the village they used basketwork jugs waterproofed with resin or pitch.

The Lipan warrior, clad in breechclout, leggings, and moccasins of hide, cut his hair at ear level on the left side of his head, but he allowed the right side to grow and tied it at shoulder level. He decorated his hair with feathers and trinkets and wore earrings. From nomadic buffalo hunters, they gradually became fierce warriors protecting their land, and then dispossessed wanderers.

The mighty Comanche drove the Apache from most of Texas and became the scourge of the plains. He traveled in bands, hunted in groups using the surround, and camped near running water when possible. The Comanche depended almost entirely on the buffalo for his livelihood. He used all the buffalo, eating the meat and making his clothing and shelter from the hide. He made rawhide bags, called parfleches, from the skin of the buffalo and used them to store food. His bow was strung with the sinew of buffalo, and his tools were made from buffalo bones. The hide of the buffalo made the Comanche saddle, and rawhide thongs were used as rope.

The following is a description of the Plains Indians as seen by Coronado's chronicler.

I came to a settlement of Indians who are called Querechos, who travel around with these cows, who do not plant, and who eat the raw flesh and drink the blood of the cows they kill, and they tan the skins of the cows, with which all the people of this country dress themselves here. They have little field tents made of the hides of the cows, tanned and greased, very well made, in which they

live while they travel around near the cows. . . . They have dogs
which they load, which carry their tents and poles and belongings.[2]

When the Lords of the South Plains rode into battle, they
were an awesome sight. They daubed their faces, their lances,
and the heads and tails of their horses with red paint. They
wore headdresses of feathers and carried painted shields decorated with bear teeth and feathers. Their weapons were a
fourteen-foot lance and a small, but powerful, bow. Their hair
was parted in the middle with braids falling on each side and a
decorated scalp lock falling from the top. When a Comanche
warrior died, his war equipment was buried with him, and his
favorite horse was slaughtered over the grave. The Spaniards
gave the Comanche his name, which in the Ute language
means "One who fights me all the time." And the Comanche
lived up to his name, warring with both the Spaniard and the
Apache for Texas.

But in Texas, as in other parts of the world, these native
peoples were to become victims of the march of civilization.
Time ran out for the Plains Indians in the last quarter of the
nineteenth century. The white man's numbers and technology
had become overwhelming. The Colt revolver gave the Ranger
an edge on the brave for the first time. The railroad provided
a means of transporting buffalo hides to the East where people
wanted to buy them. In the end the Comanche lost the huge
domain he had taken from the Apache and others after he left
his home in the Pacific Northwest. But so long as men admire
horsemanship and respect courage, the Plains Indian will live
in memory.

The Coming of the Spanish

The Spanish established their claim in the New World when
Columbus, sailing under the Spanish flag of their supreme
highnesses King Ferdinand and Queen Isabella, landed on a

---

[2]George Parker Winship, "The Coronado Expedition, 1540-1542," *Four-
teenth Annual Report of the Bureau of Ethnology* (2 pts.; Washington, 1896),
I, 491-583. Reproduced in Wallace and Vigness, *Documents of Texas History*
(Austin: Steck-Vaughn Company, 1963), 6-8

beach at San Salvador on October 12, 1492. Although Columbus believed that he had found a new and shorter trade route to the Indies, later explorations revealed that he had instead discovered a new continent. With the discovery of the vast natural resources of the New World, the rulers of Spain, France, and England, vying for supremacy in Europe, realized its true importance.

The Spaniards looked to the new land to fill their country's coffers with gold and to swell the number of converts to the Catholic religion. A love of adventure, desire for gold, and religious fervor led expedition after expedition of conquistadores and missionaries to the New World and opened the Spanish century, one hundred years in which Spain's naval superiority enabled her to protect her conquests. Spain's interest for most of the sixteenth century concentrated on islands in the Caribbean and on conquests in Central America, Peru,

George Catlin produced this and many other paintings of the Comanche Indians.

and Mexico. There the conquistadores found lands rich in silver and gold and advanced civilizations.

The Conquest of Mexico. In 1519 Montezuma, the Emperor of the Aztec Empire, received word that eleven ships, 553 men, and sixteen monstrous beasts—horses—had landed on the shores of his mighty empire. After a bloody campaign that lasted several months, Cortés conquered the Aztecs and destroyed the ancient capital city of Tenochtitlán. On the ruins of the Aztec capital he built a city and named it Mexico. From this base, he sent out parties of explorers to investigate this new center of Spanish civilization in the New World.

Spanish Entradas. However, the first Spanish expedition to land on the shores of Texas came from Jamaica, searching for the mythical Strait of Anian that would lead to the Pacific Ocean. In 1519, the same year in which Cortés landed his ships on the shores of Mexico, Alonso Alvarez de Piñeda contracted with Governor Francisco Garay of Jamaica to find this legendary water passage to the Orient in order to establish trade routes. Piñeda spent forty days at the mouth of the Rio Grande and mapped the Texas coastline. Piñeda reported to Governor Garay that where the Rio Grande, or the Rio de las Palmas as he called it, met the Gulf of Mexico would be an excellent site for a colony, but no colonization resulted from Piñeda's exploration.

However, other Spaniards came to Texas. Pánfilo de Narváez landed on the coast of Florida in 1528. When his fleet failed to return, he attempted to cross the Gulf of Mexico in crude boats, fashioned under the direction of a Greek member of the party who knew something of shipbuilding, Doroteo Teodoro. After a difficult journey along the coast, the expedition was shipwrecked, probably on Galveston Island, in November 1528. Of the three hundred men who had landed in Florida with Narváez, only four reached civilization again. One was a black man, Esteban. Another was Alvar Núñez Cabeza de Vaca, treasurer of the expedition.

Although the Spaniards were captives of Indians, probably the Karankawas, they were given a certain amount of freedom. Cabeza de Vaca traded with the Indians and used prayers and an elemental knowledge of medicine to establish himself as a

24

powerful healer. The four survivors of the expedition managed to escape in 1534 and wandered for many miles until they reached Mexico. De Vaca reported his adventures to the Viceroy of New Spain, who read the report with great interest. De Vaca described the interior of Texas, detailing the customs and habits of the Indians and describing the buffalo and other animals.

De Vaca reported that he had seen the Indians living in poverty, but he repeated the stories the Indians had told him of great cities with much gold. The viceroy appointed Fray Marcos de Niza to lead an expedition guided by Esteban in search of the golden cities. Just outside the first of these cities Esteban was killed by the Indians. When Fray Marcos, following behind, heard of this, he turned back after viewing the city from a distance.

The Indians that Esteban encountered were the Zuñi pueblo dwellers of what is now New Mexico. Fray Marcos did not enter the first of the seven cities, but friendly Indians told him stories of great riches in all seven, and said that the one he observed was the smallest and poorest. Fray Marcos's report led the viceroy to appoint Francisco Vásquez de Coronado to investigate and claim the Seven Cities of Cíbola for Spain. Coronado left Mexico with a party of over one thousand men— Portuguese, Italians, Frenchmen, Scotsmen, and Germans, as well as Spaniards. However, Coronado's expedition found only the Indian pueblos near the Arizona-New Mexico border, and the explorers were rewarded with corn instead of the gold and silver they expected.

Coronado sent expeditionary parties across the plains to scout the area for the rich cities and moved his men to Tiguex for the winter. There Coronado met an Indian the Spaniards called the Turk, who told them of a fabulous city, Quivira, where the streets were lined with silver and the natives ate from golden dishes. He spoke of trees hung with golden bells and of rivers with fish as large as horses. For forty days Coronado and his men followed the Turk's imaginative stories across the Great Plains of Texas. They found only mud and grass huts, and instead of fish as large as horses, they found buffalo. Defeated and dejected, Coronado returned to Mexico. In 1542, his fortune lost and his health broken by a fall from a horse, he submitted his report to the viceroy.

A report filed by Luis de Moscoso de Alvarado, who traveled through East Texas, helped give Viceroy Mendoza some idea of the geography and the natives of much of Texas. Both reports cited the favorable conditions for settlement, but the Spanish government was interested in gold and silver. The Spaniards concentrated their colonization efforts in Mexico and in Peru.

The French in Texas

While Spain maintained her territorial right to Texas, France looked to North America with the idea of establishing trading posts there. French traders had penetrated the interior of North America from Canada, and in 1682 René Robert Cavelier, Sieur de la Salle, expanded France's claim in the New World when he followed the Mississippi River to its mouth.

Texas Memorial Museum

Fort St. Louis was located here, on high ground beside Garcitas Creek in Victoria County.

La Salle claimed the river and the lands drained by it in the name of Louis XIV of France and named the land Louisiana in his honor. La Salle saw the Mississippi as a natural avenue of commerce, and he realized that whoever controlled the mouth of the river would hold the destiny of the whole Mississippi River valley. He persuaded the king of France to grant him a commission to establish a permanent colony at the mouth of the Mississippi. Bad weather and mistakes in navigation caused La Salle's ships to stray off course. He first landed near present Port Arthur, Texas, on New Year's Day, 1685, and began skirting the Texas Gulf Coast. Finally La Salle entered Matagorda Bay and established a colony, Fort St. Louis, on Garcitas Creek near present Inez, Victoria County. The settlers constructed a fort from the timbers of their wrecked ships as protection against the hostile Karankawas.

The Indians, lack of food and water, and disease quickly reduced the number of settlers, and La Salle determined to seek help from Canada. With a band of men he set out to find the Mississippi River and follow it to Canada. La Salle was murdered by one of his men somewhere in East Texas, and even though six members of the expedition finally reached Canada, no help arrived to save the colonists.

Spanish alarm at the French intrusion into East Texas led to efforts to locate and destroy the settlement, but the Spanish arrived to find their work already done by the Karankawas. The Spanish padre, Father Damian Massanet, who arrived at the site of Fort St. Louis with Alonso de León in 1689, described the abandoned site: "There was a great lot of shattered weapons, broken by the Indians—firelocks, carbines, cutlasses. . . . We found two unburied bodies, which I interred, setting up a cross over the grave. There were many torn-up books and many dead pigs."

The rivalry between Spain and France made the colonization of East Texas imperative. Since large numbers of Spaniards were not available to come to the New World for purposes of colonization, the Spaniards knew that they would have to colonize the Indians and attempt to use them as a bulwark against the French. Since the Caddoes were the most stable, and since they lived on the edge of French country, they were the key to the retention of Texas. And so the world of western men came to the Caddoes, making them a pawn in a gigantic European chess game.

Discuss

1. Compare the way the Indians of Texas dealt with geography and their environment to the way later inhabitants of the state have dealt with them.

2. Illustrate the ways in which geography affects man by comparing the way that the Caddo Indians of East Texas lived with the way the Comanche Indians of West Texas lived.

3. What was Texas's real importance to Spain? How did the Spanish reaction to the establishment of Fort St. Louis show this?

4. How do geography and climate affect the way modern Texans use the land?

5. Give some examples of ways modern Texans use the land that are different from the ways the Indians used it. What has made this possible?

6. Explain the relationship between the ease with which a people obtain the necessities of life and the complexity of their social and material cultures. Use three examples: the Coahuiltecans, the Caddoes, and yourself and your family.

7. Identify the characteristics common to the three best-known cultural groups of Texas Indians. Explain why you think these similarities existed. Which of these characteristics can you identify in modern society? What conclusion might be drawn from this?

8. What problems did the early explorers face which were caused by the geography of the Great Plains?

Identify

Coastal Plains
Great Plains
North Central Plains
Mountains and Basins
Paleo-Americans
Cortés
Cabeza de Vaca
Coronado
La Salle

Karankawas
Caddoes
Coahuiltecans
Jumanos
Apaches
Comanches
Piñeda
Fray Marcos
Quivira

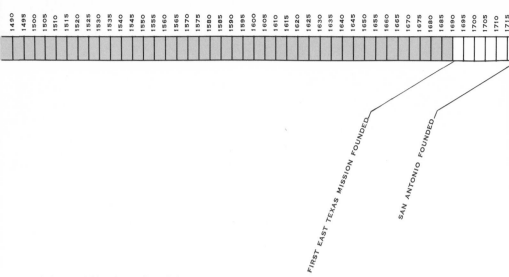

1490 1495 1500 1505 1510 1515 1520 1525 1530 1535 1540 1545 1550 1555 1560 1565 1570 1575 1580 1585 1590 1595 1600 1605 1610 1615 1620 1625 1630 1635 1640 1645 1650 1655 1660 1665 1670 1675 1680 1685 1690 1695 1700 1705 1710 1715

FIRST EAST TEXAS MISSION FOUNDED

SAN ANTONIO FOUNDED

Archives Division, Texas State Library

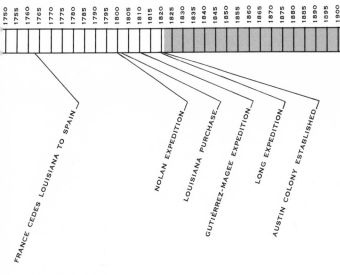

FRANCE CEDES LOUISIANA TO SPAIN

NOLAN EXPEDITION

LOUISIANA PURCHASE

GUTIÉRREZ-MAGEE EXPEDITION

LONG EXPEDITION

AUSTIN COLONY ESTABLISHED

CHAPTER 3

"Bold, Restless Men"

During three centuries of Spanish rule, the fertile land of Texas lay waiting to be settled. The early nineteenth century saw in the United States a wave of westward migration whose crest was to break upon the distant shores of Texas. The Treaty of San Ildefonso and the Louisiana Purchase opened the door to settlement of Texas from the United States. The historian George Bancroft stated that "the Anglo-American race was pushing westward and southward. Bold, restless men, impelled by the fascination of wild adventure, made their way into new regions, reckless of danger and hardships."

The First Missions

When Alonso de León came to Texas in 1689, he found Fort St. Louis in ruins, but the French threat still existed. De León

31

THE ABANDONED SAN SABÁ PRESIDIO IS A SYMBOL OF
SPAIN'S FAILURE TO COLONIZE TEXAS.

wanted to establish a string of fortresses across Texas, but Spanish officials decided that missions were more economical and practical. De León and Father Massanet returned to East Texas in 1690 with "20 mules laden with wine, wax, and so on, also clothing for distribution among the Indians, and six loads of tobacco."

The Caddo Indians welcomed the Spaniards and helped them to erect a mission, San Francisco de los Tejas, near present Weches, Houston County. A few months later the friars began another mission nearby, Santísimo Nombre de María. The Texas mission frontier was officially open. Floods and raids by hostile Indian tribes spelled failure for the early missions, and when the French threat subsided for a time, Spanish officials decided that the missions should be abandoned. Father Massanet protested, but when the friars learned that supposedly friendly Indians planned to massacre them, they hastily buried the mission bells and abandoned Texas. Not a soldier or a missionary remained north of the Rio Grande by the end of 1693, two hundred years after Spain came into ownership of that land.

Texas remained on the periphery of Spanish interest, serving as a buffer between Mexico and interlopers into Spanish territory. Renewal of the menace from France forced the Spaniards to reoccupy territory in Texas. In 1716 new missions were founded as far east as Mission San Miguel de Linares, where Robeline, Louisiana, stands now, and Mission Dolores de los Ais near present San Augustine, Texas. In 1721 the Spanish established a presidio, or fort, near the Mission San Miguel de Linares, and the resulting settlement of Los Adaes became the capital of Texas.

The need for a supply base between the East Texas missions and the closest settlement in Mexico, San Juan Bautista on the Rio Grande, led to the establishment of what were to be Spain's most successful missions in Texas. The Spanish government appointed Martín de Alarcón governor of the province of Texas and sent him to establish a way station between San Juan Bautista and East Texas. Alarcón led his troops to the San Antonio River and founded Villa de Bexar in May 1718, and Father Antonio Olivares established Mission San Antonio de

Valero, which at another location in later years was to be known as the Alamo. In 1722 the Marquis de Aguayo, who served as governor of the provinces of Coahuila and Texas, was instrumental in founding Mission Espíritu Santo and Presidio La Bahía on the Gulf Coast, which were removed in 1749 to a site on the San Antonio River near present Goliad.

The Spaniards considered the mission system in East Texas poorly situated and open to attack by Indians, and, due to the need for economy, the missions were moved in 1731 to the Bexar location and named San Francisco de la Espada, San Juan Capistrano, and Nuestra Señora de la Purísima Concepción. The five missions in the Bexar area served more than one thousand persons.

In 1729 an effort was made to people Texas when the king ordered that four hundred families from the Canary Islands be settled in Texas. The fifteen families who responded arrived in Bexar in 1731 and founded Villa San Fernando across from the presidio. The viceroy made each Canary Islander and his heirs hidalgos, Spanish noblemen, and these settlers formed the nucleus of a permanent ranching and farming community at San Fernando de Bexar.

The friars established missions along the San Gabriel River beginning in 1747. San Francisco Xavier, San Ildefonso, and Nuestra Señora de la Candelaria were founded near present Rockdale, Milam County. The Indians in the area were anxious to have the Spaniards help them protect their land against raids by the warlike Apaches. In 1757 the San Sabá Mission was founded near present Menard to serve the Lipan Apaches; the mission lasted only a year before the Comanche and Wichita Indians destroyed it. In an expedition against the Wichitas, who had a large village on the Red River at present Spanish Fort, the Spaniards found the Indians armed with French weapons. The San Sabá Presidio carried on the war against the Comanches for another ten years, but no more efforts were made to establish missions among the Apaches.

Some of the problems faced by the early missions and presidios were due to geography. The geographic conditions discussed in the following selection made the maintenance of the San Sabá Presidio difficult.

The presidio is located between two ravines which lie open in unequal distances to the north and south. The enemy can come and station themselves in these under cover for the purpose of attacking this presidio. . . . They can make . . . a great deal of trouble helped by their proximity and the shelter of the underbrush. The thickness of this and the fertility of the soil which allows it to grow back so quickly prevents its being kept cleared away by so small a garrison. . . .

. . . The ease with which the enemy has been seen to maintain himself in its vicinity without being molested, added to the opportunities offered for their maintainance by the numbers of creeks and flowing springs, the abundance of buffalo which is their principal food, deer, wild turkeys and other animals will someday suggest to them the ease with which this presidio can be surrounded. . . . [1]

The Spaniards' fear of French encroachment ended with the termination of the French and Indian War in 1763. According to the terms of the Treaty of Paris, France ceded to England Canada and all her land east of the Mississippi River, with the exception of New Orleans. She ceded to Spain New Orleans and all her territories west of the Mississippi. When the English colonists were forbidden to move west of the Appalachian Mountains in 1763, Spain's possessions seemed secure.

Five years later, in 1768, the Marquis de Rubí recommended the abandonment of the presidios and missions in East Texas. A royal order gave the settlers in East Texas the choice of settling at San Fernando de Bexar or on the Rio Grande. Gil Antonio Ybarbo, a rancher and trader, led a group of discontented settlers who petitioned the Spanish government to allow them to return to East Texas. Permission was granted to return as far east as the Trinity River, where they established Bucareli. The settlement was abandoned in 1779, and Ybarbo led the settlers back to Nacogdoches.

Ybarbo, Martín de León, and Tomás Sánchez founded the

[1]"A copy of the report sent to his Excellency the viceroy, Marquis de Croix regarding the advantages of the maintaining or removing the presidio of San Sabá, August, 1767" (Archivo General de Indias, Audiencia de Guadalajara, 1768–1722, 104-61-13, Sevilla; Dunn transcripts, Archives, University of Texas Library, Austin. Reproduced in Wallace and Vigness, *Documents of Texas History* (Austin: Steck-Vaughn Company, 1963), 19-22.

Inside the mission walls were living quarters. San José Mission in San Antonio also preserves stone ovens.

original privately owned cattle ranches of Texas. Sánchez was granted permission to form a settlement in Texas in 1755, and his settlement—Laredo—became a crossroad for people entering Mexico from Texas. Sánchez held the offices of alcalde and chief justice for almost forty years. De León was a rancher who later became a colonizer. He began his ranching in Texas in Refugio County, but he later moved near San Patricio.

Mission Life

The mission was planned to serve as a self-contained compound in case of attack by Indians. Inside its fortified walls stood the church, quarters for the missionaries and Indians, workshops where the missionaries taught the Indians simple crafts and skills, and quarters for the soldiers. Crops were grown outside the walls, and goats and cattle were raised nearby. The missionaries taught the Indians the rudiments of a

Christian education and encouraged the Indians to learn to govern themselves. The Indians had their own chosen officials, who were closely supervised by the friars. When an Indian had learned a craft, the Christian religion, and how to farm and ranch, he became entitled to hold land and be a citizen of Spain.

Although many Indians moved within the mission walls for protection from enemy tribes, the missionaries kept them under guard to prevent their escaping. It was often difficult to convert the Indian to Christianity and to get him to give up his native rituals. The friars introduced Spanish dances, taught to the accompaniment of the violin and the guitar, as a more acceptable substitute for the Indians' native rites. Despite the dedicated efforts of the friars, relatively few converts were made among the Indians. After four years of labor at the Mission Rosario near La Bahía, only twenty-one baptisms had been performed—all of them at the deathbed.

Catholic Spain observed her church rituals with both splendor and solemnity, and the missionaries brought a love of grandeur and ornamentation to the Texas missions. The churches were often of the ornate style of Spanish architecture called *churrigueresque,* and the ornamentation of windows and doorways was often of a style of carving called *plateresque,* from the Spanish word for silver. The tracery decoration of the Rose Window at San José Mission shows the influence of the *plateresque* style on mission architecture.

Father Juan Agustín de Morfi, the historian of the Franciscan order, visited San José Mission in 1777 and wrote, "No one could have imagined that there were such good artists in so desolate a place." Despite a lack of materials, Indian artists devoted countless hours to decorating the missions and to creating beautiful and colorful images of Christ and the Virgin Mary. Among the most interesting are the images made of cornstalk and pitch that are found at Mission San Juan Capistrano.

Don Christobal de los Santos Coy established the first nonmission school in Texas at San Fernando de Bexar in 1746. The school was jointly sponsored by the church and by the people. Some years later, Ignacio de los Santos Coy, a native of Texas and probably the son of Christobal, taught at the same school.

Although several other such schools were established, no organized system of education was started in Texas by the Spanish government.

The Filibusters

Although the mission system introduced the Christian religion to the Indians of Texas and defied the French threat, the missions and presidios could not defend the area against adventurers who looked to the region with an eye for riches and a lust for conquest. The expeditions into Texas during the early 1800s were composed of men of many nationalities—adventurers all—who looked at Texas and saw the opportunities that it offered. Sometimes Spanish authorities granted permits of trade to the adventurers. However, many expeditions were illegal, and their leaders' dreams of conquest and empire ended in tragedy.

French trading posts along the Red River in Louisiana supplied the Indians with trinkets and ornaments in exchange for furs and horses in the early eighteenth century. In 1714 a French trader, Louis St. Denis, caused official concern when he arrived at the Spanish outpost of San Juan Bautista on the Rio Grande. Bernard de la Harpe established a French trading post on the Red River in 1718 and traded with the Texas Indians. The Spanish alarm over the French presence in Texas caused them to reestablish the missions in East Texas.

An adventurous horse trader from Ireland, Philip Nolan, spent five years in Texas capturing wild horses and trading them. The Spaniards became suspicious of Nolan's activities in Texas when they discovered he had mapped the region and that he had met with the American vice-president, Thomas Jefferson. The Spaniards issued an order for Nolan's arrest should he again enter Texas. In December 1800, on what he called a mustanging expedition, Nolan built mustang pens near present Waco and established his force of eighteen men there. With Nolan were fellow Irishmen Michael Moore, William Dublin, and Simon McCoy; the Negroes Caesar and Robert; some Germans, and several Spaniards.

One hundred fifty Spanish soldiers supported by a small

cannon rode out to arrest Nolan and his men. A young Anglo-American from Tennessee, Peter Ellis Bean, wrote of the ensuing battle and his plan to charge their attackers: "I told them . . . if we stood still all would doubtless be killed; that we must take the cannon, or retreat." Retreat they did, but the Spaniards killed Nolan and imprisoned most of his men.

On October 1, 1800, Spain returned Louisiana to France by the Treaty of San Ildefonso. Under the terms of the treaty, Spanish citizens living in Louisiana could retain their Spanish citizenship and resettle in Spanish territory. Moses Austin, an Anglo-American resident of Louisiana, was to use this condition to gather colonists for his proposed settlement, and many others living in Louisiana as Spanish subjects began considering a move to Texas.

The United States acquired the Louisiana territory from France by treaty of cession on October 21, 1803. Before 1803 the Spaniards had managed to keep the Anglo-Americans out of Texas by using Louisiana as a barricade between Texas and the United States. Now the eastern border of Texas was far from the control of Spanish officials in Mexico and close to the western border of the United States.

At the time of the Louisiana Purchase, the western boundary of Louisiana had not been accurately determined. The Americans claimed the Sabine River was the boundary, while the Spaniards contended that it was the Arroyo Hondo tributary of the Red River, a few miles to the east. The result was a no-man's land between these two waterways, into which outlaws poured. In 1819 the Adams–D'Onis Treaty created the present boundary, but Mexico had become independent of Spain before the treaty was ratified. The boundary was finally confirmed by a treaty between the United States and Mexico in 1828.

Thomas Jefferson, president of the United States at the time of the Louisiana Purchase, had always been interested in exploration of the country west of the Appalachians. In addition to the Lewis and Clark and Pike expeditions into the Louisiana Territory, he authorized an expedition under the command of Thomas Freeman to explore the upper Red River. In 1806 Freeman led a group of men up the Red River to camp in Caddo country. Jefferson had given Freeman strict instructions to avoid a clash with the Spanish, and when Freeman was challenged by a Spanish force under the command of Francisco Viana near the old French fort established by La Harpe, he turned back. However, the reports brought back by the Freeman, Pike, and Lewis and Clark expeditions stimulated interest in Texas as well as in the Louisiana Territory.

The Republican Army of the North. The Mexican people since the time of Cortés had felt the weight of Spanish domination. On September 16, 1810, a revolutionary leader and priest in the small town of Dolores, Mexico, called on the Mexican people to rise against Spain. He and a group of revolutionary leaders seized the prison in Dolores and raised the *Grito*, the call to arms. Within a year Father Hidalgo was dead and many of the revolutionary leaders were in prison. However, the revolutionary movement under Hidalgo inspired other revolutionists, and Mexico eventually gained her independence from Spain in 1821.

While Father Hidalgo was initiating insurrection in Mexico, Juan Bautista de las Casas was plotting with a group of army officers at Bexar to overthrow Spanish rule in Texas. Casas and his allies moved against Governor Manuel María de Salcedo and Commander Simón Herrera. Athough Casas was appointed governor of the province by the followers of Hidalgo, after the revolution failed he was tried for treason and executed.

Another ardent follower of Father Hidalgo's, Bernardo Gutiérrez de Lara, set out for Washington to seek aid after the revolution failed. Returning in 1812, Gutiérrez organized an expedition with other adventurers, including Augustus Magee, a West Point graduate. Calling themselves the Republican Army of the North, immigrants of many nationalities joined the effort to overthrow the Spanish. Troops under the command of Magee started from Natchitoches, Louisiana, in August 1812 and crossed the Sabine River to join Gutiérrez.

The forces captured Nacogdoches without firing a shot. They then captured La Bahía, and Magee's successor, Samuel Kemper, took San Fernando de Bexar in April 1813. Gutiérrez then made several mistakes which led to failure. He lost the support of some of the Americans when he allowed the execution of fourteen prisoners, including Governor Manuel Salcedo.

More Americans left when Gutiérrez declared Texas to be independent and formed a state government which was to become part of Mexico when she gained her independence from Spain. Faced with mounting opposition from both the Mexicans and the Americans, Gutiérrez resigned. The forces of the expedition fell into an ambush set by the Spanish general Arredondo and were wiped out. Only a few survivors escaped to the United States, and the first "Republic of Texas" fell.

Freebooters and Privateers. Gutiérrez and Magee were not the only adventurers with dreams of empire in Texas. French freebooter Louis-Michel Aury and privateers Pierre and Jean Lafitte occupied Galveston Island off the Texas coast from 1816 to 1821. When Mexican revolutionaries proclaimed Galveston a port of the short-lived Mexican Republic in 1816, Aury was appointed resident commissioner. But while Aury was on an expedition to Mexico, Jean Lafitte took over Galveston Island and established his town, Campeachy.

The Long Expedition. In 1819 Dr. James Long organized the last of the filibustering expeditions. He offered a league of land to every man who would follow him into Texas. Long appealed to Lafitte to supply him with materials and men, offering the pirate the position of governor of Galveston. Lafitte declined. At the first sign of Spanish resistance, Long and his men fled. However, Long returned to Texas in 1820 and entered La Bahía without resistance on October 4, 1821. Ironically, the very thing for which the filibusters had been striving—the

Jean Lafitte, ruler of Galveston Island, refused to ally himself with Dr. James Long.

From Thrall:
A PICTORIAL HISTORY OF TEXAS

overthrow of Spanish rule—had been accomplished seven months earlier by revolutionaries in Mexico. Long soon lost his position as president of his "Republic of Texas," as he was defeated by Mexican forces October 8. Long was imprisoned in Mexico and was shot by one of his guards while in Mexico City to plead with authorities for his release.

Dr. Long's widow, Mrs. Jane Wilkinson Long, gained the title "The Mother of Texas" by her brave stand against the elements and the Indians while Long was filibustering. When Long's expedition was marching toward La Bahía, Mrs. Long was left behind to face the Karankawas with only a twelve-year-old Negro servant, Kian, and her five-year-old daughter. She and Kian successfully kept the Indians from attacking the fort until settlers could rescue them.

The Empresarios

Dr. Long's expedition marked the end—temporarily—of efforts to establish an independent Texas. However, developments in the United States led to various attempts to colonize Texas. Americans were feeling a growing spirit of interest in their nation. The Louisiana Purchase doubled the size of the nation, but more than that it led to explorations which focused the attention of the people on the West. Manifest destiny, the idea that America was destined to rule from sea to sea, was becoming popular. And the young republic, alarmed by the establishment of Russian trading posts in Northern California, made clear its interest in the West by proclaiming the Monroe Doctrine.

After the War of 1812 the Indian menace west of the Appalachian Mountains was reduced, and Americans began to push westward toward the Mississippi River. The Ordinance of 1787 prohibited the holding of slaves in the states in the Northwest Territory, north of the Ohio River. The Missouri Compromise of 1820 extended that prohibition to the Louisiana Purchase above 36°30′ north latitude, except for Missouri. Southern planters seeking new cotton lands inevitably looked to Texas. Prices were rising on cotton, cattle, and grain, and farmers were buying land on credit to increase production. However, the

41

business depression of 1819 ruined many businessmen and farmers. It also caused the government to require cash payments for public lands. To a man broke and in debt, the United States no longer seemed to be the land of opportunity. But another lay just beyond the Sabine.

The effects of the depression of 1819 were felt far to the west in Missouri. Moses Austin, born in Connecticut and a veteran of the mining industry in Virginia, had obtained a Spanish land grant in Missouri. Austin entered the banking business only to be ruined when the bank failed. Looking for a means to regain the money he had lost, he headed for San Fernando de Bexar to petition Governor Martínez for a land grant in Texas. The governor ordered Austin out of Spanish Texas. However, the Baron de Bastrop, an old friend, intervened for Austin and encouraged the governor to file Austin's petition with General Joaquín de Arredondo, chief civil and military commandant of the province. Arredondo approved the grant for two hundred thousand acres and authorized Austin to settle three hundred families in Spanish Texas. However, before Austin could begin his colonization scheme he died, leaving his son to complete the plans he had begun.

So Stephen F. Austin came to Texas in 1821 and investigated lands along the coastal plains between present San Antonio and the Brazos River. The Spanish government approved his site, and the first settlers in Austin's colony arrived in December 1821 aboard the schooner *Lively*. Other settlers led by Austin arrived by land the same month. In the meantime, Mexico gained her independence from Spain.

Austin now faced a difficult problem. Would the new government honor the Spanish grant? The need for an answer to this question was urgent, as new settlers were arriving daily and Austin now had no authority to issue them titles to land.

Austin went to Mexico City to obtain approval of his grant from Agustín de Iturbide, head of the Mexican government. After much delay, Austin obtained his grant and complete civil and military authority in his colony. Settlers in the province were expected to be loyal to the Mexican government and to become members of the Catholic Church.

Stephen F. Austin took up
the task begun by his father.

Austin said, "From the day of my arrival on Mexican soil I
bid an everlasting farewell to my native country and adopted
this, and in so doing I determined to fulfill rigidly all the duties
and obligations of a Mexican citizen."

After 1823 settlers poured into Texas, escaping from the continually rising price of land in the United States. Immigrants
traveled overland from Natchitoches through Nacogdoches and
on to the Brazos River. Others came overland from Gaines
Ferry on the Sabine River. Some settlers journeyed by ship
from New Orleans, usually landing at Velasco, Brazoria, or
Columbia. They then traveled by land to the colony's capital,
San Felipe de Austin, founded in July 1823 on the Brazos River
near present Sealy.

Sterling C. Robertson and several other citizens of Tennessee,
including Sam Houston, formed the Nashville Company in 1822
to bring settlers into Texas. In 1825 Robertson obtained a land
grant to settle eight hundred families along the upper Brazos
River. Green C. DeWitt obtained a land grant to settle some
four hundred families on the Guadalupe, San Marcos, and Lavaca rivers. In 1805 Martín de León, descended from a wealthy
Mexican family, traveled to Texas and decided that he could
make a living raising cattle in the region. In 1823, after Mexico
had obtained her independence from Spain, De León obtained

43

a grant to settle Mexican families in Texas. He named the capital of his colony after the Mexican patriot Guadalupe Victoria. De León's contribution to the Texas province was not only in helping to build a flourishing cattle industry, but in bringing to Texas many Mexican families who helped to establish Victoria as one of the leading early cities of Texas.

Lorenzo de Zavala, a political exile from Mexico who served as minister of the treasury under President Vicente Guerrero and minister to France under Santa Anna, had obtained an empresario contract and had formed a partnership with David G. Burnet and Joseph Vehlein in 1829. De Zavala, one of the most polished men on the frontier, established his home on Buffalo Bayou and lent his political experience to the colony.

James Hewetson, an Irishman, visited Austin's colony in 1821. In 1826 he formed a partnership with James Power, another Irishman, to colonize coastal lands between the Nueces River and Coleto Creek. Power brought some three hundred fifty persons from Ireland, many of whom settled on the grant near Refugio. James McGloin and John McMullen received an empresario contract to settle two hundred families on the Nueces River in 1828. The Irish families who settled there named the leading settlement San Patricio in honor of the patron saint of Ireland, Saint Patrick.

Early visitors to Texas marveled at the nationalities represented in the province. In late 1821 Nacogdoches was described as a town of about one hundred Spaniards, Frenchmen, Americans, and free Negroes. Comanche Indians traded hides and dried buffalo meat at San Antonio and referred to the thriving town as "our rancho." A visitor to San Antonio wrote, "The traveler hears around him a confusion of unknown tongues, the red natives, in their different guttural dialects, the swarthy Spaniard of scarce brighter hue, the voluble Frenchman, a small number of the sons of Green Erin, and a goodly few of Uncle Sam's nephews or half expatriated sons."

Under Mexican Government

In 1824 the Mexican government adopted a federal system of government similar to that of the United States. Texas became

Land such as this near Smithville appealed to Austin's colonists.

part of the state of Coahuila y Texas. Certain restrictions were imposed on the colonists under laws enacted by Mexico in 1824. All settlers would become citizens of Mexico. They were required to develop the land within a specified period of time, adopt the Catholic religion, and obey the laws. Settlements could not be made within twenty leagues of a foreign boundary, nor within ten leagues of the coast without special permission.

With the adoption of the 1824 constitution the stage was set for the break which would occur a dozen years later. People who had been subjects of a monarchy for three centuries had adopted a written constitution providing for a federal system and popular republic. Those who had always lived under kings would not take a written constitution as seriously as frontier democrats from the United States who had always lived in a constitutional republic. There would be different reactions to executive encroachment on legislative domains and to the sacrifice of the rights of the Mexican states to the central

45

government. There would be differences of opinion over adequacy of representation and the right to criticize government and petition for redress of grievances. On top of all this there were language differences. And when the break came there was no one such as the Baron de Bastrop around to explain the two sides to each other. The old man had died earlier, so poor the legislature of which he was a part had to take up a collection for the burial of the selfless old man.

Discuss

1. Discuss the factors which made possible the rapid colonization of Texas under Mexican rule.

2. Compare the motives of the filibusters for coming to Texas with the motives of Stephen F. Austin. Compare the attitudes of the filibusters and Austin toward the government.

3. Explain how events in the United States between 1800 and 1820 stimulated interest in Texas.

4. Why were many citizens of the United States willing to give up their homes and citizenship to come to Texas?

5. Why did the early colonists restrict their efforts at settlement to the eastern portion of the state?

6. What tribes of Indians were found in the area of the San Sabá Mission? What effect did they have on the attempt to settle the region?

7. What part did geography play in the failure of the San Sabá Mission?

8. What was a principal reason for the establishment of the Spanish missions in Texas? Looking at the date of the report on the San Sabá Mission, can you give another reason for its abandonment besides trouble with the Indians?

Identify

San Francisco de los Tejas	Gil Antonio Ybarbo
Los Adaes	Tomás Sánchez
Villa de Bexar	Louis St. Denis
Treaty of Paris (1763)	Philip Nolan
Treaty of San Ildefonso	Father Hidalgo
Bernardo Gutiérrez	Jean Lafitte
Dr. James Long	Moses Austin
Sterling C. Robertson	Stephen F. Austin
James Hewetson	Martín de León

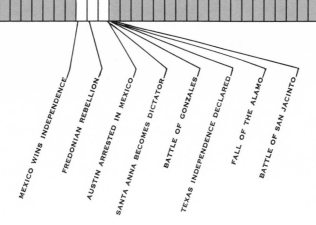

MEXICO WINS INDEPENDENCE

FREDONIAN REBELLION

AUSTIN ARRESTED IN MEXICO

SANTA ANNA BECOMES DICTATOR

BATTLE OF GONZALES

TEXAS INDEPENDENCE DECLARED

FALL OF THE ALAMO

BATTLE OF SAN JACINTO

CHAPTER 4

"Come to the Bower"

On April 21, 1836, an ill-equipped band of Texas soldiers under the command of General Sam Houston charged the Mexican army and its flamboyant general, Antonio López de Santa Anna, on the Coastal Plains where Buffalo Bayou flows into the San Jacinto River. The afternoon was hot, and the Mexican army was taking its siesta. To the tune of the Irish ballad, "Will You Come to the Bower I Have Shaded for You?" the tattered band of Texans marched to victory over the Mexican army. The Battle of San Jacinto was a brief but bloody one. The Texans swooped down on the surprised Mexican soldiers with cries of "Remember Goliad! Remember the Alamo!" The Mexicans were routed, and Santa Anna fled for his life, only to be captured by the Texans. The Battle of San Jacinto has been called one of the significant battles of history, for the events that followed in the next few years were to have a great impact on the course of world events.

49

Immigration into Texas

An understanding of the kind of men who came to Texas is necessary for an understanding of the Texas Revolution. The men who marched with Houston at San Jacinto have been described as a motley band with their clothes in tatters and their long hair and beards plastered with mud. However, among them were lawyers, doctors, teachers, and men of science. There were Englishmen, Irishmen, Scotsmen, Mexicans, Frenchmen, Germans, Italians, Poles, and Americans, white and black. Some of them had called Texas home for years, while others were recent arrivals from Europe or the United States. They had followed many paths to this land where their insistence on Santa Anna's governing according to the Constitution of 1824 led them to take up arms against the dictator.

The immigrants that poured into Texas following the establishment of Austin's first colony seemed to be possessed of few similar characteristics. They came from many countries and many stations in life. However, the fact that they came sets them apart from those who remained behind. These were bold men—men willing to undertake adventure and battle the difficulties of a frontier life. They shared the characteristics of individualism and independence. Many of them came from the frontier in the United States, bringing with them their skills of survival and the conviction that a man who wrested a living from the wilderness single-handedly owed little to a government that provided few services and little protection. They were convinced that the best government was the one that governed least. They were also certain that what government there was ought to be controlled by the people. These beliefs had their roots in the ideals of Thomas Jefferson and Andrew Jackson. Jefferson was a strong believer in limiting the powers of government, and he had faith in the ability of the common man to govern himself. Jackson, the first president from the West, was a believer both in westward expansion and in the common people. Thus, the immigrants from the United States brought with them a strong belief in local government run by the people with as little interference as possible from the central government. Many of the immigrants who came from countries other than the United States were fleeing oppressive governments; they shared the desire of the other Texans for the right to rule themselves.

The immigrants had an important trait in common. They were doers. When their position in life was not to their liking, they changed it. They regarded the right to improve their condition as one of their basic rights. But to a government far away in Mexico City, plagued by revolutions, plots, and intrigues, the exercise of what the frontiersman considered to be a basic right looked a great deal like rebellion against the authority of the central government, so the stage for revolution was set. Texans, with customs and political traditions different from those of their rulers, protested what they felt to be wrongs and injustices by using the conventions, consultations, and petitions that were traditional devices in the United States. Even worse from the viewpoint of the Mexican government, the Texans proposed changes in their form of government which, if adopted, would have resulted in less control by the central government.

The many men who immigrated to Texas brought with them a variety of skills and accomplishments as well as basic political beliefs. Many brought a knowledge of science and agriculture that helped to transform the economy of the territory. Jared Groce earned his title of "Father of Texas Agriculture" by bringing to Texas the first cottonseed. He opened the first cotton gin in the territory and encouraged other planters to come to Texas. Groce hardly fit the picture of the average frontiersman as he traveled to Texas on his thoroughbred horse, accompanied by his personal body servant. His party included about one hundred slaves, fifty wagons, and a herd of livestock.

In contrast to Groce was the eccentric Brit Bailey, who built the first brick house in Austin's colony. Bailey enjoyed frontier fights and would jump into any fight he saw with his fists cocked and the yell, "Free fight!" Bailey requested that he be buried standing up with his face to the west. He never wanted anyone to be able to walk over his grave and say, "There lies old Brit Bailey."

With farms and towns springing up, the surveyor was in demand on the frontier. George Washington Smyth, the son of a German millwright, migrated to Texas in 1830 and surveyed the land grants of Lorenzo de Zavala, Joseph Vehlein, and David G. Burnet. Smyth gained quite a reputation as a surveyor and was chosen to survey the boundary between Texas and the United States in 1839. He later served in the congress of the Republic of Texas and as a commissioner of the General Land Office. Smyth also served as a member of the Congress of the United States.

Austrian surveyor George B. Erath was an Indian fighter and soldier, serving with Houston at San Jacinto. Erath surveyed the towns of Waco and Caldwell and later served in the Texas legislature after Texas became a state.

Most immigrants to Texas regarded the land as ideal for farming and ranching, but many early settlers saw the need for other ventures. When Stephen F. Austin persuaded Samuel May Williams to act as secretary of the Austin colony, he brought to Texas one of her first businessmen and one who would contribute much to the financing of the revolution. With Thomas F. McKinney, Williams opened a successful trading post at Quintana and later moved the business to Galveston. They opened Texas to maritime commerce and operated three small steamboats, bringing supplies to the colonists and shipping produce down the Brazos River to be transported to New Orleans. Williams and McKinney financed three schooners for the revolutionists in 1836. These three ships formed the nucleus of the Texas navy, and the traders brought in another schooner loaded with guns, supplies, and troops for the Texas army.

Gail Borden, Jr., succeeded his brother as surveyor for Austin's colony. He helped survey the new city of Houston. He founded the most successful newspaper in the Republic of Texas, the *Telegraph and Texas Register,* which was published at San Felipe de Austin. Borden realized his greatest success as an inventor, finding time while in Texas to invent a "meat biscuit" inspired by Indian pemmican and a "locomotive bath house" for Galveston ladies who wished to go swimming in the Gulf of Mexico but were too modest to be seen doing so. He achieved greater fame in his later years as the first successful producer of canned evaporated milk and founder of the Borden Company.

Doctors were rare in early Texas, and often had little formal training in the art of medicine. Borden related the secret of his success as a doctor to a friend.

It is no use to be a doctor unless you put on the airs of one. Nine times out of ten sickness is caused by overeating or eating unwholesome food, but a patient gets angry if you tell him so; you must humor him. This I do by taking one grain of calomel [a purgative] and dividing it into infinitesimal parts, adding sufficient starch to each part to make one of these little pellets . . . then glaze them over with sugar. In prescribing for a patient I caution him about his diet, warning him that the pills have calomel in them. Well, the result is that he abstains from hurtful articles of food, which is all he needs to do anyway.[1]

A firebrand lawyer, Robert McAlpin Williamson, helped Godwin Cotten found another early newspaper in San Felipe de Austin, the *Texas Gazette*. He later edited two other newspapers, his editorials calling for independence from Mexico. The Mexican government put a price on his head for the same reason Texans called him the "Patrick Henry of the Texas Revolution." Although crippled, Williamson fought at the Battle of San Jacinto. He later became a judge and legislator. He was an ardent fighter for civil liberties and helped protect the state from exploitation by outside interests.

The Negro freedman enjoyed the legal and political rights of any other citizen of Mexico under Mexican law. He was free to own land and to run for political office if he so desired. One of the Negro freedmen in Texas was Hendrick Arnold, an able scout who distinguished himself at the siege of Bexar and was with Deaf Smith's spy company at the Battle of San Jacinto. Greenbury Logan, a free Negro who immigrated to Texas from Kentucky, served under James W. Fannin at the Battle of Concepción and marched with Ben Milam into Bexar. William Goyens was a Negro who served the Mexican and Texan governments in dealings with the Cherokee Indians. He helped

[1]Noah Smithwick, *The Evolution of a State* (1900; reprint ed., Austin: The Steck Company, 1936), 312.

Santa Anna aroused the enmity of many Texans by suspending the Constitution of 1824.

General Sam Houston negotiate a treaty with the Indians during the Texas Revolution and was awarded land near Nacogdoches for his service to the Republic. Goyens became a successful trader in land and horses and acquired considerable wealth.

Beginnings of Discontent

Although attempts were made by both Texans and Mexicans to resolve difficulties, problems increased daily. Land titles were disputed, trade routes closed, immigration restricted, customs and taxes unequally distributed and levied, and many persons imprisoned for unjust cause.

The unstable political situation in Mexico City was responsible for much of the friction. Major revolutions rocked the capital periodically, and Stephen F. Austin likened Mexico City to a volcano. Such a climate of revolution and intrigue did nothing to increase the respect of the Texans for their government. Moreover, each new regime tried to maintain itself by increasing the strength of the central government. Such actions soon aroused the opposition of those who favored democracy.

The Rise of Santa Anna. Mexico's turbulent politics can best be described by the spectacular rises to, and falls from, power of Santa Anna. In 1821 Mexico won her independence from Spain by the Treaty of Córdoba.

On May 18, 1822, Agustín de Iturbide was elected Constitutional Emperor of Mexico with the title of Agustín I, but

54

revolutionary forces led by Santa Anna rose against him. Iturbide was exiled and later executed. In 1823 the Republic of Mexico was formed, and Guadalupe Victoria was elected president under a constitution closely resembling that of the United States. Victoria managed to serve his entire four-year term, but after he left office there was constant turmoil, and military leaders became more prominent. Spain tried to invade Mexico in 1829, but her forces were defeated by an army led by Santa Anna. Now a national hero, Santa Anna became president in 1833, one of many times he found himself at the head of the Mexican state.

Despite such upheavals, the Texans still considered themselves loyal subjects of the Mexican government, and in 1826, when Haden Edwards and his brother Benjamin established the Republic of Fredonia in Nacogdoches over a land title dispute with Mexican officials, Austin and his followers helped quell the rebellion. Austin called the leaders of the Fredonian Rebellion "infatuated madmen." The tone of the rebellion, with its flag inscribed "Independence, Liberty, and Justice," aroused the suspicion of the Mexican officials who thought that Edwards was in league with the efforts of United States president John Quincy Adams to purchase Texas. When the Indians failed to ally themselves with the rebel forces, many

The Old Stone Fort at Nacogdoches was the focal point of the Fredonian Rebellion.

of the leaders, including Benjamin and Haden Edwards and Martin Parmer, who called himself "The Ringtailed Panther from the Forks of the Creek," fled across the Sabine River.

Mexico Tightens Control. Mexican reactions to the Fredonian Rebellion included sending General Mier y Terán to Texas in 1828 to study the situation. The general's report, stating that Americans outnumbered Mexicans by ten to one, alarmed the government and resulted in the Law of April 6, 1830. The law was designed to stop immigration from the United States, increase immigration from Mexico and Europe, and halt the introduction of slaves into Texas. It also opened coastal trading to foreigners for four years and attempted to set aside the contracts of the empresarios. Texans, faced with economic problems and considering themselves falsely accused of disloyalty, opposed the law.

The Mexican president, Bustamante, took steps to enforce the law. In 1831 the forts at Goliad, San Antonio, and Nacogdoches were reinforced and an additional fort was set up at Anahuac. A series of events led to armed conflict in 1832. Mexican colonel John Davis Bradburn arrested the government land agent at Anahuac in February 1831, causing delay in the issuance of land titles, and further antagonized the settlers by using their slaves without compensation. William Barret Travis and Patrick Jack were arrested for opposing Bradburn. A company of men raised to free them persuaded Bradburn's superior to relieve Bradburn of his command, but not before fighting had taken place. Learning that Santa Anna was at that same time leading a revolution in Mexico, the Texans then adopted the Turtle Bayou Resolutions supporting Santa Anna, who promised a return to democratic government under the Constitution of 1824. Mexican garrisons all over Texas declared their support of Santa Anna also, and most left for Mexico to aid in the revolution. When Santa Anna became president, Texans believed that their requests for governmental reforms would be heeded.

The Convention of 1832. The colonists formed Committees of Safety and Correspondence, much like those used before the American Revolution, to keep the settlements informed on problems with the central government. The committees named

56

delegates to a convention held at San Felipe de Austin on October 1, 1832. The delegates to the Convention of 1832 requested modification of the Law of April 6, 1830, to allow additional immigration to the colony, to permit a land commissioner to issue land titles in East Texas, and to separate Texas from Coahuila. However, the governor of the province ruled that the convention was illegal, and for various reasons the petitions were never presented to the Mexican government. This was the first attempt to convene an assembly representing all of Texas; however, San Antonio did not send delegates.

The Convention of 1833. The Convention of 1833 repeated the requests made a few months earlier. Then the delegates drew up a proposed constitution for a new state of Texas separate from Coahuila. Austin was sent to Mexico City to present the petition to the Mexican government. Austin successfully convinced Santa Anna to accept all the colonists' requests with the exception of separate statehood. While in Mexico City, Austin wrote a letter to officials in San Antonio urging them to organize a separate state government. Unfortunately for Austin, Mexican officials who saw the letter regarded it as a threat of revolution. Austin was arrested and imprisoned on suspicion of inciting revolution in Texas. He was held in Mexico until August 1835, although no charges were ever filed against him.

Santa Anna Becomes Dictator. The Texans believed in modification of government by democratic procedures. But the experience of Mexican authorities was with rigid government that was more easily overthrown than altered. A change as important as separate statehood smacked of revolution. In April 1834, declaring that Mexico was not ready for democracy, Santa Anna suspended the constitution, abolished the federal system, dissolved the congress and the governments of each of the states, and proclaimed himself dictator of Mexico. He sent troops to reopen the customs house at Anahuac. After Andrew Briscoe was arrested for violation of the tariff law, on June 29, 1835, William B. Travis and some two dozen others demanded that the garrison surrender and leave Texas. Santa Anna sent General Martín Perfecto de Cós to Texas with five hundred troops to insure that the tariff law would be enforced.

A Difficult Choice

Most Texans had chosen between submission to Santa Anna and resistance, but for some of Mexican descent the choice was difficult. Many had family ties in Mexico, having fled to Texas when Santa Anna rose to power. José María Carbajal had served as surveyor for Martín de León's colony and had married Refugio de León. Family ties drew him to the cause of Texas independence. Placido Benavides had also married into the De León family and served as alcalde of Victoria. Benavides gathered a group of ranchers and farmers and fought with the Texas army.

Agustín Viesca was governor of Coahuila y Texas in April 1835, when the legislature was dissolved. Viesca tried to move the capital to San Antonio. He was captured but escaped and came to Texas where he urged independence with his speeches to the citizens of Texas: "Your destruction is resolved upon, and nothing but the firmness and energy peculiar to true Republicans can save you."

Lieutenant Jesús Cuellar deserted the Mexican army at the siege of Bexar. His dislike of Santa Anna's policies led him to join the Texas army. Many Texans of Mexican descent held official positions in Texas and chose to side with the revolutionists. Juan Antonio Padilla, land commissioner for Martín de León's colony, and José Miguel Aldrete, who had served as mayor of Goliad and land commissioner of Coahuila y Texas, stood with the colonists. José Menchaca joined the Texas forces and served at Bexar. He marched under Juan Seguin's command at the Battle of San Jacinto, and after the war became an alderman for the city of San Antonio.

Erasmo Seguin was a close personal friend of Stephen F. Austin and many times tried to restore peaceful relations between the officials in Mexico and the Texans. His loyalties lay with the Texas cause, and he furnished great quantities of supplies to the Texans. After the Battle of San Jacinto he worked to restore civil government in San Antonio. His son Juan served gallantly in the Texas army, escaping death at the Alamo because Travis used him as a courier. After the revolution, Juan Seguin served in the Texas Senate and as mayor of San Antonio.

José Francisco Ruíz and José Antonio Navarro were the only native Texans to sign the Declaration of Independence. Ruíz was a teacher and former officer in the Mexican army. After the revolution he was the senator from Bexar to the first congress of the Republic. Navarro served on the committee which drafted the Constitution of the Republic of Texas and later was a member of the Texas legislature when statehood was attained. He spoke for many Texans when he said, "I have sworn to be a free Texian. I shall never forswear."

The Texas Revolution

In September 1835 Cós's army landed at Matagorda, bound for San Antonio. Colonel Ugartechea at San Antonio demanded that the Texans at Gonzales surrender a six-pound cannon. The cannon was of slight value, but the demand symbolized a desire to render the Texans defenseless. On the morning of October 2, 1835, the Texans fired the cannon over the heads of Mexican troops sent to seize it. The war was on. The Mexicans retired to San Antonio while the Texans celebrated their victory. Stephen F. Austin, recently returned from his long imprisonment in Mexico, had made a prophetic statement a few weeks earlier when he said, "War is our only recourse."

Noah Smithwick indicated the intrinsic value of the cannon when he later wrote his recollection of those days.

So with the old cannon flag flying at the head, and the "artillery" flying at the heels of longhorned Texas steers occupying the post of honor in the center, we filed out of Gonzales and took up our line of march for San Antonio. Our pride in our artillery soon began to wane. We had to take turns riding in its rear, and the slow pace of the oxen ill accorded with our impatient zeal. . . . and finally, after all the trouble we had brought upon ourselves in its defense, the old cannon was abandoned in disgrace at Sandy Creek before we got halfway to San Antonio. . . .

I never saw nor heard of it again.[1]

[1]Noah Smithwick, *The Evolution of a State* (1900; reprint ed., Austin: The Steck Company, 1936), 110-11.

Eleven days after the Battle of Gonzales, flying a flag bearing a drawing of the cannon and the words, "Come and Take It," Austin led three hundred men out of Gonzales to oppose Cós, who held San Antonio. At Mission Concepción the Texas army sustained its first casualty. Austin, at the direction of the provisional government, handed over his command to Edward Burleson in order to go to the United States to seek assistance for the Texans. The army then began a listless siege of San Antonio that dragged on for almost two months. Samuel Maverick reported that Mexican defenses were weak, and a deserter reported the general condition of the garrison was poor, but Burleson decided that the troops should march to Goliad instead. Some members wished to attack, but such action was postponed when one group of men refused to march without Hendrick Arnold, who was on a scouting mission. When Arnold returned on December 5, some three hundred men answered Ben Milam's call to follow him into San Antonio. House by house, street by street, the Texans advanced. Cós's forces surrendered on December 10. San Antonio had been won, but not without cost. Some soldiers, such as Greenbury Logan, were crippled for life, while the courageous Ben Milam was killed before the doorway of the old Veramendi house. Deaf Smith, who had served as a scout under Milam, wrote a poem in his memory which ended, "As bright was thy example,/So bright shall be thy fame;/And generations yet unborn,/Shall honor Milam's name."

The Consultation. The colonists called a Consultation to meet at San Felipe de Austin on October 16, 1835, but the members could not assemble until November 3. Branch T. Archer, who had served in the Virginia House of Burgesses, headed the Consultation. Many members wanted to declare Texas independent from Mexico, but most hoped to remain within the Mexican union. They drew up a Declaration of Causes similar to the Declaration of Rights and Grievances the American colonists had submitted to the British government in 1775. By a vote of thirty-three to fifteen the delegates declared their allegiance to the federal government of Mexico and petitioned for the restoration of the Constitution of 1824.

The delegates to the Consultation took several other actions.

Branch T. Archer, William H. Wharton, and Stephen F. Austin were sent to the United States to obtain financial aid. Sam Houston was elected commander in chief of an army that did not exist. A provisional government was established, but the executive and legislative branches were at odds over the issue of independence and did not cooperate. In early February 1836 the government collapsed.

Independence Is Declared. During the month of February, Texas had no government. In one of the few actions taken by the government before its collapse, the delegates called a convention to meet at Washington-on-the-Brazos in March. A norther sent its chill winds blowing through the rough, unfinished building that was rented for the meeting. Makeshift windows and doors kept out little of the cold, and the delegates huddled together. Few records were kept.

George C. Childress introduced a resolution calling for a committee to draft a declaration of independence. He wrote out the declaration, and the delegates voted Texas free from Mexico on March 2, 1836. The Committee of Twenty-one drafted the Constitution of the Republic of Texas, providing for an *ad interim,* or temporary, government, composed of a bicameral legislature, a president, and judicial powers vested in a Supreme Court and such other courts as the legislature might deem fit. Sam Houston was made commander in chief of the Texas army then gathering at Gonzales.

Sam Houston served the Republic as commander in chief, president, and congressman. After annexation he was senator and governor.

From Thrall:
A PICTORIAL HISTORY OF TEXAS

The model for the constitution of the Republic was the Constitution of the United States. The Republic's Declaration of Rights contained seventeen articles providing for freedom of speech, freedom of religion, and other rights guaranteed to citizens of the United States by the Bill of Rights. The constitution reflected the origin of its framers with its emphasis on the Jeffersonian and Jacksonian ideals of frontier democracy and the natural rights of man.

Many of the delegates to the Convention of 1836 had legislative experience in either the United States or Mexico. Lorenzo de Zavala had extensive governmental experience in Mexico. He fled from Mexico to escape Santa Anna's dictatorship, and General Cós placed a price on his head. De Zavala served as *ad interim* vice-president of the Republic and was highly esteemed for his legislative experience.

Martin Parmer of San Augustine had served in the Missouri territorial legislature, and Richard Ellis of Pecan Point had been a delegate to the Alabama Constitutional Convention of 1819. Samuel P. Carson, also of Pecan Point, had served in the North Carolina Senate and in the United States House of Representatives. Another member of the convention with experience in the United States Congress was Robert Potter of Nacogdoches, who served as *ad interim* secretary of the navy. Sam Houston, close friend of President Andrew Jackson, had served as governor of Tennessee and in the United States Congress. Houston was typical of the men who represented the West.

The Siege of the Alamo. While the provisional government was in its last days, preparations were being made to resist the return of Mexican troops to Texas. The Texas forces under Colonel James C. Neill planned to defend San Antonio from the Alamo. Although the colonists had not expected Santa Anna to march toward Texas until early spring, six thousand troops led by Santa Anna were marching toward Bexar. William Barret Travis was sent to the Alamo with a regular army detachment of thirty men to strengthen the volunteer forces. Travis and James Bowie immediately quarreled over the command of the garrison: they shared the command until Bowie fell ill.

Bowie had gained a reputation as an adventurer and duelist

before he came to Texas and became a Mexican citizen. His marriage to Ursula Veramendi, daughter of the vice-governor of Coahuila y Texas, ended when she and their two children died of cholera. Bowie then joined the revolutionists. Houston had sent Bowie to tell Colonel Neill to destroy the Alamo and retreat, but Bowie decided the Alamo should be held.

Volunteers were pouring into Texas in response to calls for assistance. Over one hundred men flying the flag of the New Orleans Greys came to Goliad. Thirty men calling themselves the Mobile Grays, among them James Butler Bonham, went with Bowie to the Alamo. Travis twice sent Bonham to seek aid from Fannin, and twice Bonham returned to the Alamo through the Mexican lines.

A few days before the siege began the legendary frontier hero, David Crockett, rode into the Alamo with a group of his fellow Tennesseans. He had served as a member of the Tennessee legislature and as a member of the United States House of Representatives before enlisting as a private in the volunteer army of the Republic. Crockett's opposition to the financial policies of Andrew Jackson and his supposed authorship of a scathing denunciation of Martin Van Buren, Jackson's choice as his successor to the presidency, led to a bitter election campaign in 1835. Defeated for reelection, Crockett joined the Texans, defending the south side of the Alamo with the same bravery he had shown fighting bears in Tennessee.

On February 24, with Santa Anna's forces garrisoned in the city and the Napoleon of the West headquartered at San Fernando Cathedral, Travis appealed for aid to "The People of Texas & all Americans in the world," saying, "I shall never surrender or retreat. . . . I am determined to sustain myself as long as possible & die like a soldier who never forgets what is due to his own honor & that of his country—Victory or Death!"

Thirty-two men from Gonzales answered Travis's call. Fannin's troops at Goliad prepared to march, under General Houston's order, to the aid of the men at the Alamo. However, a cart broke and Fannin turned back. Travis and his small band would have to stand alone. The defenders, flying a flag with the numerals 1824, referring to the constitution they supported, mounted the parapets to wait for Santa Anna's troops

The storming of the Alamo

to charge. In full view flying from the San Fernando Cathedral was the red flag signifying that no quarter would be given.

Before dawn on March 6 the sombre notes of the traditional song of no quarter, the *degüello*, broke the chill morning air. Santa Anna's infantry advanced toward the Alamo, carrying ladders. The cavalry rode behind, ready to cut off any defender who tried to escape. The first shots rang out, and after desperate fighting the Mexican battalions scaled the walls. The men were reduced to fighting hand to hand, and even though the Mexican army suffered severe casualties, their great numbers overwhelmed the Texans. Travis fell over his cannon; Bowie died on his cot, too ill to stand; Davy Crockett held his position to the end.

Within an hour it was over. Not a defender lived. Slaves, women, and children were the only survivors of the battle. Mrs. Almeron Dickenson, her child, Mrs. Horace Alsbury, and Travis's Negro servant Joe survived to carry the news of the Alamo to the Texans. The alcalde of San Antonio, Francisco

Ruíz, hurried to the fortress to attend the wounded. He reported that the bodies of the defenders, 182 in number, were piled in heaps and burned. The monument to their heroic stand at the Alamo reads: "Thermopylae had her messenger of defeat; the Alamo had none."

Santa Anna's army suffered over a thousand casualties. Moreover, the thirteen days the Alamo held gave the Republic time to prepare for Santa Anna's advancing army. On March 6, the day the Alamo fell, Houston left Washington-on-the-Brazos to take command of the forces at Gonzales. Wearing a buckskin coat and vest, high-heeled boots, Mexican spurs with three-inch rowels, and a hat crowned with a billowing feather, he arrived in Gonzales on March 11. When news of the fall of the Alamo reached him on the thirteenth, Houston ordered Fannin to destroy the fort at Goliad and retreat to Victoria.

The Goliad Campaign. Fannin delayed for six days after receiving the order to retreat. When he finally began his retreat, he was short of ammunition and food and his oxen and horses were growing weak from hunger. Fannin halted his troops on an open prairie about three miles from Coleto Creek in order to let the livestock graze and was immediately surrounded by Mexican forces under General José Urrea. Fannin withstood the attack as best he could. However, the Mexicans received reinforcements, and Fannin, wounded, realized the cause was lost and surrendered.

Urrea marched the prisoners back to Goliad. Santa Anna, hostile to men who had entered Texas from the United States to join the Texas army, ordered that all prisoners were to be executed. On Palm Sunday, March 27, Urrea's men divided the some 390 prisoners into three groups and marched them from the fort to be shot. Fewer than thirty escaped. To the cry of "Remember the Alamo," the Texans could now add "Remember Goliad."

Attitude of the United States. Stephen F. Austin and William H. Wharton, in the United States to gain money and support for the Texas cause, were desperate. To possible lenders, the fall of the Alamo meant the Texans were unlikely to win their independence and would be unable to repay any loans. On April 15 Austin published an open letter to President Andrew

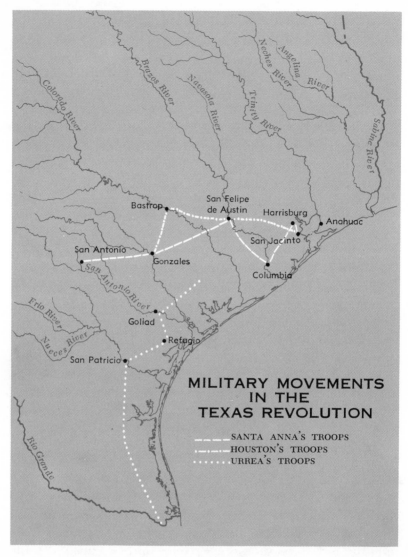

MILITARY MOVEMENTS
IN THE
TEXAS REVOLUTION

－－－－－－SANTA ANNA'S TROOPS
■－■－■－HOUSTON'S TROOPS
∙∙∙∙∙∙∙∙URREA'S TROOPS

Jackson, asking for United States intervention on behalf of Texas. While Jackson was sympathetic to the Texans, he believed the United States should honor its obligations to Mexico and maintain a strict neutrality. He also believed that intervention might disrupt the Democratic party and involve the United States in a war with Mexico.

The Runaway Scrape. In Texas the colonists were panic-stricken. The Alamo had fallen. Houston had abandoned Gonzales and was in retreat. Santa Anna's forces were advancing, and news of Goliad left no one with the desire to risk capture by the Mexican army. The settlers packed what they could, abandoned the rest, and began the Runaway Scrape to safety across the Sabine River. Old men, women, children, and deserters from the army fled before Santa Anna's advance.

Doctor Pleasant Rose's daughter, Dilue Rose Harris, described the terror of the fleeing settlers: "On the 12th of March came the news of the fall of the Alamo. A courier brought a dispatch from General Houston for the people to leave. . . . Then began the horrors of the 'Runaway Scrape.' We left home at sunset, hauling clothes, bedding, and provisions on the sleigh with one yoke of oxen."

The Battle of San Jacinto. Houston's forces were exhausted and mutinous because of the continual retreating. Spring rains flooded the creeks and made a marsh of the countryside. Rations were scarce, and the soldiers declared that Houston was a coward and a madman. Houston wrote to his friend, Secretary of War Thomas Jefferson Rusk: "I consulted none—I held no councils of war. If I err, the blame is mine." Despite hardships, Houston reached Groce's Ferry where the steamboat *Yellowstone* was commandeered to ferry the troops across the Brazos River.

Santa Anna marched to Harrisburg with a portion of his army, hoping to overtake the officials of the *ad interim* government, who had fled to Galveston Island. Troops under Generals Sesma and Filisola were on the way to join Santa Anna's forces. The tiny Texas navy, four ships strong, managed to keep lines of supply open for the Texans and to thwart attempts by the Mexicans to bring in provisions.

Santa Anna's pursuit of the politicians took him toward Galveston, and when he returned to cross the San Jacinto River near Harrisburg, he found Houston and his army waiting. The two armies faced one another across the plains of San Jacinto. Houston held Lynch's Ferry across the San Jacinto River, and he had Deaf Smith destroy Vince's Bridge, the only other avenue of escape for either army.

Houston held a council of war and ordered his men into position on the afternoon of April 21. Santa Anna, confident that the Texans would be waiting when he chose to destroy them, had settled the Mexican army down for a nap. The "Twin Sisters," a gift from the citizens of Cincinnati, loosed a salvo. Shouts of "Remember the Alamo! Remember Goliad!" awakened the sleeping Mexicans. In eighteen minutes the Texans won the Battle of San Jacinto and their independence from Mexico. The next day Santa Anna, disguised in the uniform of a private, was captured and taken before Houston, who had received an ankle wound. Houston stipulated that all Mexican armies should be withdrawn beyond the Colorado River before negotiations could begin. Santa Anna's message to General Filisola began, "The small division under my immediate command having had an unfortunate encounter yesterday afternoon, I find myself a prisoner of war." It was only due to Houston's intervention that Santa Anna did not become a casualty himself, for a number of Texans wanted to hang him.

At Velasco on May 14, 1836, Santa Anna signed two peace treaties with the Texans. The public one ended the war and promised the withdrawal of Mexican troops from Texas and payment for supplies and property taken by the Mexican army. The Mexicans agreed to exchange their prisoners of war, and Santa Anna was to be sent back to Mexico. In the secret treaty Santa Anna agreed to work for Mexican acknowledgment of Texas's independence from Mexico and recognition of the Rio Grande as the southern border of Texas.

Settlers were still fleeing toward the Sabine River. Dilue Rose Harris reports that a rider signaled the frantic families and shouted, "Turn back! The Texas army has whipped the Mexican army and the Mexican army are prisoners. No danger! No danger! Turn back!" The weary settlers returned to their homes. The Republic of Texas had begun.

Discuss

1. What basic differences in political philosophy were a contributing factor to friction between Texans and Mexicans?

2. Documents adopted by the Texans at the Conventions of 1832 and 1833 and at the Consultation stress that the Texans were trying to achieve local self-government and were loyal to the Mexican Constitution of 1824. Discuss the reasons the Texans might have had for taking this stand, and tell which reason you feel is the most valid, and why.

3. How did Mexico's internal political troubles lead to a desire among Anglo-Americans in Texas for independence?

4. Why did Mexico become alarmed over immigration to Texas in 1830? How did the situation that developed over Mexico's attempt to solve the problem further worsen relations between Texas and Mexico?

5. Describe some of the specific situations that led to friction between the Anglo and Mexican peoples in the Republic of Mexico.

Identify

Jared Groce	James Fannin
George Washington Smyth	Treaties of Velasco
	Robert M. Williamson
Samuel May Williams	Hendrick Arnold
Gail Borden, Jr.	William Goyens
General Mier y Terán	Santa Anna
Turtle Bayou Resolutions	Republic of Fredonia
	Greenbury Logan
Convention of 1833	Convention of 1832
Juan Seguin	General Martín Perfecto de Cós
José Antonio Navarro	
Consultation	Battle of Gonzales
George C. Childress	Sam Houston
José Francisco Ruíz	William B. Travis
James Bowie	Runaway Scrape
David Crockett	

From Thrall: A Pictorial History of Texa

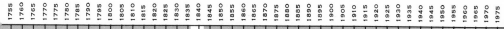

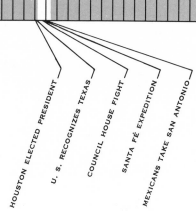

HOUSTON ELECTED PRESIDENT

U. S. RECOGNIZES TEXAS

COUNCIL HOUSE FIGHT

SANTA FÉ EXPEDITION

MEXICANS TAKE SAN ANTONIO

CHAPTER 5

"Our Sister Republic"

In Thomas Jefferson's dream of American empire he had envisioned a series of sister republics extending across the continent. These republics would be based on the American model and devoted to the ideals of republicanism and democracy set forth in the Constitution of the United States. The Republic of Texas seemed to be a step toward fulfillment of Jefferson's dream. The preamble of the Constitution of the Republic of Texas gives a good clue as to the origins of most of the ideas in that document: "We, the people of Texas, in order to form a government, establish justice, ensure domestic tranquility, provide for the common defense and general welfare; and to secure the blessings of liberty to ourselves, and our posterity, do ordain and establish this constitution."

71

The Republic

The *ad interim* government under President David G. Burnet had functioned during the hectic days of the revolution. Following the defeat of the Mexican army at the Battle of San Jacinto, President Burnet set in motion the machinery for establishing a true republic. An election was held in the fall of 1836, and Texas formally became an independent state with a popularly elected government. The election provided an opportunity for the citizens of the Republic to elect government officials, ratify the constitution, and vote on whether the Republic should seek to be annexed to the United States.

Texas Politics. In the election of 1836, all but a few votes were in favor of annexation by the United States. The constitution also received overwhelming approval. Sam Houston was elected president; Mirabeau B. Lamar was elected vice-president. This first election in the Republic set a pattern for the politics of Texas that has continued into the twentieth century. The strong sense of individualism inherent in frontier democracy led to the selection of political leaders with strong ideas and temperaments. Texas politics over the decades has continued to produce forceful and controversial leaders.

Problems of the Republic. The leaders of the Republic had to face many problems as they pulled people of many races and backgrounds into a self-governing republic. Financial difficulties, disposition of the public lands, Indian raids, trouble with Mexico, and the task of gaining recognition from the United States and other foreign countries plagued each of the three presidents of the Republic of Texas. Overshadowing all these problems was the question of annexation. Most Texans had voted in favor of seeking annexation to the United States, but a number of obstacles kept Texas from statehood for almost a decade.

Recognition of Texas independence was more easily obtained; the United States became the first nation to appoint a diplomatic agent to Texas on March 3, 1837, when President Andrew Jackson appointed Alcée LaBranche as chargé d'affaires to Texas. France followed suit in 1839, appointing Count Alphonse de Saligny chargé d'affaires. Saligny got involved in a dispute with his Austin landlord over the landlord's pigs invading Saligny's stable, and there was the matter of some unpaid bills and counterfeit notes, so Saligny went back to France in a huff. His report to the French minister of finance (Saligny's brother-in-law) may have contributed to Texas's failure to obtain a much-needed loan from France.

Slavery constituted the major obstacle to Texas annexation to the United States, and foreign countries such as Great Britain were reluctant even to extend diplomatic recognition to a government which permitted slavery to continue. The freedman was forbidden to remain in the Republic without special permission from the congress; thus free blacks like Hendrick Arnold and Greenbury Logan, who had fought for the independence of Texas alongside whites, had to ask for permission to remain in Texas.

Houston's First Administration

Houston took office in October 1836. He appointed Stephen F. Austin as secretary of state, but the Father of Texas died shortly after the appointment. Houston's main problem was that of establishing and maintaining a government with an almost empty treasury and no means of providing revenue. Houston considered the wisest course to be one of carefully husbanding all resources while Texas recovered from the war and developed sources of revenue. Houston's administration inherited a debt of approximately $1.25 million, and taxation proved to be a problem. Although congress passed poll taxes, occupation taxes, property taxes, and a tax on goods imported into the state, the people were too poor to pay the taxes. Houston attempted to minimize the inevitably increasing debt, but many expenses of the infant Republic were unavoidable.

Houston considered a standing army to be a menace to civil government, but danger from Indians and the constant threat of invasion from Mexico made protection a necessity. However, alarmed by unrest among the inactive troops and pressed by growing debts, Houston furloughed the majority of the army, leaving frontier protection up to the militia and a few bands of Rangers.

Houston used his wide experience among the Indians to advantage in his term as president of the Republic. Serving as Indian agent in 1836, Houston had convinced the Cherokees near Nacogdoches to remain quiet during the fight for Texas independence. The Indians feared the encroachment of the white man, realizing that he wanted to displace him and gain his land. Mexican spies among the Indians encouraged them to attack the white man. The Cherokees had good reason to be suspicious of the white man, having been forced to sell their land in the southeastern United States. However, Houston had promised them titles to their land and fair treatment from the government. But the Texas Senate refused to ratify Houston's treaty with the Indians.

Although most of the Texans of Mexican descent residing in Texas during the revolutionary period chose to become citizens of the Republic, Vicente Cordova, a resident of Nacogdoches, opposed the revolution. He ambushed Texas troops marching to the siege of Bexar in 1835, and in 1838 he organized a force of several hundred Cherokees and other settlers and established headquarters on an island in the Angelina River. Cordova sent word to President Sam Houston that he and the members of his army would not swear allegiance to the Republic. However, when the Texas militia pursued Cordova, his army fled and he escaped to Mexico, returning to Texas in 1842 with the army of General Adrian Woll.

Houston opposed the establishment of a general land office and tried to protect the rights of the Indians. Many settlers wanted a more generous land policy and feared the Indians and their dominance of the land. When Houston's term came to an end, his policies had caused him to lose some of his popularity with the people. The constitution of the Republic provided that the president could not succeed himself, and Houston retired from office. Lamar, Houston's vice-president, was elected president of the Republic of Texas.

Lamar's Administration

Lamar's liberal education policy was in sharp contrast to the severity of his policy toward the Indians. Lamar's Indian policy was supported by Secretary of War Albert Sidney Johnston. Lamar and Johnston considered the Indians to be encroachers on the land. They also felt that settlers had the right to take Indian lands without interference from the government. Furthermore, many Texans believed that the Indians were allied with the Mexican government against the Texans. Lamar's belief in the expansion of Texas, perhaps to the Pacific, was

SETTLEMENT OF
TEXAS TO 1846

illustrated by his desire to have the capital located as far west as possible, so it would be centrally located in the Texas of the future. Austin was selected as the site in 1839.

Fighting broke out and Johnston led a punitive expedition against the Cherokees in East Texas. Chief Bowles, the leader of the Cherokees, was killed, and the Cherokees were forced to retreat across the Red River. The following year quarrels between leaders of the Comanches and the Texas government led to bloodshed in the Council House Fight in San Antonio. Over thirty Indians were killed. The Indians retaliated with raids down the valley of the Guadalupe River as far as Victoria and Linnville, a small town on the coast. Bands of militia formed to pursue the Indians. Volunteers under the command of Felix Huston and Rangers under Ben McCulloch overtook the Indians at Plum Creek, near Lockhart. The Comanches were beaten badly. In October 1840 a Texas force attacked a Comanche village far up the Colorado River and killed most of the inhabitants to demonstrate Texas's retaliatory capabilities. Lamar's Indian campaigns were costly ones, both in lives and in money. The immediate gain was the opening of some rich agricultural land in East Texas to settlement and the safety of the Republic from Indian attack on the frontier.

When Lamar became president of the Republic, he called for congress to set aside lands for educational institutions. His message to congress in December 1838 stated that "[a] cultivated mind is the guardian genius of democracy." The congress provided fifty leagues of land for the establishment and endowment of two colleges or universities. (A league was equal to 4,428 acres.) However, the Republic lacked funds for continuing any type of higher education, and it was not until after statehood was attained that the legislature could provide funds for a state college. The congress also provided for land to be set aside in each county to finance a general system of education. Another aspect of Lamar's land policy was the passage of a homestead law that had its origins in legislation of Coahuila y Texas. The law provided that a man's home and tools for making a living could not be seized and sold to satisfy debts. That law, with slight modifications, has been carried forward to our own time.

Lamar sought to solve financial problems by establishing a government-operated bank, supported by a loan from the United States government. However, opposition to the bank was rooted in a frontier democracy founded on Jacksonian principles, and congress failed to pass legislation for the founding of the bank. At the end of Lamar's term of office, the finances of the Republic were in an appalling condition. Commenting on the state of the economy, Houston stated, "There is not a dollar in the treasury. The nation is involved from ten to fifteen millions. The precise amount of its liabilities has not been ascertained. . . . We are not only without money, but without credit, and for want of punctuality, without honor." Most of the liabilities of the Republic were in the form of interest-bearing notes issued by the government and circulated as currency. Depreciation rendered most of these notes virtually worthless, and Texans relied mostly on the barter system. The lack of money was so severe that at one time the treasurer of the Republic had to send a thousand dollar bill to New Orleans to be changed so the money could be spent.

A shortage of money in the Republic forced the settlers to resort to barter, although some came up with an ingenious solution to the problem of transacting business in which a cow and her calf formed the security for an issue of paper money.

Mrs. H., a widow living near me, having need of merchandise, for which the cash was not on hand, offered a cow and a calf in lieu thereof, a cow and calf being rated at ten dollars. The tender was accepted, Mrs. H. reserving the use of the cow during the milking season. The bill of sale being made out, the merchant paid off a debt with it and the creditor likewise passed it on. That bit of paper passed from hand to hand, always with the original reservation, till it paid about one hundred dollars; when the widow made a deal and bought the cow back again before it went dry. That was a fair illustration of the potency of confidence. We all felt satisfied that the cow was safe in the widow's keeping and would be forthcoming on demand, the only risk being the possible death of the cow.[1]

---

[1]Noah Smithwick, *The Evolution of a State* (1900; reprint ed., Austin: The Steck Company, 1936), 234.

Houston's Second Administration

When Houston took over the reins of government for a second term in 1841, a policy of financial retrenchment was called for. The public debt during Lamar's term of office had risen to an alarming amount, while revenues remained low. Many of Houston's policies and actions during his second presidential term were based at least partially on the poor financial condition of the nation.

Houston set about repairing relations with the Indians and establishing trading posts to furnish the tribes with goods and supplies. The Waco and the Comanche tribes signed treaties with the Texas government, and Houston's second administration was relatively free from Indian threats. However, Houston was forced to call out the militia to quell civil disorders in East Texas between the Regulators and the Moderators, vigilante groups who were causing trouble in Shelby County and adjoining areas.

Houston inherited the problems created by President Lamar in his relations with Mexico. In trying to force Mexico to recognize the independence of Texas, Lamar had unwisely permitted Yucatan revolutionaries to make use of the Texas navy. He also sent an expedition to establish control over the Mexican city of Santa Fé. Although the attempt was a failure, the reaction of the Mexican government was to reply in kind.

In March 1842 Mexican troops moved into San Antonio, Goliad, and Refugio in retaliation for the Santa Fé expedition. However, they soon retired from Texas soil. Congress voted to declare war and appropriated 10 million acres of land to pay the expenses. The Republic could not afford a war, particularly an unnecessary one, so Houston vetoed the war bill on the grounds that the appropriation was insufficient.

In September 1842 General Adrian Woll and a Mexican force occupied San Antonio. When they withdrew, taking a number of officials as prisoners, General Alexander Somervell assembled a force of militia and started for Laredo. After taking Laredo, Somervell suggested that the force disband and retreat to Gonzales. Many obeyed, but a force led by William S. Fisher crossed the Rio Grande and attacked a Mexican army in the town of Mier. After a two-day battle, running short of supplies and ammunition, the Texans decided to surrender to General Pedro Ampudia and were imprisoned in Mexico City. A few escaped enroute; the rest drew beans from a jar to see who would be executed for the attempted escape—the seventeen black beans signified death by firing squad. Many who drew white beans later died in prison.

The troubles with Mexico gave President Houston an excuse to move the government archives from Austin to Houston. Houston had long objected to the capital being placed on the exposed western frontier. He ordered the archives taken to Houston, but residents of Austin, warned by a Swiss hotel owner, John Wahrenberger, and led by another hotel owner, Mrs. Angelina Eberly, used a cannon to repulse the men sent by Houston. The Archive War helped Austin retain the capital.

Part of the cause for continued trouble with Mexico was the desire of the Mexican government to prevent the annexation of Texas by the United States. Houston asked that the United States, Britain, and France demand that Mexico either recognize or declare war on Texas. Santa Anna offered peace if the Texans would acknowledge Mexico's sovereignty and not seek annexation. Houston proclaimed a truce, and an armistice was signed between the two nations to smooth the way for negotiations. However, sentiment in Texas was strong for annexation, and it is probable that Houston was more interested in the armistice than in the negotiations.

Jones's Administration. When Houston stepped down from the presidency of the Republic for the second time, his secretary of state, Dr. Anson Jones, became president. Jones favored Mexican recognition of Texas independence instead of annexation of the Republic by the United States. Since annexation took place during Jones's administration, however, his name is usually associated with the attainment of statehood, though Houston and others had been working for annexation for years.

The "Texians"

The colonists of the Republic of Texas were generally referred to as "Texians," a term first introduced by a writer in the *New*

Orleans Bee and picked up by Gail Borden for use in his *Telegraph and Texas Register.* And the number of "Texians" was growing rapidly. In 1834 there were approximately 24,700 people in Texas; in 1845 there were 125,000 residents. Many people came from the southern United States—Tennessee, Alabama, and Georgia—looking for land on which to grow cotton. With the invention of the cotton gin by Eli Whitney in 1793, the economy of the South had been revolutionized. However, much of the land of the Southern states had been worn out by the continuous one-crop planting of cotton, and the spread of the cotton culture meant the spread of slavery.

The rich soil of Texas attracted people from outside the United States. Germans, Frenchmen, Swiss, Englishmen, Scotsmen, and Irishmen poured into Texas and began transforming the wilderness into farms and towns. Following Frederick Ernst's example, German settlers flocked to the Republic of Texas.

German immigration to the new Republic increased in 1842 when a group of German nobles formed a society to promote German settlement in Texas. The *Mainzer Adelsverein* or "Society for the Protection of German Immigrants in Texas" constituted one of the most important European immigration influences in early Texas. Prince Victor of Leiningen and Count Joseph of Boos-Waldeck came to Texas in 1843 seeking grants of land. Boos-Waldeck founded Nassau Farm in present-day Fayette County. Nassau served as a recreation resort for many of the nobles who later came to Texas as representatives of the *Adelsverein.*

The German noblemen fell victim to many schemes to divest their proposed colonists of funds, and they obtained many grants that were virtually worthless. However, in 1844 Prince Carl of Solms-Braunfels was elected commissioner general of the *Adelsverein* and began negotiations to obtain lands near other settlements. In 1845 he obtained from the Veramendi family in San Antonio the rich agricultural land on the Comal River that was to become New Braunfels. The settlement flourished and was one of the most successful German communities in Texas. Prince Carl's successor, John O. Meusebach, expanded the holdings of the *Adelsverein,* and the years im-

John O. Meusebach insured
the safety of Fredericksburg
by negotiating a treaty with
the Comanches in 1847.

mediately following annexation were very successful ones for
the German settlements.

On February 15, 1842, Henri Castro, of Portuguese and
French descent, obtained a contract to settle a colony west of
the Medina River. On September 3, 1844, the colony of Castroville was established west of San Antonio on the Medina River,
and Castro's settlers later founded Quihi, Vandenburg, and
D'Hanis. French, German, and Swiss settlers—more than five
thousand strong—settled in the colonies established by Castro
between the years 1843 and 1847.

Svante Magnus Swenson, founder of the SMS Ranches near
Stamford, arrived in Texas in 1838 from his native Sweden.
Swenson sponsored many other Swedish immigrants who
wished to come to Texas and provided them with jobs on his
extensive land holdings. Swenson encouraged his uncle, Svante
Palm, to immigrate to Texas, and in the 1850s Palm served the
city of Austin as alderman, justice of the peace, and postmaster.

Scotsmen, Irishmen, and Englishmen were all successful
colonizers and settlers during the days of the Republic. Robert
Hamilton, of Scottish descent, settled near Pecan Point on the
Red River in 1834. He was a highly successful trader. Lawyer,
doctor, and geologist Francis Moore, Jr., was a surgeon in the
Texas army and publisher of the *Telegraph and Texas Register*.
His newspaper articles helped to promote immigration to Texas,

and his *Maps and Description of Texas,* published in 1840, added much to the scientific knowledge of the Republic.

Although he had lost a leg to a cannonball at the siege of Bexar and an arm firing a cannon to celebrate Texas Independence Day, Irish architect Thomas William Ward constructed the first capitol building in Houston. Later Ward served as the commissioner of the General Land Office and was sent by Houston to remove the archives of the Republic from Austin, an occasion which again found him under fire, this time from Mrs. Eberly. William Kennedy published his *The Rise, Progress, and Prospects of Texas* in 1841. Kennedy traveled in Texas for two years before completing his two-volume work, and his book encouraged immigration to Texas. Later Kennedy served as consul from Texas to the British government in London.

Thomas William House, an Englishman of Dutch ancestry, migrated to Texas in 1838 and rose from the proprietorship of a Houston confectionery shop to become a prominent businessman instrumental in developing the resources of the city. House was one of the developers who helped organize the first company to extend the ship channel and make Houston a leading port city. His son, Edward M. House, was a power in Texas politics and adviser to President Woodrow Wilson. The

Charles B. Normann's painting of Svante Palm commemorates an immigrant who made great contributions to Texas.

Austin-Travis County Collection, Austin Public Library

82

Englishman Arthur Ikin negotiated treaties between the Republic and Great Britain and the Netherlands. Serving as consul from Texas to England, Ikin published a guide for British emigrants and businessmen interested in the financial affairs of the Republic. His book, *Texas: Its History, Topography, Agriculture, Commerce, and General Statistics,* was published in London in 1841.

Not all writers saw Texas as the ideal democratic republic. The English writer Nicholas Doran P. Maillard warned prospective immigrants that they would find the land a "wretched, sickly place." His *The History of the Republic of Texas,* published in London in 1842, attempted to discourage British recognition of the infant Republic. However, when the newly founded Republic was in financial need, the English writer William Bollaert encouraged British investors in her behalf. His writings reflected his interest in geography, topography, and the natural resources of the state.

The impact of the immigrants on the Republic was varied and long-lasting. Cultural contributions are only a part of their legacy. Hard-working and courageous, the immigrants helped lay the foundation for an agricultural economy that was to carry Texas through the Civil War with far less suffering than might otherwise have been the case. Their pioneering spirit helped push the frontier back with a speed that is almost unbelievable. In 1836 the frontier lay along a line from San Antonio to Nacogdoches and then north to the Red River. By the end of 1845, the line ran from San Antonio to Austin to Dallas and on to the Red River, and before the end of 1846 the Germans had settled Fredericksburg far to the west of that line.

Life in the Republic

In the relative calm that prevailed after the revolution and Runaway Scrape, the settlers could concentrate on developing the resources at hand. The settlers began to strive toward making the cotton economy a productive one, although little cotton had been exported previously. Times were hard and food was often scarce. Agriculture remained at the subsistence level for

The Varner-Hogg Home is an example of the Southern influence on Texas architecture.

many settlers. However, many were diversifying and growing sugar cane in the coastal areas and wheat, rye, and oats in the interior. German settlers were experimenting with growing tobacco.

The basic food crop was corn, and a typical diet was composed of corn dodgers, beef, venison, sweet potatoes, and coffee. The growing of vegetables was not popular, and when game was scarce, many settlers lived on a diet of corn bread and coffee three times a day. Early travelers complained of the lack of variety in the food and the fact that whatever meat was served was usually fried. The German and French settlers were instrumental in cultivating a broader taste for vegetables, and settlers began to grow cabbages, turnips, potatoes, peas, and pumpkins. The Irish introduced the Irish potato, originally a staple crop of the South American Indian. The Mexican settlers used corn in many original ways. An army officer in Corpus

84

Christi tasted a Mexican preparation called *themales* (tamales) and wrote, "I know of nothing more palatable." Mexican food preparation and a variety of Mexican foods were soon to be associated with Texas.

The homes of the "Texians" revealed the utilitarian bent of the pioneer settlers. Houses were commonly of the dog-run variety—two log cabins joined by a covered porch. An open central hall allowed an occasional breeze to provide ventilation. The houses were originally constructed of rough-hewn logs, but soon sawed planks were being used. Houses were located near wood and water. In later years the children of the settlers merely added second stories, porches, and wings to these houses to create a type of architecture that was both expansive and practical.

Homes in San Augustine and Galveston reflect a growing interest in a type of architecture more indigenous to the South than to the frontier. Greek Revival style houses and hotels, with their galleries, columns, and porches, linked frontier Texas with the Old South and with an architectural style introduced into the United States by Thomas Jefferson.

Mexican architecture lent originality and practicality to houses in San Antonio and Goliad. Colonel Juan Almonte, aide to Santa Anna at the Battle of San Jacinto and an observant inspector of Texas in 1834, commented on the houses of Spanish design with their stone and adobe walls and flat roofs. The houses were planned to adapt to both terrain and climate. Homes throughout the Southwest today reflect the timelessness and the colorfulness of these homes. Patios, colorful tiles, and ornamental grill work retain the essence of Mexican architecture in the Southwest.

The clothing of the settlers reflected a practical bent with a strong desire for individualism and color. Buckskin was not unusual wear for the frontier, but often shirts and pants would be trimmed with fringe and beads. Cotton homespun was also a common material for clothing, but broadcloth and silk gowns brought from the East were treasured for Sunday wear. Women carded cotton, spun the thread, wove and dyed the material, and made the clothing for the entire family. Men adopted the colorful and practical Mexican poncho for their outerwear, and coats were made from bearskin, buffalo hide, or heavy blankets.

Culture on the Texas Frontier

The scrape of fiddles and the shuffle of feet along a log-cabin floor marked many festivities in the early days of the Republic. Any occasion was a chance for fun and frolic. Rail splittings, housewarmings, and quilting bees were as popular as parties in honor of San Jacinto Day, amateur theatricals where men took all the parts, and horse racing. The Texans enjoyed themselves with typical frontier gusto, and dancing and singing enlivened their existence. German singing societies grew up in many of the communities, and pianos and other musical instruments were a vital part of many homes. The strains of frontier dance tunes such as "Money Musk" and "Piney Woods," sometimes banged on a tin plate, rivaled the shuffling of boots on puncheon floors.

The Mexican fandango was a lively part of the dance tradition of Texas. As early as 1828 the Mexican settlers in San Antonio celebrated *Diez y Seis de Septiembre* by performing their waltzes and reels to the light of candles in Main Plaza. In the days of the Texas Republic, the name *fandango* was applied to the dance hall itself. Dr. Ferdinand von Roemer described a fandango as "a long narrow room dimly lighted by three wax candles fastened to the walls." Prettily dressed women sat on benches waiting for their partners to choose them.

Amateur theatricals were supplemented by the touring companies that often played the Southwest. The appearance of a professional company was the highlight of the season in Houston in 1839. Residents of the Republic saw such standards as Sheridan's *School for Scandal* and Shakespeare's *Macbeth*. Melodramas, minstrel shows, and traveling circuses added to the theatrical enjoyment of the settlers, and amateur groups often presented plays written by Texas authors. A former Texas army officer wrote a stirring play, *The Fall of the Alamo, or, The Death of Col. Crockett,* which had a great appeal to the frontier Texas audience.

Fandango came to mean the hall as well as the dance; both appear in this old drawing.

A surprising number of people on the frontier took time to engage in artistic pursuits. Artists of the Republic came from widely varied backgrounds. Jefferson Wright painted while serving as an Indian agent in Nacogdoches. An artist who came to Texas as a soldier, Seth Eastman, captured scenes of Indian life and the Central Texas landscape. William M. G. Samuel, a law officer in San Antonio, captured the charm of the city on canvas to decorate the courthouse.

Adventure and exploration were favorite topics for books then as now. George Wilkins Kendall, publisher of the *New Orleans Picayune,* joined the Santa Fé expedition and spent two years in a Mexican prison. In 1844 he published his widely read account of the expedition, *Narrative of an Expedition Across the Great South-western Prairies from Texas to Santa Fé: Narrative of the Texan Santa Fé Expedition.*

On December 22, 1837, Dr. Ashbel Smith, Connecticut-born and educated at Yale, wrote the following to his friend Henry Barnard, first United States Commissioner of Education and founder of the *American Journal of Education:* "We have established a Philosophical Society. . . . It is composed of the first men of the Republic. You will be gratified to see that your old friend is Vice President. The President of the Society is General Lamar; Ex-President Burnet is Corresponding Secretary. . . ." The Philosophical Society of Texas devoted itself to various subjects, many of them as current as "Ought the Texian government to have put Santa Anna to death in 1836?"

Education in the Republic

Although private seminaries and academies flourished, only Houston established a public school. From early morning to late in the afternoon, children in the rural schools bent their heads over their Webster's *Speller* and McGuffey's *Reader.* In more isolated areas families employed a teacher and provided an ill-equipped schoolhouse for their children.

School buildings often left much to be desired, as the following description of the schoolhouse at Webber's Prairie, near Austin, points out.

School teachers in those times were not to be envied. There was no public school fund to draw upon and no private fund, either, to speak of, except such surplus produce as farmers happened to have. Our first school was taught by Captain Beach, in a log cabin having neither floor nor window, or even a door. A couple of the lower logs being left uncut in the doorway, over which the little tots had to be lifted, prevented the ingress of the pigs.[2]

---

[2]Noah Smithwick, *The Evolution of a State* (1900; reprint ed., Austin: The Steck Company, 1936), 231.

In 1845 Hermann F. Seele opened the first German-English school at New Braunfels. Seele was one of the early educational and cultural leaders in the German community and later served as mayor of New Braunfels during the Civil War and in the legislature of the state of Texas.

Reverend Louis Ervendberg arrived in Texas in 1839 and dreamed of a German-English university to be located near Industry. Although he sold stock and even erected a building, the school never opened. However, Ervendberg later served as minister to Protestant German immigrants in New Braunfels, which was founded in 1845. Ervendberg never gave up his dream of founding an educational institution among the German settlers, and in 1850 he obtained a charter for a university to teach scientific agriculture. When his plan failed, he migrated to Mexico.

However, the need for an educational system was strongly felt during the days of the Republic, and many citizens advocated the education of girls to the same degree as boys. Seminaries for young ladies were established, and the girls learned reading, writing, arithmetic, grammar, geography, and history, and in many schools such advanced subjects as chemistry, philosophy, botany, French, and Latin. Desire for a system of higher education in the Republic led to the founding of many private and denominational colleges. The Methodists opened Rutersville College in 1840. Galveston University opened the next year. The University of San Augustine began operation in 1842. The career of this institution of higher learning gives some insight into the Republic. It was housed in a two-story building about fifty feet square for which was paid a league of land. Courses offered ranged from French and Greek to fortifications and gunnery, and discipline was reported to be firm. The university suffered an unfortunate demise in 1847 when its president was shot.

Literary societies, debating clubs, theatrical groups, and the study of the classics were signs of growth and the beginnings of maturity, for it was necessary that the Texans first provide for food, clothing, and shelter before they could devote appreciable efforts to art, literature, and education of more than rudimentary content.

Discuss

1. Compare the preambles of the constitutions of the Republic of Texas and the United States.

2. Why did the practice of printing paper money and issuing promissory notes for currency fail to solve the financial problems of the Republic of Texas?

3. For each of the major difficulties faced by the Republic of Texas, compare the policies of Houston and Lamar on the subject and decide which man you believe followed the better course of action.

4. Investigate the history of the Cherokee Indians before they came to Texas. Analyze their attitude toward white men in light of their past experiences. Analyze the attitude of the white men toward the Cherokees.

5. Why do you think Texans preferred annexation by the United States to independent statehood?

6. Did Texas or Mexico seem to be more responsible for the trouble between the two nations after 1836? Explain your answer.

7. Describe the role played by immigrants in the development of the Republic of Texas.

8. What reasons did people have for coming to Texas from the United States? From Europe?

9. Characterize the society of the Republic of Texas. You may find it helpful to compare the society that existed then with modern society.

10. Compare education in the Republic of Texas with education as you know it.

Identify

David G. Burnet

Mirabeau B. Lamar

Vicente Cordova

Archive War

Prince Carl

Robert Hamilton

fandango

Council House Fight

General Adrian Woll

Mier Expedition

Mainzer Adelsverein

Henri Castro

Thomas W. House

Dr. Ashbel Smith

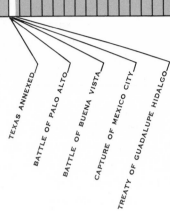

TEXAS ANNEXED

BATTLE OF PALO ALTO

BATTLE OF BUENA VISTA

CAPTURE OF MEXICO CITY

TREATY OF GUADALUPE HIDALGO

CHAPTER 6

"This Great Drama"

On February 19, 1846, the Lone Star Flag was lowered and the Stars and Stripes was raised over the capitol of Texas. Anson Jones, the last president of the Republic of Texas, stated, "The final act in this great drama is now performed; the Republic of Texas is no more." Jones relinquished his authority to J. Pinckney Henderson, who served as the first governor of the state of Texas under the United States, and Texas officially became the twenty-eighth state in the American union. The annexation of Texas had been a major issue in the politics of the nation for a number of years. Involved in the annexation controversy were issues pertaining to the extension of slavery by virtue of Texas being slave territory, nationalism, westward expansion, the relations between the United States and Mexico, and England's interest in the cotton economy of Texas.

93

Annexation

The topic of the annexation of Texas to the United States was first discussed in political and diplomatic circles as early as 1803, when the United States purchased Louisiana. Advocates of expansion argued that because of the French claim to Texas established by La Salle, Texas was part of the Louisiana Purchase. Therefore, they argued, Texas should never have been part of the treaty of 1819 between the United States and Spain, which resulted in the western boundary of the Louisiana Territory being set at the Sabine River. These expansionists claimed that Texas had really belonged to the United States, and therefore should be "re-annexed."

Annexation Is Delayed. Shortly after Texas achieved her independence from Mexico in 1836, the citizens of the Republic voted in favor of annexation. Although President Andrew Jackson favored annexation, he failed to push the issue with Congress. He recognized Texas as an independent nation, but he did not support the cry for annexation because he feared arousing antislavery sentiments in the North; neither did he wish to provoke Mexico. However, it was no longer a question of whether or not Texas would enter the Union; it was merely a matter of when. Jackson's successor to the presidency, Martin Van Buren, chose to maintain the status quo on the problem of annexation. Many people in Texas shared a dream of manifest destiny, whereby Texas would stand as an independent nation stretching from the Louisiana boundary to the Pacific coast. So the issue slumbered fitfully for a decade.

Interest in Annexation Is Reawakened. The Santa Fé and Mier expeditions brought Texas once more to the attention of people in the United States. President Tyler worked for the annexation of Texas. Tyler believed in manifest destiny. He encouraged the expedition of John C. Frémont to explore the Rocky Mountain area, and he had supported Dr. Marcus Whitman's efforts in the settlement of Oregon.

Slavery was the issue on which many of the politicians in the United States opposed the annexation of Texas. After being twice rejected, the Texans started cultivating the English. Both Britain and France wanted a strong and independent Texas to check the expansion of the United States. Mexico certainly did not want Texas to join the United States. It was the prospect that Texas might become a satellite of Great Britain that moved President Tyler to negotiate a treaty of annexation.

Several legislatures in the Southern states passed resolutions favoring the annexation of Texas, and on April 22, 1844, Secretary of State Calhoun laid the treaty of annexation before the Senate. Calhoun skillfully pointed out the interest of England in the cotton economy of Texas to win support for his treaty. President Sam Houston also used the desire of France and England to prevent annexation to generate interest in the United States in the Texas situation. When the votes were counted, however, the treaty received only sixteen yeas to thirty-five nays. President Tyler mourned, "Alas for annexation!"

As the United States presidential election of 1844 approached, annexation was a major issue in the campaign. Henry Clay, the popular Whig candidate, opposed annexation for fear of war with Mexico. Clay was to regret his stand, as he failed to judge the strength of public demand for the annexation of Texas. The Democrats turned from former president Martin Van Buren in favor of James K. Polk of Tennessee, who campaigned with the slogan "re-occupation of Oregon and re-annexation of Texas." Clay lost the election. The Democrats also obtained a majority in both houses of Congress, a significant indication that the people of the United States stood for manifest destiny and the annexation of Texas.

The following stanzas from the poem "The Plea of Texas," written by Mrs. Mary Austin Holley in 1844, express the sentiment for annexation by the United States and warn of the possible consequence if annexation is rejected.

Admit us—we would deem it shame,
Of other lands such boon to claim,
For we are free and proud.
But we a mother's love may seek,
And feel no blush upon our cheek,
Before her to have bowed.

. . . .

We love your flag, your laws, your land—
Wishing to worship, see we stand
At Freedom's Temple door.
Admit us now for it may be,
That tost on Time's tempestuous sea,
We part, to meet no more.[1]

Texas Is Annexed. President Tyler interpreted the election results as favoring the immediate annexation of Texas and called for a joint resolution of Congress annexing Texas to the United States. As passed by Congress, the resolution annexed Texas provided that the people of Texas voted their approval by January 1, 1846. The resolution further provided that Texas would keep her public lands to pay the Republic's debts, that all other public property would revert to the United States, and that the land of Texas might be used to create as many as four new states, with slavery to be prohibited above 36°30′ north latitude. The United States accepted all responsibility for settling disputes over the boundaries of Texas.

Andrew Jackson Donelson, United States chargé d'affaires, presented the annexation terms to the government of Texas, with the newly inaugurated President Polk urging the Texans to support immediate annexation. President Anson Jones called a convention to consider the offer and to determine whether Texas should join the United States or accept a peace treaty Mexico was offering in an attempt to prevent annexation. The voters of Texas overwhelmingly approved the terms of annexation and ratified the constitution drawn up by the convention. President Polk signed the act of annexation on December 29, 1845. The transfer of authority from the national government to the state officials took place the following February, and the curtain came down on the "great drama."

The Constitution of 1845. When the framers of the Texas Constitution of 1876 chose a working model for their constitution, they chose the Constitution of 1845. The constitution adopted by the newly created state was a model of clarity and

---

[1]Philip Graham, ed., *Early Texas Verse* (Austin: The Steck Company, 1936), 23.

a tribute to its makers. The governor was elected for a two-year term. Any one governor could serve no more than four years out of any six-year period. The governor had the power to appoint the secretary of state, attorney general, justices of the Supreme Court, and district judges, with the approval of the senate.

The legislature of the state met in biennial sessions. Representatives were elected from districts set up according to population; they served two-year terms. Senators served four-year terms. The hostility that many Westerners felt toward private corporations and banks was embodied in the provisions that all corporations had to obtain a two-thirds vote of the legislature to be incorporated and that no banks could be established within the state. The state could not incur debts over $100,000, and property was to be taxed in proportion to its value. In addition, the consent of the wife became necessary for the sale of homestead property, and homesteads not in excess of two hundred acres were exempt from execution and sale for debt.

Texas benefited from the setting up of the United States postal system and by federal aid in frontier defense and Indian affairs. The establishment of United States currency as the legal tender did much to facilitate commerce. With the election of Thomas J. Rusk and Sam Houston to serve in the United States Senate, the state was assured of outstanding representation in Washington.

The Mexican War

Upon the annexation of Texas, Mexican minister Juan Almonte informed the United States government that the Mexican government considered annexation an act of war. Almonte demanded his papers and left the United States, and the American minister to Mexico was ordered to return. Although the United States offered to settle the matter peacefully, Mexico began arming for a fight and stated that she intended to reconquer Texas. Texas was just as much a political question in Mexico as it was in the United States, and no Mexican president dared sacrifice his political career by ad-

The Battle of Palo Alto marked the beginning of the Mexican War.

mitting that Texas was truly lost, as it had been for nearly a decade.

In 1836 the Texas Congress had passed legislation setting the southern and western boundary of Texas at the Rio Grande. The Mexicans claimed the boundary was the Nueces River, which at some points was over a hundred miles north of the Rio Grande. While annexation was pending, President Polk sent John Slidell to Mexico to offer conditions to the Mexican government. Polk proposed to pay all claims held by American citizens against the Mexican government if Mexico would recognize the Rio Grande as the boundary of Texas. In addition, he proposed to buy New Mexico for $5 million and California for $25 million.

Fighting Begins. When Slidell's mission became known in Mexico, the Mexican government was incensed and refused to recognize him. Slidell informed the president of the warlike mood of the Mexicans and warned him of the possibility of war. In January 1846 Polk ordered General Zachary Taylor to move an army of three thousand men from the north bank of the Nueces River into the territory claimed by both nations. A skirmish took place between American and Mexican troops on April 24, and on May 8, 1846, Mexican troops crossed the Rio Grande and engaged Taylor's army in the battles of Palo Alto and Resaca de la Palma in the disputed area north of the Rio Grande.

War Is Declared. Polk delivered a war message to Congress on May 11, 1846, stating that Mexican troops had invaded the United States and "shed American blood on American soil." Mexicans believed that American troops had invaded Mexican territory, as the land south of the Nueces River lay under Mexico's claim. Polk further entreated Congress that "As war exists, and, notwithstanding all our efforts to avoid it, exists by the act of Mexico herself, we are called upon by every consideration of duty and patriotism to vindicate . . . the honor, the rights, and the interests of our country." On May 13, 1846, Congress declared war against Mexico.

Texans in the War. Texas governor J. Pinckney Henderson took a leave of absence to command Texas troops and enrolled Mirabeau B. Lamar to serve on his staff. President Polk offered Sam Houston a commission as major general in the army, but Houston refused. Texas Rangers, including Bigfoot Wallace, marched under Colonel Jack Hays and served well at the Battle of Monterrey and at Mexico City. Samuel H. Walker, whose name was to become a household word on the Texas frontier for his suggestions to Samuel Colt which were incorporated into the six-shooter known as the Walker Colt, served with Hays's Rangers and as a scout for General Taylor at the battles of Palo Alto and Resaca de la Palma. He fought under General T. J. Worth at the Battle of Monterrey and transferred to General Winfield Scott's army to combat guerrilla bands besieging the American supply routes. Walker was felled by a Mexican bullet, and his body was returned to Texas for burial.

Ben McCulloch, friend of Davy Crockett and renowned Indian fighter, organized a company of Rangers to serve as a scouting company under General Taylor at the Battle of Buena Vista. John Salmon Ford served with Hays's regiment and had the unhappy duty of informing families of the death of soldiers in the regiment. Ford often added the words *Rest in Peace* to the messages he sent, and when fighting grew heavy, he often wrote only *R.I.P.* He was henceforth known as Rip Ford.

Hamilton P. Bee resigned as secretary of the Texas Senate to march with Ben McCulloch's Rangers. Richard King, founder of the famous King Ranch, and his partner, Mifflin Kenedy, transported troops and supplies for General Taylor's army. Henderson Yoakum, an early enthusiast for the annexation of Texas, closed his law office to take part in the Mexican War. Yoakum was an accurate observer, and when the war ended, he returned to Huntsville and began composing his *History of Texas from Its First Settlement in 1685 to Its Annexation to the United States in 1846.* Yoakum relied heavily on the reminiscences of his close friend and legal client, Sam Houston, and although his history is inaccurate in some details, he successfully built a narrative around the development of Texas from the earliest Spanish settlements to the drama of annexation.

The United States Is Victorious. President Polk guided the strategy of the Mexican War with the idea of moving for swift victories. In May 1846 "Old Rough and Ready," as his soldiers named General Zachary Taylor, crossed the Rio Grande at Matamoros and moved toward Monterrey. The forces under Taylor marched some two hundred tortuous miles over the mountains and dry plateaus of northern Mexico. Guerrilla attacks and yellow fever hindered the troops. On reaching Monterrey, Taylor's forces engaged the Mexican army led by General Pedro Ampudia. Despite numerous casualties, Taylor forced Ampudia to surrender and to declare an armistice. Polk ordered Taylor to march to Saltillo and to wait there, but Taylor, his mind set on glory, marched to Buena Vista to meet the Mexican forces under General Santa Anna.

Since the Mexicans outnumbered the Americans almost four to one, Santa Anna offered to allow Taylor to surrender, then attended a high mass before the attack. With much pomp the Mexicans charged, and Taylor's forces were repulsed. A regiment of Mississippi riflemen commanded by Jefferson Davis, future president of the Confederacy, counterattacked. Santa Anna charged again, only to be met by artillery under the command of Braxton Bragg. Santa Anna charged once more, but was met by staunch resistance and finally retired from the field, retreating southward to oppose an advance on Mexico City. Taylor's men expected another charge, but found they had won the greatest American victory of the war. Taylor

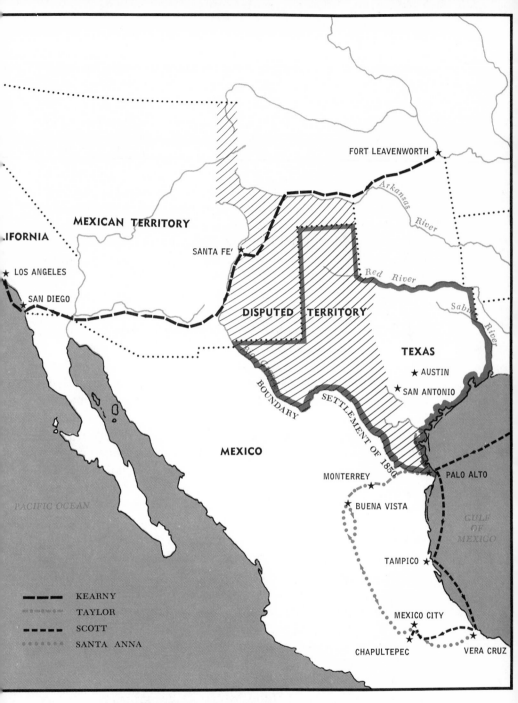

THE MEXICAN WAR AND THE
BOUNDARY SETTLEMENT OF 1850

was acclaimed the "Hero of Buena Vista" and began his rise to the presidency of the United States.

General Winfield Scott, "Old Fuss and Feathers," as his men called him, was approaching Vera Cruz with an army of ten thousand men. On March 9, 1847, he began his march inland to Mexico City. Captain Robert E. Lee scouted Santa Anna's defenses and helped Scott's army defeat the Mexicans at the narrow mountain pass of Cerro Gordo. Lieutenant Ulysses S. Grant also distinguished himself in the battle. Scott's army advanced toward the capital of Mexico, winning victories at Churubusco, Molino del Rey, and Chapultepec. On September 14 Mexico City fell to the Americans, and Scott's men paraded in Montezuma's city.

California Is Conquered. In May 1846 John C. Frémont mounted an expedition to wrest California from Mexican control. While Taylor and Scott were fighting in Mexico, Frémont successfully led an uprising in California and proclaimed California to be part of the United States of America. Colonel Stephen Kearny led a successful expedition to take over New Mexico and marched on to California to subdue remaining Mexican forces.

The Treaty of Guadalupe Hidalgo. President Polk tried to negotiate an end to the fighting in Mexico when Scott's forces were descending on Mexico City. Polk sent Nicholas P. Trist, chief clerk in the State Department, to negotiate with Santa Anna. Although moves for an end to hostilities failed, Trist managed to negotiate a treaty with the Mexican government after the fall of Mexico City. On February 2, 1848, in the little town of Guadalupe Hidalgo, Mexico ceded to the United States what is now California, Nevada, and Utah and parts of Arizona, New Mexico, Colorado, and Wyoming and accepted the Rio Grande as the boundary between Mexico and Texas. In return, the United States paid the Mexican government $15 million and assumed the claims of United States citizens against the Mexican government.

Another Boundary Dispute. Texas claimed part of the area annexed to the United States as part of her property. Slavery was an issue, as sentiment in the South favored a policy of extending slavery into any territory gained for the United States.

102

Free-soil advocates opposed the extension of slavery. The Texas legislature created Santa Fé County extending into the territory of New Mexico. Zachary Taylor, who succeeded Polk as president of the United States, opposed the Texas claims. The problem of the boundary was not solved until 1850, when Texas gave up the disputed land in return for $10 million to pay off her public debt. The money provided enough funds to pay for a new capitol building and a governor's mansion. Two million dollars was put into the Permanent School Fund, and enough was left over to provide operating expenses for the state government for six years, freeing county taxes for improvements on a local level.

Crowds of Enterprising Immigrants

With the annexation of Texas to the United States and with the end of hostilities with Mexico, immigration increased. The generous land policy founded during the Republic continued to draw settlers to the state. Numerous accounts by travelers, early settlers, and scientists continued to interest people in the frontier life of Texas. The discovery of gold at Sutter's Fort in the Sacramento Valley of California caused a mass migration to the West. The forty-niners surged across North Texas, and the route through Gainesville became known as California Street. Many of the seekers for gold liked the looks of the land they crossed and settled permanently in the Lone Star State. A series of unsuccessful revolutions against tyrants in Europe caused many educated and energetic men and women to flee to the New World to escape persecution.

During the 1840s and 1850s France was experiencing a severe agricultural and industrial depression. Many Frenchmen regarded frontier Texas as a land of freedom and economic opportunity. The philosophy of Francois Marie Charles Fourier motivated the founding of the Icarian Colony near modern Justin, north of Fort Worth. The colony was based upon equal rights for all (including women), opposition to slavery, and brotherhood. It was to be a perfect socialist community. But sickness and crop failure caused the colony to break up.

The Icarian Colony was only one of a number of experiments

103

in utopianism in Texas. The Germans founded the Bettina Colony near Llano, and the French established another settlement, La Reunion, near Dallas. Victor Prosper Considérant, the founder of the cooperative settlement La Reunion, traveled in Texas in 1852 and wrote a book, *Au Texas,* which was widely read in many European countries. People of many nationalities settled at La Reunion and many were both well educated and highly skilled. The colony flourished for several years, but poor soil hindered agriculture and few of the settlers were experienced as farmers. When the colony dissolved, many of the settlers moved to Dallas and added much to the cultural life of the city.

Allyre Bureau, a musical composer and conductor from Paris, France, was director of La Reunion from 1856 to the end of the colony in 1857. Bureau imported the first piano into the Dallas area. When the colony dissolved, the members of the Reverchon family turned to farming, and Julien Reverchon turned his interest in natural science into an avocation that resulted in a botanical collection of over twenty thousand specimens which enhanced the Missouri Botanical Garden. Reverchon also taught at Baylor University College of Medicine.

A young artist, Theodore Gentilz, came to Texas with other French immigrants to settle in Castroville. Many of the immigrants visited San Antonio, and Gentilz explored the strange city with its exotic customs and people. The scenes of Mexican life stimulated the young painter, and his paintings of *The Funeral of an Angel, The Fandango,* and *Mexican Oxcart and Jacal* illustrate his absorption with the cultural life of the Mexican community. Gentilz worked as a surveyor, platting many sections of land in the vicinity of Castroville and in the western part of the state, as well as across the Rio Grande in Mexico. While he was surveying, Gentilz sketched the Indians and their various ways of life, filling in details when he returned to his studio. Gentilz made friends with a Comanche chief by giving him a small sketch and a pouch of tobacco. In return, the chief posed for him, dressed in his full paraphernalia. Gentilz immortalized the Comanche, the Lipan Apache, and the Kiowa Indians of Texas. In his later years he had a studio on North Flores Street in San Antonio and taught painting at St. Mary's College.

Men were not the only talented artists in Texas. A French-woman, Eugenie Aubanel Lavender, came to Texas with her husband Charles Lavender in 1852. Mrs. Lavender traveled about Texas with her husband, painting many portraits and religious subjects, replenishing her supply of paints from clays and the juices of wild plants. A German woman, Louisa Heuser Wueste, fled with her family from Germany to escape the reaction to the revolution of 1848. In the spring of 1860 she opened a studio in San Antonio, and her portraits, particularly those of children, were well received. In her later years Mrs. Wueste became absorbed with life along the Mexican border, and her paintings reflect this interest.

The prosperous German colonies attracted many men of talent and artistic skill to Texas, among them Friedrich Richard Petri and Hermann Lungkwitz. Working in and around the New Braunfels and Fredericksburg areas, the two artists painted many scenes of frontier life and the Indians. Petri worked primarily in watercolor and crayon, capturing the pensive quality of the Indian. His scenes of *The Pioneer Cowpen* and *Going*

The University of Texas, Institute of Texan Cultures at San Antonio

Hill Country, by Hermann Lungkwitz, illustrates the artist's absorption with the land.

105

Visiting are typical genre paintings of frontier life. (Genre paintings depict scenes from everyday life.) Lungkwitz painted landscapes around Austin. Lungkwitz's painting *Hill Country* reflects his mastery of nineteenth-century landscape style.

Lungkwitz shared an interest in the new science of photography with another German artist, Carl G. von Iwonski, and the two artists set up a photography studio in San Antonio. Iwonski traveled extensively in Texas for twenty-seven years before returning to his native Germany. Iwonski painted portraits, landscapes, and genre studies. His paintings of everyday scenes reflect exuberance and humor. Iwonski's oil studies of the Lipan Indians and his portrait of Houston and the studies of his home show the versatility of this nineteenth-century artist.

The artists preserved scenes of Texas for future generations, the landscapes expressing the dream of manifest destiny. The limitless spaces, the abundant wildlife, the beautiful scenery seen through a romantic haze—all these characteristics of the nineteenth-century landscapes expressed the artists' feelings about their new home.

Decorative and useful arts were highly prized by the prosperous German settlers of Texas. They decorated the ceilings and walls of their homes with stencils and original designs, both colorful and amusing. The German immigrant artist Rudolph Melchoir excelled in striking decorations, and examples of his work have been preserved and restored at the Winedale Inn and in other homes in the community of Round Top.

A traveler in Texas just prior to the Civil War was impressed by the contrast between a typical frontier settlement and the German town of New Braunfels.

The main street of the town . . . was very wide—three times as wide, in effect, as Broadway in New York. The houses . . . were small . . . yet generally looking neat and comfortable.

. . . We agreed to stop at an inn and get dinner. . . . It was a small cottage of single story, having the roof extended so as to form a verandah, with a sign swinging before it, "Guadalupe Hotel, J. Schmitz."

I never in my life . . . met with such a sudden and complete transfer of associations. Instead of loose boarded or hewn log walls, with crevices stuffed with rags or daubed with mortar, which we have been accustomed to seeing during the last month, on staving in a door . . . we were in Germany.

. . . A long room, extending across the whole front of the cottage, the walls pink, with stenciled panels, and scroll ornaments in crimson, and with neatly-framed and glazed pretty lithographic prints hanging on all sides; a long, thick, dark oak table, with rounded ends, oak benches at its sides. . . .

. . . An excellent soup is set before us . . . two courses of meat . . . two dishes of vegetables, salad, compote of peaches, coffee with milk, wheat bread from the loaf, and beautiful and sweet butter—not only such butter as I have never tasted south of the Potomac before, but such as I have been told a hundred times it was impossible to make in a southern climate. . . .

As we rode out of town, it was delightful to meet again troops of children, with satchels and knapsacks of books, and little kettles of dinner, all with ruddy, cheerful faces . . . smiling and saluting us—"*guten morgen*"—as we met. Nothing so pleasant as that in Texas before, hardly in the South. . . . [2]

Many German settlers became successful businessmen and ranchers. Captain Charles H. Nimitz, a riverboat captain, arrived in Fredericksburg in 1847 and erected a hotel, which he later expanded to include a casino, general store, and brewery. The hotel served as a favorite recreation spot on the road between San Antonio and El Paso, and such distinguished visitors as Robert E. Lee, Ulysses S. Grant, and Rutherford B. Hayes, along with the bandit Jesse James, enjoyed Captain Nimitz's hospitality.

Ottomar von Behr, a pioneer rancher, introduced practical ranching and farming methods near the village of Sisterdale. Von Behr's book, *Good Advice for Immigrants,* explored the possibilities of sheep raising in Texas and introduced German settlers to the more scientific aspects of the agricultural economy.

[2]Frederick L. Olmstead, *A Journey through Texas; or, A Saddle-Trip on the Southwestern Frontier* (New York, 1860), 115-117. Reproduced in Wallace and Vigness, *Documents of Texas History* (Austin: Steck-Vaughn Company, 1963), 183-186.

The last survivors of the Polish settlers who came to Bandera in 1855 gathered in 1930.

Panna Maria, in central Karnes County, was founded by Polish immigrants from Silesia in 1854. Named for the Virgin Mary, Panna Maria was the first permanent Polish colony in Texas. Another group from Poland settled near Bandera in 1855.

Many Europeans immigrated to Texas after the unsuccessful revolution of 1848 in Europe. Many Czech citizens abandoned the idea of a free Slavic state under the reign of the Hapsburgs when the liberal uprising failed. The first Catholic priest from Czechoslovakia, the Reverend Bohumir Menzl, served the settlers of Castroville and D'Hanis from 1849 to 1856. Czechs fleeing from political revolutions in their homeland settled the community of Dubina in 1856. Joseph Peter, Jr., established a cotton gin, post office, and general store in Dubina and represented Fayette County in the legislature.

A Norwegian settlement near Brownsboro was formed through the efforts of Johan Reinert Reiersen in 1846. Settlements in Bosque County attracted a number of Norwegian immigrants during the 1850s. After settling many Norwegians

108

in Minnesota, Cleng Peerson came to Texas and settled in 1850, encouraging other Norwegians to come to Texas. Palm Valley, a Swedish settlement in south central Williamson County, attracted many immigrants. Swedes settled in Austin, Round Rock, Taylor, Elgin, Georgetown, Manor, and Kenedy, and many pursued an agricultural way of life. Present among the Swedish immigrants was the naturalist Gustave Wilhelm Belfrage, who collected insects and sent his specimens to collections around the world. His extensive collection, including some two hundred new species that he named, is now in the Smithsonian Institution in Washington.

In 1850, 134 Swiss immigrants resided in Texas, many of them educated merchants and skilled artisans at La Reunion. Henry Boll served as city alderman of Dallas after the Civil War and Benjamin Lang served as mayor of the city. Lang willed a section of land to the city to be used as a park. Getulius Kellersberger, Swiss engineer and surveyor of Grand Central Park in New York, came to Texas in 1849 and served in the defense of Galveston during the Civil War.

The extent of immigration is shown in the 1860 census. The population of Texas increased from less than 150,000 in 1845 to over 600,000 in 1860, and by 1860 one out of every ten Texans was foreign-born. The state prospered during the 1840s and 1850s, and the increase in population was a symptom of that prosperity. But a problem was assuming crisis proportions among the states, and that problem was slavery. Secession and the Civil War were to influence Texas's economic, social, and political development during the next decade.

Discuss

1. Was the acquisition of Texas by the United States annexation or "re-annexation"? Explain your answer.

2. Why do you think the United States was willing to annex Texas in spite of the problems annexation posed?

3. What obstacles stood in the way of annexation?

4. Compare the benefits of annexation with the advantages and disadvantages of independent statehood. Do you think Texans were wise in seeking annexation?

5. How did the Constitution of 1845 reflect the ideals of frontier democracy?

6. Do you think Mexico should have accepted President Polk's offer to settle the boundary dispute peaceably and agreed to sell New Mexico and California? Why?

7. How was the Mexican War related to the controversy over slavery?

8. How did the Mexican War fit in with the idea of manifest destiny?

9. It has been said by some that the $15 million paid to Mexico under the terms of the Treaty of Guadalupe Hidalgo was "conscience money." Why do you think that might have been said?

10. How did events in the United States affect immigration to Texas?

11. Why did the revolutions in Europe in 1848 cause so many intellectuals and artistic people to come to the New World?

12. Investigate the utopian and socialist movements that inspired the founding of colonies such as La Reunion and Bettina in Texas and Brook Farm in Massachusetts. How were these movements related to social and economic conditions of the times?

13. According to Mrs. Mary Austin Holley in "The Plea of Texas," why did Texas wish to be annexed to the United States? What did she warn might happen if Texas were not annexed soon?

110

Identify

Thomas J. Rusk
General Zachary
  Taylor
Battle of Palo Alto
Icarian Colony
Friedrich Richard Petri
Gustave Wilhelm
  Belfrage

Ben McCulloch
John S. Ford
Henderson Yoakum
Treaty of Guadalupe
  Hidalgo
Theodore Gentilz
Hermann Lungkwitz
annexation

Courtesy Kenneth M. Newman, Old Print Shop, N

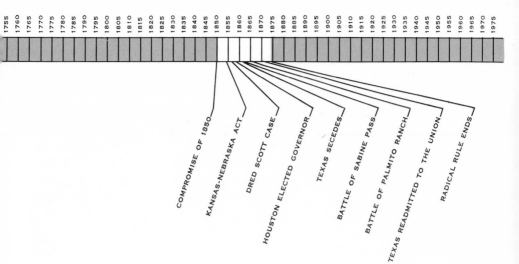

1755 1760 1765 1770 1775 1780 1785 1790 1795 1800 1805 1810 1815 1820 1825 1830 1835 1840 1845 1850 1855 1860 1865 1870 1875 1880 1885 1890 1895 1900 1905 1910 1915 1920 1925 1930 1935 1940 1945 1950 1955 1960 1965 1970 1975

COMPROMISE OF 1850
KANSAS-NEBRASKA ACT
DRED SCOTT CASE
HOUSTON ELECTED GOVERNOR
TEXAS SECEDES
BATTLE OF SABINE PASS
BATTLE OF PALMITO RANCH
TEXAS READMITTED TO THE UNION
RADICAL RULE ENDS

CHAPTER 7

"A Nation Divided"

Standing on the floor of the Senate of the United States on February 8, 1850, Sam Houston pleaded for compromise between the North and the South. Houston deplored the issue that threatened to divide the United States—the question of the extension of slavery into the new lands of the West. Houston pleaded for union and used the scriptural metaphor that Abraham Lincoln was to use later, when he closed his speech asking that "He who buildeth up and pulleth down nations will, in mercy, preserve and unite us. For a nation divided against itself cannot stand. I wish, if this Union must be dissolved, that its ruins may be the monument of my grave."

The Dispute over Slavery

Houston's sentiments were not those of the majority of Texans. The western border of the area suited to the cotton

113

culture of the South was in Texas. Many Texans, however, had migrated from other Southern states and were in sympathy with the cause of the agrarian South against the industrial North. Senator Louis T. Wigfall of Texas expressed the secession sentiment of the state in 1861, when the final bonds had been shattered and he exclaimed, "We have dissolved the Union; mend it if you can; cement it with blood!" In the spring of 1861 the boom of cannons at Fort Sumter signaled the end of peace, and sectional antagonisms founded on the slavery controversy erupted into a civil war that destroyed the economy and social order of the South.

Slavery as a Moral Issue. Slavery had long been a source of contention in America. Thomas Jefferson, writing of slavery in 1787, stated that "This abomination must have an end. And there is a superior bench reserved in Heaven for those who hasten it." John Quincy Adams said thirty years later that "Slavery is the great and foul stain upon the North American Union." Many men attacked slavery as a moral issue, and Abraham Lincoln stated in 1854 that "There can be no moral right in connection with one man's making a slave of another." The American writer Ralph Waldo Emerson wrote, "We must get rid of slavery or we must get rid of freedom." While many Southerners agreed that slavery was morally wrong, the economic advantages of the slave system silenced many voices. And the debate had assumed proportions too complex for settlement by rational discourse among men.

The Compromise of 1850. The question of the extension of slavery into new lands, temporarily answered by the Missouri Compromise in 1820, was again raised after the Mexican Cession in 1848. It was up to Congress to decide whether the lands acquired in the Mexican War would be open to slavery or would be free. In 1846 a Democratic congressman, David Wilmot, had attempted to settle the question in advance by amending a bill to read that "neither slavery nor involuntary servitude shall ever exist in any part of any territory ceded by Mexico to the United States." The Senate rejected the Wilmot Proviso because of active opposition on the part of Southern senators. However, Northern states continued to petition against the expansion of slavery into the territory. John C.

Calhoun from South Carolina argued that Congress did not have the right to prohibit slavery and that, in fact, it was the duty of Congress to protect the rights of slaveowners.

In 1849 some Southern extremists threatened disunion when California asked to be admitted to the Union as a free state. Southerners opposed the admission of California because the balance between slave states and free states would be upset. The ensuing debate in the Senate resulted in the passage of five pieces of legislation that are known collectively as the Compromise of 1850. Henry Clay of Kentucky proposed that California be admitted as a free state, but that the territories of New Mexico and Utah decide for themselves whether they were to be slave or free. Texas gave up her claim to the lands outside her present borders in return for $10 million. Another measure abolished slave trade in the District of Columbia, and a fifth law made it easier for Southerners to recover runaway slaves.

Calhoun attacked Clay's compromise on the grounds that it limited the powers of the Southern states. He argued that if the compromise passed Congress the South should be allowed to leave the Union in peace. As Sam Houston's speech of February 8, 1850, pointed out, the real issue was not the extension of slavery but the preservation of the Union. Daniel Webster said that climate and geography prevented the plantation system of cotton production in the Southwest and that a law "superior to that allowing it in Texas" would prevent the spread of slavery into the territories. Speaking "not as a Massachusetts man, nor as a Northern man, but as an American," Webster stated, "I would rather hear of . . . war, pestilence, and famine than to hear gentlemen talk of secession." Upon its passage by Congress, the Compromise of 1850 once more temporarily put the question of the extension of slavery in abeyance.

The Kansas-Nebraska Act. The slavery question, never really settled, arose again a short four years later, when the Illinois senator Stephen A. Douglas, described as "a steam-engine in britches," proposed to open the Indian territories of Kansas and Nebraska to settlement from the United States on the basis of popular sovereignty. The inhabitants of the territories were to be allowed to decide whether or not slaves would be permitted in the territory. Douglas's proposal would abolish the division of the Louisiana Territory into free and slave sections and repeal the Missouri Compromise. Senator Sam Houston opposed the Kansas-Nebraska Act and stood as the only Southern Democrat to do so. Houston defended his stand by stating that popular sovereignty would lead to conflict. Houston also pleaded for justice for the Indians who would be dispossessed of their territory and defended the Missouri Compromise with these words: "Maintain the Missouri Compromise! Stir not up agitation! Give us peace!"

Slavery was an emotional issue throughout the South. Most Texans believed that slavery was essential to the economic life of the state. Many Texans resented the intrusion of abolitionists into the state and defended their right to hold slaves as property. Meanwhile cotton prices were falling because of overproduction, while the price of slaves was rising.

The Dred Scott Case. The Supreme Court's 1857 decision in the Dred Scott case increased the furor over slavery. The case brought into question the constitutionality of the Missouri Compromise and the right of popular sovereignty. Chief Justice Roger B. Taney wrote the majority opinion, deciding that the slave Dred Scott was not a citizen of the United States. He had no right to sue in state or federal courts, and he could not claim that residence in a free territory gave him the right to freedom. At one blow the Supreme Court declared the Missouri Compromise to be unconstitutional and said that slaves were property that could be taken into any territory.

Abolitionist sentiment also was stirred over the cause of Bleeding Kansas, where settlers were fighting among themselves over the slave question. The Lincoln-Douglas debates, with Abraham Lincoln arguing against the extension of slavery and Douglas defending his stand on popular sovereignty, again brought slavery as a moral issue before the nation. On October 16, 1859, abolitionist John Brown's raid on Harpers Ferry and his call for slave uprisings horrified the South.

Houston Is Elected Governor. Houston considered both the abolitionists and the secessionists to be fanatical groups devoted to sectional causes that would split the Union. His stand on popular sovereignty had cost him any chance of reelection to the Senate. He returned to Texas in 1857 to run for the governorship, having, as he put it, some "fish to fry." He hoped to provide leadership that would give Texans a choice between Union and secession. Houston stumped the state defending his stand on the slavery issue but was defeated by Hardin Runnels, who had the support of the Democratic party in the race for the governorship.

As the controversy over slavery and secession grew stronger, Houston won the governorship in the election of 1859. Houston stood by his convictions on the danger of secession, the inevitability of war should secession occur, and the probability of the defeat of the South in a conflict. Talk of war ran rampant in the United States as well as in Texas; when Congress convened in December 1859, one member said that the only congressmen not carrying a knife and a revolver were those carrying two revolvers.

Sam Houston, in the gubernatorial campaign of 1859, stated his views on the dangers of secession. A Northerner recorded this version of Houston's remarks.

"Some of you laugh to scorn the idea of bloodshed as a result of secession, and jocularly propose to drink all the blood that will ever flow in consequence of it! But let me tell you what is coming on the heels of secession. The time will come when your fathers and husbands, your sons and brothers, will be herded together like sheep and cattle at the point of the bayonet; and your mothers and wives, and sisters and daughters, will ask, Where are they? and echo will answer, where?

"You may," said he, "after the sacrifice of countless millions of treasure, and hundreds of thousands of precious lives, as a bare possibility, win Southern independence . . . but I doubt it. I tell you that, while I believe with you in the doctrines of State rights, the North is determined to preserve this Union. They are not a fiery impulsive people as you are, for they live in cooler climates. But when they begin to move in a given direction, where great interests are involved, such as the present issues before the country, they move with the steady momentum and perseverance of a mighty avalanche, and what I fear is they will overwhelm the South with ignoble defeat. . . ."[1]

[1]Thomas North, *Five Years in Texas* (Cincinnati: Elm Street Printing Company, 1871), 93-94.

Secession and War

Daniel Webster had declared that the United States was a union of states that was "one and inseparable." John C. Calhoun expounded the theory of a compact of sovereign states that could dissolve the Union at will. Years of dissension reached a climax in the presidential election of 1860. Abraham Lincoln, the candidate of the young Republican party, gained a majority of the electoral votes to defeat Democratic candidates John C. Breckinridge, Stephen A. Douglas, and John Bell.

Southerners felt that the election of a Republican president meant an abolitionist victory. To Southerners it seemed that secession was the only way to avoid abolitionist meddling with local concerns. Six weeks after the election, South Carolina seceded from the Union. Mississippi, Florida, Alabama, Georgia, and Louisiana followed. Sam Houston argued fervently against secession, stating that Texas and the South could best benefit by remaining in the Union. Houston was besieged

This capitol building, which burned in 1881, was the scene of the confrontation between Governor Houston and the Secession Convention.

by letters and editorials demanding that he call a secession convention. Houston's opposition was overruled, and the people chose delegates to the Texas Secession Convention. Houston called the legislature into special session, stating that the convention had no legal authority. However, the legislature legalized the convention, and it proceeded with its work. Under the leadership of Judge Oran M. Roberts, president of the body, the convention adopted an ordinance of secession and annulled the ordinance of annexation, an action approved by the voters in a special election three weeks later. Texas was once again an independent state, free of the United States of America. Virginia, Arkansas, Tennessee, and North Carolina followed Texas.

The Confederate States of America. At Montgomery, Alabama, on February 4, 1861, delegates from the Southern states met to form the Confederate States of America. Jefferson Davis was chosen president and Alexander Stephens vice-president. The Confederate congress adopted a constitution by which each state retained its independence while joining in a league dedicated to further a "permanent federal government." Slavery was preserved as an institution in the Confederacy, but the importing of slaves from Africa was prohibited.

Texas Joins the Confederacy. Governor Houston recognized the secession of Texas from the Union since the act had been ratified by the voters. However, he felt that the convention had no right to attempt to join Texas to the Confederacy. President Lincoln offered to send aid to Houston to oppose the convention, but Houston felt he could not resort to force. He refused to declare allegiance to the Confederacy. The convention, therefore, declared the office of governor vacant. Lieutenant Governor Edward Clark became the first governor of Texas in the Confederate States of America.

The Civil War Begins. The Confederacy demanded the surrender of all Union garrisons in the South. General Twiggs, in Texas, surrendered his command without resistance. Fort Sumter in the harbor of Charleston, South Carolina, became the scene of the first conflict of the Civil War. Both Lincoln and Davis then called for volunteers. Texans enlisted by the thousands, many of them in units that were to gain lasting fame, such as Hood's Texas Brigade and Terry's Texas Rangers. Altogether, Texas furnished over seventy-five thousand men to one army or the other; most fought for the Confederacy.

Immigrants who had fled to America to escape oppression faced an especially difficult choice and reacted in different ways. Some made their way north to join the Union army. A group of German Unionists making their way to Mexico were attacked by Confederates near the Nueces River, and many of them were killed. Other immigrants stood with Texas. Many Czechs served the Confederacy. Augustin Haidusek knew little English but enlisted in the Confederate army. Harris Kempner, a young Pole, carried a rifle in Parson's Brigade and served throughout the war. A graduate of the French military academy, Xavier Blanchard de Bray, rose to the command of four Texas cavalry regiments and helped to defend Galveston.

Texans in the War. Lincoln's strategy for conducting the war was to have a great deal to do with the role of Texas in the war. Lincoln planned to conduct a four-pronged assault on the South. One objective was the control of the Mississippi River, which would split the Confederate states west of the river off from the rest of the Confederacy. Another objective was the capture of the Confederate capital of Richmond, Virginia, and a third objective was a drive that would split the eastern Confederacy in two. In addition, a blockade of Confederate ports was to be maintained.

The defense of Richmond involved many Texans, including a former secretary of war of the Republic of Texas, Barnard Bee. At the First Battle of Bull Run, Bee rallied fleeing Confederate troops by pointing to a steadfast Virginia commander, General Thomas Jackson, and shouting, "There stands Jackson like a stone wall!" The troops held, and Jackson had a nickname.

Texas troops saw action in the eastern theater throughout the war. Hood's Texas Brigade served most of the war under General Robert E. Lee, taking part in at least twenty-four battles, including those of Gaines' Mill, Second Manassas, Antietam, Gettysburg, Chickamauga, and the Wilderness. Of nearly five thousand men who served in the brigade, fewer than six hundred were left to surrender with Lee at Appomattox.

Texans served in the Confederate army which was defeated at Gettysburg, Pennsylvania.

Taking part in the Union effort against Lee was Milton M. Holland, a sergeant major with the Fifth United States Colored Troops. Born in Austin, Holland won the Congressional Medal of Honor for his heroism in the Battle of New Market in 1864. Another Texan, Leopold Karpeles of Galveston, also won the Medal of Honor in action against Lee's army.

The fight for control of the Mississippi River also involved many Texans. Sam Houston, Jr., was wounded at the Battle of Shiloh, as was another distinguished Texan, Ashbel Smith, former surgeon-general of Texas and later a brigadier general in the Confederate army. Their commanding general, Albert Sidney Johnston, who had been secretary of war of the Republic of Texas under Lamar, lost his life in the same battle. John Austin Wharton, son of William H. Wharton, former Texas minister to the United States, also was wounded at Shiloh.

The fall of Vicksburg to General U. S. Grant on July 4, 1863, broke the Confederate grip on the Mississippi River and isolated Texas and the western states from the rest of the Confederacy. The Confederate defeat at Gettysburg, Pennsylvania, on July 3, 1863, broke the offensive thrust of the Confederate armies in the East. General Grant moved eastward, intending to split the Deep South, and together with General William Tecumseh

121

Sherman moved against Confederate positions around Chattanooga, Tennessee. Confederates under General Braxton Bragg had earlier dealt the Union army a severe blow at the Battle of Chickamauga. The Union armies now pushed Bragg back, and General Sherman began his march to the sea.

The War in Texas. Little fighting took place in Texas. Galveston was occupied by the Union navy from October 1862 until New Year's Day, 1863. General John Bankhead Magruder resolved to free Galveston of Union control. He armored two steamships with bales of cotton and sailed down Buffalo Bayou toward Galveston. With the help of a thousand men from Sibley's Brigade, the Confederates captured four Union ships and about three hundred troops. Although the Union blockade was maintained along the coast, the Confederacy held Galveston until the end of the war.

In September 1863 General Nathaniel Banks attempted to invade Texas with five thousand troops aboard twenty ships. The Union fleet arrived at Sabine Pass to find themselves opposed by about forty Irishmen led by Lieutenant Dick Dowling. In a forty-five minute engagement, Dowling and his men captured two Union gunboats and 315 prisoners. The Federals then captured Brownsville and tried to block trade between Texas and Mexico, but were only partially successful. Troops under

Colonel Rip Ford and Colonel Santos Benavides, former mayor of Laredo, led Confederate forces in a battle against Texas Unionists under Edmund J. Davis who attempted to capture Laredo in March 1864. Benavides and Ford also served at the last land battle of the Civil War, fought at Palmito Ranch near Brownsville in May 1865 against Union troops Ford described as "swift of foot . . . like men who had important business at some other place." From their prisoners Ford and Benavides learned that the strategy of the North had at last been successful and that Lee had surrendered at Appomattox on April 9, 1865, a month earlier. The war was over.

Texans at Home. Few actual battles were fought in Texas, but the state served as a major supply source for the Confederacy. When the Union forces blockaded ports of the South, much cotton was sold across the Rio Grande. After the Mississippi River fell to the Union, Texans found it even more difficult to ship supplies to the Confederate armies. Women worked in the fields to produce the food needed by their men in the army, but transportation difficulties often prevented its delivery. John Scott, an Indian who later became chief of the Alabama-Coushattas, enlisted in the Confederate army and with the help of about twenty other Indians carried supplies on flatboats down the Trinity River.

Union-occupied Brownsville in 1863 as seen from Mexico. The United States flag flies over the city; Confederate cotton lines the Mexican shore.

Missouri Pacific Lines

123

Although the South planned to fight only a defensive war, her resources failed to hold out during the war years. The South counted on British and French demands for cotton to supply financial aid to secure victory for her troops, but the blockade prevented much exportation, and many times bales of cotton rotted on wharves, lacking the means of transportation. The meager Southern manufacturing facilities were strained to provide materials needed that could not be brought in through the blockade.

Texas's public men had little to work with as they tried to manage the state and assist the war effort. Governor Francis Richard Lubbock supported Jefferson Davis and secession in 1860. Elected governor in 1861, Lubbock found the state bankrupt. He organized a frontier cavalry regiment to quell Indian raids and set about raising money to operate the state government. Lubbock managed to sell cotton through Mexico to arm the state to fight the Union forces. He harnessed the industrial resources of the state to establish a cloth and shoe manufacturing industry and to set up a percussion cap factory and a foundry.

When he left the governorship, Lubbock served as an aide to General John Bankhead Magruder before becoming an aide to Jefferson Davis. Lubbock was captured with Davis in May 1865 and imprisoned. When he was released, Lubbock returned to Texas to serve as state treasurer and on the board of pardons. His memoirs, *Six Decades in Texas,* tell us a great deal about early Texas.

Texas was protected from the devastation of the war by her western location. In his farewell address as governor, Francis R. Lubbock assessed the condition of Texas near the end of 1863.

[Texas] has been blessed with abundant harvests and unparalleled health; and in every instance in which our people have been called to meet the ruthless invader their gallantry, with the aid of God, has been rewarded with entire success. Were it not for the great loss we have sustained in our brave men who have fallen by the sword of the enemy, and alas, too many by disease, we could scarcely realize the dreadful scenes that have been enacted in other portions of the Confederacy. Her [Texas's] internal affairs are in a most prosperous condition, and our State finances present a most encouraging view for a people engaged in so great and exhausting a war. . . . [2]

Prior to the Civil War, John H. Reagan served in the United States House of Representatives and opposed the proposed reopening of the African slave trade. Reagan served as postmaster general of the Confederacy and as secretary of the treasury. When the war ended, Reagan rode south with President Davis, carrying the treasury of the Confederacy in his saddle bags. After Reconstruction, he served in the House of Representatives and the Senate of the United States. He later served as head of the Texas Railroad Commission.

Many of the Negroes in Texas remained on the farms and plantations during the war. Meshack Roberts maintained the plantation home of his owner near Gilmer and protected the women and children. He planted crops while the owner of the plantation served with the Confederate forces. Roberts was a member of the Texas House of Representatives during Reconstruction. He founded Wiley College at Marshall to promote the education of Negro youth.

Reconstructing the Nation

The task of reconstruction was not an easy one. Southerners returned home to land devastated by war and neglect and to a reordered society. When word of Lee's surrender at Appomattox reached Texas, Governor Pendleton Murrah and other state officials fled to Mexico. Union general Gordon Granger reached Galveston on June 19, 1865. In line with Lincoln's Emancipation Proclamation, he declared that all slaves were free, the act commemorated by subsequent Juneteenth celebrations. Additional Union troops were ordered to the Mexican border and to the principal towns of Texas to maintain order and to establish a military government.

---

[2]Francis R. Lubbock, *Six Decades in Texas* (Austin: Ben C. Jones and Company, 1900), 520.

These former slaves attended a Juneteenth celebration in Austin in 1900.

Presidential Reconstruction. Although Lincoln had been assassinated in April 1865, he had previously made plans for bringing the Southern states back into the Union after the Civil War. Lincoln's plan was a generous and a constructive one, requiring only that 10 percent of the voters of a state take an oath of loyalty to the Constitution. President Andrew Johnson built a plan of reconstruction on Lincoln's, but he met opposition in Congress. Part of the opposition was due to a desire for revenge on the part of a group of congressmen called Radical Republicans, but the Southern states were also taking actions which aroused many Northerners.

Mississippi and South Carolina refused to ratify the Thirteenth Amendment abolishing slavery. None of the Southern states gave the Negro the right to vote. Southern states passed black codes—a series of laws restricting the rights of Negroes. In addition, many ex-Confederate officials and military leaders were returned to state offices and to the United States Congress. Alexander H. Stephens, the former vice-president of the Confederacy, was elected to represent Georgia in the United States Senate, and Texas sent to the Senate Judge Oran M. Roberts, who had served as chairman of the Texas Secession Convention.

Congressional Reconstruction. The Radical Republicans, many still reacting to prewar abolitionist sentiment, decided to take over control of reconstruction. The Radicals in Congress, led by Senator Benjamin F. Wade of Ohio and Congressman Thaddeus Stevens of Pennsylvania, blocked Johnson's plan. In 1867 the Radicals in Congress passed legislation putting their plan of reconstruction into effect. By refusing to permit the congressmen and senators from the South to take their seats, the Radicals dominated Congress. In an attempt to control the presidency, the Radicals impeached Johnson, but failed to convict him by one vote.

The congressional plan of reconstruction was much harsher than Johnson's plan. The South was placed under military rule. The Southern states were required to draw up new constitutions for approval by Congress. They also had to ratify the Fourteenth Amendment, which extended citizenship and equal protection of the laws to Negroes, provided that ex-Confederate leaders could not hold office, and declared the debts incurred by the states of the Confederacy were invalid.

Southerners felt that ex-Confederate leaders should be granted amnesty and the right to hold office. They also were angered by the North putting Southerners in the position of a conquered people through the use of military rule. They felt, as Lincoln had felt, that the South's economic and political life could be best restored by a prompt reunion with the North. Lastly, they resented the attempt to extend the rights and privileges of citizenship to Southern Negroes through the Civil Rights Act of 1866, which contained the same equal protection of the laws clause as the Fourteenth Amendment. With the ratification of the Fourteenth Amendment in 1868, citizenship for Negroes was extended into the Southern states.

The Freedmen's Bureau. In 1865 Congress established the Freedmen's Bureau to help freed Negroes adjust to their new status. Many were wandering helplessly about the South, hungry and without work. Few knew how to accept the new responsibility of freedom, and some could barely feed and clothe themselves.

Assistance to Negro education was strongly supported by the North. The Freedmen's Bureau established free schools in Texas for Negro children and tried to solve the social problems of the Negro. However, with the state in turmoil, many social problems became legal problems. The Freedmen's Bureau represented many Negroes in court cases against white men. The white Southerners became hostile to the bureau and felt that the states could best deal with their own social problems. Southerners accused the bureau of meddling, stirring up discontent among the Negroes, employing corrupt or incompetent administrators who wasted money, filling Negroes with false hopes of free land and jobs, and acting as a political agency of the Republican party. When the bureau was finally abolished, the federal government lost its most efficient agency for protecting Negroes' civil and political rights. Southern white reaction to the policies of the Freedmen's Bureau resulted in the rise of the Ku Klux Klan, vigilantes who attempted to intimidate Negro leaders and keep Negroes from voting.

Not all whites opposed efforts to help the Negroes. William E. Kendall offered to sell the dispossessed Negroes land in Fort Bend County. He divided plantation sites into tracts of land and encouraged Negroes to settle in the area. Warner Braxton brought his family to the area, and Benjamin Franklin Williams began raising cattle there. Williams served as a delegate to the Constitutional Convention of 1869 and later in the legislature.

The work of the Freedmen's Bureau did lead to greater opportunities for Negroes. Many Negroes assumed roles in the political life of the state and took advantage of educational opportunities. Richard Allen lived on a plantation when the Civil War broke out. Allen moved to Houston and worked as a contractor, building Houston's first bridge across Buffalo Bayou. Allen served as a city alderman in Houston and in the house of representatives. He also served as collector of customs for the Port of Houston and as a presidential elector.

Richard Henry Boyd accompanied his owner through the battles of the Civil War. He returned to Texas, got an education, and entered the Baptist ministry. He became one of the leaders of the Baptist Convention in Texas and founded the National Baptist Publishing Board in 1897.

G. T. Ruby, a schoolteacher from Galveston, took a position with the Freedmen's Bureau. Ruby was elected as a delegate to the Constitutional Convention of 1869. In the election of 1869 G. T. Ruby and Matt Gaines were elected to the state senate. During his term as a state senator, Gaines, a former slave, worked for Negro rights and opposed segregation. Norris Wright Cuney dominated the Republican political scene in Texas as a representative of the Negro and as a distinguished citizen until his death in 1897. Cuney came to Galveston during the hectic Civil War days and entered Galveston politics in 1869. He served as sergeant-at-arms in the house of representatives and was on the Galveston school board. Cuney's political influence with the Republican party resulted in his service as secretary of the state Republican executive committee and as temporary chairman of the state Republican convention in 1882. He controlled the policies of the Republican party in Texas for a number of years and served as a delegate to several of the Republican national conventions. Cuney served as collector of customs for the Port of Galveston from 1889 to 1895.

Congressional Reconstruction in Texas. Under the congressional plan of reconstruction, Texas and Louisiana were a military district under the command of General Philip Sheridan. In the June 1866 elections, James W. Throckmorton, who had voted against secession but became a Confederate general, defeated former governor Elisha M. Pease but was removed by Sheridan as an "impediment to reconstruction." Pease was appointed governor but two years later grew impatient with Radical excesses and resigned. Many Texans resented a government that they felt was being controlled by Northern carpetbaggers and Southern scalawags. As required by the congressional plan of reconstruction, a convention was called in 1869 to write a new state constitution. Texas was also required to ratify the Fifteenth Amendment, which provided that a person could not be denied the right to vote because of race or because he was once a slave. With ratification of the Fourteenth and Fifteenth amendments to the Constitution of the United States and approval of her new constitution, Texas was again admitted to the Union in 1870.

Radical Rule under Davis. Although the reconstruction period in Texas was officially over, it was not so in fact. Army support had been decisive in electing Governor Edmund J. Davis to office in 1869. Granted extensive powers, Davis was a dictatorial and vindictive executive. In September 1871, reacting to Davis's excesses, a taxpayers' convention convened in Austin and censured Davis's rule by stating that "the people . . . are governed by E. J. Davis as completely as if there were no constitutions, state or federal." The cost of government was high, and Davis had strengthened the police powers of the state and antagonized whites by abusing those powers.

Although frontier defense was improved, Davis's regime was consistently attacked, and the Democratic party regained a majority of the seats in the legislature in 1872. Former Confederates were allowed to vote in this election, and they sent Democratic congressmen to Washington. In the election of 1873 Richard Coke polled twice as many votes for governor as Davis, and the Democratic party unseated many Republicans in state offices. The Republicans filed suit, and the Texas Supreme Court, consisting of Davis appointees, declared the election void and the law under which it was held unconstitutional. Davis retained his office. He fortified the capitol and stationed troops in the building to block entry by the Democrats who had been elected to the legislature.

The End of Radical Rule. In the early morning of January 13, 1874, while Davis's guards slept, the Democrats climbed through a second story window, organized themselves as the legislature, and confirmed Richard Coke as governor. The needs of the state were soon acted upon by calling a convention of delegates to draft a new constitution. The Constitution of 1876 is the constitution under which the state of Texas is presently governed. Reacting to the excesses of the Radicals under Davis, the framers of the new constitution tried to cut the costs of government and reduce the power of the executive. Two-year terms for executive officers and biennial sessions of the legislature were provided, and salaries were reduced. Judgeships were made elective, and fewer courts were authorized.

In their efforts to safeguard the rights of the people, the men who wrote the Constitution of 1876 produced a document that was too long and too detailed to be flexible enough to meet all the great changes of the coming century. As a result, the Constitution of 1876 has been amended almost two hundred times.

Texas had been divided by the Civil War and reconstructed under a harsh, radical government. With the end of Reconstruction in 1876, Texans were able to turn to the task of re-

Austin-Travis County Collection, Austin Public Library

The inauguration of Governor Richard Coke marked the end of Radical Republican rule in Texas.

131

pairing the damage done to the state by fifteen years of war, dissension, and bitterness. It was not to be an easy task; the job is not yet finished.

Discuss

1. Sam Houston was a slaveowner. How do you explain his stand on the Compromise of 1850 and the Kansas-Nebraska Act? What do Houston's reasons for his actions tell you about the complexity of the problems the nation faced?

2. How did the Missouri Compromise of 1820 help establish the northern boundary of Texas?

3. Why did the Democratic party split over the candidates for president in 1860? How did this influence the outcome of the election?

4. Do you feel that the actions of the Radical Republicans in dealing with the South were justified? Explain your answer.

5. Compare the objectives of the presidential and congressional plans of reconstruction. What were the results of congressional reconstruction in Texas and the South?

6. What were the short-range results of the actions of the Freedmen's Bureau? The long-range results? Can you think of other means of achieving equality for Negroes that would have had better long-range results?

7. Describe the roles of the various ethnic groups in Texas during the Civil War and Reconstruction.

Identify

Compromise of 1850
Kansas-Nebraska Act
popular sovereignty
Milton M. Holland
General John B.
Magruder
Santos Benavides
Francis R. Lubbock
Reconstruction
Freedmen's Bureau
G. T. Ruby

Edmund J. Davis
Dred Scott case
secession
Barnard Bee
Albert Sidney
Johnston
Battle of Sabine Pass
John H. Reagan
Radical Republicans
Richard Allen
Norris Wright Cuney

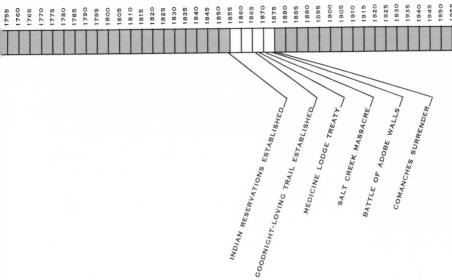

CHAPTER 8

"On the Lone Prairie"

Throughout the nineteenth century the pioneers continued their westward surge. The Mexican War opened up vast new territories for settlement, and the California gold rush lured those who were not attracted by cheap land. The passage of the Homestead Act in 1862 made it possible for anyone to own land, and the railroads built after the Civil War made it possible for anyone to get where the land was. However, until after the Civil War the vast midsection of America, the Great Plains, was regarded as unsuitable for settlement and remained the domain of the Indian and the buffalo. But the white man and the Indian soon clashed on the plains, the dugout and sod house replaced the tepee, and cattle grazed land that had belonged to the buffalo.

135

The Indian Frontier

An expanding America pushed the Indian westward and often drove him onto barren reservations. Corrupt officials and Indian traders antagonized the Indians, and many tribes were virtually destroyed by settlers or United States troops. The Indian resisted with all the defenses at his command. The Indian prized his nomadic existence, his freedom to wander the land. The tide of manifest destiny pushed the Indian before it and overwhelmed him.

Attempts were made to settle the Texas Indians on reservations before the Civil War, but these efforts met with little success. In 1854 the Texas legislature provided land for three Indian reservations. The Plains Indian depended on the buffalo for his livelihood, and the white man's insistence that the Indians not leave the reservation to hunt not only destroyed the only way of life the Plains Indian knew but also virtually insured hunger, anger, and unrest. The reservation for the Comanches in present Throckmorton County created more problems than it solved. The other western reservation was equally unsuccessful. Peaceful Caddo, Waco, and Tonkawa Indians settled on the Brazos Reserve in Young County, but white men in the area harassed and killed Indians until Governor Runnels ordered troops to the area to protect the Indians. To avoid further trouble, the Indians were moved to the Indian Territory (present Oklahoma), where an 1860 raid by Comanches left only a few survivors.

The Alabamas and Coushattas, two separate tribes who had come from the Southeast into East Texas, were granted 1,280 acres of land in Polk County. Of all the Indians of Texas, these two tribes were until recently the only ones to retain title to lands in Texas. The Alabamas and Coushattas still occupy a reservation of some four thousand acres. The Tigua Indians of El Paso came to Texas late in the seventeenth century. Recently, efforts have begun to establish a Tigua reservation.

With the outbreak of the Civil War the United States government abandoned frontier defenses, and the Confederacy had few men to spare for frontier duty. The Comanches and Kiowas took advantage of the situation and pushed eastward.

136

Late in 1862 Indian depredations became heavier than before the war. At Elm Creek in Young County on October 13, 1864, five soldiers, ten settlers, and the sheriff died in an Indian raid. The Indians carried away seven women and children, including the wife and two children of Britton Johnson, a Negro cowhand. Johnson searched for his family for two years, finally found them, and arranged for their release, along with other captives.

After the Civil War General Philip Sheridan refused to allow the state to assign a ranger force to the frontier. Like many Northerners, Sheridan believed that the defeated state should not be allowed to maintain companies of men under arms. He assigned federal troops to the frontier, but they were little help against the Indian attacks. The Indians made raids and then retreated to hiding places on the plains such as Palo Duro Canyon or to the safety of the Indian Territory. The troops could not guard all the settlements at once, so the raiders usually escaped unmolested.

The Medicine Lodge Treaty. In October 1867 the federal government and the Plains Indians held a treaty meeting in Baker County, Kansas. The treaty negotiated at the Medicine Lodge Council was the last ever made with the Comanche, Cheyenne, Arapaho, Kiowa, and Kiowa-Apache Indians. In it they agreed to accept settlement on a reservation in the Indian Territory. Tepees were erected for miles along Medicine Lodge Creek. More than seven thousand Plains Indians attended, among them the Comanche chief Ten Bears, who advocated peace with the white man and fell into disfavor with his people.

The Kiowa chief Kicking Bird also advocated peace with the white man and signed the Medicine Lodge Treaty. Kicking Bird was able to convince many of the Kiowas to remain on the reservation, but he also gained the disfavor of his tribe. The most eloquent voice heard at Medicine Lodge was that of Satanta, the White Bear, chief of the Kiowa, who held the well-deserved title "Orator of the Plains." Speaking in Spanish, Satanta said, "I have heard you intend to settle us on a reservation near the mountains. I don't want to settle there. I love to roam free over the wide prairie. When I do it, I feel free

Satanta and others opposed the Medicine Lodge Treaty.

The Smithsonian Institution

and happy, but when I settle down I grow pale and die. . . . A long time ago this land belonged to our fathers, but when I go up to the river, I see a camp of soldiers, and they are cutting my wood down or killing my buffalo. I don't like that, and when I see it, my heart feels like bursting with sorrow. I have spoken." General George Custer said of Satanta: "Satanta is a remarkable man—remarkable for his power of oratory, his determined warfare against the advances of civilization, and his opposition to the . . . quiet, unexciting . . . life of a reservation Indian."

The Salt Creek Massacre. The Salt Creek massacre near modern Graham in May 1871 resulted in a change of policy toward the Indians. A Kiowa and Comanche war party waited in ambush as a group of soldiers led by General William Tecumseh Sherman passed. A few hours later they attacked a wagon train on the same road. Seven teamsters were killed. When General Sherman heard of the deaths of the teamsters, he arrested Satanta, Satank, and Big Tree, who arrived at the reservation in Indian Territory boasting of their feat. Sherman ordered that they be taken to Jacksboro for trial. Satank sang his death song, drew a knife, and was killed in his escape attempt. Big Tree and Satanta were tried for murder at Jacksboro and imprisoned at Huntsville. The Salt Creek raid convinced military leaders of the need for offensive action against the Indians.

Before, the troops acted only to defend the frontier, but General Sherman now allowed troops to pursue the Indians onto the plains. But neither the reservation nor the United States army finally defeated the Plains Indians. Hunger did. The white man continued to slaughter the buffalo, the Indian's main source of food and clothing. General Philip Sheridan told the Texas legislature, "Let them kill, skin, and sell until they have exterminated the buffalo." Ruthlessly efficient, the buffalo hunters destroyed in a few years the millions of buffalo that roamed the plains. With the buffalo went the way of life of the Plains Indian.

Defeat of the Indians. Indians, realizing that the slaughter of the buffalo meant the end of their civilization and resenting buffalo hunters' intrusions into Indian lands, once again began raiding the white man. On June 27, 1874, a group of Comanche, Kiowa, and Cheyenne warriors under the command of Quanah Parker, last war chief of the Comanches, attacked the trading post at Adobe Walls in Hutchinson County. The Comanche medicine man promised that the Great Spirit would guide the Indian and restore his lands and his buffalo and give him victory over the white man. However, the Indian's arrows and lances were no match for the white man's long-range rifles. The last hope of the Indian to regain his land was destroyed at Adobe Walls.

Colonel Nelson Miles was ordered to force the Indians onto the reservation at Fort Sill. In August 1874 Miles encountered the Cheyenne on the rim of Palo Duro Canyon and destroyed their village. In September 1874 Colonel Ranald Mackenzie, guided by Indian scouts, attacked the Kiowas and Comanches in Palo Duro Canyon. He drove the Indians onto the Staked Plains and burned their tepees. Mackenzie's troops captured about fifteen hundred horses and slaughtered them. Afoot, defeated, and hungry, the Indians began to surrender at the reservation. Among those who returned to Fort Sill was Boin-

139

Edal, called Kiowa Dutch. He was of German ancestry, a tall, raw-boned man who spoke English with a German accent. He had been captured by the Indians in a raid and was raised to be a Kiowa warrior. Boin-Edal knew no other life than that of the Indian and wished to remain on the reservation as one. The United States troops employed Indian scouts, among them a company of Negro-Seminole scouts from Eagle Pass. Descendants of these scouts still live near Brackettville.

When Quanah Parker's Quohada Comanche agreed to retire to Fort Sill in 1875, the Indian threat to the Texas frontier was over. All of West Texas was open to white settlement and to the development of agriculture and the cattle industry. The

Texas Highway Department

Palo Duro Canyon, once the retreat of the Plains Indian, became cattle country after 1875.

grass no longer cropped by the buffalo proved to be ideal for longhorned steers, and ranchers soon began to expand their holdings onto the Great Plains of Texas and beyond. Less than two years after Mackenzie expelled the Comanches from Palo Duro Canyon Charles Goodnight established a ranch there, and others soon followed suit.

After the defeat of the Indians and their removal to reservations in the Indian Territory, the way was clear for the final great slaughter of the buffalo. One of the participants in that event left his account of the activities of one group of hunters in modern Stonewall County.

We were twenty-five miles west of the one-hundredth meridian, in plain view of the Kiowa Peak to our east and the Double Mountain to our south. We were in a veritable hunters' paradise. . . .

Too late to stop and moralize now. And sentiment must have no part in our thoughts from this time on. We must have these 3361 hides that this region is to furnish us inside of three months, within a radius of eight miles from this main camp. So at it we went. And Hart . . . started out, and in two hours had killed sixty-three bison. . . . It was now a busy time. Some days thirty and forty-odd hides, then a good day with eighty-five, and one day in February, one hundred and seventy-one; then again the same month, 203; and these 203 were killed on less than ten acres of ground. . . . [1]

A World in Itself

In Texas the cattle kingdom was the land of the longhorn, the wild descendant of Spanish cattle. South Texas was the spawning ground for millions of the beasts over the years. Tough and wiry, the longhorn could withstand the heat of summer and the cold of winter. He could protect himself when attacked by wild animals. He was agile, sturdy, indestructible. And he was a valuable part of the economy of Texas after the Civil War. There were over 3 million cattle in Texas but no buyers. But the North was a ready-made market, with buyers

[1]John R. Cook, *The Border and the Buffalo* (Topeka, 1907), 110-150. Reproduced in Wallace and Vigness, *Documents of Texas History* (Austin: Steck-Vaughn Company, 1963), 223-25.

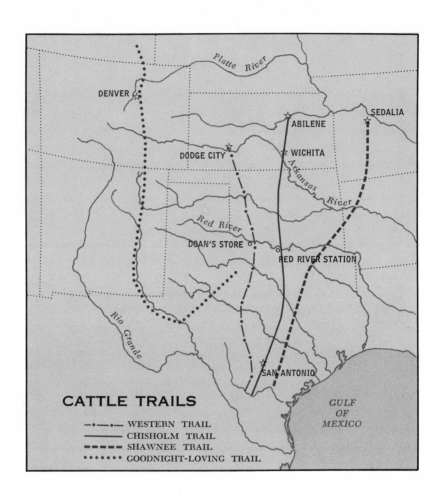

CATTLE TRAILS

—·—·— WESTERN TRAIL
————— CHISHOLM TRAIL
▬ ▬ ▬ ▬ SHAWNEE TRAIL
•••••• GOODNIGHT-LOVING TRAIL

GULF
OF
MEXICO

willing to pay from twenty to thirty dollars a head for cattle.

The Long Drives. Cattle had been driven to markets in the South, Midwest, and West before the Civil War. After the Civil War, cattle drives resumed. The first drives went up the Shawnee Trail from South Texas to Missouri, but the route was soon abandoned. A new route was needed, farther west.

Joseph McCoy, a Springfield, Illinois, cattle dealer, chose Abilene, Kansas, a site on the Kansas Pacific Railroad, as his shipping point. He built a stockyard, a livery stable, and a three-story hotel. He spread the news, by handbills, that there was a dependable market for cattle at Abilene. Part of the route to Abilene followed a trail established by Jesse Chisholm, who served as guide, interpreter, and trader in the Indian Territory. The entire route came to be called the Chisholm Trail.

The Shawnee (or Sedalia) and Chisholm trails were substantially the same as far north as McLennan County, but from Waco the Chisholm Trail ran past Fort Worth to Red River Station, through the Indian Territory to Abilene and Wichita. The establishment of the Goodnight-Loving Trail in 1866 provided an outlet to western beef markets. Charles Goodnight began cattle ranching in Palo Pinto County and fought Indians and cattle rustlers. In 1866 he formed a partnership with Oliver Loving, a longtime trail driver, and they drove cattle from Fort Belknap on the Pecos River to Fort Sumner, New Mexico. The Goodnight Trail, an extension of the Goodnight-Loving Trail, was established in 1875, providing a route from New Mexico to Granada, Colorado. Loving was killed by Indians in 1867 while on a drive in New Mexico. His last words were, "Take me back to Texas. Don't leave me on foreign soil."

A seemingly insignificant insect led to the establishment of the Chisholm Trail and later the Western Trail. Kansas passed quarantine laws against Texas cattle because of outbreaks of splenetic fever among Kansas cattle. Later the fever was found to be carried by cattle ticks. As the Texas cattle quarantine moved west with the frontier, Dodge City became the best shipping point for cattle. The Western Trail, which served Dodge City, ran from San Antonio north to Fort Griffin, crossing the Red River at Doan's Crossing and skirting the Panhandle across Indian territory. At least 5 million longhorns were taken north by 1884.

The trail drives presented many problems to cowmen handling wild longhorns. Charles Goodnight, one of the most successful trail drivers, gives some idea of the difficulties and dangers that had to be overcome.

As soon as the cattle had grazed sufficiently, they were put in moving order without delay. A column of cattle would march either slowly or faster according to the distance the side men rode from the line. Therefore, when we had a long drive to make between watering places and it was necessary to move faster, the men rode closer to the line. . . .

143

On my first drive across the ninety-six-mile desert that lies between the Pecos and the Concho Rivers, I lost three hundred head of cattle. We were three days and nights crossing this desert, and during this time we had no sleep or rest, as we had to keep the cattle moving all the time in order to get them to the river before they died of thirst. I rode the same horse for the three days and nights, and what sleep I got was on his back. . . .

When cattle are first started, the risk of stampede is great. They are nervous and easily frightened, the slightest noise may startle them into running. Some cattle are stampeders by nature. The greatest losses occurred in the night when all was utter confusion. A herd was more likely to run on a dark night than on a moonlight night. The remarkable thing about it was that the whole herd started instantly, jarring the earth like an earthquake. . . .

I was the only trailman that I know of who used steer leaders. I conceived this idea after the first trip and found it to be of great advantage. I used two steers. The bells I put on them were of the very best type—ox bells. They were arranged with a strap which would easily stop the clapper. When the signal to graze was given the man in charge of the steers would fasten down the clappers, and turn the steers off the trail. After we had been out for a month, should the clapper come loose at night, the whole herd would be on its feet in no time. The lead steers were of great advantage in swimming the rivers and in penning, for the cattle soon learned to go where the bell called them. Before starting on a trail drive, I made it a rule to draw up an article of agreement, setting forth what each man was to do. The main clause was that if one man shot another he was to be tried by the outfit and hanged on the spot—if found guilty. I never had a man shot on the trail.[2]

The Drovers. The trail drivers were of all kinds. Men such as Sam Bass and John Wesley Hardin went up the trail alongside men such as George W. Littlefield, the future founder of the American National Bank of Austin and member of The University of Texas board of regents. The long drives provided an opportunity for some young cowboys to collect enough money for a spree in a cattle town saloon, but for others they marked the beginning of a better life. The Negro cowhand Daniel Webster Wallace was one of the latter. Wallace took

[2]Charles Goodnight, "Managing a Trail Herd" (MS, J. Evetts Haley Library, Canyon, Texas); H. T. Burton, "A History of the JA Ranch," *The Southwestern Historical Quarterly*, XXXI (April 1928), 330-55.

his nickname, "80 John," from cowman Clay Mann's brand, a large "80." Wallace helped drive Mann's cattle up the trail to Dodge City and carefully saved his pay. He purchased his own ranch and stocked it with cattle, eventually acquiring over ten thousand acres in Mitchell County. Al Jones, a Negro trail boss, became well known, as was Bose Ikard, called by Charles Goodnight "the most skilled and trustworthy man I had."

The long drives died out as opposition grew among settlers whose lands the drives crossed and as the railroads came to Texas. Fencing made it possible to upgrade herds, and men from all over the world with capital to invest went into ranching on the Great Plains. Ranching was becoming a big business.

The Cattle Kings. Ranching on a large scale was nothing new in South and West Texas. Mifflin Kenedy and Richard King set the pattern for the ranches of the cattle kingdom of Texas. The giant King Ranch in South Texas pioneered many ranching practices, some of which were refinements of techniques of early Mexican ranchers such as Martín de León and Tomás Sánchez. Ben Leaton was one of the first Anglo-

Trail drivers Al Jones and George Glidden were two of Texas's many black cowboys.

The University of Texas Archives,
Barker Texas History Center

Americans to attempt to tame the Big Bend section of Texas. He made peace with the Apaches, and he brought pioneering agricultural techniques to the rugged land he ranched, constructing irrigation ditches to raise vegetables and wheat. The largest operator in the Big Bend before the Civil War was Manuel Músquiz, who ranched the canyon that now bears his name. An Apache raid in 1861 caused him to abandon his ranch.

Milton Favor was a powerful man in the Big Bend, where he settled in 1854 near modern Presidio. He raised money for his ranching enterprise by working as a freighter and by running a general store. His cattle grazed over hundreds of square miles between the three fortresses he erected, and Favor made his own laws and meted out his own justice. But Favor did not keep up with the times. He failed to establish ownership of his land and livestock, and with the advent of barbed wire fences and the branding iron, Favor lost many of his cattle, and much of his land was taken in by other men. Finally he retired behind his fortress walls and died almost penniless.

Abel H. ("Shanghai") Pierce bought 250,000 acres in Texas and formed the Pierce-Sullivan Pasture Company. The company sent thousands of cattle up the trails into Kansas and shipped other thousands north by railroad. Pierce searched Europe to find a breed of cattle immune to ticks. He came back without a definite answer but with a strong suspicion that Brahman cattle were best suited to be immune. After his death his estate imported Brahman cattle, foundation stock for present Texas Brahman herds.

The cattle business took on different characteristics after the end of the long drives. The establishment of a ranch was no longer a matter of branding wild cattle and defending them from the Indians. Ownership of the land became necessary to protect one's holdings, and large amounts of money were needed to finance a ranch. Foreign investors were attracted both by potential profits and by the romance of owning a ranch.

Englishmen found the cattle business fascinating, and many made substantial investments in Texas land and cattle. Captain William Turner was one of the first English settlers in the Fort Concho area, where he founded the Whitbarrow Ranch. The

Earl of Aylesford settled near Big Spring, Texas, and became known for his eccentricity. He bought the local hotel to insure himself a room, bought the butcher shop to be sure his meat was cut to order, and bought the local saloon to insure himself an adequate supply of whiskey. Less dramatic but more long-lasting in his effect on Texas was another Englishman, E. E. Risien, who made a great contribution to the pecan industry. Risien improved native varieties of pecans and developed new varieties, appropriately named Comanche, Apache, and Wichita.

English-owned companies invested in Texas land and acquired holdings of more than 20 million acres in the 1880s. The Rocking Chair Ranche Company, Ltd., was called "The Nobility Ranch" by the native Texans in Collingsworth and Wheeler counties. The ranch never did well financially, and the English sometimes failed to get along with their neighbors. They called their tenant farmers "cottagers" and their cowboys "cow servants." The individualistic hands showed a lack of tolerance for the foreigners, and they probably took some ribbing from other cowboys who saw humor in the "cow servants" having a boss named Sir Dudley Coutts Majoribanks, Baron of Tweedmouth.

The largest ranch in Texas, the XIT, was the result of payment for a new capitol building. When the state capitol burned in 1881, the legislature appropriated 3 million acres of land to finance a new structure. The Capitol Syndicate was organized and the XIT Ranch established to use the land until it could be sold. The Capitol Freehold Land and Investment Company, Ltd., was incorporated in London to stock the ranch and to provide money for operating expenses. The XIT Ranch spread across the 3 million acres and was stocked with over one hundred thousand head of cattle. Hereford, shorthorn, and Angus cattle were introduced to improve the herds, and over fifteen hundred miles of barbed wire fence were built. Gradually the extensive holdings were sold to other ranchers, such as George W. Littlefield, and to farmers. By 1912 all the XIT cattle had been sold.

The Irishman John George Adair formed a partnership with Charles Goodnight to establish the JA Ranch in Palo Duro

The legislature appropriated land rather than money to pay for the present capitol, shown under construction.

Canyon. When Adair bought Goodnight's interest, he expanded the ranch to include almost 2 million acres owned or leased and stocked it with some one hundred thousand head of cattle. Such large ranches were necessarily run as businesses and often returned profits that enabled the owner to live quite well. The most opulent house in frontier West Texas belonged to the Frenchman Ernest Carlin. Carlin's ranch house, with its porcelain bath tubs and servants' quarters, astounded his neighbors.

An interesting factor in the settlement of West Texas was the Franco-Texan Land Company, established by Frenchmen and capitalized by the Texas and Pacific Railroad. Jot Gunter, of French ancestry, and others founded the T-Anchor Ranch north of Palo Duro Canyon. Gunter moved to San Antonio at the turn of the century and established the famous Gunter Hotel, which was for years cattlemen's headquarters.

Eric and Albin Swenson, sons of the Swedish pioneer Svante Magnus Swenson, continued the SMS Ranches near Abilene after their father's death. The Swenson Land and Cattle Company is still being operated by their descendants. Some of the holdings were land grants purchased by Swenson from rail-

148

roads building to the area. The Swedish Horse Society, an organization founded to aid ranchers in retrieving stolen horses, pioneered in the recording of cattle brands.

Railroads, Barbed Wire, and Windmills. Railroads, encouraged by huge grants of public land, aided in the opening of West Texas. Barbed wire came into use in 1879. For the first time fencing was available that was both effective and inexpensive. Barbed wire would turn a steer, but did not require the timber or the labor that traditional wooden fences did. The open range began to disappear as miles of Texas ranch- and farmlands were enclosed. The windmill freed the rancher from dependence on streams for water for his livestock, so that fences could be erected to obtain the most efficient use of the range.

In 1857 a Swiss ironworker named Grenninger made a crude barbed wire fence to enclose his Austin orchard, but his neighbors feared injury to their cattle and prevailed on him to take down what may have been the first barbed wire fence. By the early 1880s barbed wire had caught on in Texas. The King Ranch purchased two hundred thousand pounds of wire, and Charles Goodnight began the fencing of the huge JA Ranch in 1881. The fencing of the XIT Ranch required some three hundred freight carloads of materials, including six thousand miles of wire and a carload each of staples and gate hinges. The success of barbed wire in Texas was partly brought about by an inventive young salesman, John W. ("Bet-a-Million") Gates. In 1877 Gates set up a barbed wire corral on San Antonio's Main Plaza and bet that the wire would hold in a herd of longhorn steers. The ranchers took his bet, and Gates won. Gates sold so much wire that the company he represented could not fill all the orders, so he began organizing his own companies and in eight years had established five companies producing barbed wire. Always one to see the possibilities in a new venture, a few years later Gates invested in the Texas Company, which now operates worldwide under the name Texaco.

The First Farmers. Although the Great Plains were to remain the province of the cattleman for a while, some farmers came soon after the Comanches left. The first two Panhandle

149

towns, Mobeetie and Tascosa, were established to serve ranching country, but the third town, Clarendon, was founded by colonists who were farmers. Farming on the South Plains was pioneered by Paris Cox, who exchanged his Indiana sawmill for railroad lands in Texas. He sold acreage in Crosby County to Quakers in 1879. Their settlement, Estacado, flourished, and the Quakers, with their knack for farming, grew good crops and extensive orchards. George Eames Barstow organized the Barstow Irrigation Company near the Pecos River and pioneered in irrigation and water conservation. Barstow was one of the first men to recognize the need to conserve water, a matter of vital importance to all Texans today and especially to the people of West Texas, where irrigation is depleting groundwater resources.

Frontier Hero. Brief as the time of the cattle drives was, only about thirty years, it produced a wealth of folklore. The cowboy was the purest example of the American hero. Before, he had been Daniel Boone, and David Crockett, and others who preceded other men into wilderness yet unexplored. The cowboy, the new hero, was a plainsman, whereas Boone, in Kentucky, and Crockett, in Tennessee, lived in the woods. But both had Indians and wild animals to contend with, and new country to explore. The cowboy's self-reliance, initiative, perseverance, and strength made him the perfect hero for Americans on the eve of a technological age. Americans thought of the cowboy in terms of the ballad that goes, "O bury me not on the lone prairie."

Walter Prescott Webb described the cowboy as a typical Westerner. "He swears like a trooper, drinks like a fish, wears clothes like an actor, and fights like a devil. He is gracious to ladies, reserved toward strangers, generous to his friends, and brutal to his enemies." The Western novelist Emerson Hough said of the cowboy: "He never dreamed he was a hero." And yet hero he became, lauded in lore and legend, celebrated in song and movie.

The cowboy represented the West, but he originated in Mexico. The Spanish charro tradition with its glittering costumes and brilliant *charreadas,* or riding stunts, made horseback riding as popular in Mexico as the bullfight. The Mexican

150

vaquero, the working cowboy, brought his *amor al ganado* or cowsense to Texas with him. He brought his equipment and his way of life to the Texas cattle trails, and the Texas cowboy quickly adapted them to his life on the plains. The vaquero's braided *reata* was used to rope the longhorn either *mangana,* by the forefeet, or *pial,* by the hindfeet. Knowledge about the care of the horse passed from vaquero to cowboy. They loosened the *cincho,* or cinch, raised the saddle and blanket, and let the air pass over the horse's back. Around the horse's nose fitted the *jaquima,* soon anglicized to hackamore. Bits, saddles, and other horse equipment brought to the New World by the Spanish were the basis of the cowboy's equipment, with refinements and changes to fit local conditions. The cowboy wore the practical working gear of the vaquero. His *sombrero* protected him from rain, his *chapas* protected his legs from brush and saddle burns, and his bandanna shielded his eyes and nose from the dust and sand.

Rustlers and Renegades. As legendary a part of the West as the cowboy is the badman, and American folklore has transformed many a murderer and thief into a Robin Hood of the range. In the wide-open days of frontier Texas, the renegade and the cattle rustler were as much a part of life as the farmer and the lawman. Sam Bass worked as a cowhand, but quit to race a quarterhorse named the Denton Mare. After working as a trail driver, he drifted toward the Dakota Territory and lost all his money gambling. He fell in with a band of outlaws and helped rob a train in Nebraska, an adventure which netted them sixty thousand dollars. Bass came back to Texas to organize his own band of outlaws. They robbed four trains near Dallas, and the Texas Rangers under Major John B. Jones took to the trail after Bass and his gang. Hiding out near Round Rock, Texas, Bass managed to keep ahead of the Rangers, but a member of his gang informed the Rangers that Bass planned to hold up the local bank. On July 19, 1878, Bass's gang and the Rangers shot it out in a gun battle, and Bass died of his wounds.

John Wesley Hardin, the son of a Methodist circuit preacher, killed his first man when he was fifteen. A trip up the Chisholm Trail in 1871 netted him nine more victims. He surrendered to the sheriff of Cherokee County in 1872, but broke out of jail soon after and became involved in the Sutton-Taylor Feud. Sentenced to twenty-five years in prison, Hardin studied law and taught the prison Sunday school, trying to escape the entire time. He received a pardon in 1894 and was admitted to the Texas bar to practice law. However, Hardin's reputation followed him to El Paso, where Constable John Selman shot him in the back in 1895.

While some Texans recounted the adventures of men like Bass and Hardin, others remembered the cattle rustler and renegade Juan Cortina. Cortina claimed leadership of a movement to secure justice for his countrymen. Cortina led an army of some five hundred renegades in cattle rustling swoops into Texas. During the Civil War, Cortina cooperated with both Union and Confederate troops and supported Maximilian in the French effort to take over Mexico. The liberal Mexican government under Benito Juárez granted Cortina amnesty, and he continued his adventurous cattle rustling escapades across the Rio Grande. Finally the Mexican government took Cortina into custody, and he remained paroled in Mexico City for the rest of his life.

Gregorio Cortez became as legendary a folk hero as Billy the Kid or Jesse James. The *corrido* (ballad) of his adventures was sung from San Antonio to Mexico City. Born in Mexico, Cortez and his family moved to Manor, Texas. In 1889 he joined his brother in Karnes County, where they worked as vaqueros. When he and his brother were unjustly accused of stealing a horse, Cortez killed Sheriff Brack Morris, who gunned down Cortez's unarmed brother and then tried to kill Cortez. Cortez fled for Mexico, pursued by posses numbering up to three hundred men. In a ten-day chase, Cortez rode more than four hundred miles and walked another hundred miles before being captured by Texas Ranger captain J. H. Rogers. The shooting of Sheriff Morris was ruled self-defense, but Cortez was sentenced to life imprisonment for the murder of another sheriff who was killed during the pursuit. Governor Oscar B. Colquitt pardoned Cortez in 1913.

Lawmen. Those who enforced the law were usually as colorful as those who broke it. Judge Roy Bean, "the Law West of

152

the Pecos," drifted to Texas during the Civil War days. He owned a saloon in California and was jailed for dueling. Strung up by a rival suitor in New Mexico, he was fortunately cut down by his sweetheart. In San Antonio he gained a reputation as a bill dodger and moved west operating a tent saloon serving railroad construction workers. In 1882 Bean settled near the present site of Langtry, Texas. Bean claimed he named the town in honor of the famous actress, Lily Langtry, but other citizens said it was named for the track foreman of the Southern Pacific Railroad. The lawless conditions in West Texas led to Bean's appointment as justice of the peace.

Bean's reputation as a justice of the peace was widespread. When he married couples, he told them to come back for a divorce if the marriage did not "take," even though Texas law gave him no jurisdiction over divorce cases. When a corpse was found with a gun and forty dollars, Bean fined the corpse forty dollars for carrying a concealed weapon. Dispensing what he took to be justice from a mail-order catalog bound in sheepskin, Judge Roy Bean was never a success as a businessman, but his shrewdness and courage brought some order to his part of the state.

A lawman as crusty as Roy Bean was Ben Thompson, who began and ended his career on the dark side of the law. In his youth he shot a playmate; a few years later he fought a duel that became legendary—Bowie knives in a dark, locked icehouse. He served as a hired gunman in Mexico and Colorado before returning to Texas, where he was elected city marshal of Austin. Thompson's idea of recreation was to sit in a saloon beneath a print shop and fire a fusillade of bullets through the ceiling to see how fast the printers could vacate the premises. Although crime rates in Austin plummeted, Thompson's misdeeds rose to new heights, culminating in his shooting of a prominent San Antonio citizen in 1882. Acquitted of the crime, he returned to San Antonio two years later and was murdered by unknown assailants.

The Texas Rangers were effective frontier defenders. They were fine marksmen and expert horsemen. Armed with the Colt six-shooter, the Ranger became a threat to Indian and bandit alike. Leander McNelly, a slender, soft-spoken man who had fought in several Confederate campaigns, was Ranger captain after the reorganization of the force in 1874. He settled feuds among cattlemen and pacified the border. When Mc-Nelly's Rangers first moved against armed bands of men stealing cattle and horses and burning ranches in South Texas, they took no prisoners. The Ranger policy of "shoot first, ask questions later" eliminated much of the outlaw element on the border and frontier, but some Texans opposed the Rangers because of the deaths of innocent people who were mistaken for criminals.

The Texas Rangers rose to the height of their fame under McNelly and Major John B. Jones, a former Confederate who became commander of the Frontier Battalion of Rangers. Much of the energy of the Rangers in the 1880s and 1890s was spent in tracking down fence-cutters, who objected to the fencing of the open range—usually because they owned little land themselves or found themselves blocked off from water by someone else's fence. In 1884 the Texas legislature made fence-cutting a crime but required that owners provide gates at least every three miles. Problems with fence-cutters continued into the twentieth century.

With Pen and Paintbrush

Lawman, cowman, rustler, and renegade—all were part of the western cattle kingdom. And all formed the image of the West reflected in song, story, and art. From history by R. N. Richardson to novels by Benjamin Capps, from dime novels to the Western of movies and television, the West lives on. The ballads of the cowboy and the folksongs of the cattle country were first collected by John A. Lomax, and the songs of the trail express the loneliness and the vigor of the cowboy's life. Stories by Owen Wister, O. Henry, and Eugene Manlove Rhodes created a picture of life in the West. Andy Adams's *Log of a Cowboy* and his other writings describe the trail driving days. Dorothy Scarborough's novels deal with the life of the farmer on the plains.

The Irishman John Armoy Knox was a sewing machine agent in Texas before becoming a journalist. His articles in

154

Louis Hoppe's engraving of *Julius Meyenberg's Farm* near La Grange reflects the more substantial architecture developed as the frontier retreated westward.

Texas Siftings gained national acclaim. Knox collaborated with Alexander Sweet on the novel *On a Mexican Mustang through Texas*, which was first published as a serial in *Texas Siftings*. The Englishman Frank Collinson worked on ranches in Texas and hunted the buffalo over the Great Plains. In later life he wrote of his adventures.

Many artists went west with surveying or exploring parties and captured the spirit and the romantic vision of the West which made landscape painting a nineteenth-century phenomenon. The vastness of the West inspired artists to paint huge panoramas, one so large that it was displayed in motion by being wound from one reel to another, there being no room big enough to display it all at once. Artists such as John Kensett, Albert Bierstadt, Frederick Church, and George Inness idealized the American West.

Prints became an effective means of portraying Texas cities and scenery. A draftsman and surveyor, William H. Sandusky, created scenes of Austin, and the subjects of German printmakers Erhard Pentenrieder and Helmuth Holtz were San Antonio and Matagorda. Louis Hoppe created a pastoral genre scene of Texas farm life in his engraving *Julius Meyenberg's*

155

Farm. The Frenchman A. de Vandricourt's *Rio San Pedro* captures the Texas landscape, and John E. Weyss's *Brownsville, Texas* the relationship of man and land.

The End and the Beginning

The end of the West of cowboy and Indian marked the beginning of a new age. A quiet, retiring schoolmaster who had tried to invent a self-winding clock before he left Germany tinkered with steam engines in his spare time in Fredericksburg and San Antonio. By 1863 he had built a prototype of an airplane which had wings, a rudder, and a propeller. Jacob Brodbeck labored for more than twenty years to perfect his airship, which was powered by coiled springs. With financial backers, including San Antonio physician Ferdinand Herff, standing by, Brodbeck got his airship into the air, but the spring could not be rewound in flight, and the plane crashed. The successful flight of a heavier-than-air plane had to wait for the development of the internal combustion engine.

At the time Brodbeck began work on his flying machine, another Texan three hundred miles away was trying to bring oil from under the ground. Lyne Taliaferro Barret manufactured drilling machinery with the help of a local blacksmith and drilled an oil well near Melrose, Nacogdoches County. The well produced only about ten barrels a day, and Barret lost his financial backing, but he lived to see the Spindletop well bring in a new era.

Discuss

1. Why did the practice of putting Indians on reservations do little to stop Indian raids until after 1875?

2. What factors made possible the rise of the cattle industry?

156

3. Why do you think Americans have come to idealize the cowboy? What do your reasons reveal about the values of those who idealized the cowboys? Do you think new heroes will replace cowboys? Why? What characteristics would you expect the hero of the future to have?

4. The destruction of the buffalo brought an end to the Indians' way of life. What events might cause our own way of life to undergo a drastic change? What can be done to prevent such events from taking place?

5. What does Satanta's speech at Medicine Lodge reveal about the Indians' concept of the nature of the struggle between the white man and the Indian?

6. What developments changed ranching from an individual enterprise into a big business?

Identify

reservation
Alabama-Coushatta
  Indians
Tigua Indians
Britton Johnson
Quanah Parker
Joseph McCoy
Daniel Webster
  Wallace
E. E. Risien
John W. Gates
Gregorio Cortez
Leander McNelly
Jacob Brodbeck

General Philip
  Sheridan
Medicine Lodge Treaty
Satanta
Salt Creek massacre
Colonel Ranald
  Mackenzie
Charles Goodnight
Ben Leaton
XIT Ranch
Swedish Horse Society
John Wesley Hardin
Roy Bean
John Armoy Knox

Part 2

THE DYNAMIC CENTURY

THE 1880S SAW FARMERS, SUCH AS THESE IN EL CAM
PO, PRODUCING GOODS FOR SALE RATHER THAN HOM
CONSUMPTION.

CHAPTER 9

"The Great Railroad Octopus"

The key to development of the interior of Texas was transportation. Rivers spanned the state, but for most of their lengths they were useless as highways for goods and passengers. But wherever the railroads went, towns and commercial farms were possible. Adequate transportation was a boon to development. But as soon as tracks were laid, railroads began abusing their patrons, causing the Farmers' Alliance to ask, in 1890, "Shall the great railroad octopus be shorn of its talons?"

The Snort of the Iron Horse

The linking of the East and the West by the transcontinental railroad in 1869 marked the beginning of a new era in the

German immigrants bound for New York, some of whom perhaps found their way to Texas.

settlement of the West. Once the continent was spanned, railroad companies turned their attention to building feeder lines, connecting towns to the main lines and making it possible for cities to grow up where none had been before. Texas, possessed of vast public lands and desiring railroads, offered huge grants to the railroads. The Texas Constitution of 1876 provided for a grant of 10,240 acres for every mile of track laid. The resulting explosion of track-laying occurred in every part of the state. By 1882 over 35 million acres of public lands had been granted to railroads. From fewer than seventeen hundred miles of track in 1870, none lying west of a line from Denison to Dallas, Waco, Austin, and Corpus Christi, the network of rails grew to almost ten thousand miles in 1900.

This building often took place in underpopulated areas where there was little business. It was in the interest of the railroads to see that those areas were settled. In addition, state law required that the railroads sell their granted land within twelve years or ownership would revert to the state. Thus the railroads had a double motive for encouraging immigration to unsettled areas. The railroads sent agents to Europe to encourage immigrants to come to America. The agents found interested listeners in many parts of Europe, where economic and political conditions had many people eager to seek a new life across the Atlantic.

Many immigrants from Europe poured into the United States, and many found their way to Texas. Organizations were formed to promote areas for settlement. The frontier disappeared and towns arose. Agriculture expanded, and railroads were the best means of moving produce to market. Farmers planted thousands of acres of cash crops where they once engaged in subsistence agriculture alone.

A Tide of Immigrants. While immigration of German, French, English, Irish, Swedish, and other northern European ethnic groups to Texas continued, the late nineteenth and early twentieth centuries saw an influx of Greek, Lebanese, and Chinese immigrants to swell the population of the state and to make significant contributions to the culture of Texas. Although the immigration of Lebanese to Texas began after the Civil War, it increased from 1890 until the end of World War I, reaching its peak before 1914. Lebanese settlers concentrated in Dallas, Houston, Beaumont, El Paso, Austin, and San Antonio. Immigrants formed ethnic clubs such as the Lebanese Club and the Lebanese and Syrian Brotherhoods. Eight Joseph brothers arrived in Austin, and soon a block of Austin's business thoroughfare, Congress Avenue, had six stores headed by Josephs.

When Abraham Kazen, Sr., arrived in Laredo from K'nat, Lebanon, in 1890, he founded one of Laredo's leading business and public service families. Kazen, with his brothers Anthony and Joe, founded a wholesale and retail business in Laredo. They had to learn both English and Spanish in order to deal with their customers. Abraham Kazen became an interpreter for the United States Customs Service. His son Charles served as district collector of the United States Customs Service; another son, James, is a district judge in Laredo; Philip is a distinguished lawyer; and Abraham, Jr., was a state senator and now represents the Laredo district in Congress.

Greeks immigrated to Texas from their small, agricultural

Abraham Kazen, Jr., is a member of a Laredo family with a long history of public service.

country to escape Turkish oppression, drought, crop failures, and economic depression. The first Greeks settled as tenant farmers in Fort Bend County in 1883. The first Greek Orthodox community was established in Galveston in 1885. Father Theoclitos served as the first priest of Saints Constantine and Helen Serbian and Greek Orthodox Church in the city.

The network of railroads fanning out across the state brought the first Chinese to Texas. The Houston and Texas Central Railroad employed some three hundred Chinese laborers. When the three-year railroad contract was completed, some 150 workers returned to the Brazos River valley to settle.

The concept of a railroad running from New York City to Mexico City moved Count Giuseppe Telferner to take advantage of the state's liberal land grant policy for railroad construction. The count brought Italian laborers to Texas to construct the railroad: their families settled along the line. In 1881 the crews began work on the New York, Texas, and Mexican Railroad, and by July 1882 ninety-one miles had been completed at a cost of $2 million. When the state repealed all land grants to railroads, work on the "Macaroni Line" ceased, and Telferner eventually sold his interest in the railroad to the Southern Pacific.

164

Danish settlers began arriving near El Campo in 1894. They shared the hardships that the farmer in Texas was experiencing at the time. Fire had ravaged much of the land. Storms and floods pelted the region. Their livestock died of starvation. The Danes brought to Texas a farming experience based on grain crops and livestock raising. They were unfamiliar with cotton, but they were industrious and willing to learn. By 1897 the Danes produced enough cotton to require a cotton gin. They founded Danevang in 1904.

Ribbons of Steel. Without an efficient system of transportation, a state cannot develop its industries. Prior to the construction of the railroads, goods and produce had been transported to market in carts and wagons. Although Texas was spanned by a number of rivers, few were navigable in the nineteenth century. Freight and passenger rates were high. Roads were few, and none were paved. The first railroads were crudely built, roadbeds were poor, and railroad equipment was often unsafe. Iron bridges were seldom seen: the first was constructed in Bell County in 1886. The railroads became slightly more efficient after the Civil War. Steel rails allowed the use of larger locomotives and cars.

When the Civil War ended, Texas had only 395 miles of track in use, and most railroad equipment was damaged and deteriorated. The Houston and Texas Central Railroad began

Crossing the Brazos River, early trains navigated tracks resting on a flatboat which could be moved to allow river traffic to pass. Passengers usually walked across.

construction after the war and connected Houston with the Midwest and East by meeting, at Denison, the Missouri, Kansas, and Texas, which had arrived in 1872. The Texas and Pacific, at Texarkana, provided another eastern outlet. After the Constitution of 1876 made such liberal allowances for railroad land grants there was much activity. More than half the track laid in the nineteenth century was built between 1875 and 1885. It was the state's discovery that the whole supply of available public land had been exhausted that resulted in repeal of the granting law in 1882.

In addition to land payments by the state, railroad officials often required bonuses from communities for the promise of a place on the line. Fort Worth, expanding as an important center for shipping cattle to market, paid bonuses to all of its railroad lines. The smallest of these bonuses was $78,000. Communities which were bypassed, such as Jefferson, withered.

The railroads stimulated the growth of industries. An expanding lumber industry contributed wood for buildings, crossties, fuel, and bridges. A burgeoning state agriculture provided food for the railroad construction gangs and the animals required in constructing the lines. Construction camps became towns—Abilene, Eastland, Sweetwater, Colorado City, Big Spring. Every aspect of business was stimulated by the construction and presence of the railroads, but then began criticism of unfair railroad practices. Rebates granted to favored shippers, unfair rates, inadequate service, the issuance of free passes, and the influence of the railroads in the state legislature became matters of concern to many Texans, especially to farmers who depended on railroads to haul their produce to market at a rate that would allow them to earn a living.

Rain Follows the Plow

The advance of the settlers into West Texas did not wait on the railroad. Four years after Quanah Parker's surrender, settlement had reached Vernon on the north and Ballinger on the south, an explosive movement that thrilled such West Texans as the Jacksboro editor who thought it would require Mexico and the Indian Territory to accommodate all those who were migrating. West Texans were optimistic, such as the one who said that if a man wanted to die he would have to go somewhere else to do it. And people invented reasons for settling on the plains. One of the myths that persisted was that where a farmer began cultivation of the land, rain would follow due to some interaction between the tilled soil and moisture in the sky. Rain did fall in above normal amounts for several years after the immigrants began pouring in, but a severe drought in 1886 disillusioned many settlers. A return of the rains the following year brought another surge of the hopeful to test their mettle against the locusts, droughts, and hailstorms that inevitably came.

Technological advances seemed to hold the promise of a brighter future for the farmer. The United States Congress passed the Morrill Act in 1862 providing for land grant colleges to specialize in agricultural and mechanical skills, and the Texas farmer profited from the establishment of the Agricultural and Mechanical College of Texas and the agricultural experiment stations set up to improve farming methods.

Problems of the Farmer. While improved equipment and techniques helped the farmer increase production, the resultant oversupply of farm produce caused prices to fall. Faced by falling prices, the only answer seemed to be increased production, on the theory that the farmer could make the same amount of money as before by selling more. However, increased production caused prices to fall even lower. Many farmers found themselves unable to meet the mortgage payments on their land and equipment. Banks foreclosed on the farmers, and many became tenant farmers on the land that had once been theirs. Other men unable to buy a farm because of rising land prices also became tenant farmers.

Whether working to pay off a mortgage or to pay the rent, the farmer had to grow crops that could be sold for cash. A new agricultural economy was developing—one which was based on the production of crops for sale rather than for food. American agriculture, like American industry, was becoming specialized.

The specialization of agriculture led to a greater need for credit. The farmer no longer raised or made all the necessities of life on his own farm. Some things had to be purchased, yet for most of the year there was no cash income. Farmers borrowed to pay expenses, but for most it seemed that the harvest never brought in enough money. The goods the farmer needed rose in cost, while the price of farm produce fell. One solution that had some appeal was expansion of the currency supply. It seemed logical that if the government put more money into circulation, dollars would be easier to get, prices for farm produce would go up, and debts could be paid.

The railroads were a problem, too. Railroad rates were discriminatory, arbitrary, and unreasonable. The free lands offered to railroads had tempted speculators to build some railroads that were economic failures. Many small lines were acquired by larger companies. By 1882 more than half the railroad mileage in the state was controlled by two men, Jay Gould and Collis P. Huntington, who divided the state into north and south zones and virtually eliminated competition between the two systems. The trunk line railroads formed an association to fix rates. Railroads charged more for short hauls than for long hauls, granted rebates to large shippers, and charged high rates where they had no competition. The railroads also gave free passes to anyone with any political influence.

Farmers believed that regulation of the railroads and an expansion of the money supply were needed. Individually they could do little, but as a group they would have influence and could cause the existing political parties to pay attention to their needs. The farmers organized, and the ideas first put forth by them became the foundation of present government regulation of parts of the economy.

The Agrarian Crusade

The farmer who plowed his own acreage and maintained a self-sufficient unit could afford to be an individualist. His responsibility was only to his family. But those concentrating on the wheat or cotton crops were becoming businessmen. They were forced to concern themselves with the economic conditions affecting other farmers and other segments of the society they lived in. Gradually the farmer began to see that

168

Economic difficulties aggravated by the overproduction of cotton drove prices down and forced farmers to seek reforms.

through organization he could hope to accomplish the ends he sought. The farmer ceased to function as one individual and began to look toward organizations to express his discontents and to press for political and social action in his behalf.

The Grange. The earliest farm organization to express the needs and discontents of the farmer was the Patrons of Husbandry, or the Grange. Organized as a national social society in 1867, the Grange sought to advance the social and cultural activities of people living in rural areas. Bell County was the site of the first Texas chapter of the Grange, and by 1875 the Grange was recognized as an important force. Although the Grange was nonpolitical, it kept pressure on the legislature for favorable action on behalf of the farmer. With Texas primarily an agricultural state, the very size of the farm vote made the Grange a potent force in state politics. The Grange exerted considerable influence in the convention which wrote the Constitution of 1876.

The Greenback Party. A third-party movement resulted when farmers pressed for an inflated currency. During the hard times of the 1870s the Greenback party gained in strength among farmers across the nation, and it reached Texas during 1878. The Greenbackers held a party convention in that year and fielded candidates for both state and national offices. By 1884, as economic problems lessened and the Greenback party failed to deal effectively with the money issue, many of its members returned to the Democratic party.

The Farmers' Alliance. During the hard years of 1874 and 1875 the Farmers' Alliance was formed in Lampasas County. Although the first efforts were negligible, a second Alliance was founded in 1879 and spread quickly throughout the state and the South. In 1887 the leader of the Texas Alliance, Dr. C. W. Macune, organized the National Alliance, which grew rapidly. A similar organization began in the midwestern states, and the two agencies pressed for the betterment of the farmer's life. The Alliance worked for reform without resorting to political action. However, the demands called for by the Alliance were so significant that many found their way into the platform of the Democratic party. The Farmers' Alliance advocated significant changes in banking, reform of the currency system, government ownership of railroads and telegraph systems, and reductions in national and state taxes.

The demands of the Farmers' Alliance caused the Democratic party, in its state platform in 1888, to advocate railroad and trust regulation. Regulation was a new concept to a nineteenth century steeped in the Jeffersonian belief that the best government is the one which governs least. The Alliance in Texas appointed a special committee to represent the interests of the farmers before the legislature. Laws were passed for the regulation of trusts in 1889. The continued demands of the Alliance resulted in the Democratic nomination for governor of a railroad commission advocate in 1890, James Stephen Hogg, who won easily. In 1891 the legislature established the Texas Railroad Commission with power to regulate the railroads.

The Populist Party. Populism had its roots in the agrarian unrest of the 1870s and 1880s and in the principles expressed by the Farmers' Alliance. The spread of Populism through the West and the South resembled a religious revival, an evangelical crusade based on the farmers' demands for an equal voice in the government. Throughout the West and the South a new breed of politician sprang up, proclaiming the discontent of the farmers. Kansas sent Sockless Jerry Simpson to

Congress. Mary Ellen Lease exhorted the farm element. In Minnesota Ignatius Donnelly preached of an international conspiracy against farmers, and General James B. Weaver of Iowa ran for president of the United States on the Populist ticket. The agrarian rebel Tom Watson was elected to Congress by the small farmers of Georgia. Pitchfork Ben Tillman of South Carolina sponsored legislation for the regulation of railroads.

The Populist platform of 1892 included a number of reform measures that eventually became laws: a graduated income tax, the secret ballot, and the direct election of United States senators. The platform also included single terms for the president and vice-president, the use of the initiative and the referendum, and shorter hours for all laborers. The basic principles and goals of the Populist party are outlined below.

The fundamental ideological concept behind the People's Party is to be found in the old American doctrine of the equality of man. . . . Not only were men created equal; they had certain equal and inalienable rights, of which justice demanded that they be not deprived. The old Alliance doctrine was summarized in the words "Equal rights to all, special privileges to none," and People's Party publicists were not able to improve upon that idea.

The second great hypothesis of Populism, which rested directly on the doctrine of equality and equal rights, may be stated in these terms: Despite the essential and natural equality of man there exist certain economic inequalities which weigh heavily on all workingmen but more especially on the agricultural classes. These inequalities must be eliminated if justice is to be done, and this can be accomplished effectively only through government assistance. Therefore the farmer desired government regulation; then, if that should prove unavailing, government control; and finally, as a last resort, public ownership, not of all industries but only of those affected with the public interest.[1]

The Populist party backed the Democratic candidate for the presidency in 1896. The Democrats had adopted the Populist demand for an expansion of the money supply. The "Boy

[1]Roscoe C. Martin, *The People's Party in Texas* (Austin: University of Texas Press, 1970), 46.

Orator of the Platte," William Jennings Bryan, thundered that mankind was being crucified on a cross of gold. Bryan advocated the coinage of silver at a sixteen-to-one ratio with gold. Bryan campaigned tirelessly and with a fervor that William Allen White, a Kansas newspaperman, described as a "religious frenzy," but William McKinley won the presidency and the Republican party gained control of both houses of Congress.

The Populist party lost much of its strength by backing Bryan as the Democratic candidate rather than nominating a candidate of its own. The reforms that the Populists preached had to wait until the twentieth century to become law. In 1913 the Sixteenth Amendment to the Constitution provided for the graduated income tax, Congress passed the Federal Reserve Act creating a government-controlled, decentralized banking system with the power to expand the money supply, and the Seventeenth Amendment put the election of senators into the hands of the voters.

Populism in Texas. The Populist party in Texas drew its support primarily from small farmers, sheep ranchers, and laborers. The Populists effectively used newspapers, public speakers, and camp meetings to spread the Populist message.

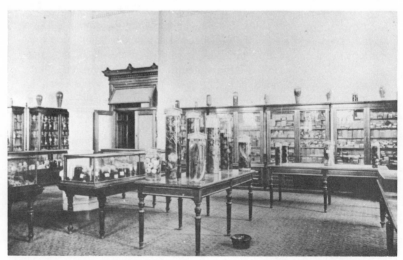

From ART WORK OF AUSTIN

The importance of agriculture to Texas was shown by this display of Texas produce in the capitol.

Through the *Texas Advance* and the *Southern Mercury,* Texas Populists carried their reform program to the people. The number of Populist newspapers grew to a total of seventy-five during the height of the Populist fervor. The Populists nominated candidates for political office from 1892 to 1904 and managed to send members to both the state house of representatives and the state senate. Although they failed to capture many seats in the state government, the Populists caused the Democratic party in Texas to adopt many reform measures and to attune the party to the importance of the farmer.

Regulation of the Railroads. The regulation of freight rates in Texas became a major political issue in 1890. As early as 1875, the Farmers' Alliance had called for regulation of railroad rates, and Congressman John H. Reagan introduced a bill in 1878 which called for the federal government to prohibit railroad pools, rebates, drawbacks, and the fixing of discriminatory rates. Reagan was the joint author of the bill that passed Congress in 1887 to establish the Interstate Commerce Commission.

Another significant piece of regulatory legislation was the Sherman Antitrust Act of 1890. The two laws showed that some Americans were expecting protection from the monopolistic tendencies of big business. Under the Interstate Commerce Act, the railroads were forbidden to charge discriminatory rates, could not form pooling agreements, and were forced to publish the schedules of their rates. The Interstate Commerce Commission could supervise the enforcement of the act, but could enforce the law only through the courts. It could not require witnesses to testify and had no power to enforce the law itself.

Intrastate railroads did not fall under the jurisdiction of the Interstate Commerce Commission. Texas would have to regulate these lines if they were not to be free of supervision. The Twenty-first Legislature debated the matter at length. A bill authorizing a railroad commission passed the house of representatives but failed in the senate, where lobbying by railroad forces was more effective. Many members of the senate thought that the bill was unconstitutional, so the advocates of the railroad commission proposed a constitutional amendment to remove any doubt. Hogg made the need for a railroad commission a major issue in his governor's race. The voters approved both Hogg and the amendment.

There was heated debate on whether the members of the commission should be elected or appointed. United States senator John H. Reagan helped draft the bill, which provided for a three-member commission appointed by the governor. The commission had the authority to regulate rates and eliminate abuses of intrastate railroads. Hogg persuaded Senator Reagan to accept the position of chairman of the commission. The railroads kept the commission tied up in court for two years, but in 1894 the constitutionality of the commission was upheld. In that same year the three railroad commissioners became elective officers. Rates and practices of the railroads came under regulation. The granting of free passes to legislators and other persons of influence was not stopped until the early part of the twentieth century. Although the establishment of the commission curbed many abuses, farmers claimed it was a "lawyer commission" and that the railroads regulated the commission instead of the commission regulating the railroads.

The Changing Role of Government

When Richard Coke became governor in 1874, Texas's paramount needs were for a new constitution and financial stability. Coke was a Virginian, a graduate of William and Mary, a Confederate captain, and a Waco lawyer who had been removed from the Texas Supreme Court by General Sheridan as "an impediment to Reconstruction." Coke's efforts to reduce expenditures and pay the state debt helped Texas recover from the financial exhaustion of the Civil War and Reconstruction. When Coke was elected to the United States Senate in 1876, Lieutenant Governor Richard B. Hubbard succeeded him. The Democratic convention of 1878 failed to renominate Hubbard and chose instead Oran M. Roberts, a lawyer who had served as president of the Texas Secession Convention. Roberts was elected governor in 1878 and 1880.

Roberts continued the policy established by Coke and Hub-

174

bard of paying off the state debts and of trying to put the state government on a cash basis. Laws were passed to improve methods of assessing and collecting taxes. Speculation in government land followed Roberts's attempt to sell as much of the public domain as possible.

Roberts advocated lowering the appropriation for the public schools, a highly unpopular move, but the public gradually became convinced that retrenchment was necessary to reduce the public debt. When Roberts's administration closed, the governor could point with pride to a successful financial policy that had lowered the state debt by a million dollars, cut the tax rate, and left a surplus in the treasury. The establishment of The University of Texas Roberts considered the high point of his administration. He was on the faculty of the university and was a founder of the Texas State Historical Association.

Governor John Ireland, Roberts's successor, acquired the nicknames "The Sage of Seguin" and "Honest John" because of his wisdom and integrity. While serving in the state senate, Ireland opposed grants of land or money for the construction of railroads and was called "Ox Cart John." Ireland instituted a stricter regulation of the sale of public lands. He continued the policy of financial retrenchment set by prior governors. During his tenure of office, the present capitol was built and fence-cutting laws were passed.

Former Texas Ranger captain Lawrence Sullivan Ross was the fifth Confederate veteran to be elected governor of the state. Governor Ross called for the regulation of the railroads, but it fell to his young, crusading attorney general, James Stephen Hogg, to establish the railroad commission. After he left the governorship, Ross became president of the Agricultural and Mechanical College of Texas. Sul Ross State University at Alpine was named in his honor.

James Stephen Hogg, the first Texas-born governor of the state, seized the political spotlight with his reform platform. The son of Confederate general Joseph Hogg, Jim Hogg became a printer and newspaperman in Quitman and Longview. Hogg studied law and won a statewide reputation as a crusading district attorney. While attorney general of the state, he fought land frauds depriving the state of public lands and prosecuted out-of-state insurance companies doing business in Texas illegally. Hogg helped write the Texas Antitrust Act, signed into law by Governor Ross in 1889, by which corporations were forbidden to conspire to fix prices, to restrict trade, or to limit production. Congress enacted the Sherman Antitrust Act the following year.

With the Hogg administration, an era of reform and regulation began in Texas. The government had, for the first time, agreed to supervise the activities of a segment of the business community. The need for reform would be a constant one in the following years. Within a generation Texas had made such progress that instead of having to worry about survival and protecting citizens from Indian attack, it could concern itself with establishing universities and adjusting inequities between farmers and railroads.

Discuss

1. What factors led to the rise of the reform movement?

2. What change in attitude toward railroads occurred between 1860 and 1890? What other areas were affected by this change in attitude?

3. How was the role of government in society changed by the Populist movement?

4. Why do the reforms worked for by the Populists seem less radical today?

5. What effects did railroads have on the economic development of the state? What effect did they have on your community?

6. "The basic problem of the nineteenth-century American farmer was simple: he was too efficient." Analyze this statement. How does it apply to modern farmers?

7. What factors led to the rise of organized farm groups in the late nineteenth century? Why did they disappear?

8. How do the political actions taken by the farmers of the nineteenth century affect us today?

9. How did economic conditions influence the role of government in society between 1860 and 1900?

10. Farmers argued for an expansion of the currency on the premise that more money in circulation would mean higher prices. What is the modern term for this? What fact or facts did the farmers overlook? How would creditors feel about the expansion of the money supply?

Identify

Abraham Kazen, Sr.
Count Giuseppe Telferner
Danevang
James Stephen Hogg
Interstate Commerce Act
Texas Railroad Commission
Oran M. Roberts

Lawrence Sullivan Ross
Morrill Act
Grange
Farmers' Alliance
Populism
Sherman Antitrust Act
Richard Coke
John Ireland

178

THE FOUNDING OF THE UNIVERSITY OF TEXAS WAS
SIGNIFICANT STEP TOWARD BETTER EDUCATION F
TEXANS.

CHAPTER 10

"The Spirit of Education"

On November 17, 1882, at the laying of the cornerstone of The University of Texas, Dr. Ashbel Smith, first president of its board of regents, quoted Thomas Jefferson: "Make the university as good as possible, and the spirit of education will permeate the masses, in the end securing them the highest possible attainments." The opening of The University of Texas marked the beginning of a new age, one in which Texans could begin to develop the state that had so recently become wholly theirs. More importantly, it was an age in which they could begin to develop themselves through education and the arts.

Higher Education

A University of the First Class. The establishment of a university was not a new idea. The constitution of the state of Coahuila y Texas had noted the need for higher education. The Texas Declaration of Independence cited as a grievance the failure of the government to establish any public system of education. In 1839 the Congress of the Republic of Texas provided for "fifty leagues of land . . . for the establishment and endowment of two colleges or universities." In 1858 the state legislature provided funds and lands for the university and designated its administrative heads—the governor, the chief justice of the Texas Supreme Court, and eight other administrators to be appointed by the governor. However, the Civil War halted any constructive work toward the establishment of the university. Higher education facilities consisted of the fifty-odd private and church schools founded since 1840.

The Morrill Act of 1862 made possible the founding of the Agricultural and Mechanical College of Texas, which opened in Brazos County in 1876. The university was still postponed. The Constitution of 1876 made specific reference to the establishment of the university and provided that the Agricultural and Mechanical College should become a branch of the university. Many Texans opposed the establishment of a separate university devoted to the arts, literature, and the sciences and felt that the Agricultural and Mechanical College constituted a satisfactory university. They cited the fact that the state already had a number of denominational and secular colleges. However, Ashbel Smith and Governor Oran M. Roberts traveled extensively to explain the need for a university and a system of higher education.

Experience as a teacher, school superintendent, and legislator led Smith to see the founding of the university in a practical light. Not only would state funds provide students with an education, but the graduates of the university would increase the wealth and the potential of the state. Dr. Smith and Governor Roberts constantly stressed the importance of agriculture, industrial subjects, modern languages, and geology and science as part of the curriculum of the university. They believed that a first-class state university would encourage common school education and promote the state's economic interests. Appropriations for the university and the public schools has been a political question through the years.

The presidency of the Agricultural and Mechanical College of Texas was offered to former Confederate president Jefferson Davis, who declined but suggested Thomas Gathright. After a couple of years Gathright and the other five faculty members were dismissed. In 1879 John James closed down the military school he had run at Austin and took his faculty to the Agricultural and Mechanical College, where he was president for four years. The board of regents of the Agricultural and Mechanical College established a school for Negro students in 1876, but when few students enrolled for agricultural courses, in 1879 the school became Prairie View State Normal School, devoted to the training of teachers.

Education for the Negro Youth of Texas. In 1914 during President Woodrow Wilson's administration, legislation was passed providing for a system of agricultural extension based on cooperation between the national Department of Agriculture and the land-grant colleges, with matching funds to be shared by the state and the federal government. Robert L. Smith, the last Negro to serve in the Texas legislature in the nineteenth century, served as the first head of the extension program at Prairie View. Smith established the Farmers' Improvement Society of Texas, which operated the Farmers' Improvement Agricultural College at Ladonia.

Born in slavery in Wharton County, M. M. Rodgers managed to obtain the basic rudiments of education. He began teaching Negro children and soon earned enough money to enroll in the newly founded Prairie View State Normal School. Graduated with honors in 1881, Rodgers became principal of a Negro school in La Grange and was elected to the post of city alderman. William Nickerson, Jr., was born in San Jacinto County when there was no school for the Negro youth of the area. He attended high school in nearby Huntsville and went on to study at Bishop College in Marshall and at Prairie View Normal. He devoted himself to teaching Negro youth for four years before embarking on a business career.

Officials of the Negro churches advocated the establishment of higher education facilities for the Negroes of Texas. Wiley College was established in 1873, the first of seven private Negro colleges, five of which were begun by churches. Reverend O. T. Womack and a group of ministers of the African Methodist Episcopal Church organized Texas College at Tyler in 1894 with Reverend Womack as president. Members of a Negro parish in San Antonio bought property adjoining Saint Philip's Episcopal Church and established Saint Philip's Day and Industrial School in 1898. Out of the day school grew Saint Philip's College, now part of the San Antonio junior college system.

For Teachers and Students—Education. The Constitution of 1876 set aside 42.5 million acres of land for the public schools. In 1883 rural districts were given the power to levy local school taxes, but most did little to improve the quality of the schools. The Peabody Fund, established by George Peabody in New England to aid Southern schools in establishing free public education, encouraged improvements in teacher training. Sam Houston Normal Institute in Huntsville was established in 1879 to train teachers, as was Prairie View Normal.

The legislature in 1876 established a system of community school systems which proved unworkable and unsatisfactory. Adequate funding for public schools was the primary problem facing William C. Crane, the president of Baylor University and the first president of the first association of teachers in Texas. Crane helped to promote realization of the need for a public school system across the state. With the publication of the *Texas Journal of Education,* teachers joined the movement for effective schools.

A constitutional amendment adopted in 1883 allowed the legislature to levy school taxes to provide income for a six-month school term. In addition, citizens in a school district were authorized to vote special local taxes to provide for building and maintaining schools. In 1884 provision was made for election of a state superintendent of instruction to supervise the public school system. School districts were placed under county control, and children were required to attend school from ages eight through fifteen. Teachers were required to have certificates. Annual attendance reports were required.

The responsibility for education was placed on the local level, instead of on the state level. It was difficult for rural districts to provide adequately for their students. As a result, the quality of education varied widely and was often poor by modern standards.

The rapid growth of the population also contributed to the problems of the common schools. However, many of the immigrants brought a desire to educate their children, and many of them made significant contributions to education. The University of Texas owes much to Dr. Johan A. Udden, born in Sweden and educated in Illinois. In 1903 he surveyed university lands for mineral resources and laid the basis for oil exploration which resulted in the first production on the West Texas lands of the university. Dr. Udden served as a member of the university's Bureau of Economic Geology and Technology and won world acclaim as a scientist.

Two institutions, Texas Lutheran College at Seguin and Texas Wesleyan College Academy at Austin, were founded by Swedish settlers. The Czech settlers in Texas also established schools across the state. Father Josef Chromcik built the Chromcik School in Fayetteville and taught several languages there. At their home near Brenham the Reverend Adolph Chlumsky and his wife began instructing young ladies in Bible studies. The result of the school was the Hus Memorial School established in Granger and later in Temple. Students from the school assisted pastors in Czech Moravian Brethren churches in Taylor, Caldwell, West, and Temple.

Professional Education and Practice

The rise of a new professional class—teachers, lawyers, and doctors—brought to the state a need for professional schools. Texas Medical College and Hospital in Galveston had tried to meet the needs of a growing state for doctors, but when The University of Texas began operating the need for a medical branch was apparent. Dr. Ashbel Smith led the campaign for the new medical school. The people chose Galveston as the site of the first state-supported medical school. The University of Texas Medical Branch opened there in the fall of 1891.

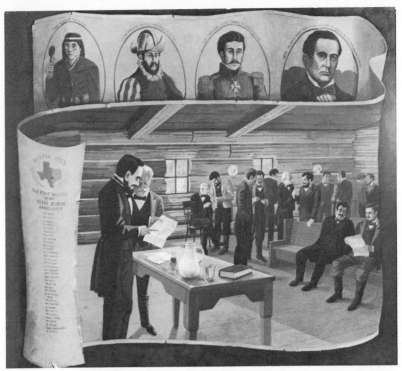

This Lynwood Kreneck painting depicts the organization of the Texas Medical Association in 1853.

The physicians of the nineteenth century sought to improve their profession by organizing the Texas Medical Association, formed in 1853. Doctors took the lead in the campaign for better medical schools.

The Edward Randall Pavilion at The University of Texas Medical Branch was originally opened in 1937 as a Negro hospital. The pavilion now serves as a clinic for psychiatric patients and was named in honor of one of Texas's pioneer doctors, Dr. Edward Randall, born in Huntsville, who served The University of Texas as a professor of medicine and as a regent.

Negroes who could not obtain medical training in Texas went outside the state to get it, and many returned to Texas to practice. From the time he entered Tillotson College in Austin and served as a page in the Texas House of Representatives, Monroe Alpheus Majors showed a flair for scholarship.

184

He enrolled in the medical branch of Central Tennessee College in 1883 and earned his diploma in 1886. He settled in Brenham in 1886 and hung out his shingle—the first Negro who was a native Texan to practice medicine in his state. He joined with thirteen other doctors to form the Lone Star Medical, Dental, and Pharmaceutical Association and continued his practice in Calvert and later in Dallas.

Dr. Benjamin Rufus Bluitt left the farm in Limestone County to attend Meharry Medical College in Tennessee. He was graduated in 1888 and returned to Texas to practice medicine in Dallas, the first Negro surgeon in Texas. Dr. Bluitt helped establish a hospital for Negroes in Dallas and helped organize the first Negro bank in the city. The state's first Negro dentist, Marcellus C. Cooper, began his career sweeping floors at the Sanger Brothers Department Store in Dallas. Cooper enrolled in dental school and practiced in Dallas. The M. C. Cooper Dental Society of Dallas is named in his honor.

Folk medicine and herbal cures, many with sound scientific bases, had been popular in Texas since the days of Gideon Lincecum, a self-trained physician who relied on herbs rather than patent medicines. In 1881 a young Mexican, Don Pedro Jaramillo, arrived at the ranch of Don Andres Canales near

Dr. Marcellus C. Cooper, Texas's first black dentist.

Don Pedro Jaramillo's herbal cures had their origins in Indian practices.

Olmos. Don Pedro had resolved to spend his life healing the sick. He became a legendary *curandero,* or faith healer, and folk hero to Mexican Americans in rural areas, who many times could not obtain professional help. His curative powers were based on faith and herbs. He carried a Bible wherever he went. Pictures of Don Pedrito hung in many Mexican-American homes. Wreaths and candles are often placed on his grave at Olmos. A firm in Laredo once sold curative herbs using his picture and the trademark Don Pedrito.

Education for a New Society. On the eve of the twentieth century, Texans were justly proud of their state. Two-thirds of a century was all that they had needed to turn an undeveloped land of fifty thousand residents into the sixth most populous of the forty-five states. Home of 3 million people, Texas had a work force of over 1 million, most of whom were still in agriculture. However, professional men and women, doctors, lawyers, and teachers composed 3 percent of the population. The transition to urban industrial Texas was already apparent: while the state had over one thousand livery stable keepers, there were almost twenty thousand railroad employees. The rising office buildings were employing a few hundred stenographers and even a few female "typewriters" who operated the new typing machines.

The Texas legislature established a college for women at Denton in 1901, now Texas Woman's University. Normal schools were turning out trained teachers, and more and more children were receiving an adequate education. Private and denominational colleges were receiving support from churches and private citizens.

Eleemosynary Institutions. Increasingly Texas was assuming a more active role in the education of her citizens and evidencing more concern for their well-being. Efforts were made on behalf of the unfortunate and the destitute, as well as the mentally ill. In 1856 the Texas legislature established the Texas School for the Blind, the Texas School for the Deaf, and what is now the Austin State Hospital. In the 1880s the Terrell State Hospital for the mentally ill began providing care for psychiatric patients, and the State Orphans' Home was founded in 1887. The year 1887 also saw the Texas Blind, Deaf, and Orphan School open, and in 1892 the San Antonio State Hospital for mental patients was opened.

The Artistic Life of the State

As the frontier closed it became possible for Texans to take a greater interest in education and the arts. More and more artists, writers, and architects, native and foreign-born, had an opportunity to develop their talents.

At the World's Columbian Exposition held in Chicago in 1893, the exhibit from the state of Texas was well attended. One of the most admired features of the Texas exhibit was the sculpture of Elisabet Ney. Born in Westphalia, Germany, Miss Ney was already famous for her busts of Bismarck, Schopenhauer, Garibaldi, George V of Hanover, and Alexander von Humboldt when she arrived in the United States.

Miss Ney was commissioned by the state to sculpt statues of Stephen F. Austin and Sam Houston for the Chicago exposition. Working in her studio, Formosa, in Austin, Miss Ney sculpted two statues of each of the Texas heroes. Her statues of Houston and Austin stand in the rotunda of the Texas capitol and in the nation's capitol in Washington.

Governor Oran M. Roberts encouraged young Stephen Seymour Thomas to continue his work as an artist after the governor saw the boy's drawing of him. The governor wrote to young Thomas, "I trust that you may be able to cultivate your great talent so that all Texans shall be proud of your fame as a painter." Thomas painted *San José Mission* and raffled it off for funds to continue his studies. Thomas painted genre scenes and crayon portraits, as well as landscapes. He exhibited his work in Paris and at the Chicago exposition in 1893.

Born in Mississippi, Ella Moss Duval came from New York to Texas. Miss Duval taught art in both Austin and San Antonio. Among her most famous portraits is one of Dr. Ferdinand Herff.

Edward Grenet's parents came to San Antonio from France, and Honoré Grenet bought the convent and courtyard of the Alamo to expand his business. Edward studied in New York and returned to Texas to paint such genre scenes as *Mexican Candy Seller* and *Mexican Hut,* as well as portraits of many of the citizens of San Antonio.

The nineteenth century saw an increased interest in historical painting. The legislators and leaders of Texas commissioned

Elisabet Ney at work in her studio

188

works of art for the capitol and other state buildings. Louis Eyth received a commission to paint portraits of David Burnet and other Texas statesmen. Eyth also painted *The Speech of Travis to His Men at the Alamo* and the *Death of Bowie.*

Orphaned early in life, the Irish painter Henry McArdle immigrated to the United States and finally to Texas. He gained experience making maps as a member of the Confederate army and was inspired to paint *Lee at the Wilderness,* showing Lee leading Hood's Brigade into battle. McArdle exhibited the painting at the state fair in Houston in 1875 and was urged to paint scenes of the Texas Revolution. *Dawn at the Alamo* and *The Battle of San Jacinto* hang in the state capitol in Austin.

William Henry Huddle painted portraits of the executives of Texas beginning with the provisional governor and continuing through seventeen state governors. Huddle also painted the *Surrender of Santa Anna,* which hangs in the capitol. Huddle's study of Sam Houston wrapped in a Cherokee Indian blanket hangs in the capitol, but his painting of Rip Ford has been lost. The University of Texas owns Huddle's painting of Governor Oran M. Roberts, and the legislature has purchased his portrait of David Crockett.

The Onderdonks, of Dutch descent, added much to Texas's rich artistic heritage. Robert Jenkins Onderdonk immigrated to Texas from Maryland. Onderdonk painted many of the scenic spots of San Antonio, and his paintings of *The Twohig House* and *Military Plaza* reflect his interest in nineteenth-century landscapes. Onderdonk's son, Julian, and his daughter, Eleanor, continued the artistic tradition set by their father. Julian Onderdonk's *Dawn in the Hills* and *A Texas Road* depict his love of nature and the scenes of his native state. Onderdonk was a member of the San Antonio Art League, an organization reflecting the civic pride that many cities in Texas were beginning to take and the patronage of the arts they were beginning to sponsor.

Pompeo Coppini followed in the tradition of his fellow Italian Frederick E. Ruffini and immigrated to Texas. Ruffini devoted himself to architecture, but Coppini studied portrait sculpture. In 1902 he came to Texas to sculpt the five statues that form the Confederate Monument on the grounds

189

of the state capitol. The Littlefield Monument at The University of Texas, the monument to Stephen F. Austin at the state cemetery, and the centennial monument in the Alamo Plaza in San Antonio are all the work of Coppini.

To the Mexican Americans of Texas, dramatizing the wonder and mystery of religion is part of their cultural heritage. In many predominantly Mexican-American communities, the observance of Christmas would be lacking in religious significance if the people could not experience *Las Posadas* and *Los Pastores*, religious dramas of the Christmas season. Brought to the New World by the Franciscan fathers in the sixteenth century, these traditional religious ceremonies have been handed down by word of mouth or by laboriously copied scripts from generation to generation. Each production varies, and added elements make for an indigenous theatrical production.

The journey of Joseph and Mary in search of shelter for the birth of the Christ Child is the subject of *Las Posadas*. For nine days before Christmas, or during a special church service, bands of performers carry figures representing Joseph and Mary on a litter from house to house or from door to door of a church. They chant or sing a litany asking for shelter but meet with refusals. Finally, the Child is washed, dressed, and laid in a cradle—a ceremony known as *La Acostada*. The figures of Mary and Joseph are placed in worshipful attitudes near the Child.

The origin of *Los Pastores*, the pastoral play, can be traced to the medieval morality plays of Europe, performed in town squares or in churches as early as the ninth century. The Franciscans imported the play to the New World and Father Antonio Margil de Jesus, the founder of San José Mission, taught it to Texas Indians. Volunteer groups in the Mexican-American communities of Texas still perform the age-old drama during the twelve days before Christmas, acquiring costumes and carefully preserving the cultural elements of the drama.

Los Pastores is a drama of the people which revolves around the medieval concept of the struggle between the forces of Good and Evil. Lucifer and the Archangel Michael duel for supremacy, with nine devils representing deadly sins as Lucifer's helpers. Comic shepherds comment on the action, and

190

Some of the twelve shepherds in *Los Pastores*

many times cowboys and Indians are added to the cast. Lucifer is beaten and Michael triumphs, with the entire audience joining in to worship the Christ Child in the finale.

Literature of the State

As the frontier became a place that existed only in memory, many Texans set down what they remembered of that era. John Wesley Hardin recorded his own adventures, and W. M. Walton wrote *The Life and Adventures of Ben Thompson.* John C. Duval authored *The Adventures of Big Foot Wallace,* and James T. DeShields's *Border Wars of Texas* was the first of his numerous books devoted to the history of the state. J. W. Wilbarger wrote of conflict on the frontier in his *Indian Depredations in Texas.*

Man in touch with nature is a theme that has often inspired poets, and the Texas frontier reflected nature at her best and at her worst. The Swedish poet John Peter Sjolander won national renown with his poems on his adopted land. *Salt of the Earth and Sea* brought Texas poetry to the nation. *Lone Star Ballads* by F. L. Allen and Lawrence Chittenden's "Cowboys' Christmas Ball" showed the pioneer flavor of Texas poetry. Newspapers reprinted the work of Texas poets, many of them anonymous. Sam H. Dixon gathered a collection of the verse into *Poets and Poetry of Texas.*

William Sydney Porter, one of America's greatest short story writers, found inspiration in Texas for much of his work. After coming to Texas from his native North Carolina, Porter lived on a ranch in La Salle County before moving to Austin, where he worked as a draftsman in the General Land Office and as a bank teller.

Porter edited a humorous weekly paper, the *Rolling Stone,* but it failed. Then he was tried and convicted on charges of embezzling funds from the First National Bank in Austin. He was sentenced to the federal penitentiary, and there he began writing the short stories that were to make him famous under the pseudonym O. Henry. His best-known short stories are "The Ransom of Red Chief" and "The Gift of the Magi." His Texas stories have been collected under the title *Heart of the West.*

By the end of the nineteenth century Texans were able to turn from the physical frontier to the more subtle frontiers of educational, cultural, economic, and social development. They stood at the threshold of an era of change unparalleled in scope and pervasiveness.

Discuss

1. Compare the need for higher education in 1875 with the need today. Why has this change taken place? Do you think the change is good or bad?

2. Why were efforts to establish a system of state-supported higher education for Texas slow to achieve success?

3. What contributions did the various ethnic groups in Texas make toward the establishment of a system of education?

4. Compare the artistic and literary development of Texas between 1830 and 1875 with development between 1875 and 1900. What conclusions can you draw from this comparison?

5. How did Texans' artistic and literary efforts reveal a pride in the history and culture of their state?

6. What problems are faced by institutions of higher education in Texas today? What effects do these problems have on you?

7. How has social change affected modern education?

8. What changes in the educational system do you foresee in your lifetime?

9. What objectives do you think the modern educational system should have?

Identify

Prairie View State Normal School	Robert J. Onderdonk
	Las Posadas
Agricultural and Mechanical College of Texas	*Los Pastores*
	O. Henry
Robert L. Smith	Dr. Johan A. Udden
Saint Philip's College	Texas Lutheran College
William C. Crane	Marcellus C. Cooper
Monroe A. Majors	eleemosynary institution
Don Pedro Jaramillo	Henry McArdle
Elisabet Ney	Pompeo Coppini

194

FIRE WAS A CONSTANT THREAT TO EARLY DRILLERS
THIS BLAZE TOOK PLACE AT SPINDLETOP IN 1902.

CHAPTER 11

"The Fuel of the Twentieth Century"

With a mighty roar, the Lucas gusher ushered in the age of petroleum on the morning of January 10, 1901. Oil shot through the top of the derrick, taking the drill stem with it. The age of petroleum had arrived. Neither Texas nor the world would ever be the same again.

The Lucas gusher ran wild for nine days, spewing out eight hundred thousand barrels of oil. Few people realized at the time that beneath the surface of the soil of Texas there lay fuel enough to light the lamps of the world, to lubricate the engines, to power the factories, the ships, the locomotives, and the new horseless carriages that wealthy men were steering down many streets of the United States. Samuel ("Golden

Rule") Jones, the progressive former mayor of Toledo, Ohio, said that "liquid fuel is to be the fuel of the twentieth century."

The Early History of Oil

Men had known of oil in Texas since the sixteenth century, when the explorer Moscoso caulked his boats with the pitch-like substance we know as asphalt. This was the first known account of oil in the New World, and Moscoso and his men found it near Sabine Pass in the vicinity of the Spindletop Field. Indians knew of the curative powers of what they called sour mud. Their medicine men used it on wounds and to cure rheumatism, skin eruptions, and minor sores.

But oil was often a nuisance to the early farmers, for it seeped into their wells and turned the water brackish and foul tasting. Even before the Civil War, the residents of Beaumont told stories of a "fountain of lemonade," and a small health resort grew up near the warm sulphur springs. A pioneer East Texas woman claimed she repulsed an Indian attack by skimming a bucket of crude oil from a pond, heating it over the fireplace, and throwing it at advancing warriors. The farmers put the black substance to good use by using it to lubricate the axles on their wagons.

Men were fascinated by the oil seeps in various sections of the state, and before the Civil War Jack Graham dug a simple oil pit and erected a crude derrick near Tar Springs in Angelina County. Oil rose to the top of the water which flowed into the hole. However, it was not until Edwin L. Drake brought in the first successful oil well near Titusville, Pennsylvania, in 1859 that a feasible means of bringing the oil to the surface was found. A new industry was born—one that would change the economy of Texas and revolutionize industry throughout the world.

The first producing oil well in Texas was drilled by Lyne Taliaferro Barret near Melrose in Nacogdoches County in 1866. Barret was forced to cap it. No one was interested in investing in an oil well in 1866. In 1878 Martin Meinsinger struck oil while trying to bring in water to supply the town of Brownwood. Meinsinger sold the oil for medicine, advertising in the newspapers that "This oil is far superior to any liniment now in use for the cure of all wounds, bruises, and sores. It cures cuts, burns, scalds, and all eruptions on man or beast caused by impurities in the blood."

Most early discoveries were accidental. George Dullnig struck oil in 1886 while searching for water on his ranch near San Antonio. He saw the potential of oil as a lubricant and sold much of the crude for this purpose. In 1889 Texas first made an appearance in official oil production records. According to federal statistics, Texas showed an annual yield of forty-eight barrels of oil and over a thousand dollars worth of natural gas—all from the Dullnig well. A water well driller struck a gas pocket five miles from Palo Pinto in 1888. The gas ignited, and it took workers several hours to extinguish the flames. The owner of the well filled it in, explaining that he was hunting "for water, not fire."

Toward Spindletop. In 1894 the city of Corsicana contracted for three water wells to supply the community's needs. Oil began to seep into the wells, and interested citizens formed the Corsicana Oil Development Company to drill for petroleum. Soon the Corsicana Field was producing more than two thousand barrels of crude a day. By 1897 the Corsicana Field had grown and was pumping more than sixty-six thousand barrels of oil a day. A Pennsylvania refiner, J. S. Cullinan, built a refinery at Corsicana in 1898, and experimental oil-burning equipment was installed in a Cotton Belt passenger locomotive running between Corsicana and Hillsboro.

At Beaumont a lumber worker named Patillo Higgins was convinced that there was oil at the Sour Spring Mound on the banks of the Neches River, and in 1892 he organized the Gladys City Oil, Gas, and Manufacturing Company, named for Gladys Bingham, a member of the Sunday school class he taught. With the help of other citizens of Beaumont, Higgins drilled three unsuccessful holes at his Gladys City development. However, due to lack of money and the presence of layers of sand, he could not drill deep enough to find the oil he felt was there, and the project had to be abandoned.

In desperation Higgins placed an advertisement in an oil field equipment manufacturing journal soliciting a lessee for

the hill with the knowledge of drilling technique needed to bring in a successful well. Anthony F. Lucas answered Higgins's advertisement, and a partnership was born that was to produce the spectacular Lucas gusher.

A native of Austria, Antonio Francisco Luchlich was graduated from the Polytechnic Institute at Gratz and the Naval Academy of Fiume and Pola. As an Austrian naval lieutenant, he visited his uncle in Saginaw, Michigan, in 1879. He stayed, anglicized his name to Anthony Lucas, and became an American citizen. He worked as a resident engineer at a salt mine in Louisiana and by 1900 had gained extensive experience in salt dome geology. When Lucas came to Beaumont, he leased land from the Gladys City Oil, Gas, and Manufacturing Company, allotting a one-tenth interest to Patillo Higgins. Lucas sank a test well but soon ran out of money. He contacted John Guffey of Pittsburgh, Pennsylvania, and Guffey and John Galey provided additional financing.

Spindletop Blows In. With the aid of the Hamill brothers, who had drilled wells at Corsicana, Lucas sank a new well. On the morning of January 10, 1901, a new bit was mounted. About two-thirds of the drill stem had been lowered into the well when suddenly the gusher blew in. Seven hundred feet of four-inch pipe were thrown through the top of the derrick;

it broke apart as it fell. Drillers scattered. Oil shot 160 feet into the air, flowing at a daily rate of some seventy-five thousand barrels. It blew for six days before it could be capped, and it took another three days to shut it down completely.

People flocked to the scene. It took dozens of guards to keep spectators away from the well. Forty farmers with teams and plows built levee after levee to impound the oil in a huge lake, while the crew fought to control the well. Others plowed oil-soaked grasslands beyond the levees to reduce the chance of fire. When the oil flow was finally halted, a black sea covering acres of land surrounded the well.

On March 3 sparks from a passing locomotive ignited the lake of oil. In the next few hours, eight hundred thousand barrels of oil went up in a mighty blaze. Fortunately, Lucas had placed a huge iron cylinder filled with sand around the wellhead. As much oil as the Corsicana Field had produced the entire year before went up in flames, but the fabulous well was safe.

Oil Boom!

In the first week after the gusher blew in at Spindletop, twenty thousand excited speculators, tourists, and oil men descended on Beaumont. Railroads advertised, "See a gusher gushing in Beaumont," and sold every seat on special excursion trains from Dallas, Houston, and Austin. Leases were bought and sold around the clock. Some land near the well sold at a million dollars an acre, and even a hundred miles from the gusher, some land was a thousand dollars an acre.

Texas had produced only 836,000 barrels of oil in 1900. With Spindletop, the state's oil production climbed to over 4,000,000 barrels in 1901, and by 1902 production shot to 18,000,000 barrels. The market was so glutted with oil that the price of oil dropped to three cents per barrel in 1901 and averaged only twenty cents per barrel in 1902. Clearly, new uses had to be found for the oil that was flowing from Spindletop. The Houston Ice and Brewing Association sent a representative to Beaumont to contract for one hundred thou-

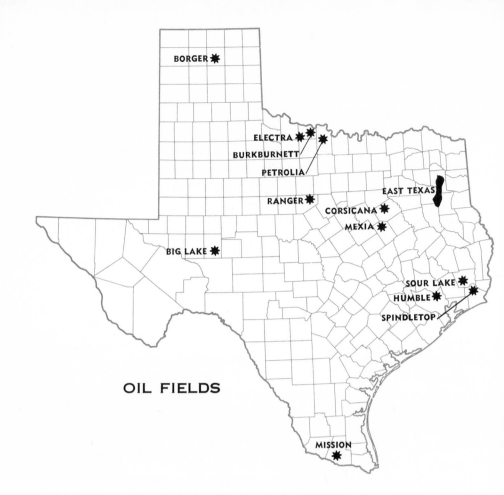

OIL FIELDS

sand barrels to be used as fuel. The Cotton Belt test at Corsicana had demonstrated the efficiency of oil as a fuel for locomotives, and the Houston and Texas Central Railroad began switching from coal to oil. The Gulf, Colorado, and Santa Fé bought its first oil-burning locomotive in 1901, and in four years had purchased 227 oil-burners, using over 1.5 million barrels of crude oil annually. The coal-burner became a relic of the past.

Within months pipelines radiated from the Spindletop Field to shipping points on nearby waterways. Refineries began to spring up. J. S. Cullinan built the Texas Company at Port Arthur, and its Texaco trademark was used as early as 1906. The first backers of Spindletop formed the Gulf Oil

Corporation. Governor James S. Hogg, then retired from office, came to the Spindletop Field to look over the investment possibilities in Texas's new resource. When an oil strike was made at Humble in Harris County in 1904, Ross Sterling, who was later to serve as governor of Texas, and other interested men formed the Humble Oil and Refining Company.

Oil, Oil, Everywhere. Boom towns sprang up across the state, with wildcatters and speculators dealing frantically in land and leases. Each new discovery brought new wealth and new people to the state. In 1904 the North Texas area was opened to the oil men by the discovery of oil and natural gas near Petrolia in Clay County. The Petrolia Field was not located on salt domes, and the shallow depths of the field made drilling an easier task. Soon natural gas from Petrolia was being piped to Wichita Falls and Henrietta, and later to Fort Worth. Southwest Texas came in with the Mission Field, and wildcatting brought in the Mexia Field, where oil had lain for centuries trapped in faults beneath the earth's surface. Corsicana had first produced and consumed natural gas commercially as early as 1901, and by 1903 sixteen gas wells were in operation in the area.

The greatest of the accidental water well strikes occurred when W. T. Waggoner, a pioneer Texas cattleman, ordered a well drilled to furnish water for his cattle. The drillers began digging on Waggoner's extensive holdings in Wilbarger and Wichita counties, and soon a gusher blew in. Until his dying day, Waggoner complained that the oil produced on his property spoiled the water for his cattle, even though the Electra Field made him one of the richest men in the country.

Oil became big business in Texas and added to the industrial wealth of the entire United States. The worldwide oil market has prospered under such companies originating in Texas as the Gulf Oil Corporation, using as its first resource the Lucas gusher at Spindletop. The Texas Company, the Magnolia Petroleum Company, and the Humble Oil and Refining Company had their origins in Texas. When the field at Spindletop ceased to flow, John W. ("Bet-a-Million") Gates offered funds to help the Texas Company open the nearby Sour Lake Field.

The rush to the oil fields created many new jobs, but new problems arose as well. The following selection points out the situation created by a lack of regulations governing oil field operations.

During the first week of October, 1903, I went to Sour Lake. Boll weevils had ruined the cotton in my part of the country, and, like thousands of others, I went to the oil field to tide over a hard time. By pawning my fiddle and six-shooter and borrowing fifty cents from a friend, I scraped up enough money to buy a ticket; I got there without a cent. . . .

For surging energy, unrestrained openness, and diabolical conditions otherwise, Sour Lake was head and shoulders above anything Texas had seen up until that time or perhaps has seen since. The site is on low ground. At that time little effort was made at drainage; and a short while after operations began, a large part of the field was worked up into such a mess of mud as can hardly be imagined.

One thing that made the mud so bad and rendered the place such an inferno in other ways was the crowded condition. There were few, if any, laws governing oil field operations; no such thing as restrictions on drilling existed. Landowners sold their land to anyone who came to buy it and in as small amounts as the buyer's purse spoke for. Aided by the ignorance of the people and the get-rich craze that swept the country, many men of small means came into the field and bought acreage. In many instances land in as small amounts as one-sixteenth, or even one thirty-second, of an acre was sold. The result was that the greater part of the field was soon a forest of derricks. As quantities of water are required to run a rotary drill, the slush which spread from these hundreds of wells and which was stirred up by the men working in it made the place a sight to behold.[1]

"Black Gold" of the Twentieth Century. The next great chapter in the saga of Texas oil was written in 1917 in Eastland County. W. K. Gordon brought in the great Ranger Field, and an oil boom followed in which thousands of speculators poured into Ranger. When World War I broke out, Ranger's oil fueled the ships of the United States Navy and merchant

[1]Charlie Jeffries, "Reminiscences of Sour Lake," *The Southwestern Historical Quarterly*, L (July 1946), 25-35.

marine. In 1918 "Fowler's Folly" brought in the Burkburnett Field, which yielded more than 40 million barrels of oil by the end of 1919.

The discovery of two major fields, one in West Texas and one in East Texas, made Texas first among the oil-producing states. As early as 1905 geologists and speculators were working in the Panhandle area searching for favorable drilling sites. Gas was discovered near Amarillo as early as 1918, and in 1923 wildcatters brought in the Big Lake Oil Field in the Permian Basin of West Texas, on land owned by The University of Texas. Dr. Johan A. Udden had become convinced the area would produce oil, and Santa Rita No. 1 proved him to be correct.

Oil and gas wells were drilled across the vast prairies of the West Texas and Panhandle regions. Towns sprang up as drillers poured in. Amarillo, Borger, Big Spring, Midland, and Odessa now form prosperous business communities growing out of the mineral resources of West Texas. Pipelines spread out carrying crude oil to refineries and seaports. Oil refineries dotted the Texas landscape.

Courtesy of Phillips Petroleum Company

Natural gas processing plant, center, and oil refinery, upper right, near Borger

203

In the piney woods of Rusk County in the fall of 1930, on the Daisy Bradford farm near Henderson, a wildcatter named Columbus Marion Joiner, known as "Dad" to the men who worked with him, brought in his first gusher. The Joiner well brought in the mighty East Texas Field—the greatest oil field in the world. By the following summer the East Texas Field was producing half a million barrels of crude a day, with one week seeing a new well completed every hour.

Proration. The first oil from the Joiner well was used to fire boilers to drill other wells. So much oil came in from the East Texas Field that drilling almost ceased in other areas. Overproduction in East Texas caused the price of oil to drop drastically. In December 1930, when tank cars began transporting oil from East Texas into the general market, the price per barrel was down to sixty cents and falling fast. When the price dropped to eight cents, the governor and some legislators realized the necessity of regulation of oil production.

As natural resources, oil and gas must be conserved; they cannot be replaced. Long before the East Texas Field came in, oil producers and refiners recognized the need for restricting production to conserve the available oil and stabilize prices. However, the presence of hundreds of small independent operators made voluntary regulation impossible. With the price of oil falling daily due to increased production, a proration plan was established. Each field and each individual oil well were assigned a specified amount of oil each month—their prorated share—that they might produce.

Proration began in the Burkburnett Field and has since been applied to all oil fields throughout the state. By this method oil and gas are conserved and the productive life of the oil field is extended for many years. The work of maintaining the system of proration and conserving Texas's oil and gas resources falls under the jurisdiction of the Texas Railroad Commission, operating under laws set by the legislature. Oil pipelines were declared common carriers in 1917 and placed under the supervision of the railroad commission. In 1919 the Oil and Gas Division of the commission was established, and that same year the legislature debated a law spacing the drilling of oil wells.

Photography by L. Milton Rudy, Houston, Texas—
Courtesy of Texas Eastern Transmission Corp.

Dual thirty-six inch pipeline for Texas petroleum products being laid across the Ohio River

With the overproduction of oil causing a drastic drop in prices in 1930, the railroad commission set the production level of the East Texas Field at 160,000 barrels a day to begin on May 1, 1931. The operators continued to exceed production quotas, however, and the price for crude oil hit eight cents a barrel.

The Texas legislature was called into special session to pass an oil control bill. Texas governor Ross Sterling closed the East Texas Fields to give the railroad commission time to hear advocates of proration and the opponents of the plan. Governor Sterling declared martial law and sent General Jacob Wolters to the fields with some twelve hundred national guardsmen to stop production and maintain order. On September 5 the field was reopened with production sharply limited.

Early in 1932 the courts invalidated Governor Sterling's martial law declaration, but much of Texas's oil had been conserved during the interim. In 1940 the Supreme Court upheld the state's authority vested in its railroad commission to limit oil production. In addition, both state and federal laws were passed making it illegal to produce and to deal in so-called hot oil, oil produced in violation of railroad commission rules.

The setting of oil allowables by the railroad commission, the taxation of oil produced in the state, and the concept of proration have all proven to be politically troublesome to the state of Texas during the twentieth century. However, the oil and gas industry and an expanding petrochemical complex have spurred the development of industry and have broadened the economy of the state. Millions of people seek employment in the expanding industries, new wells are drilled, new refineries built, and new pipelines laid. Offshore oil drilling has increased during the latter part of the twentieth century, and in the 1950s Texas's rich tidelands oil supply became an issue in national politics.

Texas's Oil Capital. Located close to the Spindletop Field and with adequate transportation facilities, including a ship channel and railroads, Houston was the ideal location for the headquarters of Texas's prospering oil industry. When the Humble Field was brought in, the Texas Company extended its pipeline to Houston to intersect with the International and Great Northern Railroad and the Houston, East and West Texas Railroad. Houston began to develop as a substantial oil transportation center, and legal and financial operations of the oil industry shifted from Beaumont to Houston. Houston, Beaumont, and Orange, situated on the flat Coastal Plains, were ideally suited for refinery locations. Large areas of land were available, fresh water was adequate, protection from storms could be provided, and ship channels could be dredged to supply deepwater shipping facilities. Galveston would have been an ideal port, but a devastating storm in 1900 destroyed her chances of becoming headquarters for the new industry.

The Galveston Flood

At Galveston on the morning of September 8, 1900, a strong wind was blowing and heavy rains were falling. By afternoon sea water covered the island and stood from one to five feet deep in the city. Communications with the mainland were cut off. At eight o'clock in the evening, the wind reached a velocity of 120 miles an hour, and a tidal wave six feet deep swept the island.

Central Galveston after the hurricane of 1900 was a scene of almost complete destruction.

When the water receded on the morning of September 9, Galveston, the world's leading cotton port, was ruined. Over half the city's homes were destroyed, and property losses totaled over $25 million. About six thousand persons lost their lives. The oil industry was establishing its headquarters while Galveston was recovering from the storm. But the storm did give Galveston the opportunity to demonstrate the virtues of the commission form of local government. Galveston was not the first city in the United States to use the commission form of city government, but it proved so successful that it spread rapidly to other municipalities. Houston was the second city in Texas to change over, and by 1915 forty cities in Texas had set up commissions.

Impact of the Oil Industry

In 1908 the Texas Company moved its headquarters to Houston, and the Gulf Oil Corporation opened its offices there in 1916. Major oil refineries were built in the Bayou City. The Houston Ship Channel rapidly developed into a major port for petroleum products. Industries relating to the drilling and refining of oil products moved to Houston. The Hughes

Tool Company, a concern that manufactures drill bits, moved to Houston.

The oil industry spawned related industries. Houston was not the only city that benefited from the new wealth oil brought. The forest of derricks required lumber, steel, machinery, and labor. Thousands of workers poured into the state to drill wells, lay pipelines, and become consumers of goods and services. Transportation facilities expanded, and capital from other states was invested in Texas. The oil and gas lobby became a potent force in state and national politics.

Industrial development expanded as petroleum freed industry from its dependence on coal. Manufacturers moved to Texas. The internal combustion engine used petroleum products, and with the rising popularity of the automobile the oil industry prospered. From a few experimental models built before 1900 the number of automobiles climbed to 9 million in 1920 and almost 30 million in 1930. The automobile was to become the means of locomotion for millions of Americans in the twentieth century—and Texas would supply much of the gasoline and oil they needed.

Education and the state government reap large revenues from oil and gas production. Discoveries on lands belonging to The University of Texas have made that institution one of the nation's wealthiest. Cities have grown up around oil fields and refineries. Industry, transportation, society, politics—in fact, almost every facet of Texas life—have been profoundly affected by the mineral Carl Coke Rister called the "titan of the Southwest."

Discuss

1. What is the economic importance of oil to Texas?

2. What sources of fuel will someday replace petroleum? How will our lives be affected?

3. Why was little use made of oil and natural gas before the twentieth century?

4. Which is more desirable—proration of oil or lower prices resulting from unregulated production?

5. How have the uses of oil changed since its discovery? What has made these new uses possible?

6. What effect does the oil industry have on your community? Assess the effects if the oil industry ceased to exist.

7. How has oil been politically troublesome in Texas?

8. Do you agree or disagree with Governor Sterling's action in declaring martial law and stopping production in the East Texas Field? Why?

9. Do you think alternative sources of power will be fully utilized before petroleum is depleted? Why?

10. What role did geography play in the development of Houston and Galveston?

Identify

Spindletop
Lyne T. Barret
J. S. Cullinan
Patillo Higgins
Anthony F. Lucas
gusher

Petrolia Field
Electra Field
Big Lake Oil Field
East Texas Field
proration

TEXAS IN THE EARLY TWENTIETH CENTURY, LIKE THES
LEE COUNTY ROAD WORKERS, WAS ATTEMPTING T
MEET NEW PROBLEMS WITH OUTDATED METHODS.

CHAPTER 12

"A New Era"

On the site of the Spindletop gusher a monument commemorates that January 1901 date. Its inscription reads, "On the tenth day of the twentieth century a new era in civilization began." Texas was the place most immediately affected by that new era. Texas was rich in natural resources, and many of her leaders envisioned a future in which factories contributed more to the state's economy than farms and ranches.

Population growth, technological advances, and the growth of cities were factors that stimulated changes in the economy. Larger factories producing goods for larger markets not only brought new benefits but new problems.

A Changing Economy

A Desire for Growth. Texas's 1850 industrial output had a value of only a million dollars. In the last years of the cen-

211

tury organizations were formed to encourage industrial growth and investment in Texas; after the Civil War northern capital helped found many businesses in the state. In 1899 Governor Joseph D. Sayers was urging the industrial development of the state. His efforts caused New York businessmen to charter a special train to survey investment opportunities in Texas. Later governors such as James V. Allred and John B. Connally sought economic growth. The Texas Bankers Association, the Texas Industrial Congress, and the Texas Manufacturers Association were among the statewide organizations formed to promote business and industry. Local groups, such as chambers of commerce, which began to increase in the 1920s, advanced the economic life of their cities. All of these organizations sought favorable legislation for business and industry to attract new investment and keep businesses healthy.

Changes in Industry. With vast natural resources, an excellent geographic location, an expanding population, and a rapidly improving system of transportation, Texas was prepared for the increase in her industrial facilities which would change her from a predominantly rural, agricultural entity into an urban, mechanized society. The first manufacturing centered around the rich natural resources of the state—lumber, stone, and brick—needed for the growing number of homes and buildings that an expanding population called for, and around the agricultural produce of the state. Early Texas industry produced goods to meet local needs. The twentieth century brought the change to manufacturing new products for worldwide markets.

Farm and ranch products formed the basis for Texas's first moves toward industrialization. With cotton the staple agricultural product of the state, textile mills were an early industry at Bastrop, New Braunfels, and Waco. Cotton mills were also located at Houston, Hempstead, Tyler, and Gonzales. Later textile firms were established at Dallas and Sherman. The by-products of cotton growing, such as cottonseed oil and cotton meal, formed the basis for other industries. A small mill at High Hill in Fayette County began producing cottonseed oil in 1867, and by 1900 the processing of cotton by-products was a major enterprise.

212

In 1885 a Chicago firm purchased an unsuccessful Fort Worth packing plant and was planning to move it from the state. A Jewish immigrant, Isaac Dahlman, campaigned to save the plant for the city and succeeded. Fort Worth had been a cattle town in the days of the trail drives and was still conveniently located for cowmen. With the aid of capital from the eastern part of the United States and from England, Dahlman acquired the packing plant and began shipping meat in refrigerated cars to New Orleans. Eventually, he shipped beef by refrigerated ship to England. With Fort Worth expanding as a major railroad center, it became a natural location for both stockyards and packing plants. By 1902 both the Swift Company and Armour had begun constructing plants there, and by 1906 Fort Worth ranked as the fifth largest cattle market in the United States, trailing Chicago, St. Louis, Kansas City, and Omaha.

From Pine Cones to Profits. The East Texas counties that make up the Pine Woods represent the most important forest area of the state and produce almost all of the commercial timber cut in Texas. With rapid population growth, sawmills

Texas Forest Service

Horses pulled logs to the railroad running to the sawmill.

Replanting cutover land provides future generations with forests for recreation and building materials.

flourished in Beaumont, Orange, and throughout East Texas. Businessmen in the area (among them H. J. Lutcher, G. B. Moore, and John Henry Kirby) realized the economic potential of East Texas forests. With eastern financial backing, Kirby alone acquired millions of acres of valuable southern pine and hardwood forests.

Sawmills in the area began cutting millions of board feet of pine lumber annually. As the expanding railroads sprawled across the state, lumbering flourished. Rails were laid on wooden crossties, and depots, section houses, repair shops, roundhouses, and water towers were of wood, as were the boxcars that passed over the rails. Workers felled the huge trees, limbed and bucked them into logs. The logs were then hauled to the mills on crude horsedrawn wagons. More and more sawmill owners rushed in to get their share of the virgin timber. "Cut out and get out" became the watchword as the stately pine trees fell, and one of Texas's most valuable natural

214

resources was in danger of depletion. It seemed likely that in a few years Texas would be stripped of all its lumber resources.

For over forty years, the main manufacturing industry in Texas was lumbering. As huge numbers of the lofty pines were fed to the sawmills and the supply began to dwindle, the lumbermen began to see the error of their ways. New timber was planted in the old cutover land, and the need for intensive forest management to perpetuate forests was gradually realized. Conservation and good forestry practice resulted in more productive forests in the East Texas region. As the second growth timber matured, many revolutionary features of the forest industry were developed in Texas. Lumber production in Texas reached its peak in 1907, when the state ranked third among all lumber-producing states.

Since that time Texas has remained among the top lumber producers in the country, and the state has pioneered many manufacturing and forestry "firsts." The first kraft paper mill in the South was built at Orange, Texas, and in 1911 Edward H. Mayo pioneered in producing sulphate paper pulp from yellow pine. The first mill to use southern yellow pine in the manufacture of newsprint was constructed at Lufkin, and gas-fired dry kilns and electronic lumber sorters were first used in Texas. From the Kirby Lumber Corporation grew the East Texas Pulp and Paper Company, which turns out hundreds of tons of pulp, paper, and paperboard every day. In 1939 Champion Paper and Fibre Company built a pulp mill near Houston and began manufacturing paper in a nearby plant. The tall timbers of East Texas have proven to be "green gold" to the economy of the Lone Star State.

Public Utilities. Technological advances have played an important role in the development of new industries. Texas's public utilities have developed steadily in the twentieth century. In 1854 the Red River Telegraph Company began service from New Orleans to Marshall and gradually extended its lines to other parts of East Texas. The Western Union Telegraph Company brought small companies under its control in 1866 and extended service throughout the state.

The first telephone exchange was established in Galveston in 1879. The editor of the *Galveston News* had the first telephone installed after he saw Alexander Graham Bell's new invention exhibited at Philadelphia in 1876. Soon the exchange had over three hundred subscribers. Dallas had forty telephone customers in 1881. The first long distance line connected Houston and Bryan, but it was only partially successful. The Houston listener heard the speaker from Bryan ask, "Say, what kind of rooster are you down thar, anyhow?" By 1883 Texas had over two thousand telephones.

The first electric power plant began operation in New York City in 1882, and Houston and Galveston had installations generating electricity later in the same year. Local plants produced their own electricity until 1912, when the Texas Power and Light Company constructed the state's first high voltage transmission line, stretching from Waco to Fort Worth at the outset, then branching off to Hillsboro, Waxahachie, Ferris, Dallas, and Corsicana. By the 1920s more than six hundred communities in Texas received power service, and rural electrification became a reality in the 1930s.

Transportation for Everyone

By 1890 Texas had some eight thousand miles of railroad track, and by 1900 the total had climbed to ten thousand miles. By the 1920s over sixteen thousand miles of track spread out across the state. The railroad provided massive stimulation to the development of Texas's economy, and both population and business followed the tracks.

However, steam locomotives could go only where tracks were constructed. A new type of vehicle was called for that could carry small loads for short distances economically. The automobile could substitute machinery for animal power but could retain the mobility of the horse. The automobile was a reality before the opening of the twentieth century, but it remained a rich man's toy for a generation. Then it became a mover of freight as well as passengers, a reducer of distances, requiring roads and gasoline stations and calling into being the automobile mechanic, the tourist court operator, and a number of other crafts and businesses.

The first automobile in Texas was driven at such an alarm-

216

Early automobiles and roads were primitive by modern standards.

ing speed that it covered the thirty miles from Terrell to Dallas in five hours and five minutes. The driver was sued by several farmers who claimed that the automobile upset their livestock. However, Dallas had forty vehicles—electric, steam, and gasoline—by 1903. Texas began to experience traffic accidents. An early hit-and-run accident occurred in Fort Worth on April 30, 1904. A "benzine wagon which turned the corner noiselessly and at a rapid speed" struck Gainesville attorney George H. Giddings and then sped on. An ordinance was passed requiring registration of automobiles and setting the speed limit at ten miles an hour.

In 1907 the Texas legislature required that all automobiles be registered in the owner's county of residence, and speed limits were set at eighteen miles an hour in the country and at eight miles an hour in town. Drivers were required to stop when they met a horse and to wait until the horse passed. In 1909 Dallas purchased an automobile for use as a fire truck, and Fort Worth had two motorized fire trucks in 1910. In 1914 Fort Worth was the largest American city without police cars. That year they bought the first patrol car, but Fort Worth retained fifteen policemen on bicycles until 1917.

217

The Ford Motor Company opened a sales and service unit in Dallas in 1909. Texas registered 32,000 motor vehicles in 1913 and 194,000 in 1917.

The Campaign for Good Roads. With the increasing use of the automobile, campaigning for better roads increased. In 1900 there were no hard-surfaced roads in Texas outside the major cities, where some streets were paved with bricks. Most roads were simply trails graded by dragging a split log over them. The better roads were surfaced with a mixture of sand and clay, and perhaps gravel. A heavy rain rendered them impassable.

The responsibility for building and maintaining roads rested with the county. State law required every able-bodied man between the ages of twenty-one and sixty to work on the roads for five days each year. The law was abolished in 1917, but until that time the county commissioners appointed road overseers to supervise citizens at work on the roads. In 1901 a statute was passed authorizing counties to use prisoners in the county jails to work on the roads.

With increased automobile ownership, the citizens of the state began to think road building should be done in a business-like fashion. Good road clubs were formed, and a Good Roads meeting at the state fair in 1910 requested that the state employ a highway engineer to advise counties on road construction. In time proceeds from bonds sold by the counties were used to pay for building roads, instead of depending upon citizen or convict labor.

Highway construction and maintenance remained the responsibility of the individual counties until after World War I, when the state assumed the responsibility for Texas highways. In 1914 the Texas Good Roads Congress, meeting at Fort Worth, called for a state highway department. In 1917, during the administration of Governor James E. Ferguson, a highway department was created in order to qualify for road building funds under the Federal Aid Road Act. A state highway commission planned the location and construction of a system of roads and granted state aid to counties on state-approved plans.

By 1910 Texas was the fifth most populous state. Between 1900 and 1910 the population of her cities increased by 80 percent, while farm population increased by only 17 percent. The rush to the cities had begun, made possible by a technology placing increasing burdens on machines, facilitating the movement of men and materials, and freeing Texans from the sole occupation of tilling the soil.

Business Opportunities for All

As the economy grew and became more sophisticated, more Texans were able to participate in the state's industrial, business, and professional life. Texas Negro businessmen, including Robert L. Smith, journeyed to a meeting of the National Negro Business League in Kansas in 1907. They decided that Texas needed such an organization and called a meeting in Fort Worth in 1908. The movement resulted in the organization of the Texas Negro Business League, a forerunner of the Texas Negro Chamber of Commerce. Smith was one of the Negro leaders who felt that Negroes should have their own banks to sponsor their business organizations, and he founded the Farmers Improvement Bank in Waco in 1908. Negro banks in Houston and Fort Worth preceded Smith's institution.

Emmett J. Scott, the son of a Houston blacksmith, rose from janitor in the offices of the *Texas Trade Journal* to secretary of Tuskegee Institute, secretary of the National Negro Business League, and secretary of Howard University in Washington, D. C. Scott gained editorial experience on the *Journal* and founded the *Texas Freemen,* a Negro newspaper. He entered politics as secretary to Norris Wright Cuney, collector of customs at the Port of Galveston and leader of the state Republican party. When Booker T. Washington spoke in Houston in 1907, Scott so impressed the Negro leader that Washington hired him as his confidential secretary. Scott wrote a study of Washington entitled *Booker T. Washington—Builder of a Civilization,* and a book devoted to the participation of the Negro in America in World War I. The Emmett J. Scott High School in Tyler commemorates this Texas Negro leader.

Other Negroes gained prominence in financial and political circles. William Nickerson, Jr., organized the American Mutual Benefit Association in Houston in 1908 and served as general

219

secretary for the organization. In 1925 he founded the Golden State Mutual Life Insurance Company, the second largest Negro life insurance company in the nation, with assets totalling over $30 million. William McDonald founded the Fraternal Bank and Trust Company in Fort Worth in 1911. McDonald gained power in the Republican party when Norris Wright Cuney began his fight against the Republican party's "lily white" attitude. McDonald was respected throughout the state as one of the outstanding public speakers of the time.

Events in Europe caused continued immigration to the United States, where immigrants contributed to the business expansion of the country. Some of the Jews fleeing anti-Semitism came to Texas, where they contributed to business, the professions, and civic endeavor. Jewish immigrants built some of the bustling mercantile empires of the state. Many set examples of public beneficence through such organizations as the Hebrew Benevolent Society, first organized in Galveston through a bequest left by Rosana Dyer Osterman. Galveston sent Leo N. Levi, a prominent Jewish lawyer born in Victoria, to the Texas legislature to represent her interests. Levi helped the American statesman John Hay formulate a formal protest against the pogroms in Russia.

El Paso merchant and civic leader Samuel J. Freudenthal served as city alderman, member of the school board, and as a county commissioner who led a reform fight against gambling. Moritz Kopperl served as president of the National Bank of Texas at Galveston and as a leading coffee importer. Kopperl served in the Texas legislature, heading the powerful House Committee on Finance. The town of Kopperl in Bosque County carries the name of this civic leader and businessman.

Washer Brothers Clothing Store in Fort Worth counted among its customers, just prior to his Spanish-American War service, then Colonel Theodore Roosevelt. Present Sanger-Harris stores in Dallas grew out of the business founded by the five Sanger brothers in 1872. Neiman-Marcus, established in this century, has long had an international reputation.

The Jewish community in San Antonio was ably served by the humanitarian Rabbi Samuel Marks, who for thirty-seven years headed Temple Beth-El in the city and served as the head of many civic organizations. Rabbi Henry Cohen established the Jewish Information Bureau in 1907 in Galveston to aid immigrants. President Woodrow Wilson called Cohen "the foremost citizen of Texas." Rabbi Cohen helped bring ten thousand persons to the United States. He encouraged Jewish immigrants to Texas to scatter themselves across the state. Jewish immigrants settled in El Paso, Galveston, Houston, San Antonio, and Dallas. Rabbi Cohen worked for prison reform, helping released prisoners find a place in society.

Italian immigrants started the only licensed winery in the state. Frank Qualia and his wife Mary carried cuttings from their grape vineyard in Milan, Italy, to Del Rio. Their winery still produces five thousand gallons of wine each year.

Antonio Mateo Bruni came from Italy to establish the Bruni Ranch in Webb County. He was active in politics in Laredo. Italian immigrants worked as lumberjacks in Angelina County. The oldest Italian-English newspaper in the South was established in Dallas in 1913 by C. S. Papa. *La Tribuna Italiana* advertised itself as the "spokesman for Justice—Freedom—Opportunity—America" under the editorship of Louis E. Adin. Joseph P. Gennaro changed the title of the paper to the *Texas Tribune* and published it until 1963.

Long avid readers of newspapers, Texans were becoming interested in more weighty literary pursuits. Citizens of Austin believed, "If it's a book, you can get it at Gammel's." Danish immigrant Hans P. N. Gammel's small bookstore grew to contain one of the largest collections of Texana in the state. His interest in books led Gammel to begin a publishing business. He salvaged state records from the capitol fire in 1881 and hung the watersoaked records on a clothesline to dry. Some of the salvaged material appeared in his ten-volume edition of the *Laws of Texas*. Gammel also published John C. Duval's *Early Times in Texas*, C. W. Raines's *Bibliography of Texas*, and other works relating to the state.

The New Politics

Thomas William House helped organize the first street railway in Houston, the first gas company, the Houston Board of

Trade, and the Cotton Exchange. His son, Edward Mandell House, was one of the most successful men in Texas political history, although he never held public office.

Edward M. House moved to Austin to be at the center of Texas politics. Governor Hogg placed him in charge of his successful campaign for reelection. In appreciation for his services, Hogg gave House the honorary title of "colonel." House successfully managed the gubernatorial campaigns of Joseph D. Sayers, S. W. T. Lanham, and Charles A. Culberson before he became interested in national politics.

House was unenthusiastic about supporting William Jennings Bryan for the presidency in the election of 1912. When he met the governor of New Jersey and former president of Princeton University, Woodrow Wilson, House knew that he had found a candidate he could back. With House managing his campaign, Wilson received the Democratic nomination and went on to defeat the Republican candidate, William Howard Taft, and the Progressive party candidate, Theodore Roosevelt. Wilson relied heavily on House's advice. Wilson said, "Mr. House is my second personality. He is my independent self. His thoughts and mine are one."

House's influence in Washington and Wilson's cabinet members from Texas brought the state to an unprecedented eminence in national politics. The growth of industry and population created economic and social problems requiring solutions. Texas shared these problems with the rest of the nation. She also shared the search for solutions.

Discuss

1. Compare the development of Texas industry and agriculture.

2. Why did manufacturing and farming begin producing for world markets rather than local markets? What effects did this have?

3. What do the histories of the oil and lumbering industries in Texas indicate about man's attitudes toward the conservation of natural resources?

4. How did the development of the automobile stimulate the economic growth of Texas?

5. What geographical advantages and disadvantages does Texas have as a manufacturing state?

6. Assess the importance of the development of a state highway department.

Identify

Isaac Dahlman	Emmett J. Scott
Pine Woods	Moritz Kopperl
John Henry Kirby	Rabbi Henry Cohen
"Cut out and get out"	C. S. Papa
Hans P. N. Gammel	Edward M. House

$1,808,483.30

THE WATERS-PIERCE OIL COMPANY FINE WAS PAID
FIVE AND TEN THOUSAND DOLLAR BILLS. THOMAS WA
GREGORY IS SEATED AT RIGHT.

CHAPTER 13

"A Giant Arouses"

Since the reform administration of James Stephen Hogg, Texas politics had been dominated by business and commercial groups. While farmers had enjoyed a period of relative prosperity that quieted their voices, the spirit of rebellion that had fostered the Grange, the Farmers' Alliance, and the Populist party lived on in Texas farmers. The state representative from Brownwood, C. H. Jenkins, stood on the floor of the state legislature calling for more state reforms and recited:

> Swing outward O Gates of the future
> Swing inward O Gates of the past
> A giant arouses from slumber
> The people are awakening at last.

The Progressives

The new reform movement—Progressivism—sweeping the United States had its roots in the agrarian protest of the Populist movement, but now it was moving to the new urban centers and including newspaper editors, lawyers, teachers, white-collar workers, and businessmen. The Democratic party in Texas had adopted many of the Populist reforms called for by the farmers: regulation of railroads, abolition of convict labor, the income tax, direct election of United States senators, and currency reform.

The problems that the Progressives faced were primarily the results of industrialization: the rise of big business, the growth of monopoly as a way of corporate life, and the problems of rapidly expanding urban centers. While the Populist movement had been composed of and mainly appealed to the farmers, the Progressive movement included farmers, small businessmen, wealthy humanitarians, intellectuals, writers, and professionals. Crusading journalists and novelists carried the evils of the corporations, the cities, the trusts, child labor, industrial accidents, and corruption in business and government directly to the people in such widely circulated magazines as *McClure's, Everybody's,* and *Cosmopolitan.* Ida M. Tarbell, in *The History of the Standard Oil Company,* showed the influence of John D. Rockefeller's industrial empire on the corporate world. Lincoln Steffens exposed evils in politics in *The Shame of Cities,* depicting a rising corruption growing out of materialism. President Theodore Roosevelt, himself a Progressive, called these writers of the literature of exposé and protest "muckrakers," and the name stuck.

Many of the Progressives were moralists who believed in reforming the morals of the people through such means as the prohibition of liquor. Many tended to look at people in terms of all evil or all good and at all big business and industry as either good or corrupt. The Progressive movement exerted a decided reform influence on the social and political life of the United States from the 1890s to the beginning of World War I. The Progressive movement was decidedly American in that it was optimistic, based on middle-class concerns, moderate, liberal rather than radical, and highly idealistic. Progressivism combined the faith of the Jeffersonians with the pragmatic action of the Jacksonians.

The reforms of the Progressive era were wide-ranging and

embraced social, political, and economic problems. Monetary reform, conservation of resources, destruction of monopolies, improvement of the lot of the immigrant, crime prevention, improved food and housing, and removing corruption from government all came under the reform banner of the Progressives. The problems caused nationwide by the shift from a primarily agricultural economy to a rapidly expanding industrial one made reform necessary. The small businessman was finding that it was difficult to survive in the wake of larger concerns that tried to monopolize the market.

By 1900 a small percentage of the population owned an inordinate portion of the wealth of the nation. The unequal distribution of the country's wealth was becoming both a social and a political problem. The influx of immigrants into the cities caused problems of housing, employment, and sanitation. Differing cultural patterns and the strangeness of a new land caused many of the immigrants in the larger cities to band together into ghettos. And the influx of immigrants from other countries caused conflict within the labor movement that had risen in response to the new industrialism.

The Labor Movement and the Rise of Unions

Labor emerged from the Civil War prepared to move toward national organization. Plentiful resources, labor reserves, and a demand for the products of new industries, plus the railroad, steel, and oil empires carved out by business leaders and financiers, created a climate for industrial growth. Monopoly was the goal of the industrialists, and the individual laborer was reduced to insignificance against the power of the great corporation. Prices and wages were no longer determined by local conditions, and nationwide economic changes required that workers organize to meet the power of industry.

The Knights of Labor began as a secret organization of Philadelphia garment workers in 1869. It expanded to other industries and grew rapidly. Texas could claim thirty thousand members of the Knights in 1886. The Knights of Labor supported the International Association of Granite Cutters against the contractors building Texas's new capitol in the 1880s. When

A labor dispute over the capitol granite quarry resulted in an early union victory in Texas.

the builder used convict labor to quarry granite for the new capitol, the granite cutters voted to boycott the job. The contractors then imported stonecutters from Scotland to finish the job. Prosecuted under the Alien Contract Labor Law, which forbade such importation of labor, the contractors were fined sixty-four thousand dollars.

The strength of the Knights of Labor was broken in Texas by an unsuccessful strike against Jay Gould's Texas and Pacific Railroad in 1886, but an investigation was held by a congressional committee on industrial relationships as a result of the strike. The decline of the Knights of Labor paved the way for the formation of the American Federation of Labor, founded in 1886.

The American Federation of Labor was organized as a combination of craft unions composed of workers engaged in a single activity or trade. The purpose of the organization was to insure that union members gained a rightful share of the profits of capitalism. Independent unions were also formed across the country, among the strongest of which were the four railroad brotherhoods.

Strikes and agitation for higher wages led to a growing hostility among the American people toward the labor unions. The American Federation of Labor called for collective bargain-

228

ing between labor and management, but it also recognized that strikes and boycotts were often the only effective means of gaining labor's demands. Also called for were an eight-hour workday, a six-day week, the abolition of child labor, tenure for union members, and the highly controversial closed shop which would permit the hiring of dues-paying union members only.

In 1898 the Texas State Federation of Labor was organized, and by 1900 the American Federation of Labor had chartered six central trades councils in cities in Texas. The Joint Labor Legislative Board was created in 1903 to insure labor's power to bargain. Although unions remained small, they were active in Texas, and their leadership was strong. The union members used newspapers to spread their message, and they worked closely with members of the Farmers' Union to effect reform.

The War against the Trusts

Antitrust Legislation. In the Constitution of 1845, the state of Texas had first dealt with the problem of monopoly. That constitution declared monopolies to be contrary to free government. James Stephen Hogg helped write a Texas antitrust act in 1889 setting penalties for combinations in restraint of trade, price fixing, unlawful limitations on competition or production, and refusal to sell or transport goods. This Texas antitrust act was the second law of its kind in the United States. The national government passed the Sherman Antitrust Act in 1890, although at first it was more often used to check the growth of labor unions than to check the growth of monopolies. John H. Reagan had helped to frame both the state and the national laws, and in each a trust was defined as an association of capital, skills, or acts by two or more persons or corporations for the purpose of restricting trade, limiting production, or controlling prices.

The United States found its champion of antitrust legislation when Theodore Roosevelt succeeded to the presidency upon the assassination of President William McKinley in 1901. Governor Hogg of Texas once stated of Roosevelt, "Well, he is a trust-buster, and not a trust-cusser." Roosevelt's antitrust program was continued under his successor, William Howard Taft.

The Texas statutes were strengthened from time to time. In 1899 each corporation in the state was required to file an affidavit stating that it was not in violation of the state antitrust laws. In 1903 farmers and labor unions were placed under the antitrust laws. The statutes were amended in 1909 to make them even more effective.

The Waters-Pierce Case. The most important antitrust case in the history of Texas was filed by Attorney General Martin M. Crane in 1897 against the Waters-Pierce Oil Company, a Missouri corporation doing business in Texas. The dispute was not settled until 1909. In the meantime it became a political issue. The first decision came in the 1897 suit. The company's permit to do business in Texas was canceled. Then the legal adviser to the company, Senator Joseph Weldon Bailey, managed to get its charter reinstated. It was discovered that the company was still in violation of Texas antitrust laws, and a second suit against the company resulted in a fine of almost $2 million and the final ouster of the company from the state.

Austin-Travis County Collection, Austin Public Library

Theodore Roosevelt, shown here at The University of Texas, visited Texas in 1905.

An Era of Reform

Elected on a platform dedicated to reform, Governor James Stephen Hogg had fulfilled substantially all of his campaign promises. The establishment of the Texas Railroad Commission was one of his greatest achievements. During his term in office, reform legislation centered on the railroad commission, laws regulating the issuance of stocks and bonds, an alien land law, and a franchise tax on corporations. Hogg had the ability to capture the imagination and the loyalty of the common man.

In 1895 Hogg was succeeded by former attorney general Charles A. Culberson, who continued Hogg's program of reform and regulation. Culberson's father had been a popular congressman, and his campaign was aided by the effective political management of Colonel House. During Culberson's administration the antitrust laws were extended to cover insurance companies, and the first suit against the Waters-Pierce Oil Company was instituted.

Following the era of reform under Hogg and Culberson, the state government reverted to conservative tendencies under the leadership of two former Confederates. Joseph D. Sayers and Samuel W. T. Lanham, backed by their political adviser, Colonel Edward M. House, occupied the governor's mansion during the first years of the twentieth century. Both governors were basically conservative; however, during their administrations several laws of a progressive nature were enacted. The state banking system was established, a child labor law was enacted, and the Texas Rangers were reorganized.

A former supporter of Governor Hogg, Sayers ran for governor against Hogg's chosen candidate, Martin M. Crane, who then lost Hogg's confidence and dropped from the race. Sayers became governor in 1899, vacating his seat in the United States Congress to Albert Sidney Burleson. Sayers was governor at the time of the great Spindletop discovery. The tragic flood that inundated Galveston and the rise of the commission form of government in that city also came during his administration. A poll tax as a requirement for voting was levied, and several colleges were established.

Sayers served the second term that was becoming customary for Texas governors and was succeeded by Colonel House's chosen candidate, Samuel W. T. Lanham. Lanham believed that the state needed little new legislation, and he stated that he thought "the fewer laws the better" would be the best guide to his administration. He did suggest legislation which would provide a more equitable distribution of the tax burden. The most significant event of the Lanham administration was the passage of the Terrell Election Law in 1905, named for Judge Alexander Watkins Terrell.

Election Reform. The Terrell Election Law designated the party primary as the main method of nominating state officials. Under its terms as first enacted, nominations were made by a combination of party convention and primary, and during the administration of Governor Thomas M. Campbell, who was elected under the new law, the legislature amended the law to make it less cumbersome. Conventions were abolished and the primary method of nomination became standard. In this manner, each citizen who was qualified to vote could take an active part in the nomination and election of officials. This was especially important since the Democratic party was the only one with enough strength to elect its candidates.

Judge Alexander Watkins Terrell, the moving force behind Texas election reform in 1905

The Terrell Election Law, as amended, had a great effect on Texas politics. The primary became all-important. State officials were, in effect, elected in the Democratic primary. Personalities became more important than before. More candidates ran for public office. High-ranking party members meeting in convention no longer nominated candidates. Anyone who could meet the requirements for office could enter himself in the primary. The Terrell Election Law originally provided for only one primary; later amendments established a run-off primary by which the two top contenders for the nomination competed if neither had a majority of the votes.

Progressivism Reawakens. By 1906 Texans were ready for a change. The conservative members of the Democratic party were split as to whom they would support for governor. Four candidates entered the race for the governorship—Charles K. Bell, Judge M. M. Brooks, Oscar B. Colquitt, a member of the railroad commission, and a lawyer from Palestine, Thomas M. Campbell. The candidates' platforms lacked variety except for one issue that had entered Texas politics as a result of the Progressive movement. Both Bell and Colquitt were antiprohibitionists, while Brooks and Campbell were for prohibition of liquor through legislative enactment. All of the candidates advocated more stringent antitrust laws, tax reform, and measures to regulate the lobby, now becoming a powerful force in the legislative process. Ex-governor Hogg supported Campbell, as did Senator Joseph Weldon Bailey. In addition, Campbell had the support of Populists James H. ("Cyclone") Davis and Harrison Sterling Price ("Stump") Ashby, who said Campbell was "the nearest approach to old-time Populism that is now before the country." Campbell won in 1906 and again in 1908.

Progressivism marked Campbell's first term. The legislature strengthened the antitrust law, limited working hours of railway employees, passed a pure food law, established rules for lobbyists, gave some cities power to regulate public utilities, forbade corporate campaign contributions, and provided for road improvements. An amendment to permit increases in local school taxes was submitted to the people and passed.

The Department of Insurance and Banking and the Texas State Library were established during Campbell's administration. The ad valorem tax rate was lowered as the $1.8 million fine assessed the Waters-Pierce Oil Company was collected. A reform bill intended to regulate insurance companies, the Robertson Insurance Law, was passed. It required life insurance companies to invest at least 75 percent of their reserves in Texas securities to secure policies on the lives of Texans. After the legislature approved the bill, twenty-one insurance companies withdrew from the state. Most of the companies later returned.

Another reform of the Campbell administration ended the practice of leasing the services of convicts to individuals and corporations. Investigation disclosed that convicts were whipped, starved, and sometimes killed. The prison system was reorganized, ending some of the worst abuses.

"Baileyism" and Prohibition. Another issue during Governor Campbell's administration aroused as much emotion as prohibition. That controversy concerned Senator Joseph Weldon Bailey and his relationships with various oil companies. Bailey was a storm center in Texas politics from 1900 to 1920. Men were judged by whether they were "Bailey men" or not. Bailey's friends boasted that he was "the ablest man sent to the Senate from the House since John C. Calhoun," and his enemies claimed that he was "the shame of Texas!"

Bailey first came to prominence in Texas politics when he campaigned for statewide prohibition in 1887. He was elected to Congress in 1890 and usually sided with progressive forces. Bailey served five consecutive terms in the House of Representatives and was the House Democratic leader when the legislature elected him to the Senate. In the Senate Bailey became more conservative, often voting with Northern Democrats and Republicans.

During his first term in the Senate, Bailey was accused of accepting a retainer of one hundred thousand dollars from the Waters-Pierce Oil Company and similar fees from the Standard Oil Company and the Kirby lumber interests. The Texas attorney general began an inquiry into Bailey's relations with the oil companies in 1906, after it had been discovered that the Waters-Pierce applications to be readmitted to Texas contained sworn untruths. The legislature convened for an investigation.

Bailey roared back to Texas with threats that he would drive all the "peanut politicians" into the Gulf of Mexico. He stumped the state declaring that he had represented oil companies as their legal counsel only when the Senate was not in session, and furthermore, that his representation of those corporations had never conflicted with his duties as a senator representing the interests of Texans.

The legislative investigating committee was mainly interested in Bailey's part in the readmission of the Waters-Pierce Oil Company. Pierce, Bailey, and John Henry Kirby testified. However, even before all the evidence was heard, Bailey's supporters forced a vote, and the legislature reelected him to the Senate. Bailey retired from the Senate to resume his law practice in 1913. However, he continued to be a factor in Texas politics.

Prohibition was the other issue that split the voters of the state of Texas. The effort to make liquor illegal was the logical result of years of progressive effort against evils in government and the economy. If the nation might be made better by ending corruption in government, it might not be out of order to end the evils flowing from the consumption of liquor. The "wets" and the "drys" had been arguing the question of prohibition since the 1870s, when the United Friends of Temperance and the Bands of Hope had organized. Those groups were pledged to total abstinence from drink and set about trying to force the issue of prohibition. The Constitution of 1876 contained a local option clause, but the prohibition forces insisted on state-wide prohibition. The Grange and the Greenback party had spoken out against the Democratic party for not submitting the issue to the voters. Finally, in 1887 a statewide prohibition amendment was submitted and defeated.

This defeat, however, was not the end of the prohibition question. The prohibitionists gained in strength, until in 1908 they were again powerful enough to get the issue submitted to the voters in the primary. Again it was defeated. Prohibition was one of the main issues in the election of 1910, when Oscar B. Colquitt, a former member of the railroad commission, was elected governor. Colquitt led the antiprohibitionists, but the prohibitionists forced the Democrats to promise the submission to the voters of a statewide prohibition amendment to the Texas constitution.

Antiprohibitionist and prohibitionist groups published their platforms in 1908 and 1910, respectively.

Resolved, that we are unalterably opposed to State wide prohibition for the following reasons:

It . . . involves an unwarranted interference with the personal happiness and liberties of the people and violates the well-established principles of government set forth in the great Declaration of Independence.

It . . . inevitably leads to a union of Church and State.

It announces the heresy that those who are governed best are governed most, in direct conflict with the vows of the founder of the Republic.

We further contend that whatever evils result from the liquor can be better cured by proper regulation and by local laws. . . .

The experience of various states that have adopted and subsequently repealed State prohibition abundantly proves that it is a failure, and that it promotes intemperance and crime rather than decreases it.[1]

The history of the liquor traffic is a history of crime, degradation, sorrow, suffering, poverty, pauperism, insanity and woeful economic waste, without a single virtue to its credit, or a sane reason for its license, toleration or existence. . . .

In Texas, it is the only business authorized or permitted by law to live which in effect is declared by various statutes to be dangerous to the morals of our youth, inimical to the cause of education, repugnant to the Christian religion, subversive of the Sabbath and workmen's rest day, menacing to our homes and firesides, a foe to the wives and female relatives of its patrons, and so destructive of the purity of its elections and the sanctity of the ballot box that it must hide its head from twelve hours before until twelve hours after the touch of a ballot by a freeman's hand.[2]

Both forces campaigned actively, and in 1911 the prohibition amendment was again defeated by a close vote. The prohibition

[1]*The Dallas Morning News,* October 13, 1908. Reproduced in Wallace and Vigness, *Documents of Texas History* (Austin: Steck-Vaughn Company, 1963), 266.

[2]*The Dallas Morning News,* December 9, 1910. Reproduced in Wallace and Vigness, *Documents of Texas History* (Austin: Steck-Vaughn Company, 1963), 266-67.

A business street in Carrizo Springs. Expanding industries and cities brought new problems in the twentieth century.

leaders charged the "antis" with having used fraudulent tactics during the campaign, but a legislative investigating committee could find nothing amiss. However, the prohibitionists were inspired by the closeness of the vote, and for the next several years continued to push for statewide prohibition.

The prohibition forces were gaining in strength across the nation. The Anti-Saloon League used the entry of the United States into World War I to push for national prohibition. In 1917 Congress adopted and submitted to the states an amendment to the Constitution prohibiting the manufacture, sale, or transportation of alcoholic beverages. The resolution providing for the amendment had been introduced by Texas senator Morris Sheppard, the "Father of National Prohibition."

In February 1918 a special session of the Texas legislature ratified the Eighteenth Amendment, and the saloons in the state were closed by legislative action in June. By July 1919 federal statutes implementing prohibition were passed, and on January 16, 1920, national prohibition became a reality.

The early twentieth century was a time of idealism and social experimentation. Reforms were grounded in the belief that man and his world could be improved. Americans were enjoying what one historian termed "the innocent years," a time of growing and maturing. But soon the belief that men could—and ought to—change things for the better would lead the Americans into a war "to make the world safe for democracy."

Discuss

1. Compare the Populist and Progressive movements.

2. "The rise of the Progressive movement was a direct response to the political, social, and economic developments taking place in the United States." Analyze the preceding statement.

3. Compare the goals of the early labor unions with those of modern unions.

4. Why do you think Texas had periods of reform alternating with more conservative periods?

5. Why are Texas officials generally elected in the primary rather than in the general election?

6. Why did the membership of the reform movement expand to include groups other than farmers?

7. Compare the reforms called for by the Progressives with reforms currently being called for in the United States.

8. Review the accomplishments of labor unions over the years. Do you think that labor unions are still needed?

9. What is your attitude toward legislation such as the prohibition of liquor and the banning of cigarette advertising on television?

Identify

Progressivism

Knights of Labor

American Federation of Labor

Joseph Weldon Bailey

Morris Sheppard

Waters-Pierce case

Terrell Election
  Law

primary

prohibition

Robertson Insurance
  Law

TEXANS IN THE WILSON CABINET WERE THOMAS
GREGORY, REAR, SECOND FROM RIGHT; DAVID F. HOU
TON, FRONT, THIRD FROM LEFT; AND ALBERT S. BUR
SON, EXTREME RIGHT.

CHAPTER 14

"We Count upon Texas"

Since the end of Reconstruction, the Democratic party had controlled Texas government. During the second decade of the twentieth century, Texas Democrats also began to make their presence felt on the national level. Texans were to play key roles in the administration of the Democratic party's first progressive president, Woodrow Wilson.

When Henry Morgenthau of New York, financial chairman for Wilson's campaign, wired Thomas B. Love, a Wilson supporter in Texas, "We count upon Texas for fifty thousand dollars," he was forecasting the influence that Texas would have on Wilson's destiny.

The Colquitt Administration

Governor Oscar B. Colquitt was elected in 1910 on a platform written in reaction to the reform movement. Colquitt pledged a period of legislative rest in which business would not suffer from adverse legislation. He also declared against prohibition, which set Colquitt at odds with the legislature. His first term was a stormy one. Colquitt's administration was plagued with other troubles also. There was much lawlessness along the Rio Grande, given impetus by the revolts against the longtime dictatorship of Porfirio Díaz in Mexico. The governor sent state troops and Texas Rangers to the border.

Financial problems constantly beset Colquitt. The rising cost of living necessitated an increase in state salaries. New departments and bureaus of the state government were established, and maintaining them called for additional expenses. A fire at the Agricultural and Mechanical College of Texas drew funds from the state treasury, and an additional sum was required to augment Confederate pensions. The prison system was again showing signs of financial mismanagement. An audit was attempted, but the financial records were in such deplorable shape it was impossible to discover how money had been spent. Faced with all these problems, the legislature was forced to raise the tax rate.

During the Colquitt administration an eight-hour day for state employees was established and an employer's liability act was passed. The "10-54" law restricting the work of women in industry to a ten-hour day, fifty-four-hour week was passed. A stronger child labor act became law.

Colquitt's second term was considerably more progressive than the first. Numerous educational laws were passed, among them a law establishing rural high schools and a law granting state funds for the teaching of vocational subjects. The legislature ratified the Seventeenth Amendment providing for popular election of United States senators, a reform called for by both the Populists and the Progressives.

The prohibitionists fought Colquitt's election to a second term as hard as they fought for Wilson's nomination. Colquitt's enemies claimed that he had pardoned fifty-one convicts on his fifty-first birthday and had freed twenty-five Mexican-American convicts, including folk hero Gregorio Cortez, on a fiesta day. Colquitt answered that he had never given pardons for political purposes.

Upon the retirement of Joseph Weldon Bailey from the United States Senate, Congressman Morris Sheppard of Texarkana, a prohibitionist, defeated the antiprohibitionist Jacob Wolters for Bailey's seat. The victory encouraged prohibitionists, although they had failed to seat their candidate in the governor's chair in the election of 1912.

The state Democratic platform of 1912 advocated a warehouse plan enabling the farmer to store his cotton until the market price was favorable. Pending sale, the farmer would receive negotiable notes for part of the value of his cotton in storage. Events in Europe precipitated a crisis before a warehouse law was enacted. More than two-thirds of the cotton crop in 1913 was exported. In the fall of 1914, the beginning of World War I caused the European cotton market to collapse, and the price of cotton fell to below eight cents a pound. A special session of the legislature authorized the commissioner of insurance and banking to lease warehouse space to farmers to keep cotton off the market. However, the measure did not solve the problems of the farmers. It was not until Governor Ferguson's administration that a law was passed giving state banks authority to lend money to farmers on their warehouse receipts. By that time the cotton market had regained its balance.

The Election of Wilson

When Woodrow Wilson, a former professor and president of Princeton University, was elected governor of New Jersey in 1910, Texas progressive and prohibition leader Thomas B. Love wired him: "I am for you for president of the United States in 1912." As governor, Wilson managed to get a conservative New Jersey legislature to provide for party primaries, to pass a corrupt practices act, to provide workmen's compensation, and to regulate railroads and utilities. Some progressives thought such a record qualified Wilson for the highest office in the land. Love served as the president of the Woodrow Wilson State Democratic League of Texas. The league invited Wilson to address the Texas Democrats at the state fair in October 1911. Wilson spoke also at Dallas's First Baptist

Church and in Fort Worth. Sizeable crowds turned out to see Wilson, giving his presidential hopes a boost. Colonel Edward M. House began organizing statewide support for Wilson.

Texas's forty delegates to the Democratic National Convention in June 1912 were committed to Woodrow Wilson. With the delegations from Pennsylvania and New Jersey, the Texans held out for Wilson over Champ Clark of Missouri, Speaker of the House of Representatives, and Oscar W. Underwood of Alabama, chairman of the House Ways and Means Committee.

The struggle for the nomination was also a contest for control of the Democratic party, and for a time Wilson's chances seemed slight. However, on the fourteenth ballot William Jennings Bryan changed his support from Clark to Wilson. On the forty-sixth ballot the Underwood forces conceded, giving Wilson the nomination. Throughout the voting the delegates from Texas stood firm for Wilson. Wilson was elected president, defeating Republican candidate William Howard Taft and the Progressive party candidate Theodore Roosevelt.

United Press International

At the Democratic National Convention of 1912 in Baltimore, confusion reigned inside and outside the convention hall.

Edward M. House, left, was Wilson's closest adviser, although he chose to remain in relative obscurity.

Governor Colquitt won a second term in the Democratic landslide which had been usual since the end of Reconstruction.

Texas's National Influence

Texans in the Cabinet. Colonel House remained Wilson's confidant and adviser. Three Texans—Albert Sidney Burleson, Thomas Watt Gregory, and David F. Houston—were given appointments in Wilson's cabinet.

Albert Sidney Burleson was appointed postmaster general. Born in San Marcos, Burleson attended both the Agricultural and Mechanical College of Texas and The University of Texas. He had served as a district attorney and went on to the United States Congress. During his eight-year tenure as postmaster general, the Post Office experienced considerable growth, and parcel post and air mail service were established. When America entered World War I, many radical newspapers protested. Burleson, as postmaster general, suppressed many of the newspapers by depriving them of their second-class mailing permits. The United Mine Workers petitioned for the removal of Burleson at about the same time campaigning was going on for the release of the Socialist Eugene Debs, imprisoned in the federal penitentiary at Atlanta, Georgia. "We try to be fair to both sides," one miner remarked. "Debs and Burleson should both be let out."

A graduate of The University of Texas Law School, Thomas Watt Gregory, became Wilson's attorney general. Gregory had served as Austin city attorney and as special counsel for the state in the Waters-Pierce Oil Company case and other anti-trust suits. Wilson appointed Gregory special assistant to his first attorney general, J. C. McReynolds, and Gregory brought federal antitrust action against the New York, New Haven, and Hartford Railroad. Wilson appointed Gregory attorney general in 1914. Gregory established the War Emergency Division of the Department of Justice and enlarged the Federal Bureau of Investigation.

When Charles Evans Hughes resigned as chief justice of the United States Supreme Court, Wilson offered Gregory the position, but Gregory declined. He resigned from Wilson's cabinet in March 1919 to serve as an adviser at the Versailles Peace Conference. When he returned to the United States, he settled in Houston and devoted much of his time to raising funds for construction at The University of Texas.

Secretary of Agriculture David F. Houston was born in North Carolina and was living in St. Louis when he was named to Wilson's cabinet. Houston had studied at Harvard University, and during his lifetime he was awarded eight honorary doctorates. He began teaching at The University of Texas in 1894. He served as dean of the faculty from 1899 to 1902. He was president of the Agricultural and Mechanical College of Texas before he assumed the presidency of The University of Texas in 1905. He resigned as chancellor of Washington University to become secretary of agriculture.

Houston was one of the designers of the Federal Reserve System. In 1920 Wilson appointed him secretary of the treasury, chairman of the Federal Reserve Board, and chairman of the Federal Farm Loan Board. After Houston resigned from the cabinet, he was a vice-president of the American Telephone and Telegraph Company.

Other Texans in High Office. Texans serving below cabinet level in the Wilson administration included Thomas B. Love, who was an assistant secretary of the treasury during World

War I; Cato Sells, head of the Bureau of Indian Affairs; and Cone Johnson of Tyler, who was a solicitor for the State Department.

In addition, many Texans made their presence felt in Congress. Robert Lee Henry of Waco was chairman of the House Rules Committee during Wilson's administration. Morris Sheppard succeeded to the Senate seat formerly held by Joseph Weldon Bailey. John Nance Garner of Uvalde was an important member of Congress. A freshman congressman, Sam Rayburn, had served as Speaker of the Texas House of Representatives. Later he would be Speaker of the United States House of Representatives longer than any other man in history.

The New Freedom

Wilson's goals were to bring a New Freedom to the American people and to revive competition in the business community. He felt that trusts and monopolies threatened the free-enterprise system, and that by eliminating trusts, reducing tariffs, and reforming the banking system, free competition could be restored.

Wilson made the first item on his legislative agenda the lowering of the tariff. The Underwood-Simmons Act, passed in 1913 after a bitter fight, revised tariff rates downward and provided for a graduated income tax under the recently approved Sixteenth Amendment. However, the most significant piece of domestic legislation passed during Wilson's first term was the Federal Reserve Act of 1913, which gave the government control over banking.

The Federal Trade Commission, created in 1914, had the power to investigate complaints of unfair competition. The Clayton Antitrust Act complemented the Sherman Antitrust Act by forbidding interlocking directorates, price discrimination leading to monopolies, and antitrust injunctions against agricultural associations and labor unions.

Assistance was extended to agriculture during the Wilson administration through the Federal Farm Loan Act of 1916 and its system of banks which extended long-term loans at low interest rates to farmers; through the Warehouse Act of 1916, by which farmers could obtain credit receipts against their crops stored in warehouses; and through legislation providing agricultural extension services through the land-grant colleges and funds for agricultural and vocational schools.

Labor received some assistance during Wilson's administration. Wilson backed the La Follette Seaman's Act, which raised the safety and health standards on ships and guaranteed seamen the right to join a union. However, Wilson refused to back a child labor law which he believed to be unconstitutional. The Keating-Owen Act prohibited the interstate shipment of goods made by factories employing children. The Supreme Court ruled in 1918 that the act was indeed unconstitutional, but a similar act was upheld by the Court in 1941. The Adamson Act of 1916 granted employees of interstate railroads an eight-hour work day with extra compensation for overtime.

Despite the progressive reforms of Wilson's adminstration, the government policy toward Negroes reflected a lack of social justice and the growing influence of Southern positions on race. Some departments became segregated. Many Negro civil servants were either removed from office or lost the status they had gained. The "new freedom" had not yet been extended to all.

Trouble along the Border

Wilson achieved notable success in domestic matters. However, he was not so successful in his dealings with Mexico, where his objective was to see established a stable government.

In 1910 Porfirio Díaz, then eighty years old, decreed a celebration honoring his thirty-four years as dictator of Mexico and commemorating the centennial of the Hidalgo revolution against Spain. Within a few months, Díaz had been overthrown by Francisco Madero and his reform government. In the next four years Mexico had nine presidents, one of whom served only twenty-eight minutes as chief executive. With Mexico in a state of revolution, trouble broke out along the Texas-Mexican border. Arms were being smuggled through Texas, and Mexican bandits were raiding Texas towns along the border.

Governor Oscar B. Colquitt appealed to President Wilson to intervene, but Wilson preferred to watch the Mexican revolutionary situation more before ordering federal troops to the border. Colquitt sent Texas Rangers to protect the lives and property of Texas citizens along the Rio Grande.

Madero was betrayed and deposed by his chief general, Victoriano Huerta, who assumed the presidency and reported Madero killed while attempting to escape. Huerta was overthrown by Venustiano Carranza in July 1914. Huerta lived in El Paso until his death two years later. Carranza became president. For a time the United States hesitated in deciding whether to recognize the Carranza government. Recognition was extended in the summer of 1915. Arms bought by Carranza in the United States were used to subdue such revolutionists as Francisco ("Pancho") Villa, who could not, by law, buy weapons and ammunition in the United States.

The Villa Raids. Villa, one of the most flamboyant of the Mexican revolutionaries, sought to overthrow Carranza. When the United States recognized Carranza's government, Villa became enraged and began raiding border towns in Texas and New Mexico. Villa had previously been friendly to the United

Archives Division, Texas State Library

Before Pancho Villa (center) began his raids, he was friendly to the United States. Pershing never got this close to Villa on the punitive expedition.

249

States but now declared himself its enemy. In January 1916 Villa's guerrilla band attacked a train traveling through the state of Chihuahua at Santa Ysabel. The Villistas removed seventeen American mining engineers (in Mexico by Carranza's invitation) and shot sixteen of them. Riding at the head of some fifteen hundred guerrillas, Villa crossed the international border into New Mexico in March 1916, raided the town of Columbus and the neighboring cavalry camp, and killed nine civilians and eight soldiers. Villa managed to escape with guns, supplies, and ammunition. Pursued into Mexico, Villa's forces suffered some 120 casualties.

American public opinion demanded action. Wilson ordered Brigadier General John J. ("Black Jack") Pershing to the border to assemble an expedition into Mexico to rout out Villa and his renegades. Among the units was the Tenth Cavalry Regiment, a Negro unit Pershing had always considered his home regiment. At Pershing's request, Charles Wycoff, a Negro sergeant from Carswell Air Force Base, Texas, played "Taps" at Pershing's funeral in 1948.

The Punitive Expedition. Pershing's punitive expedition pursued the revolutionaries into Mexico in the spring of 1916. When guerrillas raided the little town of Glen Spring, Brewster County, Texas, killing three soldiers and one boy, Congress demanded action, as did Texas governor James E. Ferguson. Wilson sent two warships to the coast of Mexico and called out the National Guard to protect the border.

Pershing fought both Villistas and Carranzistas along the border and in Mexico, but his attempts to round up the elusive Villa were in vain. Villa's guerrillas melted into the hills of Chihuahua and continued their pillage of border towns. War might easily have broken out between the United States and Mexico. Early in 1917 Wilson ordered Pershing's forces to return to El Paso. However, border incidents continued. Any number of events made it clear that Germany was involved in these border hostilities or at least that Americans were being harassed in behalf of the Germans. Villa retired to his estate in Mexico, where later he was assassinated.

Many Texans were involved in the explosive border problems. A scout on Pershing's punitive expedition was Sam Dreben, a

Members of the Tenth Cavalry, which was involved in the punitive expedition

Jewish soldier of fortune from El Paso. Dreben had fought in the Mexican revolutions and had been a gunrunner for Carranza's forces. He served in France during World War I. Dreben won the Distinguished Service Cross and France's medaille militaire and the croix de guerre.

Among the members of the Tenth Cavalry who rode into Mexico with Pershing was the Negro lieutenant West Alexander Hamilton, who rose to the rank of colonel in the United States Army. Hamilton also served in France during World War I, and as commanding officer of the 366th Infantry at Fort Devens, Massachusetts, during World War II. He ended his career as commander of the ROTC at Prairie View University. Hugh McElroy, another Negro, served with the Tenth Cavalry. McElroy had been with Roosevelt's Rough Riders in the Spanish-American War. During World War I he was awarded the croix de guerre for gallantry in action.

The San Antonio Chinese. When the expedition under General Pershing returned from northern Mexico, some five hundred Chinese followed the troops into Texas. Pershing had camped near the small community of Casa Grande, and Chinese living

251

in the area supplied the Americans with food. Villa swore vengeance on the Chinese, and many followed the Americans to San Antonio to escape Villa's wrath.

Although Chinese might not enter the United States because of the Chinese Exclusion Law designed to protect American labor, Pershing obtained special permission for their entry in June 1917. Pershing placed the Chinese under military discipline, and an immigration bureau official was assigned as civilian adviser to the group. Labor was needed at the army installations at San Antonio, and the United States Department of War provided a temporary work program for many of the Chinese at Fort Sam Houston.

Working as laborers, laundrymen, carpenters, and cooks, the Chinese helped to build Fort Sam Houston. Many became merchants in San Antonio. The Chinese Baptist Church was established, and the Chinese, eager to become citizens of the United States, attended citizenship classes at the church. Until 1947 the Chinese operated a school for their children in San Antonio. The Chinese felt a debt of gratitude to General Pershing and named many of their children in his honor. In 1921 a law was passed granting the Chinese in San Antonio the right to remain within the United States.

Discuss

1. Why did the Progressive party fail to elect a candidate to the presidency?

2. Why did Texas play a larger role in national politics during the Wilson administration than it had previously?

3. How did legislation passed during President Wilson's first term in office compare with the goals of the Progressives?

4. Do you think that Wilson's policy regarding Mexico was wise? Why?

5. Review the developments in Texas agriculture and industry from 1850 to 1916. What effects do you think Wilson's economic policies had on Texas?

Identify

legislative rest
"10-54" law
Albert Sidney Burleson
David F. Houston
New Freedom
Federal Trade Commission
General John J. Pershing

Lieutenant West
Alexander Hamilton
Thomas B. Love
Thomas Watt Gregory
Sam Rayburn
Federal Reserve Act
Pancho Villa

CARRYING A BANNER READING "KAISERISM, A MENACE ABROAD; LIKEWISE, A MENACE AT HOME," FRIENDS OF THE UNIVERSITY MARCHED ON THE CAPITOL TO PROTEST FERGUSON'S ACTIONS.

CHAPTER 15

"Peace, Preparedness, and Progressivism"

In the election of 1916 President Woodrow Wilson faced a formidable opponent in Republican candidate Charles Evans Hughes of New York. Wilson campaigned on a slogan of "Peace, Preparedness, and Progressivism." His supporters claimed that "He kept us out of war," an important consideration when so much of the world was fighting. But the United States would not long remain clear of the European struggle.

On June 28, 1914, a bullet fired by a Serbian at Sarajevo, Bosnia, killed Archduke Franz Ferdinand, heir to the throne of Austria-Hungary. Immediately Austria demanded retribution and then, backed by Germany, declared war on Serbia. Russia and France mobilized, and Germany moved against

France, violating the neutrality of Belgium. Soon all Europe was involved. Despite the attempts of the United States to remain neutral, public sentiment was stirred by stories of German submarine warfare and German atrocities in Belgium.

That summer of 1914, however, Texans were more excited about the Democratic primary than about Balkan problems. A number of antiprohibitionists had announced their candidacies for the governorship, but the candidate who seemed to be getting all of the attention was a little-known Temple banker, James E. Ferguson, who was such a political newcomer that many Texans regarded his candidacy as a joke. That illusion was soon dispelled, and Texans came to know that a reference to Farmer Jim had to do with the Bell County banker.

Farmer Jim

Ferguson promised that he would veto any liquor legislation that was passed by the legislature. Prohibitionists were outraged. Ferguson's appeal was to the tenant farmers, the largest single group of voters in the state. He proposed to set up a state agency to keep cotton farmers informed about prices. More important, he promised legislation to make it unlawful for a landowner to collect a rent of more than one-third the value of the grain crop or one-fourth the value of the cotton

Governor James E. Ferguson was a storm center of Texas politics.

Austin-Travis County Collection, Austin Public Library

crop, if the tenant furnished his own supplies and tools. Ferguson also promised better schools, a businesslike administration, and state bonded warehouses for the storage of surplus crops.

Most prohibitionists favored former congressman Thomas H. Ball, who had acted as statewide chairman of the Prohibition party in 1911. Ball declared for driving liquor from the state. Ball's platform also favored separation of the Agricultural and Mechanical College from The University of Texas, longer terms for the public schools, and improvement of the state asylums and the penitentiary system.

The Democratic primary was set for July, and the question of whether or not a prohibition amendment to the state constitution would be submitted was to be decided in the primary. Campaign charges and countercharges flew. Farmer Jim spoke to the farmers, claiming that he would represent them and "Sally and the babies," and drank from a gourd dipper, wiping his face with a red bandanna. Ball announced that he was in favor of more liberal support to The University of Texas. Washington politicians, including Love, Burleson, and President Wilson, supported Ball. Ball was known to be an active supporter of Joe Bailey, and East Texas lumber baron John Henry Kirby threw his support to Ball.

But there was no heading Ferguson. He had the common touch that had drawn Texans to the great governor James Stephen Hogg. Governor Oscar B. Colquitt's support helped Ferguson also. The people knew Colquitt, and many resented "foreigners" such as Woodrow Wilson meddling in Texas politics. Ferguson won over Republican, Progressive, and Socialist opponents in November to become the third native Texan to win the office. W. P. Hobby was the lieutenant governor.

The Ferguson Administration. Ferguson began his service on good terms with the legislature. There was only slight opposition to his farm tenant rent bill. In 1921 the law was found unconstitutional. It had been only loosely enforced.

When Ferguson took office the state was contributing only about seven dollars per year per pupil to public education. This money was derived from the Available School Fund consisting of revenue from school-owned public lands. Ferguson sought to increase amounts spent for rural schools, so he got

257

Schoolchildren such as these at Yancey were greatly benefited by education legislation passed during the Ferguson tenure.

the legislature to require that in order to receive state aid, rural schools had to levy local school taxes first. A compulsory school attendance law required all children between eight and fourteen years of age to attend school for a specified time each year. Free textbooks might be provided students.

In his first term Ferguson asked the legislature to appropriate $1 million for rural schools; during his second administration, he asked for $2 million. The legislature granted both requests, and with local school districts taxing themselves to the extent of fifty cents per hundred dollars valuation on all property, county schools were able to afford teachers and equipment undreamed of before.

In 1917 four new normal schools were authorized. Sul Ross Normal College was to be at Alpine; East Texas Normal College was accepted into the state system; and Stephen F. Austin Normal College and South Texas Normal College were founded. All of these institutions later changed their names as they achieved university status. During the governor's second term, a textbook commission was created with Governor Ferguson serving as its first chairman, and a uniform system of textbooks was set up. Districts could furnish free textbooks if they wished, but they did not have to do so.

Controversy over State Funds and Education. In 1916 two Texas political enemies, Jim Ferguson and Joe Bailey, cooperated long enough to control the state Democratic convention. The party platform endorsed Wilson for president and turned down bids for women's suffrage and national prohibition. Governor Ferguson led the state delegation to the national convention and supported Woodrow Wilson's renomination.

Ferguson's reelection campaign was a difficult and bitter one. The prohibition candidate, Charles H. Morris, charged that Ferguson had used state funds for personal expenses, that the governor had exaggerated the need for school funds, that Ferguson's first campaign had been financed in part by funds from the Houston Ice and Brewing Company, and that Ferguson had collected insurance money from a fire at West Texas State Normal and had deposited the funds—at no interest—in the Ferguson-owned Temple State Bank.

Ferguson denied the charges and mentioned that his first administration had been one noted for peace and harmony between the governor and the legislature. The voters returned Ferguson to the state house and reelected Senator Charles A. Culberson, a prohibitionist, to the United States Senate over ex-governor Oscar B. Colquitt, an antiprohibitionist. Although the Democrats again voted to submit the issue of prohibition, Ferguson chose not to do so.

Besides the progressive legislation related to public schools in Ferguson's second term, some judicial reforms were made, and judges' salaries were raised. The Texas Highway Commission was established in 1917. A state had to have such an agency or it could not be granted federal funds for highway building and maintenance. The commission handled federal road funds allocated to the state. Also in 1917 Stephenville's John Tarleton Agricultural College and Arlington's Grubbs Vocational College became part of the Agricultural and Mechanical College of Texas system. Grubbs is now The University of Texas at Arlington.

A furor arose over the location of West Texas Agricultural and Mechanical College. With cities competing for the college, the governor, a member of the five-man site committee, said Abilene had been selected. Then Lieutenant Governor Will Hobby, Speaker of the House of Representatives F. O. Fuller, and another member—three-fifths of the committee—stated that they had not voted for Abilene. Meetings were held in other West Texas towns, and an injunction was granted to prevent the college from being established at Abilene. A special session of the legislature repealed the bill creating the college, by which time West Texans had decided they needed an institution more comprehensive than an agricultural college. Texas Technological College opened in 1925, responding to thirty-two years of West Texas requests.

The Ferguson Impeachment. The Democratic platform of 1914 had called for The University of Texas to list each

Texas Highway Department

Texas Technological College opened in 1925 following a controversy over the location of a West Texas college.

item for which it asked an appropriation. The legislature complied with the method of appropriation, but authorized the board of regents of the university to make changes within the appropriations. Ferguson believed the power to alter the amounts specified destroyed the value of itemization and signed the bill after stating his reluctance.

In 1916 the board of regents of the university, most of them not appointed by Governor Ferguson, elected Dr. Robert Vinson as president of the university without consulting the governor. Ferguson demanded that Vinson dismiss six professors at the university. Vinson refused and submitted the matter to the board of regents. Ferguson demanded Vinson's dismissal and charged the university with carrying dead men on the payroll and entering false expenses in the budget.

Embittered by the fight with the university and a legislative investigation growing out of the 1916 campaign charges against him, Ferguson vetoed practically the entire appropriation for the university for the next two years. Powerful friends of the university joined Ferguson's political enemies to demand that the governor be impeached. In July 1917 Ferguson appeared before the Travis County grand jury to answer charges made against him and was indicted on nine counts of violating the law, seven of them having to do with misapplication of public funds. Speaker F. O. Fuller, using a power constitutionally reserved for the governor, called the legislature into session to consider impeachment. Ferguson countered with a call for a special session to appropriate funds for the university.

On August 1, 1917, the legislature convened and Speaker Fuller presented thirteen charges against the governor. After investigation, the house of representatives voted twenty-one articles of impeachment against the governor. The senate sat as a court to determine the truth or falsity of the articles of impeachment. Upon conviction it would be the duty of the senate to decide the penalty to be imposed.

Crowds filled the senate galleries, and newspapers across the state carried the latest news of the impeachment hearings. On September 4, 1917, Jim Ferguson was found guilty on ten of the twenty-one articles of impeachment. The senate found that he had used improper means of influencing state officials;

had made improper use of state funds; had deposited large sums of money in banks in which he had an interest, including sixty thousand dollars in the Temple State Bank; and had refused to reveal the source of some $156,500 in campaign funds. The Committee on Civil Jurisprudence of the senate filed two reports in recommending the appropriate punishment for the governor. The majority report recommended the governor's removal from office and disqualification from holding any office "of honor, trust, or profit under the State of Texas." The minority report recommended removal only. The senate adopted the majority report, and Ferguson was removed from office and disqualified from further office holding. In a futile gesture, Governor Ferguson resigned the day before the judgment was announced, saying that since he was no longer governor, he could not be convicted, and therefore could not be barred from holding office in the future. He remained a major force in Texas politics, backing candidates in every election from 1918 to 1936.

World War I

The Road to War. A few weeks before the impeachment proceedings the United States had gone to war against Germany and her allies. Texans had been sympathetic toward the cause of the French and the English since early in the conflict. In 1915, when the ocean liner *Lusitania* was sunk by a German submarine, 128 Americans were among the 1,198 killed. The Texas Senate considered a resolution asking that the nation sever diplomatic relations with Germany. Increased submarine activity stirred the entire nation. Even before America's entry into the war, Royal Canadian Flying Corps student pilots were training at three Fort Worth airfields: Benbrook, Hicks, and Everman.

The war was coming closer to the United States. On January 22, 1917, President Wilson had called for "peace without victory," hoping the belligerents could back out of the war. Shortly thereafter, Germany announced that she would resume unrestricted submarine warfare. Wilson broke off diplomatic relations with Germany and asked Congress to arm all American merchant ships. On March 1 the State Department made public a telegram from the German foreign minister, Alfred Zimmermann, to the German ambassador to Mexico. Germany proposed an alliance with Mexico against the United States in case of war. In exchange for her cooperation, Mexico was to regain Texas, New Mexico, and Arizona.

On the evening of April 2 the president appeared before a joint session of Congress to ask for a declaration of war. "We will not choose the path of submission," he declared, and received a five-minute ovation from Congress. The Bolshevik Revolution gave added meaning to Wilson's request for a world "made safe for democracy." Four days after the president had delivered his war message, Congress declared that the United States was at war with Germany. John Nance Garner, Texas congressman from Uvalde, served as Wilson's liaison with the House of Representatives throughout the war. Garner's son, Tully, said he intended to enlist, and his father answered, "I couldn't have voted to send other boys to war, if I hadn't known I was sending my own."

President Wilson also felt the tremendous responsibility of leading the nation into war.

For awhile he sat pale in the Cabinet Room. At last he said: "Think what it was they were applauding. . . . My message today was a message of death for our young men. How strange it seems to applaud that. . . ." For a moment he paused and then went on. "I want to read you the letter I received from this fine old man." As he read, the emotion he felt at the tender sympathy which the words conveyed gripped him . . . "That man understood me and sympathized."

As he said this, the President drew his handkerchief from his pocket and wiped away great tears that stood in his eyes, and laying his head on the cabinet table, sobbed as if he had been a child.[1]

Preparing for War. When the war began, about two hundred thousand men made up the American army. Fifty-five flimsy

[1]Joseph Tumulty, *Woodrow Wilson as I Know Him* (New York: Doubleday, Page and Company, 1921), 256-59.

airplanes and 130 pilots made up America's air power. Although many favored a volunteer army, it was immediately apparent that conscription was necessary. On registration day 417,689 Texans between the ages of twenty-one and thirty-one registered with their local draft boards. By the summer of 1918 the draft ages were from eighteen to forty-five. In all 989,571 Texans entered their names on the draft rolls, and 197,789 Texans served in the army, navy, and marines. Women nurses numbered 449.

Texas's climate and terrain made her an excellent training ground. By the summer of 1918, one-seventh of the United States Army, a quarter of a million men, was stationed in Texas. Fort Sam Houston at San Antonio and Fort Bliss at El Paso remained important military posts, but existing facilities were not adequate for the troops pouring into the state. Camp Mac-Arthur at Waco, Camp Logan at Houston, Camp Travis at San Antonio, and Camp Bowie at Fort Worth were constructed. Some one hundred thousand men trained at Camp Bowie alone, including the Thirty-sixth Division, composed mainly of Texans.

Kelly Field at San Antonio became the largest aviation training center in the nation. Officers trained at the Leon Springs Training Camp. A school for automobile units and military aeronautics was set up at Camp Mabry in Austin. In October 1917 the Department of War announced contracts for twenty thousand airplanes.

For many Texans, World War I brought the first glimpse of an airplane, which was a major event. In 1911 an airplane had landed at Midland, inspiring a Czech immigrant, John Pliska, to build an airplane in his blacksmith shop. Pliska needed money to purchase the engine and appealed to family and friends. His father-in-law sent word that he should stay on the ground and make a living for his family, because he could not make a living in the air.

The air force of the United States had its beginnings in Texas. The airplane that constituted the total airpower of the United States reached Fort Sam Houston in February 1910. Lieutenant Benjamin Delahant Foulois, the son of French immigrants, was ordered to teach himself to fly, and on March 4,

Unprepared for war, the United States at first housed troops in temporary quarters like these at Camp Mabry in Austin.

1911, flew the 116 miles between Eagle Pass and Laredo in two hours, seven minutes to set a world speed record. The eight planes in Foulois's unit were sent into Mexico with Pershing. Within six weeks they had fallen apart, but the experience proved valuable in World War I. Foulois commanded the United States Army Air Corps from 1931 to 1935 and retired as a major general.

"Over There." Texans were marching to war. A Czech immigrant to Texas, Dominik Naplava, tried to enlist when the war broke out, but he was rejected because he was not a United States citizen. Naplava left his adopted city, Houston, and enlisted in the Canadian army. He fell in France in November 1917, the first Texan to die in World War I. The Polish former mayor of Brownsville, Benjamin Kowalski, had six sons in the army, four of whom became officers. Thirty thousand Negro troops from Texas served in the armed forces during World War I. Spencer Cornelius Dickerson of Austin, a graduate of Tillotson College and Rush Medical College, signed up as a medical corps officer and served with the Allied Expeditionary Force in France. Dickerson, later promoted to brigadier general, was the first Negro born in Texas to be named a general in the United States Army.

The Thirty-sixth Division, composed mainly of Texans, reached France in May 1918. It was in combat only 23 days

265

but sustained 2,601 casualties. The Ninetieth Division, nicknamed the "Tough 'Ombres" (because of the T-O shoulder patch), arrived in Europe in the summer of 1918. At St. Mihiel and the Meuse-Argonne, it lost 310 officers and 9,400 enlisted men. After the war the Ninetieth Division had occupation duty in Germany. In April 1918 President Wilson asked Texas to recruit more cavalry, and General Jake Wolters and General R. H. McDill commanded the new brigades.

In late October 1918 the Germans asked for terms of surrender. The armistice which went into effect on November 11, 1918, ended the fighting. Texans were awakened at three o'clock in the morning by the firing of shotguns, the blowing of locomotive and factory whistles, and the honking of automobile horns. People jammed the streets of Texas towns celebrating the return of peace.

The Postwar Years

"Johnny Comes Marching Home." When the armistice was signed, 4 million Americans were in uniform. By April 1919 four thousand were being discharged each day. Except for the twenty thousand soldiers on occupation duty in Germany, which included the Ninetieth Division, the entire American Expeditionary Force was home by January 1920. Five thousand Texas servicemen did not return. Some of Texas's finest young men died in the war, but those who survived returned home with a greater sense of nationality than before. They had had an opportunity to see other parts of the country and know Americans from other sections.

Wilson and the League of Nations. Almost a year before the end of the war, Wilson had presented to Congress the Fourteen Points, his plan for a just peace and the elimination of the causes of war. Wilson advocated open diplomacy, free trade, freedom of the seas, a halt to the arms race, an end to imperialism, and a League of Nations. Wilson went to the Versailles Peace Conference in France determined that the League of Nations be incorporated into the treaty. He believed that the League was the best means for settling international disputes. The League of Nations was the only one of the

Fourteen Points accepted by the other major powers. The Texas legislature urged that the Senate ratify the Treaty of Versailles and join the League.

President Wilson returned to the United States to find unexpected opposition. When he realized that the Senate would not approve the Treaty of Versailles, he decided to take the issue to the people. He traveled nine thousand miles by special train, making speeches from Columbus, Ohio, to Seattle, San Francisco, and Los Angeles and back to Salt Lake City.

On September 25, 1919, at Pueblo, Colorado, the president halted several times during his speech. The extensive tour had broken his health, and he returned to the nation's capital suffering from a stroke which partially paralyzed him, forcing him to give up the fight for the treaty. The Senate turned down the Treaty of Versailles and the League of Nations. In the election of 1920 the nation chose a Republican president, Warren G. Harding, turning from the reforms of the progressive era.

Women Gain the Right To Vote. The census of Texas in 1920 showed over 4.5 million people residing in the state, almost one-third in towns. The war years had required the building of roads to move troops and matériel. The trucking industry had come into being, and other industries had developed. Texas led the nation in the production of oil, wheat, corn, meat, and rice. It ranked third in the production of cotton. The war had stimulated the economy and improved the situation of the farmers.

Prohibition had become a reality across the nation, but it was proving difficult to enforce. Crime, corruption, and a general disrespect for law followed in its wake. The Nineteenth Amendment, ratified in 1920, gave women the right to vote.

England had passed the first women's suffrage bill in 1916, encouraging feminists and other groups who had been urging Congress to grant women the right to vote since the nineteenth century. However, many Texans still believed that a woman's place was in the home, not in the voting booth. Marfa rancher L. C. Brite told a group of ladies, "Women, should you enter politics, who will wash the dishes and burn the bread, sweep the floor and fuss over us carrying in mud, take care of the house, lock the door and lose the key, attend the History Club and feed us on cold biscuits?" The feminist Carrie Chapman Catt had led a group of women who hissed Governor Jim Ferguson when he delivered the minority report against women's suffrage at the Democratic National Convention in 1916. However, Ferguson was probably glad to see women voting in 1924, when they helped place his wife in the Texas governor's chair. Texas's first female public official was elected in 1918, when Annie Webb Blanton became the state superintendent of public instruction.

Governor Will P. Hobby, who had succeeded to the governorship upon Ferguson's removal from office, sought a term of his own in 1918. The campaign was bitter. Ex-governor Ferguson had filed as a candidate, ignoring the fact that the impeachment judgment disqualified him. His enemies revived all the charges that had been used against him in the impeachment proceedings. Hobby stood on his record as the interim governor—ratification of the prohibition amendment, aid to drought-stricken communities, establishment of the run-off primary, and women's suffrage in primary elections.

Hobby felt that he was entitled to a second term, and Ferguson was asking for vindication by the people. Hobby met Ferguson's charges that he was a "governor by accident" by promising increased aid to "get the farmer out of the mud," aid to county schools, and free textbooks. Hobby, with a background as editor of the *Houston Post* and the *Beaumont Enterprise*, defeated Jim Ferguson, carrying 234 counties to Ferguson's 20 counties in the primary.

Hobby appealed to Texans' pride in their war effort when the legislature convened in 1919. He urged them now to support the state's program for education: "If Texas should have to go broke, let it be for the sake of education." The legislature responded with aid to education, a tax on oil and oil products, the creation of the State Board of Control to regulate purchasing of goods and supplies for the state, and a proposal for a constitutional convention. Although both prohibition and women's suffrage were approved, Texas voters turned down the proposition calling for constitutional revision.

The war years were a time of idealism and reform when it seemed as if all things might be possible through courage and sacrifice and love of justice. Americans sought, by shedding their blood in Europe, to make the world safe for virtue. Women were given the right to vote. A mighty effort was made to elevate society by proscribing alcoholic beverages. But the efforts to improve man's lot carried within them the seeds of failure. The United States, perhaps in reaction to her venture into the affairs of Europe, retreated behind her oceans and would not join the League of Nations. Because of inadequate policing of prohibition, disrespect for the law was developing. Then vigilantes came forth wearing hoods and robes and broke the law in the name of enforcing law and morals.

Discuss

1. To what factors do you attribute James E. Ferguson's political success?

2. Why did the sympathies of most Americans lie with Britain and France in their struggle with Germany?

3. How do you think the Zimmermann telegram affected public opinion in Texas?

4. What role did Texas play in World War I?

5. Assess the importance of legislation affecting education passed during James E. Ferguson's term in office.

Identify

impeachment
Lieutenant Benjamin D. Foulois
Spencer Cornelius Dickerson

conscription
John Pliska
Will P. Hobby
suffrage

INCREASED USE OF MACHINERY ALLOWED FARMERS
RAISE PRODUCTION IN THE 1920S, BUT PROSPERITY ST
ELUDED THEM.

CHAPTER 16

"A Turning Point"

During the war years and the 1920s the High Plains of Texas, once the grazing land for Texas cattle, were turned into flourishing wheat fields. The treeless, level land was perfectly suited to large-scale, mechanized farming. Irrigation on the South Plains opened that area to cotton. West Texas land planted in cotton grew from forty-five thousand acres in 1909 to 2.3 million acres in 1924. Cotton production rose from fifty thousand bales in 1918 to 1.1 million bales in 1924.

Cattle ranching shifted to the Coastal Plains, the Edwards Plateau, and the Mountains and Basins. Sheep and goat raising increased on the Edwards Plateau. The Lower Rio Grande Valley blossomed with citrus trees, some 750,000 by 1925. The oil industry was growing and the production of sulfur booming. All of these things were part of the great changes in the economy of Texas and the nation that Governor Pat Neff called "a turning point in civilization."

The Roaring Twenties

The Desire for Normalcy. After the stress of World War I and the reforms of the Wilson era, the American people yearned for what President Harding called "a return to normalcy." Disillusionment with the postwar world insured a Republican victory in 1920, and during the 1920s Republican administrations under Presidents Harding, Coolidge, and Hoover fostered a climate of business growth that resulted in unprecedented economic expansion. Warren G. Harding carried the 1920 presidential election by 16 million votes to Democrat James Cox's 9 million. His administration was characterized by scandals such as the Teapot Dome fraud. Harding's secretary of the interior, Albert Fall, leased government oil reserves to private oil companies and received money from them for doing so. Although Harding was innocent of corruption, key figures in his administration were involved.

The gubernatorial election of 1920 in Texas held a surprise. Ex-senator Joseph W. Bailey announced that he would resume his political career and came out of retirement to run for governor. His platform reflected his growing conservatism; he was determined to lead Texas back "into the straight and narrow path." He spoke out against unions, prohibition, suffrage for women, the League of Nations, Wilson's administration, socialism, and high taxes. Bailey faced Robert E. Thomason of Gainesville and Benjamin F. Looney of Marion County, a former state attorney general. In addition, Pat Neff of Waco, a prohibitionist and a prominent Baptist layman, announced that he would seek the office. All of Bailey's opponents were progressives and Wilson men. Neff advocated an ambitious highway building program, increased state parks, and water conservation. Former governor Jim Ferguson announced for president of the United States on the platform of his newly founded American party.

No candidate received a majority of the votes, so Neff met Bailey in a runoff primary as provided by the amended election laws of 1918. Bailey campaigned for a return to old-fashioned values and condemned such dances as the bunny hug and the foxtrot and such songs as "Oh, You Beautiful Doll!"

Neff scorned Bailey's nostalgia and read from the *Congressional Record* a Bailey speech stating that automobiles should not be allowed on Washington streets. Bailey was, Neff said, opposed to the twentieth century. Neff carried three-fourths of the counties.

Governor Neff advocated the improvement of rural schools, an expanded highway building program, and more effective law enforcement. However, he and the legislature were generally at odds. He did manage to get an appropriation bill for The University of Texas to enlarge its campus and $2.5 million for rural schools. Neff tried to enforce prohibition, but he had no more success than the others whose job it was to enforce that law.

A Time of Fear. Americans were trying to adjust to a multitude of changed conditions in the 1920s. The prohibition experiment was not working, and lawlessness in parts of the country was out of control. The news from Russia was still

Texas Collection, Barker Texas History Center

Described as "a model one-room building," this Brazoria County school suffered from a lack of facilities despite legislation recommended by Governor Neff.

273

alarming, and some anarchists and other radicals seemed bent on revolution in the United States. There developed a growing tension that burst forth in intolerance, nativism, and racism. Many people began to think that the social problems of urban life were caused by immigration. Acts establishing quotas for immigrants from certain countries were passed.

A fear of Communists and Socialists resulted in raids on anarchists, radicals, and others. Led by Attorney General A. Mitchell Palmer, federal agents deported over five hundred aliens and rounded up more than three thousand as suspected Communists. Bombings and strikes increased the fear and suspicion. Many people became suspect who criticized the American way of life or the business ethics of the country. Industrialists used the public's fear of anarchism and Communism against the labor unions. Union membership declined. Laws against anarchy, censorship of books and films, and loyalty oaths for teachers followed in the wake of fear and prejudice. Espionage and sedition acts were passed in 1917 and 1918, although Supreme Court justice Oliver Wendell Holmes, Jr., defended the right of free expression unless there existed a "clear and present danger" to the country.

Labor Strife. When Boston police struck to gain recognition for their union, there was disorder in the city. Massachusetts governor Calvin Coolidge, later to become president of the United States, sent in the National Guard on the third day of the strike. He wired American Federation of Labor president Samuel Gompers, "There is no right to strike against the public safety by anybody, anytime, anywhere."

Strikebreakers moved against the longshoremen striking against the steamship lines in Galveston in 1920. Violence broke out. Governor Will Hobby declared martial law, and the National Guard moved to Galveston. General Jacob Wolters forbade the sale or the carrying of firearms. Groups were forbidden to congregate in the city's streets, and loiterers were arrested. In early July some five hundred guardsmen still remained. Governor Hobby suspended the police since they failed to keep order. The mayor, members of the city commission, and the city attorney were permitted to continue their duties, but they could exercise no authority under the penal

274

laws. The legislature had passed the Open Port Law authorizing the governor to assume special jurisdiction over any area where there was interference with the transportation of goods.

In 1922 railway shopmen went on strike. Trouble developed between strikers and strikebreakers in Denison, Houston, and other cities. Governor Neff sent Rangers into Denison first, then the National Guard as disorder increased. Martial law continued in Denison until October 22, when the Open Port Law was substituted. Rangers had been in other cities under that act because of the railway strike. In 1926 the Open Port Law was held unconstitutional.

The New Klan. In 1915 *The Birth of a Nation,* a current movie, made heroes of post–Civil War Klansmen. On Thanksgiving night of the same year, William Simmons and thirty other men burned a cross on Georgia's Stone Mountain and pledged allegiance to the Invisible Empire of the Knights of the Ku Klux Klan. The Klan's membership grew from a few thousand in 1920 to 4 or 5 million in 1925. The greater part of this increase occurred while Hiram Evans, a Dallas dentist, was Imperial Wizard, the national leader of the Klan.

The Klan preached hatred of Jews, Negroes, and Catholics. Masquerading in bedsheets and hoods, surrounding themselves with secret grips and passwords, Klansmen held processions and meetings and passed judgment on their neighbors. When masked and in groups, they practiced violence. Otherwise they used pressure tactics. A Catholic or Jewish merchant might find his store boycotted. A minister might find his congregation had been warned away from him. A Negro might find a cross burned in his yard. Teachers were persecuted for their teachings. The Klan fast became a political force.

Klansman Z. R. Upchurch arrived in September 1920 to organize Texas. Local kleagles (Klan recruiters) enrolled Houston citizens, and the oil town of Humble north of Houston became the second Klan town in Texas. Goose Creek, Beaumont, Wharton County, and Galveston soon followed. In the Texas House of Representatives, Congressman Wright Patman introduced a resolution attacking the Klan, but it was tabled indefinitely. The *Houston Chronicle* said, "Texas Klans-

The Ku Klux Klan had a ladies' auxiliary. These Klan women paraded in 1923 in Texas.

men have beaten and blacked more people in the last six months than all the other states combined."

The Klan entered local politics to control law enforcement in towns and counties. It sought to elect sheriffs, mayors, prosecuting attorneys, and judges. Racial antagonism did not seem to be the prime reason for membership in Texas. Texas Klansmen seemed mainly interested in minding the business of others, probably in response to the breakdown in law enforcement engendered by prohibition. Most Klan violence in Texas was against whites who bootlegged or failed to support their families or otherwise failed to live up to the moral standards of those who hid their faces behind masks.

In the 1922 primary Earle B. Mayfield announced for the Senate seat then held by the elderly Charles A. Culberson, who sought a fifth term. Former governor James E. Ferguson entered the race, denouncing Mayfield as the "Klandidate" and "crown prince of the Klan." Texas voters had a choice of five candidates, and Mayfield led in the first primary and defeated

Ferguson in the runoff. Commenting on the election, the *New York World* stated, "Viewed from a distance, the choice between Mayfield, sponsored by the Ku Klux Klan and the Anti-Saloon League, and Ferguson, who was impeached while serving as governor, must have been a hard one."

In 1924 the Dallas State Fair observed Ku Klux Klan Day, and between seventy-five thousand and two hundred thousand Klansmen attended. Hiram Wesley Evans and other Grand Dragons of the invisible empire set up headquarters at the 1924 national conventions to help select presidential candidates. The Democrats split over whether their platform should condemn the Klan by name or in general terms. The controversy carried over into the nominations, and 103 ballots were needed to choose John W. Davis to oppose President Calvin Coolidge and Progressive candidate Robert La Follette.

The Fergusons Return

By 1924, with Mayfield in the United States Senate, the Klan was ready to back a candidate for governor. District Judge Felix D. Robertson had Klan support. Although James E. Ferguson had been removed from the governor's office, his wife could serve.

"Me for Ma." In 1923, while the lieutenant governor was absent, Jim Ferguson's supporters had pushed through the Texas Senate a resolution nullifying his impeachment. Upon the return of Lieutenant Governor Davidson anti-Ferguson forces repealed the resolution. The *Fort Worth Star-Telegram* ran the headline, "Ferguson Citizen for 30 Minutes!" The Ferguson forces took the issue to court, but failed to win the right to enter his name on the ballot.

Ferguson used his weekly broadside, the *Ferguson Forum*, to keep his "boys at the forks of the creeks" lined up to vote as soon as the Ferguson name appeared on the ballot. Shirtless and sitting on a hotel bed in Taylor, Jim Ferguson announced to the press that his wife was a candidate for governor in the 1924 primary. Miriam Amanda Ferguson ran against Robertson, Lynch Davidson, Lieutenant Governor T. Whitfield Davidson, and five other opponents. "Ma" Ferguson, as the press soon dubbed her, ran on a platform dedicated to vindicating her husband's name. Automobiles bore bumper stickers saying, "Me for Ma—and I ain't got a dern thing against Pa!"

The Klan accused Mrs. Ferguson, an intelligent woman, of being a "kitchen drudge" unqualified to hold the state's highest office. Campaigning in a sunbonnet with Farmer Jim, Mrs. Ferguson said, "Hate has been the slogan of the opposition. Venom is its password and slander, falsehood, and misrepresentation its platform. A vote for me is a vote of confidence for my husband," she explained. Although opposition to the Klan was building across the state, the stand of the Fergusons was a courageous one, since the Klan was a violent organization. Mrs. Ferguson ran second to Robertson in the first primary. She bested the Klan candidate by almost ninety-eight thousand votes in the runoff.

The Klan retaliated by filing suit claiming that a woman could not hold state office, that her husband had claimed in the *Ferguson Forum* that he would run the state, and that Jim would collect her salary check. However, the state supreme court upheld her. Mrs. Ferguson met strong Republican op-

Texas Highway Department

The Fergusons departed the Governor's Mansion in disgrace in 1917; in 1925 they returned in triumph.

position in November 1924 but won to become the second woman governor. Nellie Tayloe Ross had taken the oath as governor of Wyoming a few weeks earlier.

Miriam Ferguson's Administration. A woman governor in Texas made headlines across the nation. Hordes of Texans flocked to the capitol to see Ma take the oath of office after having sworn that she had not fought any duels. Outgoing governor Pat Neff left Mrs. Ferguson a single white rose, an open Bible, and a picture of Woodrow Wilson. May Peterson Thompson, former star of the Metropolitan Opera and wife of Railroad Commissioner Ernest Thompson, sang "Put on Your Old Gray Bonnet," and rode an old gray mare up the capitol steps.

Only four years after the women of the United States had gained the right to vote, Texas had a woman governor, or, as Jim Ferguson put it, "two governors for the price of one." At Mrs. Ferguson's request, the legislature made it a crime to wear a mask in public, dealing a mortal blow to the Klan in Texas. One unable to conceal his identity was responsible for his acts. Without masks there was no point in belonging to the Klan, which succumbed to a well-deserved public revulsion. But lawlessness engendered by prohibition continued as a problem.

Americans had passed a law against alcohol without providing adequate law enforcement personnel. Bootlegging, moonshining, and general disrespect for the law followed. Governor Pat Neff noted that Texas with 5 million people had a thousand murders in 1922 compared to twenty-four homicides in London, England, a city of 8 million. Felons in Texas prisons increased from twenty-four hundred to thirty-eight hundred during the Neff years, many convicted of moonshining or bootlegging.

Mrs. Ferguson had campaigned on a promise of executive clemency, and her liberal use of the pardoning power came to be known as the "open door policy" at Huntsville, the site of the state prison. The executive mansion was referred to as "the House of a Thousand Pardons." Between January and May 1925, Mrs. Ferguson pardoned 353 convicts. She promised furloughs to the convicts, stating that "No dying mother shall ever plead in vain for a chance to see again the wayward, unfortunate son before death shall claim her into eternity." She granted executive clemency two thousand times in her first twenty months in office. Neff's record was 92 full pardons and 107 conditional pardons in four years. Criticism grew concerning the governor's pardoning power, and a legislative investigating committee found that Jim Ferguson passed on recommendations for pardons and that many prisoners received pardons before they entered the penitentiary. Ferguson supporters got the legislature to pass an act pardoning and making eligible to hold office anyone who had previously been removed by impeachment. For a time Jim Ferguson gained his vindication, although the act was later declared unconstitutional because the legislature did not have the power to pardon.

Mrs. Ferguson's administration also came under fire for practices relating to the construction of highways. Governor Neff had urged a strong program of highway building, and the legislature in 1925 empowered the Texas Highway Department to build and maintain an effective system of highways. Since Jim Ferguson participated in all meetings of the highway commission, charges were made of lack of competitive bidding and personal favoritism in the awarding of highway contracts. Attorney General Dan Moody from Williamson County began an investigation of corruption in the highway department.

Moody brought suit against the American Road Company and the Hoffman Construction Company, claiming that the state had paid the companies over $7 million on contracts that would cost less than $2 million to perform. While the suit against the American Road Company was pending, Governor Ferguson and the highway commission sued Moody, unsuccessfully, to enjoin him from prosecuting the action.

The suit against the American Road Company was settled by the company's refunding six hundred thousand dollars and surrendering its right to do business in Texas. A special legislative committee investigating the highway department stated that "more than six million dollars of the people's money was awarded to these two firms, or companies, without competitive bids, and practically in secret. Had these particular contracts been let to the lowest and best bidder, there is no doubt that the same could have been bid in at a price practically one-third of that paid by the state."

Moody Versus Fergusonism

It was apparent early in Mrs. Ferguson's term that she would face heavy opposition in her bid for reelection. Many Texans felt the Fergusons had already had the traditional two terms. She had at first stated that she would not seek a second term, since her only purpose had been to vindicate her husband's name, and her election had done that. But when the courts invalidated the act granting amnesty to impeached officials, Mrs. Ferguson declared for a second term.

Dan Moody announced that he would run against Mrs. Ferguson, denouncing "government by proxy" and claiming that he would rid the state of "Fergusonism." He ran on a platform based on judicial reform, a return of honesty to state government, the elimination of excessive pardons, and efficiency in public school administration, higher education, and the penitentiary system. However, the main issue of the campaign was getting rid of the Fergusons. Ferguson said that Moody was an "upstart," lacking experience and competence. Moody answered that the Ferguson administration had been "barren of achievements."

The field was cluttered with minor candidates, including the Reverend O. F. Zimmerman, supported by the Klan and billing himself as "Zim, the Tithing Evangelist," and Edith Wilmans, Texas's first woman legislator, who promised that she would not marry while she was governor. Although her term would not end until January 1927, in May 1926 Mrs. Ferguson stated in a campaign speech that she would resign immediately if Moody led by a single vote in the first primary, if in turn Moody would withdraw from the race if he trailed by as many as 25,000 votes. Moody accepted the challenge and then led Mrs. Ferguson by some 125,000 votes. However, Moody did not have a majority of the votes, and a runoff would be necessary unless Mrs. Ferguson resigned.

Two-thirds of the county Democratic conventions passed resolutions asking Mrs. Ferguson to resign, but she refused, saying that Moody would not have kept his part of the agreement if he had trailed in the first primary, and that she would not "turn the state over to the Ku Klux Klan." Actually, Moody had made his reputation as a Williamson County district attorney by prosecuting the Klan. Moody replied that "The Klan in Texas is as dead as the proverbial doornail." The Fergusons lost much support from people who usually backed them. In the runoff election, Moody defeated Mrs. Ferguson by 225,000 votes and in November easily defeated Republican and Socialist candidates. At the age of thirty-three, Dan Moody became Texas's youngest governor.

The Moody Administration. Rather than continue the progressive government of Jim Ferguson's first administration, Mrs. Ferguson had followed a highly conservative legislative course. Dan Moody took a progressive tack. However, his legislature chose to pass only a fraction of the legislation he proposed. Public schools received adequate appropriations, and reorganization of the school system was undertaken. The voters passed a constitutional amendment creating the State Board of Education.

During Moody's administration, graft and inefficiency were eliminated from the highway department. The prison system was reformed and reorganized, and the office of state auditor was created to bring about more efficient government. The governor and businessmen tried to lure industries and businesses to the state from the North and the East, but the depression interfered. Textbook adoptions were established on a competitive basis, and the gasoline tax was increased to finance more highways and roads.

Moody's administration suffered from the effects of the depression and from a growing conservatism in the legislature. The legislators refused to enact the system of taxation that the governor called for; they enacted no reforms in the judicial system, one of the strongest planks in Moody's campaign platform; and nothing was done toward establishing a system of civil service for state agencies. Moody's first term was a progressive one. Then the stock market crash of 1929 ended the prosperity of the 1920s, the entire nation sustained severe economic damage, and everything came to a halt.

Discuss

1. What major changes took place in Texas agriculture during the 1920s?

2. Why was there a growth in antiforeigner sentiment during the 1920s?

3. What effects did World War I and the Red Scare of the 1920s have on American civil liberties?

4. What effect did the Open Port Law have on unions?

5. What led to the rise of the Ku Klux Klan in the 1920s?

6. Why were the activities of the Ku Klux Klan difficult to control?

7. Would you have voted for Mrs. Ferguson or Judge Robertson in 1924? Why?

8. Do you agree or disagree with the Ferguson pardoning policy?

9. To what factors do you attribute Dan Moody's victory in 1926?

Identify

normalcy
Pat Neff
Ku Klux Klan
Miriam A. Ferguson
American Road Company

red scare
Open Port Law
Earle B. Mayfield
"open door policy"
Dan Moody

THE RADIO BROUGHT MUSIC, NEWS, AND SPORTS EVENTS
TO A NATION HUNGRY FOR ENTERTAINMENT.

CHAPTER 17

"The Brave Endure"

The time before the Great Depression was one of tremendous growth and development. The so-called Coolidge prosperity was based upon generally good business stimulated further by innovations and inventions such as radio, the automobile, and the uses of electricity. Productivity grew and the future seemed bright. The exuberance was reflected by the stock market. As the number of Americans who traded in common stocks increased, prices reached unrealistic levels, and the economy became quite vulnerable.

Texans registered 331,721 motor vehicles in 1919; the figure was 1,376,427 a decade later. With automobiles and improved streets and roads came filling stations, garages, auto parts businesses, and tourist courts. Other economic changes occurred. No longer did businesses have to be downtown. The new national consciousness and improved transportation accelerated the extension of retail businesses into the state. Chain stores came to Texas using such innovations as self-service, cash and carry, and advertising. Billboards and advertising in magazines and newspapers and on the radio accelerated specialization. Local wholesale grocers ceased making candy or roasting coffee or peanuts and began selling national brands.

Prosperous Years

America's New Toy. In 1920 Dr. Frank Conrad of the Westinghouse Company in Pittsburgh played phonograph music and reported baseball scores over a wireless radio he used for research, and a newspaper began advertising supplies for the amateur operators who picked up Dr. Conrad's broadcasts. Westinghouse then decided a broadcasting station would stimulate sales of their equipment, and KDKA went on the air from East Pittsburgh on November 2, 1920, to report the results of the Harding-Cox election.

However, a Dallas station may have preceded KDKA. WRR, owned by the city, broadcast fire alarms to trucks equipped with radio receivers, and in 1919 or 1920 the operators began playing phonograph records between fire calls. In 1921 Harold Hough, circulation manager for the *Fort Worth Star-Telegram,* urged his employer, Amon Carter, to go into radio broadcasting. Carter agreed to risk three hundred dollars on the venture, and Hough went to Washington to obtain a station license. Herbert Hoover, secretary of commerce, issued the license to the new station and assigned it the call letters WBAP. The letters, Hoover said, stood for "We Bring a Program," and WBAP began broadcasting in 1921, signaling the opening and closing of each program with the ringing of a cowbell.

The radio boom was on when radio station WFAA of Dallas began broadcasting in June 1922. Radio advertising soared from $60 million across the nation in 1922 to $842 million in 1929. And radio brought with it a rising interest in sports. In July 1921 two hundred thousand people tuned in to hear the Jack Dempsey–Georges Carpentier boxing match. By 1929 millions were tuning in each evening to "Amos 'n Andy."

Heroes—in the Air, on the Field, and in the Ring. On the morning of May 20, 1927, a small, silver plane, the *Spirit of St.*

Louis, left Roosevelt Field, Long Island, for a flight across the Atlantic Ocean. With one engine, no radio, and few navigational instruments, Charles A. Lindbergh averaged over one hundred miles an hour to land at Le Bourget Airfield in France in 33½ hours—the first man to fly alone from New York to Paris. President Coolidge awarded Lindbergh the Distinguished Flying Cross and promoted him to colonel in the army reserve. People lionized Lindbergh on both sides of the Atlantic.

Americans found other heroes in the boxing ring, on the baseball diamond, and on the gridiron. More than eighty thousand people filled New York's Polo Grounds in 1923 to watch Jack Dempsey defeat Louis Firpo, "the Wild Bull of the Pampas." Dempsey had won the heavyweight championship in 1919 from Jess Willard, who had won it from Jack Johnson of Galveston.

Jack Johnson was the first Negro heavyweight champion. He had to leave home to pursue his career because boxing was illegal in Texas. He won the heavyweight title from Tommy Burns at Sydney, Australia, in 1908. James J. Jeffries had retired undefeated, and George L. ("Tex") Rickard of Clay County matched Jeffries and Johnson in a 1910 bout which Johnson won. Johnson held the heavyweight title until 1915. A successful Broadway play, *The Great White Hope,* was based upon his career.

The promoter who arranged Jack Johnson's first fight was Albert Lasker, a Galveston Jew who later became the founder of modern advertising and launched such products as Lucky Strikes and Pepsodent. The greatest promoter of the 1920s and manager of Madison Square Garden was Tex Rickard, a former deputy United States marshal and gold prospector in the Klondike.

Babe Ruth hit sixty home runs in 1927. Rogers Hornsby from Winters won his first National League batting championship in 1920 and went on to win six more, setting the twentieth century record of .424 with the St. Louis Cardinals in 1924. Hornsby became a successful manager and was voted the greatest second baseman in history. The Cleveland Indians, managed by Tris Speaker of Hubbard, won the World Series in 1920. Speaker was one of the best defensive outfielders of

Texas football has long been marked by traditional rivalries. Texas and SMU played to a 7–7 tie in this 1934 contest.

all time. He had a lifetime batting average of .344 and accumulated a record 793 doubles in his career. Both Hornsby and Speaker have been inducted into the Baseball Hall of Fame.

Texas football came into its own during the depression. The Heisman Trophy, football's most prestigious award, was established honoring Rice coach John Heisman. In 1930 Baylor University's Barton Koch became the first all-American player from Texas. At the close of the 1935 season both Texas Christian University and Southern Methodist University were undefeated when they met. With the score tied, SMU Mustang Bob Finley threw a fourth down pass to all-American Bobby Wilson to win the game. SMU played in the Rose Bowl the following New Year's Day, and TCU, led by Sammy Baugh, beat Louisiana State University in the Sugar Bowl. The Football Writers Association later voted Baugh the all-time outstanding college quarterback. A former SMU star, Gerald Mann, served as Texas secretary of state in 1935 and as attorney general from 1939 to 1941.

Thousands followed Bobby Jones's golfing career, and many Texans began to play golf. Ben Hogan began his successful

288

golfing career as a caddy at Fort Worth's Glen Garden Country Club. By 1932 he was making the golf circuits as a professional. Times were hard, and he was broke and living on oranges when he won sixth place in a 1938 tournament. In 1940 he was golf's leading money winner, and he returned to the top of the ranks four more times. He won the United States Open Golf Tournament four times. Hogan was elected to the Professional Golf Association's Hall of Fame and was joined by Byron Nelson from Denton and Jimmy Demaret from Houston, each of whom won the Masters Tournament at least twice.

In 1950 the Associated Press named Mildred ("Babe") Didriksen Zaharias of Beaumont the "Woman Athlete of the Century." The daughter of parents born in Norway, Babe won the AP award as "Woman Athlete of the Year" six times. She dominated women's professional golf in the United States after having excelled in almost every sport. In the 1932 Olympics she set records in the javelin throw and in the eighty-meter hurdles. The year before, at the women's track and field championships in Evanston, Illinois, eighteen-year-old Babe had constituted the Dallas "team" which won the meet. She earned a total of thirty points and broke three Olympic records. The second place team, composed of twenty members, accumulated twenty-two points.

Keeping Cool with Coolidge. With the death of President Harding in 1923, Calvin Coolidge became president of the United States. His was a relaxed administration that suited the times. He ignored the League of Nations and adopted a probusiness, isolationist policy. Americans spoke of Coolidge prosperity in referring to the good times. In 1924 Coolidge won a full term.

One group failed to share in Coolidge prosperity. The loss of wartime markets, overproduction, and higher tariffs seriously injured the farmers. Congress passed the McNary-Haugen bill providing for the government to buy surplus crops and to sell them overseas, but Coolidge vetoed the bill. Coolidge also vetoed the bill establishing a government corporation to operate the Muscle Shoals properties on the Tennessee River. These had been built during World War I, and their operation would furnish local employment and electric power to people in need of both. The contest had been over whether the facilities should be operated by private industry or government. Coolidge's veto evidenced his belief that the government should be kept out of business.

Mexican-American Organizations. As a border state, Texas faced a special problem. The number of migratory agricultural workers had grown, and this vital part of the Texas economy was especially hard hit by the decline in agriculture.

As early as the 1890s Mexican Americans and Mexicans were following the cotton harvest in Texas. They traveled the state harvesting the crops, usually returning to their homes in the slack seasons. As farm mechanization increased and tenant farming declined, the number of migrant workers grew. The increased production of citrus fruits and vegetables in the Rio Grande Valley also increased the number of migrant workers.

At the beginning of the twentieth century 68,000 Mexican Americans were living in Texas. By 1910 the number had increased to 124,238. Revolutions in Mexico increased the number of persons coming to Texas, and Mexican Americans gradually became the second largest ethnic group in the United States and the largest in Texas. During World War I the United States encouraged Mexicans to immigrate to work in factories and fields. There was no limit placed on immigration. Some 680,000 Mexican Americans lived in Texas in 1930. The depression caused wages to drop and jobs became harder to find. Many families returned to Mexico.

As they grew in numbers Mexican Americans began to feel a need for an active political voice in the state and the local community. Several organizations were formed. The Knights of America and the Sons of America, both of San Antonio, and Harlingen's Latin American League of the Valley met at Corpus Christi for the purpose of merging in April 1929. The new organization was named the League of United Latin American Citizens. The members organized local councils in Alice, Falfurrias, Edinburg, and Robstown. LULAC proposed to educate Mexican Americans in politics and civil rights, to create pride in their heritage, and to take positions on matters affecting its constituency. By 1932 there were forty-four local groups of LULAC supporters in the five states of the Southwest.

Felix Tijerina, national president of the League of United Latin American Citizens

In 1931 F. Valencia of San Antonio began publishing the organization's first newspaper, the *LULAC News*. Felix Tijerina of Houston served as the national president of LULAC and led the organization's program to teach Mexican-American children to speak English. LULAC also helped end the segregation of Mexican-American children in the schools and led the fight that resulted in the removal of covenants in deeds that prohibited persons of Mexican descent from purchasing land.

The organizers of LULAC established a set of goals to help the Mexican American feel a sense of pride in himself as a citizen of the United States and also in his Mexican cultural heritage. The organization stresses the importance of learning English and encourages good citizenship.

A National Convention. When Calvin Coolidge announced in August 1927, "I do not choose to run for president in 1928," the Republican party looked to Secretary of Commerce Herbert Hoover to head the party ticket. The national finance chairman of the Democratic party, Jesse Jones of Houston, announced that the Democrats would hold their national convention in Houston in 1928. No major party had held its convention in the South since the Democrats met at Charleston, South Carolina, in 1860. Houston was called upon to provide housing and food for twenty-five thousand delegates, newsmen, and visitors. Houston sold $2 million in bonds to pay for necessary improvements in the city. A six-story party headquarters building was erected, and the convention center, Sam Houston Hall, was constructed in sixty-four days.

The unity of purpose Houstonians showed in preparations did not carry over into the convention itself. Many Southerners resisted nomination of the front-runner, New York governor Alfred E. Smith. Smith was a Catholic, a Northerner, and an antiprohibitionist. In addition, he had past connections with Tammany Hall. The economic prosperity of the Harding and Coolidge administrations had diminished the prospects of the Democrats. The Democratic party was splintered into three sectional factions: the Northeast, with its immigrants and urban problems; the West, predominantly rural and somewhat radical; and the South, which had grown increasingly conservative, reflecting rural, fundamentalist concerns.

Hoping to mend the breach in the Democratic party, Smith's campaign managers looked to the South for a possible running mate. Many thought that Texas governor Dan Moody was the man. Moody spoke at the annual Jackson Day Dinner of the party in Washington. As a prohibitionist, a Protestant, and a Southerner, he would balance the ticket. However, Moody chose to run for a second term as governor. He led the Texas delegation to the national convention, served on the platform committee, and helped write the plank calling for rigid enforcement of the Volstead Act.

Although Southern states opposed all antiprohibitionist candidates, Smith was nominated for president on the first ballot. A young New York politician served as Smith's floor manager in the convention and planned his nominating speech for the governor with a radio audience in mind. The *New York Times* called Franklin Delano Roosevelt's nominating speech "a model of its kind." A Southerner, Joseph Robinson, received the vice-presidential nomination.

The Republican candidate, Herbert Clark Hoover, tried to remain neutral on prohibition but called it a "noble experiment." He seemed to have a more definite economic policy than his opponent. The prosperous Republican years helped give him a landslide vote, including five Southern states. The electoral vote went to Hoover with 444 votes to Smith's 87. The popular vote was 21 million for Hoover and 15 million for Smith. However, Smith polled twice as many votes as the Democratic candidate in 1924. For the first time in history, Texas's electoral votes went to a Republican. The Republicans also won control of both houses of Congress. Dan Moody was reelected governor, and Tom Connally won Earle Mayfield's Senate seat.

The Crash

President Herbert Hoover believed that government should aid, without hindering, the development of business. Hoover believed in rugged individualism in the business community as well as in life. Business was booming. Manufacturers were pouring profits into new plants; more goods and services were demanded by the consumer; wages were high. The foreign investments of the United States in 1929 totaled $7 billion. Trade associations were increasing, and businesses were merging to the degree that by 1930, two hundred corporations owned nearly half of the country's corporate wealth.

Nineteen twenty-nine was the end of an era: the deaths that year indicated as much. Charles Goodnight, born the day before the Alamo fell, died in Tucson. He had been Ranger, trail blazer, cattleman, and authority on all things Texan. Faustino Villa died at age 118. He had worked on Captain King's Rio Grande steamboats before moving to the ranch. At age 100 he swam the flooded Santa Gertrudis Creek to bring the mail to Robert Kleberg. A decade later he was lost for two days on the King Ranch in bitter cold, with no ill effects. He said, "The year I was born, real men were born." Tex Rickard died while promoting a fight. And Joe Bailey, trying a lawsuit, fell dead in a Sherman courtroom.

Americans were reading the novels of Ernest Hemingway, F. Scott Fitzgerald, and Sinclair Lewis. They were attending motion picture theatres to applaud Al Jolson, Mary Pickford, Douglas Fairbanks, and Charlie Chaplin. And more and more Americans were investing in the stock market.

The rising automobile industry helped enlarge and expand prosperity, and President Hoover commented, "In no nation are the fruits of accomplishment more secure." However, some economists looked askance at overexpansion in business, rising unemployment, the plight of the farmer, economic distress in other countries, and the overpricing of common stocks.

Speculation and marginal buying caught up with the stock market by fall. From September 3, 1929, to November 13, 1929, the price of stocks fell sharply. On Black Thursday, October 24, 1929, a large volume of selling caused panic. People scrambled to unload their stocks, and the market collapsed.

The crash of the stock market demonstrated that specialization and centralization of the production of goods had disadvantages as well as benefits. The impact of the stock market crash was felt immediately throughout the world. Oil and an agricultural economy helped Texans fare somewhat better than many others, but Texans learned the catastrophic results of a loss of confidence in the economic system. The man who lost his savings in the stock market was frightened, as well as poorer. He cut his spending and reduced the income of everyone with whom he did business. Businesses minimized expenditures. Producers sold fewer goods and needed fewer employees. The blight spread. People still needed goods and services, and they could still supply them. However, the distribution machinery, frightened into paralysis, simply ceased to function.

Depression Days. Many of the unemployed lived on their savings until the money ran out. The ranks of the destitute increased. A year after the crash over 4 million Americans were unemployed, and a year later the number climbed to over 7 million. By October 1932 over 11.5 million men were out of work. Many roamed the country, living in hobo jungles and riding freight trains. In 1933 the total unemployment figure climbed to 13 million. Among the employed, most earned a fraction of their predepression salaries.

Fortunately, over 40 percent of Texas's population lived on farms or in villages and could still raise part of their food. In addition, many city dwellers had parents or relatives on farms who could help. The diversity of the state's economy was also a factor in softening the impact of the depression. In addition to cotton, oil, and beef, Texas sold substantial amounts of sulfur, gas, wool, mohair, wheat, corn, grain sorghums, citrus fruit, truck farm crops, poultry, and lumber, as well as manufactured goods. By late 1933, 10 percent of the nation's families were on relief, compared to 7 percent of Texas families.

Secretary of the Treasury Andrew Mellon advised letting the depression run its course, citing the Panic of 1873 as a precedent. However, President Hoover pointed out that 75 percent of Americans farmed in 1873 compared to 30 percent at the time of the crash. The president believed that local government and private charity should support the jobless and that federal relief projects would destroy the character of the people.

Hoover set out to restore confidence in the economy by opposing such deflationary actions as reduced production and cuts in wages. He encouraged industry to build additional plants and to raise wages. He asked for a tax cut and more liberal credit to put more money in circulation. He signed the Hawley-Smoot Tariff Act, providing the highest peacetime tariff in United States history. Credit was extended through the Reconstruction Finance Corporation, which lent funds to banks, railroads, and savings and loan associations. Additional capital was provided to the Farm Loan Banks, and the Federal Home Loan Bank Act enabled many homeowners to avoid foreclosure on the mortgages on their homes. However, these measures failed to halt the downward movement of the economy.

The Sterling Administration. With Texas in the throes of the depression, a number of candidates entered the gubernatorial race of 1930. Governor Dan Moody contemplated running for a third term but stepped down in favor of Ross Sterling, the highway commission chairman and a founder of the Humble Oil and Refining Company. Sterling entered the primary opposing Miriam Ferguson, former senator Earle B. Mayfield, and eight other candidates. One minor candidate described himself as a "dripping wet," and another promised to divide Texas into five states if he was elected.

Sterling advocated tax and prison reforms and proposed to bring a businesslike administration to state government. Sterling believed it was the duty of the state to pay for highway building and proposed a bond issue to reimburse counties for money spent on roads in the state highway system. Thirty-three states had already adopted similar plans. When Mrs. Ferguson led Sterling in the first primary, Dan Moody took the stump for Sterling, citing Mrs. Ferguson's excessive pardoning record—in her last twenty-nine days in office she had pardoned 124 robbers, 127 liquor law violators, and 133 murderers—and praising Sterling's administration of the highway commission, which he had taken over after federal funds had been cut off because of mishandling of road money in Mrs. Ferguson's administration. Jim Ferguson promised that Ma would pardon two thousand more of "Moody's convicts." Ferguson also claimed that Sterling could "neither read, write, nor think." Sterling retorted, "I know enough to tell the state's money and my money apart." When the votes were counted, Ross Sterling, who often introduced himself as "the fat boy from Buffalo Bayou," had defeated Mrs. Ferguson. He easily bested his Republican opponent in the general election.

Perhaps appropriately, it was an oilman governor who had to deal with problems raised by the opening of the great East Texas Oil Field. The price of oil fell as the economy slowed and production rose. Finally Sterling sent troops to the East Texas Field to prevent excessive production and stabilize the price of crude oil. Cotton, the staple agricultural crop of the state, caused as much trouble as oil. Cotton prices fell to such a low level that the governor of Louisiana, Huey P. Long, got the legislature to forbid any cotton planting and called on other states to follow suit. The Texas legislature established a 50 percent reduction in cotton acreage, but the act was declared unconstitutional in 1932 on the ground that citizens might use their property as they pleased. The problem with the cotton market ran deeper than mere overproduction, and cotton prices fell to a thirty-three year low, five cents a pound.

Governor Sterling also ran into difficulties with his road bond proposal. The legislature refused to issue bonds to reimburse the counties, but it did provide that one-fourth of the tax on gasoline be paid to counties to reimburse them for funds spent on building roads that were part of the highway system. Sterling felt that state spending should be kept to a minimum and vetoed several appropriation bills. The tax on sulfur was raised, and taxes were authorized on cement and natural gas. A proposed state income tax failed to pass.

Texas Congressional Leaders. During the depression years, Texas voters sent men to Congress who were destined to play important roles in national affairs. Tom Connally, a graduate of Baylor University and The University of Texas Law School, served in the Texas legislature and later in the United States House of Representatives from 1917 to 1929. After defeating Senator Earle B. Mayfield in 1928, Connally served twenty-four years in the Senate. He was chairman of the Foreign Relations Committee which recommended that the United States join the United Nations.

In 1931 Richard Mifflin Kleberg was elected to the United States Congress. His ancestors included Robert Justus Kleberg, a German-born lawyer, and Richard King, son of Irish immigrant parents and founder of the King Ranch. Kingsville, on the original Santa Gertrudis grant, is the county seat of Kleberg County. Jim Wells County was named for one of Captain King's lawyers, and Alice, the county seat, was named for his daughter, Alice Gertrudis King Kleberg, the congressman's mother. Helping with Kleberg's campaign and accompanying him to Washington as his secretary was a young schoolteacher, Lyndon Baines Johnson.

Later, when Lyndon Johnson became vice-president, John Nance Garner of Uvalde, Franklin Roosevelt's vice-president, told Johnson, "The best way to survive this job is to keep your mouth shut." Garner was not always prone to follow his own advice. Coming to the United States House of Representatives in 1903, Garner made few speeches and introduced few bills. However, he fought for the graduated income tax and the Federal Reserve Act. He gained the confidence of Woodrow Wilson, who often called on him to serve as his representative with House members. During the 1920s Garner fought against the domination of government by business and against the Ku Klux Klan influence in politics. He opposed Secretary of the Treasury Andrew Mellon's plan to reduce taxes and the operation of the Muscle Shoals project by private utility companies.

Garner was the House Democratic leader in 1931, and when the Democrats won control of the House in that year he became the Speaker of the House of Representatives. Garner formed the Democratic Economy Committee to attempt to balance the budget. When economy failed to end the depression, Garner proposed a bill to increase federal spending. In 1932 New York publisher William Randolph Hearst backed Garner for the presidential nomination, and Garner defeated Franklin Delano Roosevelt by sixty thousand votes in the California primary. At the Democratic National Convention in Chicago, Texas congressman Sam Rayburn led the Garner forces, and Senator Tom Connally nominated Garner to be the Democratic candidate for president. Will Rogers led the demonstration for Garner. But Roosevelt was too strong. Garner accepted second place on the Roosevelt ticket.

The Fergusons Return. Garner's bid for the presidential nomination was not the only excitement. Jim Ferguson, noting the plight of the farmers suffering from drought and depression, announced that 1932 was a good "Ferguson year." Soon Pa and Ma were on the stump again, denouncing Sterling's administration as being run by the "big oil companies." Sterling defended his administration as "honest, responsible, businesslike government." He also charged that Ferguson was actually running for governor "behind his wife's skirts."

John Nance Garner of Uvalde served two terms as vice-president under Franklin D. Roosevelt.

Austin-Travis County Collection, Austin Public Library

Miriam A. Ferguson served a second term as governor during the depression. Her husband was again a prominent force in her administration.

When the votes were counted, Ma Ferguson had gained the governor's chair again by the narrow margin of 477,644 to 473,845. Sterling's forces asked for a recount of the vote, since one hundred counties reported more votes cast than poll taxes paid, and the poll tax was a prerequisite for voting. However, Mrs. Ferguson's right to hold office was upheld. The Republican candidate was no match for Mrs. Ferguson, and the Fergusons once more moved into the governor's mansion.

Governor Miriam Ferguson went into office for her second and last term in the midst of the depression. The state's financial condition was of primary concern, and Mrs. Ferguson proposed a sales tax to meet the state's financial obligations. When the legislature failed to pass the sales tax, Mrs. Ferguson proposed a corporate income tax. Instead, the legislature levied a tax on the value of oil and cut the appropriations of all state agencies. Congress had amended the Volstead Act to permit the sale of light wines and beer, and the legislature submitted to the voters a constitutional amendment reflecting this change.

Horse racing and prize fighting were legalized, and the Fergusons' liberal policy of pardoning convicts was again in effect. Relief bonds helped alleviate the financial distress of many citizens. The federal government's system of relief was also extended to the needy of the state.

Bank Holidays and Bonus Marchers. By March 1933 the economy had hit bottom. Business was at 50 percent of normal, and 25 percent of the labor force was unemployed. Fourteen hundred banks had failed in 1932. President Franklin D. Roosevelt issued a proclamation declaring a bank moratorium throughout the United States. This action was taken in order to avoid a financial panic. Banks and lending institutions were prohibited from paying out money to depositors and creditors. The bank holiday gave the nation's economy a breather and allowed the establishment of emergency measures to reopen the banks on sound financial bases.

As president of the United States, Franklin Delano Roosevelt's first job was to calm the fears of a nation suffering from depression. Events near the end of the Hoover administration had alarmed many people. In the summer of 1932 thousands of army veterans rode into Washington on freight cars and in trucks. The veterans demanded immediate cash payment on their army service compensation certificates, a bonus voted by Congress after World War I. Texas congressman Wright Patman supported the veterans' demands successfully in the House, but the Senate defeated the measure.

Without lodging or money, the bonus marchers set up a shantytown called Bonus City near the capitol. In August 1932 there was violence in which policemen were injured and two veterans killed. President Hoover ordered army chief of staff General Douglas MacArthur to disperse the bonus marchers. MacArthur's aide was Major Dwight D. Eisenhower. Bonus City was burned, and the marchers left Washington. In recalling the incident, Congressman Patman quoted: "He who hath mingled in the fray of duty that the brave endure must have foes."

A Stricken Nation. Franklin Delano Roosevelt was inaugurated as president of the United States on March 4, 1933. He inherited the seemingly impossible task of restoring the financial health of the nation and of restoring the nation's faith in itself. Recalling Henry David Thoreau's words, "Nothing is so much to be feared as fear," Roosevelt told the nation: "The only thing we have to fear is fear itself—nameless, unreasoning, unjustified terror which paralyzes needed efforts to convert retreat into advance." Roosevelt's New Deal had begun.

Discuss

1. How did the amusements of the 1920s reflect social and economic changes?

2. What recent developments have taken place concerning Mexican-American farm workers?

3. Why did many Texans oppose the nomination of Alfred E. Smith for president? Compare these reasons to the objectives of the Ku Klux Klan.

4. In what ways did rural Texans have an advantage over urban Texans during the depression?

5. Compare the Ferguson campaign of 1932 with the previous ones.

Identify

Coolidge prosperity
Charles A. Lindbergh
Barton Koch
LULAC
Black Thursday
Ross Sterling
John Nance Garner
bonus march

Jack Johnson
Rogers Hornsby
Ben Hogan
Felix Tijerina
Herbert Hoover
depression
Tom Connally

302

PRESIDENT ROOSEVELT VISITED TEXAS IN 1936. A BA▪
NER PROCLAIMED PREMATURELY, "PROSPERITY'S RO▪
BLOOMS AGAIN WITH ROOSEVELT."

CHAPTER 18

"A New Deal for Texas"

With the inauguration of Franklin Delano Roosevelt and the beginning of the New Deal, the nation was on the road to recovery. To the people, Roosevelt became a symbol of the ability to overcome adversity. After serving in the New York legislature and as assistant secretary of the navy under Woodrow Wilson, Roosevelt contracted crippling poliomyelitis. He was never again able to get about without a wheelchair, yet he became governor of New York and then president of the United States. When he said that he could get the country back on its feet, the American people tended to believe him.

The Road to Recovery

Roosevelt called Congress into session, and on March 9 began the so-called Hundred Days, a time of reform, relief, and recovery. Congress passed emergency banking legislation, extended aid to agriculture and industry, began monetary and housing reform, provided unemployment work relief, and legislated on the conservation of natural resources.

During the Hundred Days, Roosevelt sent to Congress relief measures surpassing anything the nation had ever seen. The Civilian Conservation Corps put unemployed youths to work planting trees, building dams, constructing bridges, and helping to fight floods and forest fires. The CCC provided employment and preserved and improved the land.

Relief funds were distributed to the states by the Federal Emergency Relief Administration, and many of the unemployed got jobs through the Civil Works Administration, set up in 1933. Young people were helped through after-school jobs

Austin-Travis County Collection, Austin Public Library

Public works projects made work for the unemployed and resulted in better public facilities, such as this building at Bastrop State Park.

304

sponsored by the National Youth Administration. Lyndon Johnson returned to serve as the federal administrator of the NYA in Texas.

Under the art and literary programs of the Works Projects Administration, artists and writers recorded the life and the times of the nation. Writers collected material for a study of each state. Public buildings across the nation were decorated with murals inspired by the social art of Mexico's José Clemente Orozco and Diego Rivera. The novels of John Dos Passos and John Steinbeck reflected something of the life of the nation. Carl Sandburg, Archibald MacLeish, and Stephen Vincent Benét were writing American verse. Grant Wood, Thomas Hart Benton, and Charles Burchfield captured American scenes on canvas, while Roy Harris, Aaron Copland, and Charles Ives wrote music that was both serious and typically American. The Negro folk music inspired George Gershwin's *Porgy and Bess.* American jazz and blues were undergoing the transformation into boogie woogie and swing.

The Artistic Texans. Texans were becoming known in the world of books, art, music, and the theater. Katherine Anne Porter from Indian Creek, Texas, published *Flowering Judas* in 1930 and followed it with *Noon Wine* and *Pale Horse, Pale Rider.* She was recognized as one of the greatest American writers of fiction.

The Texas farmer was the subject for George Sessions Perry and Dorothy Scarborough. Perry's *The Walls Rise Up* was published in 1939, and his *Hold Autumn in Your Hand,* a fine portrait of the tenant farmer, was made into a motion picture entitled *The Southerner.* Boosters of West Texas in the 1920s were shocked by the picture of farm life painted by Dorothy Scarborough in *The Wind.* Miss Scarborough also collected folk music in *On the Trail of Negro Folksongs.* When Carl Sandburg published *The American Songbag* in 1927, he inspired John and Alan Lomax to collect the folk songs of the Southwest. The Negro guitar player Huddie ("Leadbelly") Ledbetter furnished the material for *Negro Folk Songs as Sung by Lead Belly.* John and Alan Lomax collected the Negro folk tunes in *American Ballads and Folk Songs* and *Our Singing Country.* The Texas Folklore Society published "Juneteenth" by Negro folk-

J. Frank Dobie was a teacher, writer, and conversationalist; he excelled at all three.

lorist J. Mason Brewer as well as his outstanding collections of folk tales and songs.

J. Frank Dobie pioneered in recording the history and tradition of his state. Dobie published *A Vaquero of the Brush Country* in 1929 and followed it with *Coronado's Children* and *Apache Gold and Yaqui Silver*. Dobie's *A Texan in England* records his experiences at Cambridge, where he received an honorary master's degree inscribed in Latin with the words, "What he does not know about longhorn cattle, does not need to be known."

Dobie's two great friends, Roy Bedichek and Walter Prescott Webb, also made significant contributions to the literary life of the state. Austin's Town and Gown Club was the site of the lively discussions the three generated. Tramping the hill country, Roy Bedichek recorded his experiences in *Adventures with a Texas Naturalist*. The mockingbird's belligerence, the courting dance of the egret, the inquisitiveness of a raccoon—

all of these caught the imagination of the Texas naturalist, and he had the ability to make whatever interested him of interest to others. His *Karankaway Country* continues the exploration of the relationship of nature to civilization and to the values of mankind.

The power of the land to shape man's destiny was a major theme of Walter Prescott Webb, the greatest Texas historian. With a very readable style, he brought to the writing of history both a literary approach and an objective view. Ballads, songs, and folklore were among the facets of West Texas life he examined in *The Great Plains*, which was published in 1931. The effects of environment on history he dealt with in *The Great Frontier*. *Divided We Stand* and *The Texas Rangers* added to his stature. In *More Water for Texas* he advanced a plan for conservation.

Jules Bledsoe, a black Texan from Waco, sang "Old Man River" in Florenz Ziegfeld's New York production of Jerome Kern's *Show Boat* in 1928. He later played the lead in Eugene O'Neill's play *The Emperor Jones*. Bledsoe studied opera in Europe and sang roles in *Pagliacci* and *Faust*. He also composed a number of musical works. Inscribed on his tombstone in Waco is the last stanza of "Old Man River." Etta Moten from Weimar was the daughter of an African Methodist Episcopal preacher. She sang "The Carioca" in the motion picture *Flying Down to Rio* and appeared in the Warner Brothers' production of *The Gold Diggers* in 1933. She retired from the theater after singing the role of Bess in Gershwin's *Porgy and Bess* from 1942 to 1945.

Franklin Delano Roosevelt invited David Guion of Ballinger to the White House to play his version of "Home on the Range," Roosevelt's favorite song. Arturo Toscanini performed the orchestral version of Guion's "Turkey in the Straw" in Carnegie Hall. W. Lee O'Daniel, sales manager for a Fort Worth flour mill, wrote "Beautiful Texas" before deciding to run for governor. Gene Austin from Gainesville made "My Blue Heaven" a perennial favorite with people across the nation. Teddy Wilson from Austin studied at Tuskegee Institute before playing with the Louis Armstrong and Benny Goodman bands. Huddie ("Leadbelly") Ledbetter wrote "Goodnight Irene" while traveling the South with John Lomax helping to collect the folk songs of the Negro. Leadbelly and Josh White played lead guitar for Blind Lemon Jefferson of Dallas, who recorded for Paramount Records.

The guitar was a Spanish contribution, and Mexican influence showed in certain styles and songs such as "El Rancho Grande," but the Negro country blues singers were the ones who taught hillbilly and cowboy singers how to play the guitar as a lead instrument.

The first performer to make a commercial success of recording hillbilly music was Vernon Dalhart of Jefferson. Carl Sprague of Alvin was one of the first to record the songs of the cowboy. Gene Autry, born in Tioga, was discovered in Oklahoma by Will Rogers, who suggested that he make records. Autry later appeared in over one hundred cowboy movies. Tex Ritter from Panola County began his career as a choral singer at The University of Texas and became a singer for radio station KPRC in Houston in 1929. He started making movies in 1936, following the cowboy stereotype invented by Gene Autry. Leonard Slye of Ohio was a member of the Sons of the Pioneers, who appeared at the Texas Centennial. Slye went to Hollywood and made dozens of movies as Roy Rogers. He married Dale Evans of Uvalde.

Ernest Tubb began his career in San Antonio, and Bob Wills was one of W. Lee O'Daniel's original Light Crust Doughboys who went on to pioneer in western swing with the "Wabash Cannonball" and "San Antonio Rose." Depression era music inspired Texans Jim Reeves of Panola County, Hank Thompson of Waco, William ("Lefty") Frizzell of Corsicana, Jimmy Dean of Plainview, Ray Price of Perryville, Johnny Horton of Rusk, Buck Owens of Sherman, and Roger Miller, who was born in Fort Worth.

Movies caught the interest of many Texans. King Vidor from Galveston began directing silent movies and later did *Duel in the Sun* and *War and Peace*. Howard Hughes, a native of Houston and the owner of the Hughes Tool Company, produced and directed *Hell's Angels* with Jean Harlow at his RKO studios. He later made Jane Russell a star in the western *The Outlaw*. Mary Martin from Weatherford became one of the top musical stars on Broadway singing "My Heart Belongs to Daddy." Texans Joan Crawford, Ginger Rogers, and Ann Miller began movie careers as dancers. The little theater movement that swept the country in the wake of Hallie Flanagan's Federal Theatre Project found support in Texas.

But while singers and actors helped the nation forget, for a while, the conditions in the world outside the theater, the Great Depression deepened. All sorts of remedies were suggested and applied, but only slight improvement could be detected in the economy.

Bigness in Business. Unlike his trust-busting cousin Theodore, Franklin Roosevelt found that bigness in business was inevitable in a highly developed industrial state. The New Deal sought to stimulate the nation's economy through direct aid to business. Congress established the National Recovery Administration and the Public Works Administration in 1933 to promote cooperative action with business. The PWA, headed by Secretary of the Interior Harold Ickes, helped private construction companies build bridges, schools, and other permanent structures. Codes of fair competition for some two hundred industries were set up by the NRA under the leadership of General Hugh S. Johnson. Under the banner of the Blue Eagle, the NRA inaugurated a 36-hour week for laborers and a 40-hour week for clerks, a minimum wage of forty cents an hour, and prohibition of child labor.

The industry codes of fair competition were exempted from the antitrust law and set standards for industries to prevent ruinous competition. The NRA was subjected to much criticism, mostly on the grounds of price-fixing, the tendency to create giant monopolies, and the guarantee to labor of the right to bargain collectively. The advent of the NRA helped organized labor, which had suffered serious losses of membership during the 1920s.

When the Supreme Court ruled that the NRA was unconstitutional, Congress passed the National Labor Relations Act, sponsored by Senator Robert F. Wagner. The National Labor Relations Board was established to enforce the act, which prohibited employers from interfering with workers' right to organize and to engage in collective bargaining.

The Beginning of Recovery

Texans of diverse backgrounds were seeing signs of recovery. Hobart Taylor, Sr., became one of Texas's first Negro millionaires. Taylor made his fortune through investments in Houston real estate, insurance companies, and public transportation. His son, Hobart Taylor, Jr., served as chief counsel to President Johnson in 1966 and has since been the director of the Import-Export Bank of the United States.

Fred Farrell Florence, a Jewish citizen of Rusk, began his career sweeping floors at the First National Bank of Rusk. In 1920 he became one of the founders of The Guaranty National Bank, then was its president and chairman of the executive committee. Florence was one of the aggressive Dallas bankers who brought the Texas Centennial to the city in 1936. In 1956 President Dwight D. Eisenhower appointed him chairman of the banking committee in the "People-to-People" program. He was one of the few Jews to receive the Benemerenti Medal, which was awarded by Pope John XXIII. Two other members of the Jewish community in Dallas, Herbert Marcus and his sister Carrie Neiman, made Neiman-Marcus a synonym for quality merchandise throughout the country.

The first Greek winery in Texas was founded by George Dounson in his basement in 1934. Dounson's fruit wines became known throughout the nation. Max Manus, another Greek immigrant, took a job in a restaurant in New Orleans. Moving to San Antonio, he opened La Louisiane, a French restaurant now famous throughout the country.

Theodore Wu came to San Antonio as a teacher and became a merchant and owner of the Tai Shan Restaurant. Bobby Manziel, a Lebanese, became an independent oil operator in East Texas. Manziel had once fought Jack Dempsey and continued his interest in sports while establishing a business empire that included banks, hotels, and newspapers. Michel T. Halbouty, born of Lebanese parents in Beaumont, became one of the state's most successful geologists and independent oil operators. He was granted the first professional geological engineering degree from the Agricultural and Mechanical College of Texas and became an expert on the geological problems of the

310

salt dome area of the Texas Coastal Plains. Halbouty helped open oil fields from Alaska to Peru and authored a book, *Spindletop*, detailing the opening of that great field. The Lebanese family founded by Nahim Abraham continued his dry goods business in Canadian, and Nahim's son, Malouf, served his state in the house of representatives beginning in 1966. Cecil Lotief was seventeen when he arrived in America. He began as a peddler, became the owner of some department stores in four Texas cities, and served in the house of representatives from 1932 to 1936. He served as the mayor of Rotan in the 1950s.

Government and the Professions. Samuel C. Adams, Jr., a black Texan from Waco, joined the United States Department of State and served in government posts in Vietnam, Cambodia, Nigeria, and Mali. He later served as director of the Agency for International Development in Morocco. John H. Clouser was state treasurer for the National Association for the Advance-

Dr. Charles Pemberton, former consul for the Republic of Liberia

311

ment of Colored People and received the Knight of Saint Gregory award from Pope Paul. Charles Pemberton from Marshall was the first black doctor to serve in the health department of the Houston public school system. For his service as consul of the Republic of Liberia, he received the order of Knight Commander of the Humane Order of African Redemption.

George Benjamin Young became the first Negro from Texas to serve as a bishop of the African Methodist Episcopal Church, serving as bishop of Arkansas, Oklahoma, and Texas from 1934 to 1948. Annie M. Mathes of Longview was the first Negro licensed as a registered nurse in the state. She served as the first president of the Texas Colored Graduate Nurses Association and as the first public health nurse in Tarrant County.

Ethnic Organizations. Chambers of commerce and trade associations pointed the way for collective action by other groups. The League of United Latin American Citizens was not the only organization that grew out of the needs of immigrant groups. Many fraternities and associations were formed to help ethnic groups through the depression. Unico National, a service organization for Italian Americans, formed chapters at Houston, Galveston, and San Antonio, and does work with youth and civic projects.

The Southern Federation of Syrian-Lebanon-American Clubs was founded in 1931 to promote citizenship. Scholarships, among them the Bobby Manziel Award and the Kahlil Gibran Scholarship, are awarded to deserving students. Helping needy people became the task of the On Leong Merchants' Association. In 1935 when the relief rolls of Bexar County carried seventy-eight thousand names, not one was Chinese, partly because of the work of the association. The Hip Sing Association of San Antonio devotes itself to mutual assistance among its Chinese members. Mary Eng of San Antonio helped organize the Young Chinese League, a social and civic group.

Regional Planning and the Concept of Parity. In addition to measures designed to conserve and develop America's human resources, Roosevelt's New Deal reform program included the conservation of natural resources. Senator George W. Norris of Nebraska proposed the Tennessee Valley Authority concept

312

whereby the government owned and operated hydroelectric power plants on the Tennessee River. Seven states in the South received benefits from the TVA, and rural communities received power for the first time. In 1934 Tupelo, Mississippi, became the first city to purchase TVA power. Besides the distribution of power, the TVA embodied the concept of regional planning. Soil conservation, flood control, river development, fish and wildlife preserves, recreational facilities, and fertilizer production were projects sponsored by the TVA.

Inevitably, private power companies felt that the TVA was in competition with private enterprise. However, in 1936 the Supreme Court upheld the TVA's right to sell power and to set its own rates. Grand Coulee Dam and Bonneville Dam followed the establishment of the TVA. The Rural Electrification Administration strung power lines across forty-three states including Texas to bring power to the farmers.

The New Deal extended help to farmers by creating an economy of scarcity. Government aid to farmers had been sought since the days of the Grange, the Farmers' Alliance, and the Populists. Now the national government offered subsidies to farmers who agreed to reduce the number of acres they planted. The Agricultural Adjustment Act taxed meat packers and flour millers to finance the subsidies. To further cut production, thousands of acres of cotton were plowed under and millions of head of livestock were killed.

The reduction in foreign markets for American farm products and a depression coupled with droughts and dust storms meant catastrophe for the farmer. However, under the parity program adopted by the Agricultural Adjustment Administration, farm income rose from $5 billion in 1932 to over $8 billion by 1935. When the Supreme Court declared the AAA unconstitutional, Congress passed the Soil Conservation and Domestic Allotment Act to benefit farmers who ceased planting crops on worn-out land. The second AAA, created in 1938, extended aid to farmers using the parity concept. Parity was the average price of crops during the five years immediately preceding World War I. When the price of crops dropped below parity, the Commodity Credit Corporation would lend the farmer money on his crops at a level slightly below parity—

in effect, buying the crops at above market prices and holding them until the price went up. Farmers received credit through a Federal Farm Loan Act, and the Farm Security Administration purchased worn-out farms and helped farmers relocate on productive land.

Many farmers were helped, but Southern tenant farmers felt the effects of inequality in the AAA system. The local agencies of the AAA were controlled by landlords, and tenant farmers were displaced on a large scale, becoming restless seekers after work or a place to farm. The AAA was amended to provide that every tenant farmer was guaranteed his place for the life of his contract, but thousands of families loaded their possessions on carts, cars, or their backs and set out looking for work that was hard to find.

Reform from the Left. Although the people returned Roosevelt and Garner to office in 1936 and strengthened the Democratic forces in both houses of Congress, there was heavy criticism of the New Deal by conservative businessmen. In August 1934 the American Liberty League was chartered to protect the private enterprise system.

Equally severe criticism of the Roosevelt administration came from the radicals of the left. Huey P. Long, the Louisiana senator, advocated a Share Our Wealth program by which large fortunes would be broken up and each family in the United States would receive a minimum income of twenty-five hundred dollars. Share Our Wealth clubs sprang up across the United States, with the Shreveport minister Gerald L. K. Smith leading the organization by radio. Father Charles Coughlin entranced thousands of radio listeners with his broadcasts from "The Shrine of the Little Flower," calling for currency inflation and nationalization of banks, utilities, and natural resources. Francis E. Townsend promised handsome pensions to the elderly.

The need for reforms underlying these movements had to be met. Roosevelt asked Congress in 1935 to pass a Social Security Act guaranteeing old-age pensions and paid for by a tax on employees' incomes and a payroll tax on employers. Unemployment compensation and welfare services for the elderly, the blind, and dependent mothers and children were also provided.

Governor James Allred, shown here signing relief legislation, took office in the midst of the depression.

Texas's Centennial Governor. In the gubernatorial race of 1934 the Fergusons backed C. C. McDonald against the able young attorney general, James V. Allred. Six candidates entered the contest, including Tom Hunter, Clint C. Small, and Maury Hughes, whose platform called for "A New Deal for Texas." One of six brothers, each of whom became a district attorney or a judge, Allred was attorney general at the age of thirty. He sued thirty-one major oil companies for antitrust violations. Allred advocated strict control of lobbyists and the creation of a board of pardons and paroles.

Allred's powers as an orator helped him defeat his primary opponents by a narrow margin, but in the general election he received 96 percent of the votes. Vice-President John Nance Garner helped reelect Senator Tom Connally. That year the liberals in the United States House of Representatives gained a member when Maury Maverick, grandson of a Texas rancher whose name stood for unbranded cattle, went to the House. Maverick coined the term *gobbledygook* to describe bureaucratic verbosity.

315

Relief and taxes were the main problems that Allred faced as governor. Relief bonds were sold to help the state's needy, old-age pensions were inaugurated, and retirement systems were established for teachers and employees. Allred had campaigned for curtailment of the governor's pardoning power, and the Board of Pardons and Paroles was created to exercise clemency based on merit.

The legislature voted to bring together the Texas Highway Patrol and the Texas Rangers under the new Department of Public Safety. Liberal appropriations were made to both colleges and public schools. National prohibition had ended in 1933, and the Liquor Control Board was established. With Allred's support, statewide prohibition was repealed. A driver license law was passed, and a graduated tax on chain stores was enacted. Although the voters acted to provide aid to destitute children and to the blind, funds were not available for this purpose until 1941.

Although Allred's first administration had devoted much of its time to social welfare measures, the lack of funds hampered many programs. Special legislative sessions had to be called to provide funds for old-age assistance. Old-age insurance failed to cover agricultural workers, domestic servants, and many other workers, so these groups failed to benefit from the program. However, provisions were voted for a stronger workmen's compensation law.

Allred received considerable publicity during his first term as governor. The United States Chamber of Commerce voted him the nation's outstanding young man in 1935. At the Democratic National Convention in Philadelphia in 1936, Allred nominated John Nance Garner for reelection as vice-president.

The Texas Centennial. When President Franklin D. Roosevelt visited the Texas Centennial, Governor Allred was his host. The Centennial marked the state's hundredth birthday and was an event that introduced many Texans to the history of their state. Many years before the Centennial celebration, Texas governor James Stephen Hogg had proposed such an observance. As 1936 approached, a Centennial commission was appointed to organize the various events that would be held.

Dallas won the competition to act as host city for the observance by offering to invest at least $10 million in cash and property. The United States and the state of Texas each gave $3 million. At Gonzales in November 1935 the Centennial officially opened. Events were held and historical markers were dedicated across the entire state.

Governor Allred traveled the nation promoting the celebration. For six months Texans and visitors poured into Dallas, and attendance at the Centennial reached almost 13 million. At a cost of $25 million, buildings such as the Museum of Fine Arts and the Hall of State were erected to hold the exhibits and accommodate events. Dallas's neighboring city of Fort Worth advertised, "Dallas for culture; Fort Worth for fun," and opened Casa Mañana, a musical staged by Billy Rose and featuring Paul Whiteman's band.

Texas Highway Department

The San Jacinto Monument was built as part of the Centennial celebration. The Battleship *Texas* served in the D-Day invasion of Europe in World War II.

317

In Fort Worth the Will Rogers Memorial Auditorium and Coliseum were erected, and the city hall and the public library were built with federal and local funds. Although Houston failed in its bid to be the site of the Centennial exposition, the federal government awarded $1 million to the state to develop the San Jacinto Battleground and to erect the monument to those who fought at San Jacinto. Another $1.3 million was granted to the city of Houston to build the Sam Houston Coliseum.

The Centennial and the various events across the state were important to economic recovery, which depended upon jobs and the circulation of money. The construction of buildings required labor and materials. Attendants were employed at the events, and visitors drove automobiles and bought gasoline, food, and merchandise. Each dollar spent changed hands several times, so that its impact on the economy was multiplied to the extent of four or five dollars.

Allred's Second Term. Allred's popularity assured his winning the customary second term. Taxation and the revenue needed for old-age pensions were problems needing solutions. Allred advocated taxes on such natural resources as oil, gas, and sulfur, and he proposed that an income tax be levied. However, the legislature was more zealous in appropriating funds than in levying additional taxes, and the governor often had to veto appropriation bills. Despite the financial difficulties of his administration, it was a progressive one, with significant progress in social welfare and the economy. In the midst of the Great Depression Texans built roads and public facilities and businesses that would be important to their future.

Discuss

1. How did the depression stimulate literary and artistic development?

2. What influence did culture and geography have on the literary works of Texans?

318

3. To what changes in the role of government did the depression lead?

4. Compare attitudes toward government regulation of business in the 1920s and 1930s.

5. Regional environmental planning was a new idea in the 1930s. Discuss the importance of this type of planning today.

6. Do you agree or disagree with the practice of making parity payments? Why?

7. Compare the probable attitudes of the following types of people toward parity payments: an urban businessman, a housewife, a large landowner.

8. What effect did the Share Our Wealth schemes have on government programs?

9. What actions did Texas take to meet the needs of its citizens during the depression? Compare state and national actions.

10. What effect did the Texas Centennial have on the economy of the state?

Identify

New Deal	Huddie Ledbetter
CCC	J. Frank Dobie
John A. Lomax	Jules Bledsoe
PWA	NRA
Unico National	Dr. Charles Pemberton
Fred F. Florence	Hip Sing Association
Michel T. Halbouty	Cecil Lotief
parity	AAA
Social Security Act	Share Our Wealth

320

THIS GENERAL STORE OF 1938 SYMBOLIZES A FACET
THE DEPRESSION MOST PEOPLE COULD NOT UND
STAND: POVERTY IN THE MIDST OF PLENTY.

CHAPTER 19

"The Broken Lands"

Economic recovery required effort on the part of state and nation, government and business. It also required time. Many problems remained from the 1920s. The lawlessness of the prohibition era had not subsided, and with depression conditions contributing, a new generation of criminals had developed. A large part of the nation's farmland was eroded, abused, and worn out. In addition there was a severe drought in the nation's midsection. Labor unions, headed by militant leaders, moved toward a showdown with employers.

Labor

"Sit Down! Sit Down!" The NRA and later the National Labor Relations Act guaranteed to labor the right to bargain collectively, but many employers refused to recognize the unions. Impatient automobile workers dubbed the NRA the

321

"National Run Around." Strikes became more frequent as labor tried to establish itself.

Reacting to the craft-oriented American Federation of Labor, John L. Lewis, president of the United Mine Workers, led a group within the AF of L toward industrial unionism. Lewis's Committee for Industrial Organization was forced out of the AF of L in 1937 and in 1938 became the Congress of Industrial Organizations. The CIO moved to organize mass-production industries such as those devoted to automobiles, rubber, and steel, seeking higher wages and guarantees of year-round work.

The CIO met a major test of its strength in the automobile industry early in 1937 at the General Motors plants in Flint, Michigan. Charging that assembly lines were speeded up, requiring workers to work faster, the United Automobile Workers seized the plants and began a sit-down strike, sleeping in the factory and having food sent in by sympathizers. Finally General Motors agreed to bargain with the union's leaders, and the strike ended. Chrysler Corporation recognized the UAW in March, but the Ford Motor Company held out until 1941, two years after the courts had outlawed the sit-down strike. By that time the CIO had some 3 million members, and the AF of L had 4.5 million. Independent unions had roughly a million members.

Gangsters and G-men

The repeal of the Eighteenth Amendment in 1933 took away the incentive that prohibition had offered organized crime. However, lawlessness remained a major problem throughout the nation. Public attention was focused on the problem in 1932 by the kidnapping and murder of Charles A. Lindbergh's infant son. Indicative of the universal reaction to the crime, Al Capone, the prohibition era's most notorious gangster, offered a ten thousand dollar reward for the baby's return. Capone made his offer from a Chicago jail cell. The Lindbergh kidnapping case led to a public demand for stronger penal laws and more effective law enforcement.

The nation followed the exploits of desperadoes and their pursuers. "Gangbusters" was the most popular radio program,

The lawlessness of the 1930s led to the expansion of many law
enforcement agencies, including the Texas Highway Patrol.

and children saved box tops to join the Junior G-men and the
Junior Texas Rangers. In June 1933 Pretty Boy Floyd killed
four lawmen in Kansas City while trying to free a friend in
police custody. After Federal Bureau of Investigation agents
killed Floyd the new "Public Enemy Number One" was Baby
Face Nelson. The head of the FBI, J. Edgar Hoover, acquired
a nationwide reputation for the effectiveness of his agents.
George ("Machine Gun") Kelly dubbed the federal agents
G-men. He had kidnapped an Oklahoma City oilman and held
him for ransom in Wise County, Texas. On July 22, 1934,
agents of the FBI killed John Dillinger in front of Chicago's
Biograph Theatre.

Texas newspapers followed the outrages of Bonnie Parker
and Clyde Barrow. Headlines told of their killing twelve persons, among them nine law officers. Barrow had been imprisoned in the Texas penitentiary in 1930. In 1932 he met Bonnie
Parker while out on parole. After killings, robberies, and kid-
nappings in the Dallas area, they enlarged their territory.

In January 1934 Clyde Barrow freed Raymond Hamilton
and three other convicts from a Huntsville prison farm, killing
a guard in the process. Ranger captain Frank Hamer had
resigned in 1932 rather than serve under the Fergusons again.

Just after Barrow freed Hamilton, Colonel Lee Simmons, head of the Texas prison system, appointed Hamer as a special investigator with one assignment—bring in Clyde Barrow.

For 102 days Hamer pursued Barrow, living in his automobile most of the time and studying Barrow's habits. Barrow was always moving, often traveling side roads and driving as much as one thousand miles in a stretch. But Hamer was able to figure out the pattern Barrow was following. On April 1, 1934, Bonnie Parker and Clyde Barrow gunned down two highway patrolmen near Grapevine, bringing their total of murders to fourteen. Soon afterwards they killed a constable at Commerce, Oklahoma, and kidnapped the police chief.

Hamer pursued the pair into Louisiana and on May 23, 1934, with the help of local law officers and two Dallas County deputies, Hamer ambushed Bonnie and Clyde near Arcadia, Louisiana. When the smoke cleared, Texas's notorious killers lay dead. Their car held a small arsenal—three machine guns, two sawed-off shotguns, ten pistols, and five thousand rounds of ammunition.

Droughts and Dusters

From 1932 to 1936 the Great Plains from Texas to North Dakota suffered a crippling drought. Pastures and wheatfields withered and died, cattle fell dead, and a huge area of the plains became the Dust Bowl. In April 1934 the first great duster hit the Panhandle and West Texas, the north wind shipping topsoil ahead of it in the fashion of a huge emery wheel, cutting away the sparse grass and throwing dust and humus high into the air. It came without warning, bringing total, choking darkness.

When the dust storm passed four hours later, fields were littered with the bodies of suffocated birds and rabbits. Some fields had lost their soil down to the depth of a plowshare. In May a wind blowing from sixty to one hundred miles an hour and carrying tons of plains topsoil disrupted air service at Chicago and blocked the light of the sun for five hours in New York, Baltimore, and Washington. Ships in the Atlantic found that dust had settled on their decks. Some 350 million tons of plains soil had been dumped on the eastern United States and the Atlantic Ocean.

Captain Randolph B. Marcy, who explored the southern rim of the Llano Estacado in the middle of the nineteenth century, declared the plains to be uninhabitable. "It is destined in the future, as in the past," he stated, "to be the abode of wandering savages."

With the surrender of the Comanches and the passing of the buffalo, cattlemen took over the plains. In the middle 1880s overgrazing depleted the grass, leaving the soil exposed to the winds that swept the treeless plains. Then the farmers came, breaking the land and planting wheat. At the turn of the century, the XIT Ranch and other large holdings were broken into smaller pieces and sold to farmers.

Special trains brought prospective land purchasers from the Midwest into Dalhart. Overenthusiastic salesmen and over-optimistic settlers claimed that the climate had undergone a transformation. Drought had been banished from the Panhandle, they claimed, and settlers poured into the area. During World War I the demand for wheat soared, and the price reached $2.10 a bushel. Farmers believed it was their patriotic duty to raise and harvest as much wheat as possible. Tractors reduced the time it took to break the soil, and by 1917 machines

Texas Collection, Barker Texas History Center

Dust storms swept the Great Plains during the depression, adding to the farmer's woes.

325

were available that could harvest and thresh grain at the same time. The breaking of the plains was accelerated.

High winds had always blown across the plains, but the grass had held the topsoil built from thousands of years of decaying plants and animals. By 1933 much of the land had been plowed and lay uncovered for much of the year. The root systems of wheat, cotton, and corn were not as extensive as those of the prairie grass and thus were not as effective in holding the soil in place.

In the early 1900s experts at the Cheyenne Wells, Colorado, Experiment Station warned that certain steps had to be taken to keep the land from suffering permanent damage. Diversified farming was recommended to keep all the land from being exposed to the wind at the same time. However, the farmers failed to take the advice. There was money to be made in wheat farming. Other warnings from Cheyenne Wells stated: "Owing to the prevalency and tendency of high winds, methods to prevent soils blowing must often be devised and practiced. Control methods consist largely in keeping immediate soil surface rough on all cultivated land that is in crop."

Still the farmers continued to break more and more land and to plant more and more wheat. In 1918, 14 million more acres of wheat were harvested than in the previous year. Farmers invested their profits in more land each year and borrowed money for tractors and machinery. When wheat prices began to fall in the 1920s, farmers broke more land and planted more wheat to cover their debt payments, many times creating new debts and driving the price of wheat down even more.

Wheat kings such as Hickman Price of Plainview began farming on a large scale, believing the efficiencies of size would insure a profit in spite of low prices. Price farmed some fifty-four square miles of land, using twenty-five combines and one hundred trucks. The Agricultural Experiment Station at Spur urged Texas farmers to diversify, but farmers were usually so far in debt they had to continue wheat farming. Twenty Panhandle counties harvested 2.5 million acres of wheat in 1930. Cotton had reached the South Plains, and some corn was being grown. Cattle continued to overgraze the land.

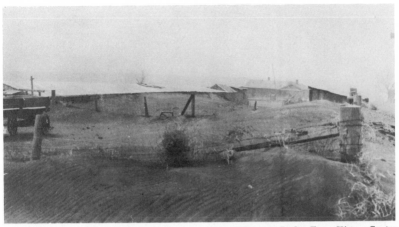

Drifts and dunes rendered much Texas farmland unusable.

The 1929 crash of the stock market caused wheat prices to fall to seventy cents a bushel. Farmers reacted as before, by planting more wheat. Increased production forced the price even lower. With an excellent harvest in 1931, twenty Panhandle counties produced 60 million bushels of wheat, and the price dropped to twenty cents a bushel. In 1932 hailstorms, cutworms, and drought devastated the crops, and the land began blowing away. Farmers by the hundreds were ruined. Some gathered their meager goods and began the trek westward, seeking jobs. Many planted in dust and prayed for rain. Sandstorms blew in, and huge sand dunes formed near Dalhart. People complained of dust fever, an infection of the lungs. On twenty-seven days in April 1935 it was impossible to see across Main Street in Amarillo at noon.

The Battle against the Dust. In June 1934 President Roosevelt asked Congress to appropriate money to buy starving cattle, to relocate destitute farmers, and to lend farmers money for seed. The AAA supported measures to help the farmers relocate and to enrich the worn-out land. Under the terms of the Soil Conservation and Domestic Allotment Act of 1936, farmers received dividends for not planting commercial crops that would deplete the soil. Instead they planted such soil-building crops as clover and soybeans.

Lister plowing and contour planting were two methods devised to help conserve the soil of the plains. To resist blow-

327

Modern farmers on the Great Plains use plowing methods similar to those of the 1930s to prevent a recurrence of the Dust Bowl.

ing, the land was plowed in such a manner as to produce a rough surface. The farmer plowed at right angles to the wind, using a plow called a lister, or middlebuster, that left a substantial furrow between the rows to collect blowing soil. However, each farmer had to plow his land for the program to be effective. For every acre left to blow twelve tended acres would blow worse than before. Abandoned farms and absentee owners jeopardized neighboring farms.

One-fourth of the farm houses in the Dust Bowl stood vacant in 1936 when President Roosevelt signed an act subsidizing farmers who would plow their fields to resist the blowing. Farmers wearing dust masks and goggles and burning the headlights on their tractors in the daytime moved from farm to farm, running the lister across the fields. But lack of cooperation among farmers threatened the program. In 1937 nine counties in the Panhandle let farmers plow vacant land and assessed the cost against the owners.

Farmers began planting alternating contour bands of tall sorghum and short wheat to break the wind and hold the soil.

328

The federal government began buying land and putting it back into grass. The government subsidized farmers' efforts to practice wind control measures and fined farmers who failed to cooperate with the program.

The federal government also aided the farmer by planting trees to form shelter belts to break the wind's force. The first planting of the trees on the plains began in 1935, the United States leasing the land for the trees at first. But farmers objected to the lease feature, so the next year the government simply provided the trees and labor to plant them and construct fences around them. By 1938 the treeless Panhandle had flourishing elm, hackberry, locust, and cottonwood trees. When World War II began, thirty thousand farms across the nation had been planted with trees to protect the land from the winds.

Dalhart's sand dunes came under the management of the Soil Conservation Service in 1936. The dunes covered some two hundred thousand acres of land and grew larger with each dust storm. "Wind intensifiers"—sand-filled gunny sacks and pieces of sheet iron—erected on top of the dunes caused the wind to cut down the part of the dunes where they were placed. By the spring of 1938 the dunes were gone.

Farmers across Texas had organized soil conservation districts by 1939. They were planting more sorghums and less wheat. There were severe dust storms in 1940 and again in 1941, but the farmers, with the aid of the federal government, had learned valuable methods of preventing soil erosion and of putting nutrients back into the soil. Man was learning that land was a valuable resource to be conserved, not an antagonist to be bested and then discarded. *Fortune* magazine commented, "It is conceivable that when the history of our generation comes to be written in the perspective of a hundred years the saving of the broken lands will stand out as the great and most enduring achievement of the time."

When President Franklin Roosevelt visited Amarillo in 1938, he spoke during the heaviest rain of the year, and West Texans spoke, hopefully, of having a mud bowl. Many people had said that the effort to try to restore the Dust Bowl lands was foolish. Roosevelt answered that if more people visited the plains, "you would hear less talk about the Great American Desert and less ridicule about our efforts to conserve water, to restore grazing lands, and to plant trees." The people of the High Plains cheered.

The Supreme Court Battle

Many Americans failed to cheer in 1937 when Roosevelt proposed a plan which would allow the president to add additional justices to the Supreme Court. The Supreme Court had invalidated the NRA and the first AAA and had ruled against the administration in five out of seven other major tests. Roosevelt wished to appoint justices who would favor New Deal measures.

Six of the nine Supreme Court justices were past the age of seventy, and Roosevelt asked for legislation providing that when a justice served six months after his seventieth birthday without retiring, the president could appoint an additional justice to the bench. Opponents viewed the move as a threat to the independence of the Court. They feared a lessening in the powers of the Supreme Court that would disturb the system of checks and balances. A precedent would be set by which future presidents might add justices to the bench any time legislation was declared unconstitutional.

Debate was bitter in Congress, and some congressmen who had supported Roosevelt's New Deal legislation defected. Although Texas congressman Sam Rayburn supported the president's proposal, Senator Tom Connally, who usually stood by the Roosevelt forces, chose to oppose the plan. Dallas congressman Hatton Sumners, chairman of the House Judiciary Committee, stated: "Boys, here's where I cash in my chips," and joined Roosevelt's opposition.

The Texas Senate passed a resolution opposing the so-called court-packing measure, but Congressman Maury Maverick, long an advocate of judicial reform, told Texas senators he would not be bound by their vote. Maverick said the Court should acknowledge "progress in the affairs of men." He added, "Mr. Lyndon Johnson supported the president's judiciary plan and was overwhelmingly elected."

When Congress failed to approve the proposed expansion of the Supreme Court, former Texas governor Jim Ferguson, long a staunch advocate of strong executive leadership, wired President Roosevelt: "Be of good cheer. Destiny or Providence will yet make it your duty to provide the judicial reform which the Senate failed to furnish. . . ." Roosevelt said he had lost the battle but won the war, for the Court began to render decisions favorable to New Deal legislation. In addition, the older justices either retired or died, and Roosevelt was able to appoint replacements.

Roosevelt Loses Support. Presidential popularity suffered from a business recession in 1937 and 1938. A group of conservative Democrats in the Senate broke with President Roosevelt and formed a bipartisan bloc with Republican senators to work against many New Deal measures, for it appeared that the government was going heavily into debt without accomplishing anything. During the congressional elections of 1938 Roosevelt sought to purge the dissident members of his party, with unfortunate results. The voters reelected those the president was trying to get rid of, and the Republicans picked up seven Senate and eighty-one House seats. Robert Taft from Ohio was one of the young Republican senators who would become prominent in his party. The strengthened opposition in Congress plus the increasing attention given to events in Europe helped to bring an end to New Deal reforms.

The New Deal reduced unemployment and human suffering and provided a means of getting through a perilous time in which popular governments elsewhere in the world were being replaced by dictators. Economic recovery was not completely realized until American industry began responding to the demands of World War II.

Pappy

The election of 1938 brought into Texas politics W. Lee O'Daniel, who was without peer as a campaigner. His announcement as a candidate for governor caused a certain amount of amusement among politicians. O'Daniel had no campaign manager and no headquarters and had not ever voted in Texas, having never paid a poll tax. But O'Daniel was a shrewd salesman with a huge radio audience.

As sales manager for the Light Crust Flour Company, O'Daniel had hired three hillbilly musicians, the Light Crust Doughboys, to broadcast over radio station KFJZ in Fort Worth. O'Daniel opened the program each noon with the line, "Please pass the biscuits, Pappy," and his listeners began referring to O'Daniel as Pappy. The show was then moved to a more powerful station, WBAP. When O'Daniel founded the Hillbilly Flour Company in 1935, the band became the Hillbilly Boys. By 1938 a million Texans heard Pappy and the boys each noon.

On Palm Sunday 1938 O'Daniel reported to his radio audience that a blind listener had written him stating that he ought to be governor. O'Daniel asked his listeners to advise him. He reported a week later that more than fifty-four thousand listeners responded, and only four suggested that he not seek the office. Those four people thought O'Daniel was too good for the job.

O'Daniel said his listeners had made the decision for him. He would seek the governorship, running on a platform measured by the Ten Commandments and the Golden Rule. He announced his motto: "Less Johnson grass and politicians; more smokestacks and businessmen." He promised old-age pensions and counted on his listeners to finance him. "I say to you in all sincerity . . . you had better take that old rocking chair down and mortgage it and spend the money in the manner you think best to get your pension. . . . We have not one dollar in our campaign fund."

Traveling across the state in an old bus and entertaining the folks with the Hillbilly Boys, Pappy was acknowledged to be "a borned actor." He firmed up his platform, offering old-age pensions of thirty dollars a month to people over sixty-five years of age. To get the $40 million needed to finance his pension plan, O'Daniel proposed to tax new industries coming into the state. He deplored the tactics of "professional politicians," and when his opponents taunted him because he failed to pay his poll tax, O'Daniel replied, "No politician in Texas is worth $1.75."

O'Daniel had a light touch and did not seem to take himself too seriously. Texans who had been through nearly a decade of economic hardship and had heard him often enough to consider him a personal friend went along. Before the primary was held a reporter asked O'Daniel what he thought his chances were of winning and O'Daniel replied, "I don't know whether or not I'll get elected, but boy! it sure is good for the flour business." Attendance at his rallies indicated that O'Daniel was doing more than selling flour, however. Eight thousand heard him in San Angelo; three thousand waited for three hours in Colorado City to hear him; at Sherman ten thousand turned out for his speech.

O'Daniel's opposition was respectable. Ernest O. Thompson was a member of the railroad commission; Tom Hunter had run against Mrs. Ferguson and Ross Sterling in 1932; and William McCraw had been attorney general. O'Daniel defeated them and nine others without a runoff. Of the 254 counties, Pappy O'Daniel carried 231 and led all his opponents combined by some thirty thousand votes.

The Immortal Fifty-six. Over sixty thousand people jammed Memorial Stadium in Austin to see O'Daniel take the oath of office. He said, "I pray that glamor and color will be eliminated from our legislative session and that seriousness and dignity will reign supreme." He stated that he would abolish the ad valorem tax and reimburse the school fund with a tax on cigarettes. He also proposed a "transactions tax," but the members of his legislature failed to see the difference between the "transactions tax" and the sales tax which O'Daniel had denounced during his campaign. The legislature opposed O'Daniel's plan to appoint a council of business advisors to aid him in running the government. The relief rolls swelled by some eighty thousand names with the enactment of O'Daniel's liberal pension program. However, the governor and the legislature could not agree on a way to finance the pensions, and each person received a smaller pension than before.

Senator R. A. Weinert proposed a 2 percent sales tax, and the senate passed the measure. The governor backed the tax, but fifty-six representatives held fast to defeat the sales tax. One of the fifty-six was Price Daniel, who was later governor,

Senator, and Texas Supreme Court justice. Homer Thornberry, who became a congressman and a federal judge, was also among the fifty-six. He later said, "I shall always be proud of the stand I took at that time."

O'Daniel's Second Term. When the campaign of 1940 began, Governor O'Daniel had to face the complete failure of his legislative program. For some months it was doubtful if he would seek a second term. Candidates opposing O'Daniel attacked his program and his lack of influence with the legislature. The opponents included Highway Commissioner Harry Hines, Railroad Commissioner Jerry Sadler, and Ernest O. Thompson. Mrs. Miriam Ferguson was also in the race. She supported Franklin Roosevelt: they were both asking for unprecedented third terms. Governor O'Daniel bested his six Democratic opponents by more than one hundred thousand votes and carried 245 of 254 counties, although most of the newspapers in the state had opposed him. The *Dallas News*

Austin-Travis County Collection, Austin Public Library

W. Lee O'Daniel, always the showman, used a huge pen to sign legislation relating to the Big Bend National Park.

stated: "The highest office in this state has been the laughing-stock of the United States for a year and a half."

Many Americans thought that Vice-President John Nance Garner would succeed Roosevelt in 1940. Garner was an out-spoken opponent of the third term Roosevelt had begun to desire. In August 1940 when a senatorial delegation headed by Harry Truman of Missouri presented him with a wicker chair for his Uvalde porch, Garner told them, "I would oppose my own brother for a third term." A Gallup poll showed 58 percent of the Democrats favored Garner if Roosevelt failed to seek a third term. However, Roosevelt received his party's nomination. Garner retired and the Democrats chose Henry Wallace, the controversial head of the AAA, as Roosevelt's running mate. Many Texans opposed the substitution of Wallace for Garner and many thought that the president should not seek a third term. However, Texas remained Democratic, with Roosevelt receiving more than four times the number of votes of the Republican candidate, Wendell L. Willkie.

Governor O'Daniel's second term was a continuation of the financial difficulties of his first term. The governor again sub-mitted the transactions tax to the legislature, along with an omnibus tax bill on natural resources and public utilities. Both bills met firm opposition in the legislature, and Representative G. C. Morris, one of the fifty-six who opposed the sales tax, introduced a bill to increase the taxes on oil and gas, sulfur, and cigarettes, impose a gross receipts tax on insurance and utility companies, and place a tax on the sales of automobiles. Although the governor denounced the bill, it was passed by the legislature. The new bill produced about $22 million per year to be divided between the pension fund and other needs of the state.

With a war going on in Europe the legislature authorized a Texas Defense Guard. The need for friendly relations with Latin American countries caused the legislature to permit each state-supported school to accept five students from each Latin American country tuition-free, and a law was passed permitting elementary schools to teach Spanish. During O'Daniel's second term, a constitutional amendment was ratified prohibiting deficit spending by the state. The state has since operated on a cash basis. In the early weeks of the 1971 session the legislature, again facing a financial crisis, turned down a plan that would have allowed the state to operate on a deficit basis.

Senator O'Daniel. Within weeks of John Nance Garner's March 1941 retirement, Texas lost another strong voice in Washington. Senator Morris Sheppard, author of the Eighteenth Amendment and chairman of the Senate Military Affairs Committee, died on April 9, 1941. With the nation facing war in Europe, Texans desired a strong man to take his place in the Senate.

It was the duty of the governor to fill the vacancy by appointment pending a special election. O'Daniel wanted the Senate seat himself, which was no surprise, but the way he managed it was. On San Jacinto Day, 1941, O'Daniel appointed Sam Houston's sole surviving son to the Senate seat his father had held ninety-five years before. Andrew Jackson Houston had served as a United States marshal during the presidency of Theodore Roosevelt and had been the Republican gubernatorial opponent of Jim Hogg in 1892. At the time of his appointment he was almost eighty-seven years old and was quite feeble. No senator had ever begun his service at such an age, and clearly he could not be expected to enter the special election. Senator Houston attended sessions of the Senate only three times and died after serving only twenty-four days.

Twenty-nine candidates filed for the senatorial seat in the special election, including Congressman Lyndon B. Johnson, Attorney General Gerald Mann, and Congressman Martin Dies. Jim Ferguson considered entering his name on the ballot, declaring that "Our crowd can put it over." However, Ferguson decided not to run, stating that if O'Daniel did not run the Ferguson support would be given to the candidate who would do the least harm in Washington. O'Daniel soon announced his candidacy.

O'Daniel declared that he would take the Ten Commandments and the Golden Rule with him to Washington and that he stood on a platform dedicated to "a common touch with the common man." He had criticized others for holding an office while running for another, but when asked if he would resign as governor while he campaigned for the Senate he said, "I should say not." O'Daniel campaigned with a hillbilly band and with what Congressman Dies called his "medicine show tactics." Congressman Lyndon Johnson ran as a Roosevelt supporter, and federal officials from Washington campaigned in Texas in his behalf. With only a plurality needed for election, O'Daniel defeated Johnson by 175,590 votes to 174,279.

Pappy was on his way to Washington, denouncing the "professional politicians" around the president and threatening to put the federal government on a cash basis. If O'Daniel's threats offended his fellow senators, his other tactics rankled them even more. Freshman senators are usually expected to remain silent, but Pappy made a speech on his second day in the Senate, breaking the record of Huey P. Long, who had made a speech on his third day. O'Daniel spoke against extending the draft at a time when England alone opposed Hitler's Germany. He proposed an antistrike bill, a ban on the use of pipelines for transporting natural gas, an investigation into the production of commercial fertilizers, and a ban on the sale of liquor near army camps.

Although the Senate failed to pass a single O'Daniel measure and the votes against his bills were large, he sought election to a full term in 1942. Two former governors of Texas, Dan Moody and James Allred, announced for O'Daniel's senatorial seat, and Pappy dubbed his opponents the Gold Dust Twins. Again the newspapers in the state called for the people to unseat O'Daniel, and the *Dallas News* called O'Daniel's campaign speeches "an insult to the intelligence of Texans." A sample line from one of those speeches was O'Daniel's declaration: "Washington is the only lunatic asylum in the world run by its own inmates."

Despite the opposition, O'Daniel defeated his opponents and returned to Washington. During the campaign O'Daniel stated: "The winning of the war does not enter into the senatorial race. Winning the war is Roosevelt's job—he's our commander in chief." At that very time, 1942, the matter of most concern to 130 million Americans was prevailing in that same war. Upon his return to Washington O'Daniel found his colleagues even less interested in listening to him than before.

Discuss

1. What problems were faced by Texans in the 1930s?

2. How were the problems of the 1930s related to developments in the 1920s?

3. Trace the historical developments that led to the Dust Bowl.

4. Why did lawlessness increase during the 1920s and 1930s?

5. How did the farmers and the government combat the Dust Bowl?

6. What soil conservation methods are practiced in your community?

7. Compare labor-management relations of the 1930s with the present.

8. Why did farmers in the 1930s fail to heed warnings about the danger to the ecology of the Great Plains? Do you think there is more or less concern today about ecology?

9. What could have resulted from Roosevelt's proposed expansion of the Supreme Court?

10. How successful was the New Deal?

11. Compare James E. Ferguson and W. Lee O'Daniel. How do you account for their success in politics?

12. Do you think Texas should engage in deficit spending? Why?

Identify

CIO
John L. Lewis
G-men
Bonnie and Clyde
Dust Bowl
W. Lee O'Daniel

Andrew Jackson Houston
diversified farming
subsidize
shelter belt
court-packing

MEMBERS OF THE THIRTY-SIXTH DIVISION IN ITALY
DECEMBER 1943. IN THE MIDST OF WAR, THE SOLDIE
THOUGHTS WERE OF HOME.

CHAPTER 20

"Winning the War"

At 7:55 on Sunday morning, December 7, 1941, Japanese dive bombers attacked the United States Naval Base at Pearl Harbor, Hawaii. Two hours later eight United States battleships, three destroyers, a number of other vessels, and about 175 aircraft were destroyed or badly damaged. United States military forces stationed at Pearl Harbor reported thirty-four hundred casualties. The next day President Roosevelt asked Congress to declare war on Japan. Only one representative recorded a dissenting vote. Germany and Italy issued declarations of war against the United States on December 11, and Congress responded in kind. For the second time in the twentieth century the country was engaged in a massive war.

World War II

Conflict in the Pacific. In the 1920s the founder of the Chinese Republic, Sun Yat-sen, had begun to unify a China torn by internal strife. His successor, Chiang Kai-Shek, extended Nationalist rule and resisted the efforts of the Japanese to extend their empire into Manchuria. The Japanese sought coal, oil, tin, and rubber from other countries in Asia; and China, torn by a power struggle between the Nationalists and the Communists, lost Manchuria to the Japanese.

In 1937 Chiang Kai-Shek hired Claire L. Chennault to help train the Chinese air force to turn back the Japanese. Born in Commerce, Chennault had attended Louisiana State University and was retired from the United States Army for deafness at the age of forty-seven.

In 1941 Chennault organized the American Volunteer Group, the Flying Tigers, to defend the Burma Road from the Japanese. From near Rangoon they fought, with never more than seventy pilots or forty-nine planes at any time. In the seven months after Pearl Harbor they destroyed 297 Japanese planes and killed over fifteen hundred troops, frustrating Japanese invasion plans. Chennault was recalled by the United States Army Air Corps to command the Fourteenth Air Force, which operated in China until the end of the war.

The March of the Dictators. China was not the only country in danger. Americans found conflict on all sides by the late 1930s as the world depression created unrest and bred dictators. Benito Mussolini, prating of the glory that was the Roman Empire, began building up the Italian army and navy. Many people praised Mussolini for improvements such as causing Italian trains to run on time. Then he moved against Ethiopia and made it part of a new Italian empire. The Germans, defeated and embittered by the Treaty of Versailles, turned to the Nazi party and its leader, Adolf Hitler. Germany withdrew from the League of Nations, and Hitler set out to build Germany into a military power.

In Spain General Francisco Franco led a revolt against the republican government in 1936. The Soviet Union and France backed the Loyalists, but Germany and Italy supported Franco's dictatorship. Although many Americans were sympathetic to the Loyalist cause, isolationist sentiment in America was at high tide, heightened by revelations of a Senate investigating committee of the profits made by American industrialists

342

and businessmen during World War I. Fearful of war, Congress passed a series of neutrality acts. The result was that Spain's Loyalists received only slight help from Russia while Germany and Italy furnished heavy support to Franco.

Hitler began his conquest of Europe in 1936 with the remilitarization of the Rhineland, an act contrary to the Treaty of Versailles. Two years later Germany annexed Austria. When Germany threatened to move against Czechoslovakia, President Roosevelt urged Britain and France to oppose the move. Both countries had treaties binding them to the defense of Czechoslovakia, but neither was anxious to back up its commitment. In September 1938 British prime minister Neville Chamberlain and French premier Daladier conferred with Hitler at Munich, and Hitler assured them that his ambitions included only the Sudentenland of Czechoslovakia. Chamberlain returned to England believing "peace has been achieved in our time." The following March Hitler annexed all of Czechoslovakia. Mussolini moved against Albania.

Poland was Hitler's next target, but he did not want to risk a general war. Since the same governments were in power that had made the agreement at Munich, he did not feel there was much chance of English or French opposition. In August 1939 Germany and Russia signed a ten-year non-aggression pact. The blitzkrieg, a fast-moving German military offense, swept into Poland on September 1, 1939. Two days later France and England declared war on Germany. In the spring of 1940 Hitler's troops marched into Denmark, Norway, the Netherlands, Belgium, and Luxembourg. They outflanked the French forces along the Maginot Line. Mussolini attacked France from the south. Britain's forces were pushed to the English Channel and evacuated at Dunkirk. The crisis forced Neville Chamberlain from office, and Winston Churchill took the leadership of Britain.

France fell, and Hitler held the Continent. Only Britain stood between Hitler and the total conquest of Europe. President Roosevelt sent his special assistant, Harry Hopkins, to survey the capabilities of American aircraft factories. The president proposed measures to aid the British without involving the United States in a European war.

343

Mobilizing a Nation. With war in Europe and in Asia, it was difficult for the United States to continue to pursue a policy of isolationism. Congress concerned itself with the question of national defense. Vice-President Garner objected to shipping oil and scrap iron to the Japanese, saying "settlers never ought to sell scalping knives to Indians."

At the close of 1940, the British were almost without funds, and their need for supplies was increasing rapidly. World War I debts were still outstanding. Rather than get involved in the question of the payment of those debts, Roosevelt proposed loans of war materials, instead of money, to the Allied nations. In March 1941 Congress authorized spending $7 billion for such lend-lease goods. A survey showed 76 percent of Texans favoring lend-lease, whereas only 56 percent were in favor nationally. On the question of whether we should convoy those goods to the Allies, the Texas legislature urged the president and Congress to do what was necessary to get those goods delivered. After Hitler attacked the Soviet Union in June 1941, lend-lease was extended to the Russians.

Congress greatly increased appropriations for the armed services in 1940. The Selective Service and Training Act was passed requiring men to register for one year's military service and training—the first time the nation had drafted men while the nation was at peace. The draft was extended in August 1941, and some 31 million men were registered.

Texas was again to serve as a training ground for the armed forces. In the summer of 1940 Fort Sam Houston and Fort Bliss were enlarged, and new bases such as Camp Barkeley at Abilene were planned. Texas served, once again, as a training ground for Royal Air Force pilots. Fifteen major military bases, more than forty airfields, and several naval installations were located in Texas; by the summer of 1941 some 160,000 soldiers were stationed in the state. The Corpus Christi Naval Air Training Base, set up to train thirty-six hundred pilots a year, was the largest of its type.

Brownwood was selected as a training center, and within six months the new Camp Bowie grew into an installation of hundreds of buildings and fifty-two miles of paved roads on several thousand acres. The Thirty-sixth Division of the

344

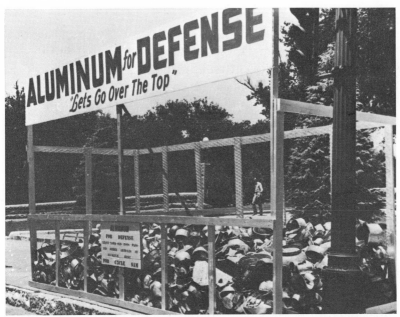

With slogans such as "Let's go over the top" and "Get in the scrap," Americans collected material to use in the war effort.

Texas National Guard was ordered to the unfinished camp, and in 1941 thirty thousand men were stationed there. Two years later the number had grown to sixty-seven thousand. Gainesville became the home of Camp Howze and an air base. Also located in Texas were twenty-one prisoner of war camps.

GI Joe—Texas Style. When war was declared against Japan in 1941, Texans began enlisting. From farms and cities men and women left their homes and jobs to further the war effort. Texas contributed a larger percentage of her population to the armed forces than any other state in the nation. Three-quarters of a million Texans served in the war, among them some twelve thousand women. Over twenty-three thousand Texans died while serving in the armed forces. The Agricultural and Mechanical College of Texas sent twenty thousand men to the armed forces, fourteen thousand as officers.

Among the 155 Texans to hold the rank of general was General Ira Eaker, born in Field Creek, Llano County. Eaker had set a world's endurance record piloting an army airplane in 1929 and made the first transcontinental instrument flight

345

in 1936. He led the first American bombing attack on western Europe in World War II. His commands included the Eighth Air Force and later the Fifteenth Air Force, and he served as chief of the air staff at the war's end.

General Lucian Truscott of Chatfield, Navarro County, led the Allied troops in the breakthrough at Anzio, Italy, in 1944 and later led the amphibious landings in southern France. Colonel Oveta Culp Hobby of Houston, wife of former Texas governor Will P. Hobby, helped organize the Women's Army Corps and served as its first commander. Twelve Texans served as admirals, including Chester W. Nimitz of Fredericksburg, commander of the Pacific Fleet. Grandson of pioneer Texas hotel man Captain Charles Nimitz, Admiral Nimitz was graduated from Annapolis in 1905. He was named Admiral of the Fleet in 1944 and served as chief of naval operations until the time of his retirement. Nimitz was present at the surrender of the Japanese to the United States aboard the U.S.S. *Missouri* in 1945.

The most-decorated soldier of the war was a Texan. When sixteen-year-old Audie Murphy of Farmersville tried to join the Marines and the paratroopers, recruiting officers turned him away. Murphy had barely a hundred pounds on his five-foot seven-inch frame. By the time he was eighteen he had gained enough weight to enlist in the Army. He served in nine major battle campaigns from North Africa to Germany. Before he was old enough to vote, Audie Murphy had received more medals than any other American in any other war. In addition to decorations from the French, British, and Belgian governments, he received every American combat citation except the Asiatic-Pacific service ribbon.

A young black sailor from Waco, Doris Miller, was awarded the Navy Cross by Admiral Nimitz in 1942. As a boy Miller's shooting practice had consisted of dropping squirrels from trees on the Brazos River bottom. He enlisted in the navy at the age of nineteen. He was below decks when Japanese dive bombers raked the U.S.S. *West Virginia.* Rushing to the aid of a wounded machine gunner, Miller manned the gun and brought down four Japanese bombers. Miller was later killed, and Waco citizens named their YMCA center in his honor.

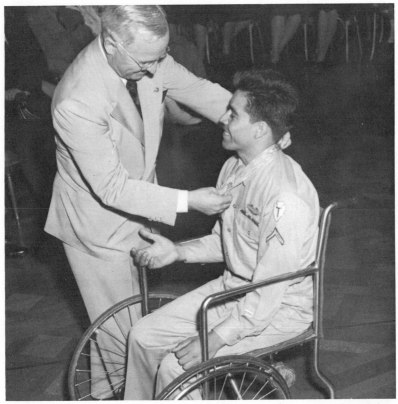

President Truman awarded the Medal of Honor to Silvestre Herrera in Washington, D. C., in August 1945.

The war correspondent Ernie Pyle wrote one of his best-
known dispatches about a Texan, Captain Henry Waskow,
whose grandparents were born in Germany. As commander
of Company B, 143d Regiment, Thirty-sixth Division, Captain
Waskow was killed on Mount Sammucro in Italy on December
14, 1943. Among the tributes paid to the young Belton officer
by the soldiers who served under him were these: "He always
looked after us. He'd go to bat for us every time." "I've never
known him to do anything unfair." "After my father, he came
next." Pyle said, "Never have I crossed the trail of any man
as beloved as Captain Henry T. Waskow."

Several Mexican Americans were among the thirty-six Texans
who won the Congressional Medal of Honor. Sergeant Luciano
Adams of Port Arthur was cited for a single-handed assault on

347

a German force, and Sergeant Macario Garcia from Sugar Land was cited for bravery under fire. Medal of Honor winner Private Silvestre P. Herrera from El Paso continued to attack until his companions could capture an enemy position, although he had sustained terrible injuries from the explosion of a mine. Sergeant Cleto Rodriguez of San Marcos and another soldier attacked a railroad station held by three hundred enemy troops. Although his companion died in the assault, Sergeant Rodriguez managed to rout the enemy. Sergeant José M. López of Brownsville won the Medal of Honor for bravery under heavy artillery fire.

Jimmie and Mike Cokinos of Beaumont were sons of a Greek restaurant owner. During World War II, Mike won the Silver Star and Purple Heart for service in Germany, and Jimmie was awarded the Bronze Star for service in the Philippines. After the war, Jimmie Cokinos was a Beaumont city councilman for ten years. In 1956 he became Texas's first mayor of Greek parentage.

Preparing for the invasion of southern France, members of the Thirty-sixth Division made practice landings near Naples in August 1944.

In 1943 Congressman Lyndon B. Johnson suggested that the name of the Del Valle Army Air Field be changed to Bergstrom Field to honor Captain John August Earl Bergstrom, son of a Swedish immigrant. Captain Bergstrom was believed to be the first Austin area soldier to die in World War II.

Benjamin Franklin Ogata of Dallas served with the all-Japanese 442d Regiment. Adopting as their slogan, "Go For Broke," the regiment became the most-decorated unit in the history of the United States. When it was attached to the Thirty-sixth Division, Governor Coke Stevenson made all members of the 442d honorary Texans. Among its other exploits the 442d Regiment rescued the Lost Battalion, a unit of the Thirty-sixth Division which had been surrounded by Germans for a week, and for which all hope had been given up.

The Thirty-sixth Division was the first American division to land at Salerno, Italy, in September 1943 and thus became the first American division to invade Hitler's Fortress Europe. The Texans were at the invasion of southern France, fought through France and into Germany, and were in Austria at the end of the war. The members of the division experienced nineteen months of combat, fought in five major campaigns, and captured over 175,000 prisoners. The Thirty-sixth Division suffered the third highest number of casualties of any American division in the war.

The War Boom. The war years stimulated industrial growth, and farmers prospered as they produced food for millions of uprooted people and hungry servicemen all over the world. In 1940 the leading industries in Texas, ranked by product value, were petroleum, meat-packing, cottonseed processing, flour and other grain products, oil field machinery and oil field tools, and bakery products. Then industry was required to diversify, as defense contracts totaling billions of dollars were granted to Texas firms. Full employment was needed to man the giant defense plants and factories turning out goods and materials for the war effort. In Texas during the years 1938 to 1945, the number of factory workers increased from 127,000 to 380,000. The value of manufactured goods rose from $1.5 billion in 1939 to $6.5 billion in 1944.

With major pilot training programs located in Texas, it was

natural that the aircraft industry should establish factories in the state. North American Aviation chose Dallas County, and Consolidated Vultee Aircraft Corporation put one of the largest plants of its kind in the world at Fort Worth. Beaumont, Orange, Port Arthur, Houston, Brownsville, and Rockport all had shipyards. Houston Shipbuilding Corporation near Deer Park began turning out Liberty ships and Victory ships. The first Liberty ship was launched in 1942 and required 254 days to build. Soon workers were able to turn out a ship every 53 days. Thirty-five thousand workers were employed at Houston Shipbuilding Corporation and Brown Shipbuilding Corporation. Thousands of Texans—men and women—left the farms for jobs in industry.

Houston and Daingerfield had substantial steel mills. The Ford plant in Dallas turned out over one hundred thousand jeeps and trucks. The war gave birth to the state's chemical industry. Humble Oil and Refining Company, which produced more than a billion gallons of aviation fuel for America's warplanes, also turned its efforts to explosives, as did the Shell Oil Company. General Tire Company, Monsanto, Goodyear, Sinclair, and Dow produced synthetic rubber. The area from Harris County to Jefferson County, already heavily engaged in refining, became a petrochemical center.

At some time during the war, Texas became an urban state as people poured into the cities to work in plants and factories. In 1940 just over 45 percent of the population resided in urban centers, while in 1950 just short of 60 percent of the population lived in incorporated towns of twenty-five hundred or more. The rural population dropped by four hundred thousand in that decade.

Victory! After Pearl Harbor the United States committed everything to the war effort. The Pacific Fleet was badly crippled, and Hitler sat within his Fortress Europe in no great hurry to snuff out the British threat. The United States had to mobilize fully and had to devise appropriate plans for the far-flung campaigns that would be required. There followed many months of defensive warfare, as Russia and Britain tried to hold off the Germans and as the United States attempted to slow the Japanese in the Pacific.

The overall strategy was to defeat Germany first, because of its more potent industrial capacity. In the meantime every effort was made to contain the Japanese. By May 1942 the Americans were able to stop the Japanese at the Battle of the Coral Sea. In the next month a Japanese invasion fleet was neutralized at Midway. Containment had been realized, and it was possible to take the offensive in the Pacific with whatever forces were not needed for the European theater of operations. American forces successfully invaded Guadalcanal late in 1942.

Field Marshal Bernard Montgomery's British Eighth Army turned back Field Marshal Erwin Rommel's Afrika Korps at El Alamein in October 1942. On November 8 Americans and British landed in Algeria and Morocco. American and British troops forced the surrender of the last Germans and Italians in North Africa in May 1943. Now the Allies could consider the invasion of Europe. In July Sicily was invaded. In September 1943 the invasion of Italy began. The Germans had been badly damaged by bombers based in England, and Allied airpower kept growing. By early 1944 the Allies were raiding Germany day and night in thousands of bombers and fighters, reducing war production and transportation to such an extent that the German air arm was unable to turn back the invasion of France in June 1944.

General Dwight D. Eisenhower, who was born in Denison, was appointed commander of Operation Overlord, the invasion of France. On June 6, 1944, four thousand Allied ships were off the coast of Normandy. Tanks, trucks, and jeeps filled their holds, and hundreds of thousands of men lined the decks. Allied soldiers parachuted into France. Thousands of Allied planes flew cover for the landing force, and the ships' guns pounded at German defensive positions. The tides were with the Americans, and the Germans were expecting the invasion at another place. By nightfall, after heavy fighting and many losses, the Allied forces had established a beachhead. Two weeks later there were a million Allied troops in Normandy.

In four months the Germans were swept out of France. Despite the warnings of his military advisers that the cause was hopeless, Hitler threw all his resources into defending Germany. The German army counterattacked in the Battle of the Bulge, a slaughterhouse of Allied troops, and the Germans were deep into Allied territory at Christmas 1944. By January the American and French forces had erased the German gains and were pushing on toward Berlin from the west, while the Russians pounded the German lines from the east. With Berlin under heavy bombardment, Hitler committed suicide. On May 7, 1945, the Germans surrendered to Allied troops, and millions of free people celebrated the victory.

Although Americans lifted their voices in cheering the end of the war with Germany and Italy, the nation was mourning the loss of her leader. On the afternoon of April 12, 1945, Franklin D. Roosevelt died of a cerebral hemorrhage. Roosevelt's vice-president, Harry Truman of Missouri, led the nation through the last days of the war.

The Allies now concentrated on defeating the Japanese. General Douglas MacArthur had been forced to evacuate the

United States Navy

Fleet Admiral Nimitz at the surrender ceremonies aboard the U.S.S. *Missouri* in Tokyo Bay. General MacArthur stands with hands behind his back at right.

Philippines in 1942. The Allies were island-hopping, pushing the Japanese back to their homeland after besting them at Guadalcanal. Gradually the Allies overcame Japanese resistance in the Solomon, Gilbert, and Marshall islands. Guam, Saipan, the Philippines, Iwo Jima, and Okinawa took a heavy toll of American lives, and President Truman knew that the death rate would mount as the Allies drew nearer the Japanese homeland.

President Truman warned the Japanese that the Americans possessed a weapon powerful enough to devastate Japan if they failed to surrender by August 3, 1945. The president waited in vain for a response. After a week of waiting the atomic bomb was dropped on Hiroshima, killing at least eighty thousand people. Still the Japanese army leaders refused to surrender, and a second atomic bomb was dropped on Nagasaki. After hurried negotiations, the Japanese surrendered to the Allies. The final terms were signed on September 2, 1945, aboard the Battleship *Missouri*.

The Postwar Nation

Preserving the Peace. At the formal surrender General Douglas MacArthur stated: "We must go forward to preserve in peace what we won in war. A new era is upon us." The task of leading the world in peace was as important as that of winning the war. In 1943 a resolution had been introduced in the Senate proposing American leadership in founding a world organization. Representatives from fifty nations met at San Francisco on April 25, 1945, to frame the charter for the United Nations. Senator Tom Connally of Texas was one of the signers of the document, which was ratified by the Senate in July 1945. America did not repeat her error of 1919, when she tried to retire behind her oceans and take no part in the keeping of the peace.

From Soldier to Civilian. Americans found that the United States had been transformed into a nation with tremendous industrial and economic potential. The people were anxious to use their new productive potential to satisfy human needs and wants. Servicemen were anxious to shed their uniforms

353

and return to a normal life. Since rationing had limited consumption during the war while many people were making high salaries, more people had savings than ever before—and people were anxious to buy.

The transition from war production to providing for the needs of consumers was not easy. Many feared mass unemployment as the war machine was dismantled and veterans returned. The government moved to soften the impact of the return of the veterans by passing the Servicemen's Readjustment Act in 1944. This GI Bill of Rights, as it came to be known, provided each serviceman with twenty dollars a week unemployment compensation for up to a year. It guaranteed low-interest loans for veterans to buy homes or farms or to establish businesses. The construction boom that followed alleviated a housing shortage caused by restrictions on wartime building and by population growth.

Probably the most significant provisions of the GI Bill concerned education. The United States paid for the college tuition, books, and supplies of veterans and provided them with living allowances as they attended college or took other training. In addition to providing them with an education, the program kept large numbers of veterans off the labor market at a time when there were many men without jobs. The living allowances let the veterans remain consumers, stimulating the economy of the nation.

Uncle Sam's investment paid off. Men became college graduates who otherwise would not have considered higher education for themselves. With more education came increased earnings and increased ability to pay taxes. Better education permitted veterans to make greater contributions to the nation's economy and society than would have been possible otherwise. Education furnished veterans by a grateful nation in the late 1940s provided the necessary knowledge and insights for the highly technical decades that followed.

Colleges and universities across Texas felt the impact of the veterans as the student base broadened. The veterans were older, more experienced, and brought a seriousness and maturity to their studies that challenged professors. Programs were developed to meet their aims and needs. Enrollments soared.

State-supported colleges and universities had enrolled 22,354 students in 1944-45. The next year the effects of the GI Bill were slightly evident, with the student population increasing to 26,866. However, by 1946-47 the student enrollment doubled to 54,321. The largest previous enrollment in state-supported colleges had been 39,338 in 1940-41. Increased funding was required to support the state institutions of higher education. Texas spent nearly $12 million on higher education in the years 1946-47, while two years previously it had appropriated $6.8 million.

The American GI Forum. Many Mexican-American veterans returned to Texas to find discriminatory practices still existing in education, employment, housing, and medical care. A young medical corps veteran, Dr. Hector P. Garcia of Corpus Christi, founded the American GI Forum to combat discrimination against Mexican-American veterans. By making complaints to many of the agencies involved, the organization curtailed many of the abuses.

With membership open to all veterans regardless of race or color, the GI Forum became a national organization, helping the Mexican-American veteran achieve equality of opportunity.

Dr. Hector P. Garcia,
founder of the American
GI Forum

The University of Texas,
Institute of Texan Cultures
at San Antonio

The GI Forum encourages its members to participate in politics and supports candidates and legislation of interest to Mexican Americans. President Lyndon B. Johnson appointed Dr. Garcia to the National Advisory Council on Economic Opportunity, and Dr. Garcia has also served as a representative to the United Nations.

Discuss

1. What factors helped bring on World War II? Could the war have been avoided?

2. Compare the American attitude toward involvement in world affairs during the 1930s with the current attitude.

3. Why was lend-lease rather than loans used to aid the Allied nations?

4. Compare the role of Texas as a training ground in both world wars. What reasons can you give for this?

5. What effects did World War II have on the economy of Texas?

6. What effects did World War II have on population distribution in Texas?

7. Why did America join the United Nations, when she had rejected the League of Nations?

8. What was the significance of the GI Bill of Rights?

9. Why was the American GI Forum organized?

10. In what ways were America and the world changed by World War II?

Identify

Claire L. Chennault
Benito Mussolini
Adolf Hitler
Thirty-sixth Division
General Ira Eaker
Audie Murphy
Silvestre P. Herrera
Benjamin F. Ogata
General Dwight D.
  Eisenhower
blitzkrieg

Winston Churchill
lend-lease
Admiral Chester Nimitz
General Lucian Truscott
Doris Miller
Jimmie Cokinos
Lost Battalion
Harry Truman
Dr. Hector P. Garcia
Servicemen's Readjust-
  ment Act

VETERANS RETURNED FROM SERVICE IN WORLD WAR
TO A NATION WITH CHANGED ECONOMY, SOCIETY, AN
POLITICS. LYNDON B. JOHNSON BECAME A PROMINEN
POLITICAL FIGURE.

CHAPTER 21

"Party Lines Are Down"

Texas politics remained relatively quiet during World War II. Coke Stevenson from Junction guided the state through the war years after gaining the governor's chair when W. Lee O'Daniel resigned in August 1941 to serve as United States senator. Stevenson had many years of legislative experience in addition to long service as lieutenant governor. He was reelected in 1942 and again in 1944.

National politics were quite turbulent during the war years. Sentiment against the New Deal, the controversy over Roosevelt's third term, and the replacement of Vice-President John Nance Garner with Henry Wallace in 1940 had been some of the issues that resulted in controversy over the country, and those problems plus the Supreme Court decisions opening the Democratic primary to Negroes led to fragmentation of the Democratic party in Texas. Wendell Willkie, the Republican nominee for president in 1940, had been a Democrat and had supported Roosevelt in 1932. Willkie summed up the opposition to the New Deal and the factional division in his acceptance speech: "Party lines are down."

Political Turmoil

The extent of the split among Texas Democrats was clear after the election of 1940. Wendell Willkie polled more than twice the usual Republican vote in Texas, and Roosevelt's total was about one hundred thousand votes behind that of Democratic senatorial candidate Tom Connally. Nevertheless, Roosevelt won an unprecedented third term. The threat of war helped Roosevelt, for many voters were reluctant to change administrations at such a critical time.

The Bolt of the Regulars. Predictably, opposition to Roosevelt's fourth-term bid was even stronger. Some East Texas Democrats were suggesting an uninstructed delegation to the national convention in 1944. On May 23, 1944, the state convention of the Democratic party erupted into pandemonium, and the Roosevelt supporters, led by representatives of the railroad brotherhoods, walked out of the hall to the strains of "The Eyes of Texas." Those who remained behind, the anti-Roosevelt faction, organized as the Texas Regulars. Lyndon Johnson chaired the meeting of the Roosevelt supporters, with Speaker Sam Rayburn and Senator Tom Connally named delegates-at-large to the national convention. As a result of the split, two Texas delegations attended the Democratic National Convention. The Texas Regulars were determined to frustrate Roosevelt's nomination to a fourth term, and each group hoped to unseat the other.

The Regulars envisioned a revolt against Roosevelt throughout the South (many Regulars were really more alienated by Supreme Court decisions favorable to Negro voting than by the fourth-term issue), and the Texas group worked with Mississippi party leaders to organize opposition to Roosevelt there.

360

Southern representatives opposed to Roosevelt met in Louisiana before the national convention. The efforts of the Regulars to unseat Roosevelt were in vain. Each of the rival delegations was permitted to cast half the Texas vote. The Regulars gave twelve votes to Senator Harry Byrd of Virginia and twelve to Roosevelt. The other faction cast their twenty-four votes for Roosevelt. Both factions voted for Senator Harry Truman of Missouri as the vice-presidential candidate.

The Regulars filed a list of electors pledged to vote for a Democrat other than Roosevelt in the November 1944 election, establishing themselves as a separate party. Senator Byrd was the Regulars' choice, but he refused to allow his name to be placed on the ballot. The Regulars' platform advocated states' rights, white supremacy, and the limiting of presidents to two terms.

Governor Thomas E. Dewey of New York was the Republican nominee for president. Senator John Bricker of Ohio had second place on the ticket. Senator Bricker made a Dallas appearance on behalf of the Republicans, and Sam Rayburn, campaigning for Roosevelt, said Dewey had endorsed every plank in the Democratic platform except the fourth term. Congressman Johnson and Senator Connally urged Texans to support Roosevelt. Senator Harry Truman spoke in Houston, hosted by former governor Allred and John Nance Garner. Secretary of Commerce Jesse Jones declared Roosevelt's reelection essential to a lasting peace. Democratic congressman Richard Kleberg declared for the Republicans.

Rumor had it that the Regulars would support the Republicans, but the party would not give up its identity. Late in the campaign Senator W. Lee O'Daniel joined the Regulars, delivering twenty-four speeches as Texans' "hired hand on the state of the nation." However, O'Daniel had lost much of his appeal, and he was greeted by boos, hisses, and some rotten tomatoes. The 1944 results were Roosevelt, 821,605 votes; Dewey, 191,425 votes; and the Regulars, with no stated candidate, 135,439 votes.

Academic Freedom. The Democratic split had not affected Governor Stevenson's second-term bid. Although the Regulars ceased to function as a formal political party after 1944 and participated as Democrats in Democratic state conventions, the Democratic party in Texas still suffered from an ideological division. In the gubernatorial campaign of 1946 the split once again became apparent. Stevenson retired, and a bitter struggle followed.

A former president of The University of Texas, Homer P. Rainey, announced his candidacy. In 1944 Rainey had been fired by the board of regents of the university as a result of differences over how far the regents might properly go in the internal management of the university. By 1946 the arguments for and against Rainey's removal had been made again and again, and sides had been chosen and other issues injected into the controversy. The election resolved itself into a contest over vindication of Rainey's definition of the regents' proper role. Rainey proposed improvements in education, health, old-age pensions, and farm-to-market roads, all of which would have required increased taxes and state spending—a marked contrast to the frugal policies of Stevenson.

Rainey's opponents branded him a radical and an ultraliberal. The Texas Regulars backed Railroad Commissioner Beauford

Texas Highway Department

Farm-to-market roads, a campaign issue in 1946, received increased funding after 1949. This is a section of FM 2220 near McAllen.

362

Jester, whose political views were strictly middle of the road. Jester urged voters to follow the "people's path," and he castigated both ultraconservatives and ultraliberals. He correctly sensed that Texans were concerned over inflation, the threat of Communism, and rising taxes. He stood firmly for states' rights and urged the rejection of federal grants. Jester's victory set the pattern for the political campaigns of the successful candidates who followed him.

The Jester Administration. In Governor Jester's administration expenditures for state agencies were increased, and the state ad valorem tax rate was set at the maximum level allowed by the constitution. Hospitals, orphanages, and eleemosynary institutions were enlarged and received generous support. A state right-to-work law was passed as a result of the Taft-Hartley Act, passed by Congress over President Truman's veto. The Taft-Hartley Act gave the states power to abolish the union, or closed, shop. The Texas right-to-work law declared it illegal to deny employment to anyone because of union membership or nonmembership. The law also prohibited any contract between an employer and a labor union that would result in a closed shop.

Tragedy struck Texas City in April 1947. The French ship *Grandcamp*, loaded with chemicals, exploded in the harbor. Fires and explosions rocked the little town, killing at least 461 persons and injuring about four thousand. An additional 115 persons were reported missing. Property damage exceeded $67 million.

Landslide Lyndon. Governor Jester was reelected in 1948 without a runoff, but the race for W. Lee O'Daniel's Senate seat attracted considerable political interest. Two days following the release of a poll showing that only 15 percent of the people of Texas felt he adequately represented them, O'Daniel announced that he would not seek reelection. Congressman Lyndon Johnson, who had been defeated for the seat in 1941 by 1,311 votes, announced his candidacy. Since the 1941 election, Johnson had served in the United States Navy and had built a reputation as an able congressman.

Of the ten other candidates, Johnson's main opponent was Coke Stevenson, who prided himself on having brought the

363

state through World War II without a financial deficit. Stevenson ran on a platform devoted to states' rights, individual freedom, and economy in government. Johnson's platform reflected attitudes and beliefs acquired during the New Deal years. He was in favor of foreign aid, federal aid to the states, higher pay for federal employees, and a stronger air force.

The campaign was colorful and hard-fought. Congressman Johnson stated it was not enough for a candidate to campaign over the radio and in the newspapers. He flew about the state in a helicopter—its first use in a Texas campaign—swooping down for a rally whenever he spotted a gathering of people. During the campaign he made from seven to nine scheduled speeches a day.

Stevenson traveled over fifty thousand miles in an old car, buying five gallons of gasoline at a time, shaking hands and talking to people. Stevenson ran on his record as governor, and some of his opponents accused him of having no platform. Johnson reminded voters of the eleven years he had spent in Congress. In the first primary Stevenson led by 477,077 votes to Johnson's 405,617.

Stevenson had led in the big cities, so Johnson changed his tactics during the bitterly personal runoff primary. He abandoned the helicopter and went into the cities, hoping to cut Stevenson's strength there. Big city newspapers chose sides, with the *Houston Post* coming out for Johnson, and the *Dallas News,* long an anti–New Deal voice, standing for Stevenson. The voters went to the polls in August to choose a senator, but it was several days into September before the final result was determined.

The delay was caused by the closeness of the race. Reports and revised reports of the election counts poured into Austin. At one time on the day following the election Stevenson led by eight votes, and a week later Johnson led by seventeen votes. The Democratic executive committee canvassed the returns and voted to decide the nominee, but the vote was a tie. However, one member arrived late and broke the deadlock by voting to enter Johnson's name on the ballot as the official party nominee. Stevenson's supporters refused to accept the count and appealed the verdict of the state committee to the state and federal courts. They managed to get a federal judge to issue a restraining order to keep Johnson's name off the ballot. The Stevenson supporters also called for an examination of the returns in Duval, Jim Wells, and Zapata counties, where they contended that more votes had been cast than there were voters.

The restraining order was overturned by a ruling that a federal court had no jurisdiction over state elections, and charges and countercharges continued to fly. The Johnson forces called for a recount of the East Texas boxes where Stevenson had racked up large majorities. The controversy over the election continued for months, but Johnson was finally declared the victor with an eighty-seven vote margin out of some nine hundred thousand votes cast, the closest election in Texas history and one of the closest in the history of the nation. Stevenson swung his support to the Republican candidate, Jack Porter, in the general election, but Johnson prevailed. Although Johnson had come closer to occupying the middle of the road than in any of his previous campaigns, the contest reflected the growing liberal-conservative split among Texas Democrats.

Democrats and Dixiecrats. The 1948 presidential election was also hard fought. Democrats from Southern states rebelled at the strong civil rights plank in the Democratic platform. Some of these, basing their opposition on a theory of states' rights, bolted the party and formed the States' Rights, or Dixiecrat, party. Many Texas political leaders aligned with the Dixiecrats, who nominated South Carolina governor Strom Thurmond for the presidency. The Democrats chose incumbent Harry Truman as their candidate. The Republicans chose Thomas E. Dewey.

Truman condemned his Republican Congress as the "Do-nothings" and established a Committee on Civil Rights, calling for the strengthening of civil rights laws. The Dixiecrats were strongest in the Southern states with the highest Negro populations. Racial policies had less to do with the political split in Texas. Anti–New Deal sentiment continued, and the conservative elements that had dominated the Texas Regulars were evident in the anti-Truman, anti–civil rights movement. How-

Sam Rayburn from Bonham was Speaker of the House of Representatives for almost seventeen years.

ever, the conservatives failed to prevent the state Democratic convention from endorsing Truman. Republicans were jubilant over the nationwide split in the Democratic ranks and confidently predicted a Dewey victory. Early returns deceived many, some in a most embarrassing manner. The *Chicago Tribune,* on the morning after Truman was reelected and the Democrats had regained control of both houses of Congress, headlined a Dewey victory.

With the Democrats in control of Congress, the Texas delegation became perhaps the most influential in Washington. Speaker Sam Rayburn was the leader of the lower house. Senator Lyndon Johnson was the Senate Democratic whip, and Senator Tom Connally was chairman of the Senate Foreign Relations Committee. In August 1949 President Truman named his former attorney general, Tom C. Clark, to the Supreme Court, the first Texan to be so honored.

The Road to Civil Rights

Truman's insistence on a strong civil rights plank in the Democratic platform led many Negroes to support him for reelection. The number of Negroes voting in 1948 was partially the result of court decisions lifting restrictions long imposed on Negro voting in the South. Residence requirements and literacy tests were among the means used to disfranchise the Negro. In Texas and other states the poll tax prevented many people from voting. Schools were segregated. But change was coming—in fact, was already occurring.

Several Supreme Court decisions stand out in the opening of Texas primary elections and institutions of higher education to Negroes. Parts of the reasoning behind the Court's decisions in three of those cases point out the nature of the means by which Negroes were denied equal rights and opportunities.

Nixon v. Herndon

. . . The statute of Texas . . . assumes to forbid negroes [sic] to take part in a primary election . . . discriminating against them by the distinction of color alone. States may do a good deal of classifying that it is difficult to believe rational, but there are limits, and it is too clear for extended argument that color cannot be made the basis of a statutory classification affecting the right [to vote]. . . .

Smith v. Allwright

The privilege of membership in a party may be, as this Court said in *Grovey* v. *Townsend,* no concern of a state. But when, as here, that privilege is also the essential qualification for voting in a primary to select nominees for a general election, the state makes the action of the party the action of the state.

Sweatt v. Painter

Whether the University of Texas Law School is compared with the original or the new law school for Negroes, we cannot find substantial equality in the educational opportunities offered white and Negro law students by the State. In terms of number of the faculty, variety of courses and opportunity for specialization, size

367

of the student body, scope of the library, availability of law review and similar activities, the University of Texas Law School is superior.[1]

The White Primary. The Constitution of the United States prohibited discrimination in national elections, but the Southern white primary was an effective means for disfranchising the Negro at the state and local levels. In setting up its primary, the political party stated that it held such elections as a private organization choosing its nominees and that the primary was not a part of the state election process. Negroes were not allowed to vote in the Democratic primary. Since Texas was effectively a one-party state, Democratic nominees were certain to win the general election. Therefore, Negroes were denied any meaningful voice in choosing state and local officials.

In 1923 the Texas legislature forbade Negro participation in the Democratic primary. A. Maceo Smith, the state president of the National Association for the Advancement of Colored People, and other officials of the organization enlisted the help of NAACP attorney Thurgood Marshall, later a justice of the Supreme Court. Dr. L. A. Nixon, an El Paso dentist, filed the first case in 1927, charging that he had been denied the right to vote in the Democratic primary because he was a Negro. In *Nixon* v. *Herndon* the Supreme Court held that the 1923 statute violated the equal protection clause of the Fourteenth Amendment to the Constitution.

The legislature then provided that the Democratic state executive committee might prescribe voting qualifications for participation in primaries, and that committee adopted a rule forbidding Negro voting. In a 1932 case, *Nixon* v. *Condon,* the Supreme Court held that the state might not by statute authorize the Democratic party to discriminate. In that case Justice Benjamin Cardoza stated that the Fourteenth Amendment "lays a duty upon the Court to level by its judgment these barriers of color."

[1]237 U.S. 536-541, 71 L. ed. 759-761. 321 U.S. 649, 88 L. ed. 990-998. 339 U.S. 629-636, 94 L. ed. 1114-1120 (1950). Reproduced in Wallace and Vigness, *Documents of Texas History* (Austin: Steck-Vaughn Company, 1963), 271-72, 276-77, 280-81.

368

The *Nixon* cases held that the legislature might not forbid voting based upon race and that it could not authorize another organization to discriminate. Then, without any state legislation on the subject, in May 1932 the Democratic state convention resolved that Negroes were not entitled to vote in Democratic primaries. Since the party was not an arm of the state and its action was not authorized by the state, there was no constitutional question. The Supreme Court in *Grovey* v. *Townsend* held there was no violation of the Constitution since the Democratic party was a private organization. However, in *United States* v. *Classic,* a case brought to court in Louisiana, the Court ruled that where the primary was authorized by statute, it was part of the state's election process.

Therefore, when Houston dentist Dr. Lonnie Smith filed suit against an election official in Harris County after being refused the right to vote in a primary election, the Supreme Court overruled *Grovey* v. *Townsend,* held the Democratic primary to be part of the election process, and declared that Dr. Smith was entitled to participate. *Smith* v. *Allwright,* decided by the Supreme Court in 1944, declared that the white primary was unconstitutional where the primary was authorized by law.

The Jaybird case arose from an attempt to evade the *Smith* v. *Allwright* decision by holding a preprimary primary. Evidence showed that every county official in Fort Bend County since 1889 had first won the Jaybird primary before entering the Democratic primary. In 1953 after the Jaybird Democratic Association of Fort Bend County attempted to prevent Negroes from voting in Democratic primaries, the courts decided that a primary was part of the election process whether or not it was authorized by state law. Negroes could not be refused the right to vote in any primary.

School Integration. Although significant legislation dealing with civil rights was passed during President Eisenhower's administration, the 1954 school desegregation decision, *Brown* v. *Board of Education,* was the actual beginning of the entry of Negroes into the mainstream of society. The NAACP formulated the brief on which the Supreme Court based its decision. Two separate decisions were handed down in the *Brown* case, one in 1954 and one in 1955. Both decisions were written by Chief Justice Earl Warren. The first decision did away with adherence to the principle of "separate but equal," holding that separate schools for Negroes could not be equal and were a denial of equal protection under the law as provided in the Fourteenth Amendment. The purpose of the second decision was to implement the first, and it ordered integration to proceed "with all deliberate speed."

In the *Brown* case the Supreme Court cited as a precedent *Sweatt* v. *Painter*, a 1950 case which invalidated the law forbidding the admission of Negroes to The University of Texas Law School. Heman Sweatt had sued to compel the president of the university to admit him. Although a law school was opened at Texas Southern University while the case was pending, and Sweatt was eligible for admission there, the Court held that the two schools were not substantially equal and ordered Sweatt's admission to The University of Texas.

The *Sweatt* case broke the color barrier at The University of Texas. Herman A. Barnett was the first Negro graduate of the medical school at Galveston, and he established a surgery practice in Houston. Ollice Maloy, Jr., was graduated from The University of Texas Law School and became Texas's first Negro assistant district attorney, serving in Tarrant County. Charleola Farris was among the first Negro women to be admitted to the State Bar of Texas. She received her law degree from Howard University and returned to practice in Wichita Falls.

The school desegregation cases have had a far-reaching influence on American life. A major drive to extend civil rights was begun during the 1960s by President Kennedy. Lyndon Johnson was the only senator from a former Confederate state who refused to protest the Supreme Court decision in the *Brown* case. As president, Johnson provided effective leadership in civil rights legislation.

Modernizing the State's Schools

Education was of great importance to a developing urban and industrial state. Part of the American dream was higher

370

Consolidation of school districts has made possible the construction of modern schools such as this at Victoria.

education for all who sought it. The GI Bill brought this goal closer to realization and stimulated interest in education at all levels. In 1949 the Texas legislature passed the most significant legislation concerning education in its history.

In 1947 Governor Beauford Jester had vetoed an education bill because of its inadequacy, pointing out that the state was helping to support some four hundred schools whose average daily attendance was less than ten pupils each. The governor recommended that the state pay its teachers a minimum salary of twenty-seven hundred dollars and called for other needed reforms in the public schools.

Representative Claud Gilmer of Rocksprings and Senator A. M. Aikin of Paris, longtime advocates of educational reform, headed a committee that studied the educational system. When the Gilmer-Aikin committee published its findings, three bills were introduced in the legislature as emergency measures to reform Texas public education.

The first bill reorganized the administration of the schools and established a State Board of Education, with a member to be elected from each congressional district. The board was authorized to appoint a Commissioner of Education to head

371

the Texas Education Agency. The agency was established to handle school accreditation, the allocation of state school funds, the certification of teachers and teacher training programs, and the supplying of uniform textbooks to all schools.

The second bill established a Minimum Foundation Program providing each child in the public school system with a minimum of nine months of schooling each year. The bill also made a college degree and professional education training mandatory for each teacher. A minimum salary of $2,403 was established for beginning teachers, with raises for experience and additional training.

The third Gilmer-Aikin bill provided for automatic financing of the schools without the need for the legislature to appropriate funds each biennium. Previously, the state's school districts never knew the exact amount of state funding that they could expect to receive and were unable to plan ahead adequately.

The Gilmer-Aikin bills were highly controversial, with many teachers and administrators opposing the legislation when it was first introduced. The bills passed the senate by wide margins but met stiff opposition in the house. Amendments were introduced to cripple the bills, and delaying tactics were used to block action and to force a special session of the legislature.

Governor Jester came to the rescue of the Gilmer-Aikin bills by stating that the legislation was of unusual importance and urging legislators to act. The first bill to come to a vote passed by a vote of 86 to 30, with thirty-three members absent from the house when the vote was recorded. Seeing that further resistance was futile, some opponents hastened to put their names on record in favor of the legislation, and the two remaining bills passed easily by votes of 113 to 22 and 116 to 22. A few days before he died, Governor Jester signed the Gilmer-Aikin program into law.

Improvement of the state's schools was made easier by a system of adequate roads and bus transportation which helped eliminate one-room schools with few pupils. School districts consolidated to provide better facilities and programs. The state had some 7,840 separate school districts in 1929.

The interior of this modern Texas school is an example of innovative architecture. Such schools contrast sharply with those of the early twentieth century.

By 1948 the state had only 4,474 school districts, and after passage of the Gilmer-Aikin bills the number dropped to 2,748 in 1950. By 1969 the number of districts was only 1,244, although the scholastic population grew from 1.5 million in 1947 to 2.6 million in 1969.

The quality of public education has risen steadily as state funding has increased. In 1900 the state spent $4.25 per pupil. By the 1946-47 school year, the amount had risen to $41.00 per pupil. The state spent $89.40 per pupil in 1967-68. Many school districts now pay teacher salaries higher than the state minimum. Federal aid has become an important source of money for education, especially for programs to supplement those funded by the Minimum Foundation Program.

373

The primary sources of state funding for schools are occupation and motor fuel taxes. Interest earned by the Permanent School Fund provides additional revenue. Oil leases on school lands also contribute money. The state ad valorem tax, long a source of school revenue, is being phased out under the provision of a constitutional amendment adopted in 1968, but local districts continue to rely on the ad valorem tax. Maintaining an adequate school system offering the facilities and programs demanded by the public remains one of the state's problems in the 1970s.

Discuss

1. What led to the split in the Democratic party during the early 1940s?

2. Evaluate Franklin Roosevelt's chances for election to a fifth term, had he lived.

3. Discuss the meanings of the terms *liberal* and *conservative*.

4. Why have most successful twentieth-century Texas politicians been middle of the road in their political views?

5. Review the issues and outcomes of the gubernatorial election of 1944 and the senatorial election of 1948. What conclusions can you draw about public opinion on the issues involved?

6. Compare the Texas Regulars and the Dixiecrats.

7. What was the white primary? What conclusions can you draw from a review of the procedure by which the white primary was eliminated in Texas?

8. How did the Gilmer-Aikin bills influence the quality of public education?

Identify

Wendell Willkie
Texas Regulars
Homer P. Rainey
Beauford Jester
Coke Stevenson
Dixiecrats
Tom C. Clark
Nixon v. *Herndon*

Nixon v. *Condon*
Grovey v. *Townsend*
Smith v. *Allwright*
Jaybird primary
Brown v. *Board of Education*
Sweatt v. *Painter*
Minimum Foundation Program
Texas Education Agency

WORLD WAR II STIMULATED THE DEVELOPMENT OF
TEXAS INDUSTRY AND TRANSPORTATION. SHOWN IS
A BEAUMONT SHIPPING TERMINAL FOR TEXAS SULFUR.

CHAPTER 22

"Powerhouse of the United States"

By the middle of the twentieth century, Texas had become an integral part of the nation's political, economic, and cultural life. A Texan was Speaker of the House of Representatives. One Texas senator was chairman of the powerful Foreign Relations Committee, and the other was the second-ranking member of the Democratic caucus, the whip. Sam Rayburn, Tom Connally, and Lyndon Johnson were only part of a strong Texas delegation in Washington. Texas industries supplied oil, natural gas, petrochemicals, helium, carbon black, and sulfur. From her farms and ranches came cotton, rice, beef, wool, and mohair. The shift had been made from an agricultural, rural economy to an industrialized, urban society. Excellent highways spanned Texas and linked her with the nation. Airlines made it possible to reach either coast in the time it had taken to get to the county seat twenty years before. Texans were performing in movies and on the stage. They were writing books and music. Dallas was becoming important as a fashion center due in large part to the reputation of Neiman-Marcus.

Television brought world events into Texas living rooms. National advertising and distribution meant Texans used the same products as Oregonians and New Yorkers. But as they grew closer to the rest of the nation, Texans offered a certain resistance. They welcomed the benefits of advancements in business, transportation, and communications, but they wanted to maintain their autonomy as a state.

"Unlimited Growth"

As Texas entered the 1950s, Governor Allan Shivers predicted, "I think the growth of Texas is unlimited." And with over half a billion dollars invested in industry each year in the decade since the end of World War II, Texas became a leading industrial state. In the nine years following 1949 the value added by manufacturing in Texas increased by almost 200 percent. Abundant natural resources spurred industrial growth. Oil was an economical fuel for factories located in Texas. By ship, rail, truck, and pipeline, petroleum products were sent to the rest of the world.

Texas produced enough natural gas to supply half the nation's needs. Gas processing and subsidiary petrochemical industries grew rapidly. Resources such as stone, clay, granite, limestone, and timber added to the industrial output. Abundant land and water, a plentiful labor supply, cheap fuels, and low taxes induced major industries to move to Texas. Oil field and construction machinery plants, aircraft and automobile factories, and plants producing scientific and technical instruments were among the industries of the state. Farm and ranch products generated canning and freezing facilities. By 1958 Texas had thirty cotton mills and three woolen mills.

Although agriculture remained an important source of income, industry became the state's largest producer of wealth.

Industrial development caused people to concentrate in the cities. In 1956 *U.S. News and World Report* informed its readers, "Texas, an empire within a republic, is shaping up as the new powerhouse of the United States. In the Lone Star State, oil fields are booming. Big, new industries are springing up. Quiet towns are being transformed, almost violently, into large cities with towering skylines."

The Politics of Oil

The Tidelands. During the 1950s Texas politics were enlivened by the addition of the tidelands issue. As its main natural resource, oil was of great economic importance to the state. It was also important to the nation, for there was much talk of American petroleum reserves being exhausted in another generation. The controversy over the tidelands concerned which government, state or federal, should own the land beneath the ocean beyond the three-mile limit and regulate drilling there.

In 1933 the courts had upheld the right of the state to regulate oil production through the Texas Railroad Commission. The Interstate Oil Compact Commission was created in 1935 to facilitate the exchange of information on petroleum conservation among the oil-producing states. The duties of the Texas Railroad Commission expanded as the petroleum industry grew and became more complex. Railroad Commissioner Ernest O. Thompson stated that the commission's conservation function was to leave unclaimed "the least possible amount of oil never to be recovered by man." This objective included saving natural gas, which was required to raise crude oil to the earth's surface. Until the end of World War II, much natural gas had been discharged into the air or burned as waste, since it had limited commercial value. The railroad commission stopped the wasting of natural gas in the 1940s. Extensive pipeline building resulted in the delivery, by 1950, of Texas natural gas to every part of the nation except New England and the Pacific Northwest.

The railroad commission enforced conservation by regulating the spacing of wells. Too many wells in a given area wastes

Offshore drilling in the Gulf of Mexico led to the tidelands controversy.

gas, so that some of the oil cannot be brought to the surface. Economic waste was prevented by limiting the production of each well. Rules were also set up prescribing the manner of abandoning a well to protect against such hazards as the pollution of groundwater by salt water from abandoned wells.

The fact that oil is subject to depletion, or being used up, led Congress in 1926 to permit oil producers to deduct 27.5

percent of their gross income from oil production on their tax returns. Critics have considered the depletion allowance to be an unjustified windfall for oilmen. Supporters have subscribed to the argument made by Railroad Commissioner Thompson in 1953 before the House Ways and Means Committee. Thompson maintained that the allowance was justified because of actual depletion—every barrel pumped from a well means the well is one barrel nearer exhaustion—and because oil exploration represents a gamble on the part of the driller. The depletion allowance softened the impact of the nonproductive wells oilmen inevitably drilled. In 1969, after a stiff congressional battle, the depletion allowance was reduced to 22 percent.

Tidelands oil became a national political issue at midcentury. Offshore drilling had proven the existence of oil beneath the Gulf of Mexico. Geological surveys indicated that within thirty miles of the state's coastline lay some 245 structures showing the promise of oil. In 1948 Governor Beauford Jester testified before the House Judiciary Committee that oil revenues from the submerged lands could exceed a billion dollars, all of which was pledged to the state's Permanent School Fund.

Texas claimed that her boundary extended three leagues, or 10.36 miles, into the Gulf of Mexico by virtue of an 1836 act of the Congress of the Republic of Texas setting the boundary at that point. Texas contended that when she was annexed the United States accepted the 10.36-mile boundary, but the United States position was that Texas's boundary lay only three miles offshore. The controversy then had to do only with the submerged lands between the three-mile and the three-league limits, but the amount involved was in the hundreds of millions of dollars.

In 1946 President Truman vetoed a bill giving up the federal government's claim to the submerged lands. In 1947 in *United States* v. *California* and *United States* v. *Louisiana,* the Supreme Court upheld the federal government's rights to submerged lands claimed by those other states. Anxiety among Texas oil producers increased. They feared the federal government would be more difficult to deal with than the state, and that oil production on the submerged lands would be less profitable under federal control. Petroleum exploration and drilling in the Gulf of Mexico slowed due to the confusion over ownership. Then a 1950 Supreme Court decision held that Texas's ownership of the submerged lands beyond the three-mile limit became subordinate to that of the federal government upon annexation. Two of the justices abstained, and the majority opinion was supported by only four of the seven remaining justices. The decision did not deny Texas's ownership but held that the ownership of the United States, growing out of annexation, was paramount. For state ownership to be of value, the federal government would have to waive its interest. Many Texans were infuriated, feeling that the United States was taking something that belonged to Texas. The newspapers and some officials called it "the tidelands grab." It was clear that they did not consider the issue closed.

Democrats for Eisenhower. In the presidential election of 1952 General Dwight Eisenhower, the Republican nominee, defeated Democrat Adlai E. Stevenson by a margin of 353 electoral votes. In the popular vote Eisenhower led by 6.6 million of 61 million ballots. Eisenhower carried areas that had been longtime Democratic strongholds in the South and the large cities. The Republicans won control of the House by eight seats. Since the Senate was evenly split, the vote of Vice-President Richard Nixon made it possible for Republicans to organize it. Lyndon Johnson was the Senate Democratic leader.

For the second time in history, a Republican candidate received Texas's electoral votes. Eisenhower had 1,102,878 popular votes to Stevenson's 970,128. Eisenhower benefited from anti–New Deal sentiment that had colored Texas politics since 1944. The Truman administration had been unpopular with many Texans. The Korean War had broken out, and the end did not seem to be in sight. The exposure of graft and corruption in the Internal Revenue Service weakened the Democrats. Senator Joseph McCarthy of Wisconsin warned of Communists in the government and accused some administration officials of attempting to conceal evidence of Communist espionage in their departments. Although McCarthy never proved any of his charges, he had some supporters in Texas. Truman lost some popularity by his removal from command

382

of General Douglas MacArthur in a dispute over MacArthur's conduct of the Korean War.

After twenty years of Democratic rule, some people simply felt it was time for a change. The tidelands issue was the determining factor for many Texas voters. Some remembered that General Eisenhower was born in Texas. Texans were grateful for Eisenhower's service in World War II, and some simply "liked Ike." Eisenhower was born in Denison on October 14, 1890. His father was employed by the Missouri, Kansas, and Texas Railroad. Dwight Eisenhower grew up in Abilene, Kansas, and won an appointment to West Point. During World War II Eisenhower commanded United States forces in Europe. After the war he was president of Columbia University and commander of North Atlantic Treaty Organization forces.

Both the Democrats and the Republicans approached Eisenhower to run as their candidate for president. Eisenhower was enormously popular with Americans. At the same time he gave an impression of strength. Russia was determined to dominate Eastern Europe. Communist China had instigated the Korean War. As a military man and a war leader, Eisenhower seemed competent to cope with the ambitions of Communism.

In national Republican politics a power fight developed between conservatives backing Ohio senator Robert Taft and the more liberal Republicans sponsoring Eisenhower. In January 1952 the *Houston Post* declared Eisenhower to be the choice of its readers. He was also the heavy favorite in Texas Republican precinct and county conventions, but the state convention chose Taft delegates to send to the national convention. Eisenhower supporters prevented the seating of the pro-Taft Texas delegation at the Republican National Convention. The failure of the Texas state convention to send Eisenhower delegates after Eisenhower was the choice of the precincts and counties backfired and ruined Taft's chances. Eisenhower received the nomination and selected Senator Richard M. Nixon of California as his running mate.

Texas Democrats went into the Democratic National Convention favoring Senator Richard Russell of Georgia, but sentiment for Governor Adlai Stevenson of Illinois was too strong. Governor Allan Shivers and Attorney General Price Daniel, learning that Stevenson would not support legislation giving the tidelands to Texas, announced they would refuse to support the national Democratic ticket. Eisenhower was against federal ownership of the tidelands because it would "bring about steady progress toward centralized ownership and control," which he opposed.

Shivers and Daniel called themselves Democrats for Eisenhower. At the September state Democratic convention Shivers appealed for a split ticket, Eisenhower for president and Democrats for state offices. In November Shivers ran on both Republican and Democratic tickets. He defeated Austin district judge Ralph Yarborough in the primary. Daniel had announced for the Senate, causing Tom Connally to retire. Then Daniel defeated Congressman Lindley Beckworth of Gladewater. Both Yarborough and Beckworth were Stevenson supporters.

For the first time, both presidential candidates campaigned in Texas. President Truman toured in behalf of Stevenson. General Eisenhower was introduced by Price Daniel in Houston and by Shivers in San Antonio. Former Democratic governors Hobby, Moody, and Coke Stevenson spoke on television in Eisenhower's behalf. The excitement resulted in a huge vote in Texas, some 2 million ballots, an increase of 72 percent over the previous high. President Eisenhower obtained legislation quitclaiming the tidelands of Texas in 1953, resulting in receipt of $163 million, by 1967, from leasing of the submerged lands.

Many Texans held high positions in the executive branch of the national government in the 1950s. Robert A. Lovett, a native of Huntsville and a graduate of Yale, was appointed deputy secretary of defense in 1950 and served as secretary of defense from 1951 to 1953. He was later a special adviser to President John F. Kennedy. Mrs. Oveta Culp Hobby, wife of former Texas governor Will P. Hobby, became the first secretary of the newly created Department of Health, Education, and Welfare. She resigned in 1955 to assume the management of the *Houston Post* when her husband became ill.

Houston lawyer Dillon Anderson was the president's special assistant for national security affairs and a delegate to the

1955 summit conference in Geneva. He was the author of the very successful *The Billingsley Papers* and *Claudie's Kinfolks*. Robert B. Anderson, a native of Burleson and a graduate of The University of Texas, was the general manager of the W. T. Waggoner estate when he was named, in late 1952, secretary of the navy. From 1957 to 1961 he served as secretary of the treasury, and in 1961 he became secretary of defense.

The Shivers Years

Governor Beauford Jester died in July 1949 in his second term. Lieutenant Governor Allan Shivers succeeded Jester. Shivers became Texas's first three-term governor in 1954, defeating Ralph Yarborough. Through his bolt of the Democratic party and his unprecedented filing on both the Democratic and the Republican tickets, Governor Shivers attracted national attention. Shivers's main concern was the protection of the state from encroachment by the federal government, but he also pushed through the legislature many important measures.

During 1951 the legislature faced its chronic problem of lack of funds. Rapid growth and urbanization required higher expenditures for highways, education, and welfare. The population shift to the cities created such pressure for increased urban representation in the legislature that the state was redistricted for the first time in thirty years. Constitutional limitations on urban representation kept the cities at a disadvantage. The senator from Harris County represented 806,701 people, whereas the one from the area around El Campo had 136,756 constituents after the redistricting was done. A member of the lower house from a Panhandle district might represent only 30,000 people, while a Houston legislator represented 100,000. The need for drivers to be financially responsible for damage they might do resulted in a financial responsibility act and an automobile inspection law.

Hospital facilities were expanded, with the governor describing the situation as "Texas, the proud Lone Star State—first in oil, forty-eighth in mental hospitals." He urged prison reform, highway building, old-age pensions, aid to the blind and to dependent children, and unemployment compensation.

The growth in state government and higher education since
World War II has required many new buildings. Both the capitol
complex and The University of Texas have grown greatly.

The 1953 legislature voted a six hundred dollar teacher pay
raise but failed to appropriate adequate funds. Because of
the constitutional prohibition on deficit spending the comp-
troller could not permit payments under the measure.

The 1953 legislature submitted and the voters approved a
number of constitutional amendments, including higher legislative salaries and jury service for women. Sarah Hughes of
Dallas had spent a decade as judge of the 14th District Court,
but she had never been eligible to be a juror. Other amendments authorized the operation of a turnpike between Dallas
and Fort Worth and permitted establishment of the State
Building Commission.

Shivers tried for a third term in 1954. His opponent, Ralph
Yarborough, defeated by Shivers in 1952, demanded that
Shivers explain profits he had made in certain business deals
and land sales. The governor ran on a platform of completing
his program. He won 775,008 to 683,132. Although Price

Daniel and John Connally later served three terms each, Shivers had the greatest length of service because of the portion of the Jester term he served in addition to his own six years.

In the 1954 campaign Shivers referred to the recent Supreme Court decision in *Brown* v. *Board of Education.* Shivers promised that if he were reelected he would maintain segregation in the public schools. He declared, "If we bow down to the Supreme Court decree, if we artificially and arbitrarily enforce the mixing of white and colored children in the classroom, we are going to blight the education of whole generations of children from both races." Shivers sent Texas Rangers in 1956 to intervene in the integration of the Mansfield high school, where Negro students had been admitted by court order and a mob was creating disorder. The Negro students withdrew. Shivers charged Communist influence in desegregation and unionization. He denounced the Political Action Committee of the CIO and striking labor unions in the Beaumont–Port Arthur area.

Governor Shivers's third term was marred by scandal. A great number of Texas insurance companies had become insolvent, some eighty-six in the decade ending in 1955. Laws were enacted to correct the situation, but failures continued. It was found later that some legislators were financially involved.

The state had established a program to lend money to veterans to buy farms. The Veterans Land Board, composed of the governor, the attorney general, and the land commissioner, was to supervise the program. Bascom Giles, the land commissioner, was sentenced to the penitentiary after investigations disclosed that the state had been defrauded of millions of dollars through irregular land sales.

Price Daniel resigned from the Senate to run for governor in 1956. Ralph Yarborough, making his third race for the governorship, charged Daniel with laxity in fulfilling his responsibilities when he was a member of the Veterans Land Board. Daniel led Yarborough and four others, including W. Lee O'Daniel, who polled 347,000 votes. In the runoff Daniel defeated Yarborough by only thirty-two hundred of 1.4 million ballots cast.

Governor Shivers announced that he would lead the Texas delegation to the 1956 Democratic National Convention to oppose the candidacy of Adlai Stevenson. However, Speaker Sam Rayburn led a group of loyal Democrats to form the Democratic Advisory Committee to rebuild the party in Texas. Lyndon Johnson was nominated as a favorite son candidate for president, and the Rayburn forces swept the precinct conventions and controlled the Texas delegation to the national convention.

The Politics of Pollution

The 1950s were drought years in Texas. The lack of moisture went deep, so that when heavy rains came in the spring of 1957 the powdered topsoil washed away. Texans were reminded of the need for water management. The State Board of Water Development, later renamed the Texas Water Development Board, was created in 1957 to plan for development of water resources and flood control. In May 1957 a cloudburst dumped some ten inches of rain on Burnet and Lampasas counties. The resulting floods caused five deaths, rendered hundreds of families homeless, destroyed 168 business and industrial establishments, and caused $6.5 million in property damage. The long shortage of water followed by disastrous floods was not an unusual situation.

Congress had passed the Watershed Protection and Flood Prevention Act of 1954 to help prevent excessive water and silt from pouring into major rivers. Coauthored by Congressman W. R. Poage of Waco, the act required each participating locality to acquire land, share in the cost of construction of dams, and maintain the project when completed. The dams were planned to aid in flood control, store water for industrial and city use, and provide recreational facilities. Large lakes would gain some protection against siltation by the sediment caught in the watershed dams. Unfortunately, three dams which had been authorized for the Lampasas area had not been constructed in 1957.

Decreased rainfall coupled with increased usage of groundwater supplies caused falling water tables. Texans in some areas were faced with a critical shortage of water that was to grow during the 1960s. Houston reported the water level in

Texas lakes provide flood control, electric power, and recreational opportunities as well as water conservation.

its wells falling at a rate of eight feet a year. Nacogdoches noted that its water table was retreating almost as rapidly, and other cities experienced a diminishing water supply at the same time demands were increasing. Adding to the problem was the dumping of untreated or inadequately treated sewage into lakes and streams, which polluted the water supply of cities downstream and made some bodies of water unsafe for swimming. Congress passed the Pollution Control Act in 1956, offering matching funds to municipalities agreeing to modernize sewage treatment facilities. Texas cities were slow to act, although the amount of effluents reaching lakes and streams kept increasing.

As population and industry grew, Texans needed to find new sources of water as well as to conserve existing supplies. Texas had only 8 major reservoirs in 1913. By 1969 there were 157 major reservoirs existing or under construction, plus a number of smaller ones. The legislature established the State Board of Water Development in 1957 and the Texas Water

Quality Board in 1961 to establish means of developing new sources of water supply, help conserve existing water resources, and combat pollution of Texas's surface and groundwater supplies. Port Mansfield, Willacy County, has operated a plant for purifying salt water since 1965, and the 1968 revised plan of the Texas Water Development Board to meet water needs for the next half century included bringing water from the Mississippi River.

Texas—Space Center, U.S.A.

For years Americans led the world in technology. Then in the fall of 1957 the Russians launched a manmade earth satellite, Sputnik I. Soviet prestige rose, and America rushed to catch up in the space race. The American reaction to Sputnik, a new emphasis on scientific research and education and the acceleration of the American space effort, brought Texas into a new era.

The American space age became possible by virtue of the massive calculations of which computers are capable, the miniaturization of electronic gear permitted by transistors and integrated circuits, and an economic system which freed most Americans from growing food, constructing housing, and making their own clothing. In 1954 Gordon Teal of Texas Instruments at Dallas invented the silicon transistor. In 1958 Jack Killry of Dallas invented the integrated circuit, which combined transistors, resistors, and capacitors—all of the elements of an electronic circuit—in one tiny unit.

Space exploration would answer questions long pondered. More importantly, money spent in the space effort would create additional employment (needed since a recession had begun) and stimulate the society as well as the economy. A multitude of inventions and innovations would result, with applications in areas from fuel to physiology.

In November 1957 the Russians orbited Sputnik II, carrying a dog as a passenger. American newsmen called it "Muttnik." Speaker Sam Rayburn and Senate majority leader Lyndon Johnson pushed through Congress President Eisenhower's requests for space funds and programs. Emphasis was placed upon education at all levels to catch and stay with the Russians. Texas's appropriations for education were increased somewhat, but the chronic problem of inadequate funds would remain until the adoption of a new broad-based tax.

In January 1958 the United States launched its first satellite, Explorer I, weighing some eighteen pounds. It did not compare favorably with either Sputnik. Explorer I was designed to measure cosmic rays and temperature and to radio data to earth, but its main purpose was to show that America could launch a satellite. Russia's Nikita Khrushchev scoffed at American attempts, saying in 1959, "You send up oranges while we send up tons." In April 1961 the Soviets launched a five-ton manned capsule. In August a Russian manned vehicle orbited the earth seventeen times.

John F. Kennedy was inaugurated in 1961. He named Vice-President Lyndon Johnson head of the National Aeronautics and Space Council and made it clear that he expected results. On recommendation of the space council, President Kennedy committed America to "achieving the goal, before this decade is out, of landing a man on the moon and returning him safely to earth." The National Aeronautics and Space Administration sought a location for the Manned Spacecraft Center, a giant complex designed to serve as a research facility, mission control center, astronaut training base, and receiving laboratory for men and material returned from the moon. Congressman Albert Thomas insisted that Houston would be a perfect location. Lyndon Johnson encouraged consideration of a Texas site.

In September 1961 the National Aeronautics and Space Administration announced that it would build a $60 million facility southeast of Houston on a thousand-acre tract donated by Rice University. The site is ideal for the space center, as it lies approximately equidistant from each coast. Transportation, climate, and the supply of labor were all good, and there were suitable universities and other research facilities close at hand.

The space center contributed to the growth of Houston and the state. The building of the gigantic complex created new jobs and put money into the economy. Supporting industries

391

located facilities nearby. Housing had to be provided for personnel involved in designing and building spacecraft, training astronauts, and planning the space program. The Humble Oil and Refining Company announced that it would build a commercial, industrial, and residential development near the space center involving an investment of $900 million and creating twenty-five thousand new jobs.

The University of Houston, Texas A&M University, and Rice University received grants for space research programs. In 1953 Rice opened the nation's first space science department. The demand for highly specialized personnel increased the demands on higher education. At the end of five years, the Manned Spacecraft Center had some forty-eight hundred employees and a $50 million payroll. The center attracted some 125 business firms to the Houston area. For each one hundred persons employed at the space center an estimated sixty-five new jobs had been created in the surrounding area.

NASA

Technicians in the Lunar Receiving Laboratory of the Manned Spacecraft Center at work on material brought back by Apollo 14

The Manned Spacecraft Center launched the United States successfully into the space race. Houston became the gateway to the moon. Before the end of the decade the objective stated by President Kennedy was achieved. Not only did the Americans land a man on the moon in July 1969: they took a television camera along so that the whole world might see Neil Armstrong take man's first step on the moon. Moments later, Edwin Aldrin became the second man to walk on the moon.

The Soaring Sixties

The space race was only one of the important developments in Texas during the 1960s. The population continued its shift to the cities. In 1960 Texas stood sixth in the nation in population with 9.5 million people, an increase of almost 25 percent since 1950. The ten-year increase was greater than Texas's entire population in 1880.

The trend toward urbanization resulted in 75 percent of Texans living in towns and cities in 1960. As the number of farms decreased, the trend toward large farms accelerated. In 1940 there had been almost as many tenants on farms as there were owners. By 1960 owners outnumbered tenants by four to one. In 1960 Texas had twenty-one metropolitan areas—more than any other state. The standard metropolitan statistical area includes a city or cities of at least fifty thousand persons plus the county in which the city is located. It also includes adjoining counties economically and socially integrated with the central city. During the 1960s Texas's metropolitan areas increased to twenty-three, including thirty-eight Texas counties. In 1970 these metropolitan areas had about 70 percent of the state's population and 85 percent of the manufacturing.

Texas's problems were much the same as those facing other American industrial states in the turbulent 1960s. Inflation, the war in Vietnam, crime, welfare, civil rights, poverty, education, unemployment, and ecology all demanded solutions. Americans were going to the moon through the efforts and genius of thousands and thousands of people. They believed these other problems, though not capable of being handled by tech-

393

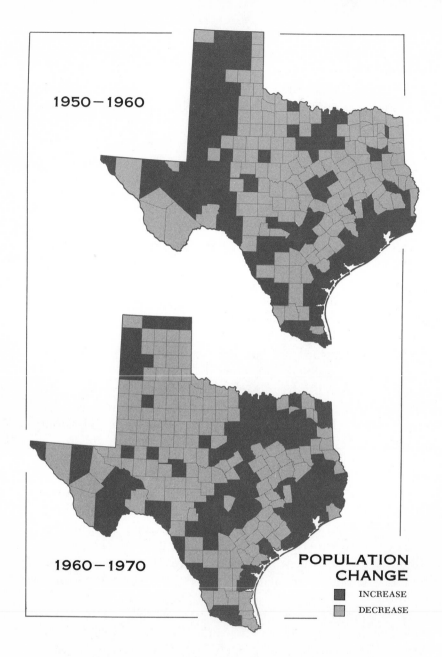

1950–1960

1960–1970

POPULATION
CHANGE

■ INCREASE

▨ DECREASE

nology alone, might well yield to the approach which had broken man away from the gravitational pull of the earth: the making of rational plans and their execution in cooperation, optimism, and faith.

Discuss

1. What factors have aided the development of industry in Texas?

2. Why was the tidelands dispute of concern to all Texans?

3. What factors enabled Eisenhower to carry Texas in the election of 1952?

4. Compare the problems Texas faced in 1900 with those she faced in the 1950s.

5. Why are the issues of pollution and water conservation closely linked?

6. What steps were taken in Texas in the late 1950s and early 1960s to conserve Texas's water supply?

7. What effect did the launching of Sputnik I have on the United States?

8. What factors contributed to the selection of a Texas site for the Manned Spacecraft Center?

Identify

Allan Shivers
oil depletion allowance
tidelands dispute
Democrats for Eisenhower
Oveta Culp Hobby
Robert B. Anderson
Bascom Giles
Manned Spacecraft Center
Price Daniel
Ralph Yarborough

Watershed Protection
and Flood Prevention
Act
Pollution Control Law
Texas Water Develop-
ment Board
Sputnik I
Explorer I
standard metropolitan
statistical area

PRESIDENT JOHNSON SIGNED THE CIVIL RIGHTS ACT
1964 BEFORE AN ASSEMBLAGE OF DISTINGUISHED CO
GRESSIONAL AND CIVIL RIGHTS LEADERS.

CHAPTER 23

"To Catch a Vision"

Historian Walter Prescott Webb was an acute observer. The industrial and economic progress of the South after World War II caused Webb to say, on the eve of the 1960s, "What the South needs today more than any other one thing is for its people to catch a vision—not of a glorious past, but of a far greater future."

Everything seemed to be changing, and changes came with ever-increasing rapidity. Abroad, the United States was on guard to prevent the spread of Communism. At home, after a delay of centuries, the Negro was moving in the direction of equality. The growth of population and cities resulted in a multitude of social, political, and economic problems. The productivity of the economy promised greater leisure as well as abundance. Above all, the 1960s were years of concern over individual rights and freedoms and United States involvement in international affairs.

The Road to the Sixties

The Daniel Administration. In the election of 1956 President Eisenhower carried Texas as he turned back Adlai Stevenson once again. Governor Shivers was retiring after a record seven and a half years in office. In the Democratic primary former senator Price Daniel narrowly defeated Ralph Yarborough for the gubernatorial nomination.

Upon Daniel's resignation from the United States Senate, William Blakley from Dallas was appointed to serve until the April 1957 special election. Ralph Yarborough defeated Blakley and eighteen others to capture the Senate seat. Yarborough served until his defeat by former congressman Lloyd Bentsen in 1970.

A 1957 legislative investigation revealed that several legislators had accepted fees from large corporations. One representative was convicted of taking a bribe. Because of the failure of a number of insurance companies, the legislature reorganized the State Board of Insurance Commissioners and provided for stricter regulation of the insurance business. In other actions, the legislature passed a teacher pay raise and raised tuition at state-supported colleges.

Among the constitutional amendments submitted to the voters in 1958 was one permitting the state to advertise for tourists and industry. Voter approval paved the way for the establishment of the Texas Tourist Development Agency, which was made an independent board in 1969. The voters also considered an amendment providing for annual legislative sessions and higher salaries for legislators. The amendment was defeated, and the question of annual sessions remains a recurrent one.

Governor Daniel was reelected in 1958. He defeated state senator Henry B. Gonzalez, who later was elected to Congress from San Antonio. Gonzalez served on the San Antonio city council and was the first Mexican-American state senator since José Antonio Navarro ended his term in 1849.

The major problem of the 1959 legislature was the usual one—a need for more money. The days when taxes on oil supported a large part of the cost of Texas government were long since past. Imported oil kept Texas production down, so that severance taxes could not be depended upon as in those times. Three special sessions of the legislature were called to pass taxes for the necessary $100 million in additional revenue. The financial needs of the state remained a major issue while Texans put off levying the broad-based tax they knew was inevitable.

In 1960 Governor Daniel announced for a third term. He defeated Jack Cox of Breckenridge in the Democratic primary and Republican William Steger in the general election. Senator Lyndon Johnson became vice-president, and a special election was called to fill the resulting vacancy in the Senate. Republican John Tower of Wichita Falls won the election to become Texas's first Republican senator since Reconstruction. Senator Tower was reelected in 1966.

John B. Connally, former administrative assistant to Lyndon Johnson, was appointed secretary of the navy by President John F. Kennedy. Connally, a native of Floresville, returned to Texas in 1962 to run for governor. Governor Daniel announced that he would seek a fourth term but ran a poor third in a six-man race. In the runoff, Connally defeated Don Yarborough of Houston by twenty-six thousand votes. Jack Cox, who had become a Republican, made a strong showing against Connally in the general election. Republican Ed Foreman of Odessa was elected to the United States Congress. Republican congressman Bruce Alger of Dallas was reelected, and eight Republicans won seats in the Texas House of Representatives.

The State, the Nation, and the New Frontier

The Kennedy Years. The space race, emphasizing education, growth, and progress, made the nation more youth conscious than ever before. The result was that in 1960 the presidential candidates were both in their forties, and on the following inauguration day the oldest president in the history of the nation turned over the government to the second youngest. Forty-three-year-old John Fitzgerald Kennedy defeated Republican vice-president Richard M. Nixon, forty-seven. Nixon had an advantage over Kennedy in that he was a member of the party in power. However, Republican chances had been

Speaker Sam Rayburn placed Lyndon Johnson's name in nomination for president at the Democratic National Convention in 1960.

damaged by an economic recession and a liberal-conservative split in the Republican party. Lyndon Johnson had made a serious try for the Democratic nomination. Speaker Sam Rayburn placed his name before the Democratic National Convention, but the Kennedy forces were too strong, and Johnson had to accept second place on the Democratic ticket.

Kennedy, winner of a 1957 Pulitzer Prize for his book *Profiles in Courage,* faced a formidable task. He was not as well known as Nixon, and he was aware that no Catholic had been elected president. The only major candidate to have made the attempt, Governor Al Smith of New York, had been defeated. Speaking before the Greater Houston Ministerial Association on September 12, 1960, Kennedy urged the abolition of religion as a campaign issue. Kennedy's candidacy was helped by his television debates with Nixon.

John Kennedy promised a New Frontier and warned, "The world is very different now, for man holds in his mortal hands the power to abolish all forms of human poverty and all forms of human life." Kennedy had served three terms in the United

400

States House of Representatives and had been a senator since 1952. He believed that the president should be a "vigorous proponent of the national interest" and that the nation's capitol should be "the vital center of action." Kennedy carried Texas by a narrow margin of 46,000 of 2.3 million ballots cast. Nationally the difference was 118,000 out of nearly 69 million, a minute plurality of 49.77 percent compared to Nixon's 49.59 percent. Thirteen minor candidates accounted for the other .64 percent.

As Kennedy took office, unemployment was rising and the economy needed stimulation. He urged business to hold down prices and asked labor not to demand increased wages. Congress extended unemployment benefits and increased the minimum wage. In 1962, when United States Steel and five other steel producers announced a price increase, Kennedy charged them with acting in "defiance of the public interest." By 1963 the economy was turning around. The gross national product had increased. Prices were fairly stable, but unemployment continued high since profits were too low to permit vigorous industrial expansion.

President Kennedy requested that Congress enact a broad plan of federal aid to education, saying "failures of our educational system breed failures in our social and economic system." Congress extended aid to higher education, vocational education, and basic education for adults in 1963. Education became an instrument of reform: it had not only to keep pace with society but to help create a better society.

Kennedy's civil rights message to Congress in February 1963 stressed the need for equal voting rights for minorities, an end to school segregation, and equal employment opportunities. When Congress failed to pass appropriate legislation, Negro leaders such as Dr. Martin Luther King, Jr., head of the Southern Christian Leadership Conference, and Roy Wilkins, executive secretary of the NAACP, intensified their efforts toward equality.

Defenders of Freedom and Democracy. The Mexican Americans in Texas had worked in the president's behalf in 1960. An outgrowth of the Viva Kennedy clubs was the Political Association of Spanish-speaking Organizations. A potent political force in Texas, PASO encourages Mexican Americans to register and vote and works for the election of candidates sympathetic to organization goals. In 1963 PASO backed five city council candidates in Crystal City, all of whom were elected.

In 1960 just under 15 percent of the population was Mexican-American, yet no Texas congressman was Mexican-American. Henry B. Gonzalez was elected to Congress the following year. Eligio de la Garza from Mission, who had served six terms in the legislature, was elected to Congress in 1964 and has been reelected three times. A member of LULAC, Congressman De la Garza earned a law degree from St. Mary's University Law School in San Antonio.

President Kennedy appointed Reynaldo G. Garza of Brownsville as district judge for South Texas in March 1961. Garza has served on the International Good Neighbor Council, the Governor's Committee of Twenty-five on Education Beyond the High School, and the Texas Educational Standards Committee.

State senator Joe J. Bernal of San Antonio was a member of the Texas House of Representatives before entering the senate in 1966. He serves on committees concerned with vocational education, slums and poverty. He has been a strong advocate of education for children of migrant workers. Representative Honoré Ligarde of Laredo is of Mexican and French ancestry. He was state Democratic executive committeeman in the early 1960s. Other Mexican Americans in the Texas House of Representatives are: Oscar Carrillo, Sr., Raul L. Longoria, Robert L. Vale, Tati Santiesteban, Raul Muniz, Lauro Cruz, Henry Sánchez, Jr., J. A. García, Jr., Paul C. Moreno, and Carlos Truan.

Mexican-American participation in local government has grown in recent years. Albert Peña, Jr., a Bexar County commissioner, has written numerous articles about the Mexican American. His writings are a study of the problems of Mexican Americans. Peter Torres, Jr., and Felix Trevino were members of the San Antonio city council. M. C. Gonzales, one of the founders of LULAC, has served for many years as an assistant district attorney of Bexar County.

Dr. Edward T. Ximenes, whose term on the board of regents of The University of Texas expired in 1971

Edward Cazares, an aide to Senator Lyndon Johnson, was an assistant attorney general and is an assistant city attorney in Houston. Felix Tijerina, another founder of LULAC, was a teacher and has been chairman of the Houston Housing Authority.

Many Texans of Mexican descent have entered the professions. George I. Sánchez of The University of Texas faculty has written a number of studies of the Mexican American. Dr. Edward Ximenes of Floresville served on Governor Connally's Committee on Aging. He was a regent of The University of Texas. Dr. Mario Palafox of El Paso is an orthopedic surgeon. Dr. Gregorio Canales from Hebbronville also practices orthopedics. Dr. Aureliano Urrutia, Sr., of San Antonio is a thoracic surgeon. Six of Dr. Urrutia's sons have become physicians or surgeons.

Tragedy in Dallas. Dissension among Texas Democrats had caused President Kennedy much concern. With a lead as narrow as he had had in 1960 he could not afford for feuding Democrats to let the Republicans take Texas in 1964. He decided on a goodwill trip, hoping to bring together Governor John Connally and Senator Ralph Yarborough, the chiefs of the warring factions. On November 21, 1963, the president and

403

Mrs. Kennedy flew to Texas, making appearances in San Antonio and Houston and spending the night in Fort Worth.

On the morning of November 22 some five thousand people stood in a light rain across from the Texas Hotel as the president spoke from the back of a flatbed truck. "There are no faint hearts in Fort Worth," he said, "and I appreciate your being here this morning."

The crowd cheered. Someone yelled, "Where's Jackie?"

The president laughed, pointed to an eighth floor window, and said, "Mrs. Kennedy is organizing herself. It takes her a little longer; but, of course, she looks better than we do when she does it."

Kennedy called out to Uvalde to pay his respects to John Nance Garner, who was celebrating his ninety-fifth birthday. At a breakfast sponsored by the Fort Worth Chamber of Commerce the president was presented with a cowboy hat and Mrs. Kennedy was given a pair of boots. The president told his audience, "Two years ago, I introduced myself in Paris by saying that I was the man who accompanied Mrs. Kennedy to Paris. I am getting somewhat the same sensation as I travel around Texas. Nobody wonders what Lyndon and I wear." He mentioned that his brother Joe, who was killed in action in World War II, had flown his B-24 Liberator bomber from Fort Worth to Europe.

By the time the presidential airplane touched down at Dallas Love Field, the day was bright and clear. The president was met by enthusiastic crowds which grew larger as his limousine proceeded through Dallas. Governor Connally sat in the jump seat in front of the president. Mrs. Connally occupied a similar position before the First Lady. Mrs. Connally said to the president, indicating the cheering crowd, "You certainly can't say that the people of Dallas haven't given you a nice welcome."

At approximately 12:30 P.M., shots were fired from the Texas School Book Depository as the motorcade passed. Both the president and Governor Connally slumped, wounded by a single bullet. The president sustained a second wound. At Parkland Hospital, physicians pronounced President Kennedy dead at 1:00 P.M.

Austin-Travis County Collection, Austin Public Library

John F. Kennedy was to have spoken here in Austin's Municipal Auditorium on November 22, 1963.

Word of the tragedy reached the world instantly. Accused assassin Lee Harvey Oswald was arrested at the Texas Theatre in Dallas's Oak Cliff section less than an hour after the president's death. Two days later a bystander shot and killed Oswald as he was being transferred from the city jail to that of the county.

President Kennedy was buried in Arlington National Cemetery on Monday. A part of his legacy was his challenge to the American people "to reject the temptations of prejudice and violence and to reaffirm the values of freedom and law on which our free society depends."

The Great Society

Texan in the White House. Perhaps no man ever came to the presidency better prepared than Lyndon Johnson. Johnson had spent most of his adult life in national politics. His public service, begun as a schoolteacher, included terms in the House of Representatives, the Senate, and then the vice-presidency. More than thirty years on Capitol Hill as secretary to Congressman Richard Kleberg, as a congressman close to Speaker Rayburn, as Senate Democratic leader, and as vice-president had

405

enabled him to build the influence that made it possible for him to convert into law many ideas proposed by John Kennedy which Congress failed to adopt. But the United States military action in Southeast Asia, which grew and seemed endless, provided a focus for dissent within the nation and caused him not to seek reelection in 1968.

Johnson had tried hard to win the Democratic presidential nomination in 1960. After defeating him, Massachusetts senator John Kennedy asked Johnson to join him on the ticket. The Kennedy-Johnson relationship was a highly complex one. Referring to his years in the Senate before becoming president, John Kennedy said, "After all, I spent years of my life when I could not get consideration for a bill until I went around and begged Lyndon Johnson to let it go ahead." Vice-President Johnson told Congressman Franklin Roosevelt, Jr., that the vice-president's duty was not to compete with the president and that the president should not permit competition. Johnson said, "Your daddy never let his vice-presidents put their heads above water." Johnson visited thirty-three countries and made 150 speeches for the president.

Five days after Kennedy's death, President Johnson delivered a message to a joint session of Congress, urging passage of New Frontier legislation pertaining to civil rights, tax reform, and the war on poverty. "Let us continue," he said, and sparked the greatest enactment of domestic legislation since the early New Deal. The Revenue Act of 1964 reduced taxes over $11 billion, the largest cut in federal taxes since the 1920s. The president urged an "unconditional war on poverty," and Congress, with the Economic Opportunity Act, set up the Office of Economic Opportunity, the Job Corps, Volunteers in Service to America, and vocational training for youths. Civil rights legislation was equally dramatic.

As a senator, Johnson had supported strong civil rights laws. In 1964 he proposed civil rights legislation which easily passed the House of Representatives. However, in the Senate a filibuster threatened the bill. Republican senator Everett Dirksen of Illinois led the movement to cut off debate and succeeded. It was the first time that cloture had been invoked on a civil rights issue.

When Johnson became president, some people felt that a Southerner would not pursue a forceful civil rights policy. President Johnson's remarks on the subject dispelled any doubt.

Perhaps no prejudice is so contagious or so unreasoning as the unreasoning prejudice against men because of their birth, the color of their skin, or their ancestral background. Racial prejudice is dangerous because it is a disease of the majority endangering minority groups. . . . for those who would keep any group in our nation in bondage I have no sympathy or tolerance. Some may feel moved to deny this group or that the homes, the education, the employment which every American has the right to expect, but I am not one of those.[1]

On July 2, 1964, President Johnson signed the Civil Rights Act of 1964, which gave federal law enforcement agencies the power to insure the voting rights of black people, opened to them all public accommodations, and banned discrimination in employment. Other groups, such as women, benefited from removal of discriminatory barriers in employment. The Voting Rights Act of 1965 attempted to obliterate discrimination in elections.

President Johnson concluded the settlement in 1964 of the Chamizal problem, a boundary dispute nearly one hundred years old. The flooded Rio Grande had changed its course in 1867, moving south and west to somewhat its present location and leaving some 630 acres north of the new river bed between El Paso and Juárez. Both Mexico and the United States claimed this area, called Chamizal because the chamizo, a shrub, grew there. The problem of ownership of the Chamizal became serious, and boundary commissioners met in 1894 to decide the precise dividing line on the El Paso-Juárez bridge. The commissioners failed to agree, and the matter was finally submitted to arbitrators in 1911. Mexico contended that the boundary should be determined by the course of the Rio Grande as it was when treaties were signed in 1848 and in 1853. The arbi-

[1]William S. White, *The Professional: Lyndon B. Johnson* (New York: Houghton Mifflin Company, 1964), 211.

407

trators rejected the contention of the United States that the boundary had moved with the river. The United States refused to accept the arbitrators' decision because of the impossibility of locating on the ground the boundary stated by the board.

The boundary dispute smoldered for years, with Mexico resenting the fact that no settlement was made. Development of the area was retarded because of the unsettled question of ownership. On September 25, 1964, President Johnson met with Mexico's president, López Mateos, in the middle of the international bridge to commemorate the successful conclusion of the boundary settlement, which had been worked out by President Kennedy. The course of the Rio Grande was to be relocated and lined with concrete. Mexico was to receive 437 acres of land and pay for structures located on the land. The United States would acquire the land from individual owners before conveying it to Mexico.

Victory. Johnson's legislative successes gave him broad-based popularity as the election of 1964 approached. Two of his major proposals were still before Congress, one providing medical care for the aged and one offering federal assistance to depressed areas. At San Francisco, the Republicans nominated conservative Arizona senator Barry Goldwater and New York congressman William E. Miller to oppose the president and his running mate, Minnesota senator Hubert H. Humphrey. Goldwater took a tough approach in foreign affairs and proposed a reduction in government programs.

Goldwater carried his home state and five Southern states, one of which, Alabama, had no Johnson electors. Johnson was returned to the White House with the largest percentage of the popular vote in history. He polled 43 million ballots to Goldwater's 27 million. In the electoral college the count was 486 to 52. Only the 1936 Roosevelt-Landon electoral balloting was more lopsided. In addition, the Democrats gained one Senate seat to control the Senate 68 to 32. With 38 additional congressmen the Democrats outnumbered Republicans in the House 295 to 140. Two defeated Republicans were from Odessa and Dallas.

Americans had overwhelmingly approved the president's Great Society, with its emphasis on education, research, attention to urban problems, assistance to underdeveloped sections of the country, countering rising crime rates, and removing voting obstacles. Again Congress responded to the president's call for legislation dealing with equal employment opportunities, education, health care, problems of the cities, and the beautification of the country. Congress extended federal assistance to Appalachia. The Elementary and Secondary Education Act of 1965 appropriated funds for schools, disadvantaged children, educational service centers, the National Teachers Corps, higher education, and migrant and minority groups. In 1965 Medicare was extended to every American sixty-five and over, and additional health services and facilities were funded. The Department of Housing and Urban Development was established in 1965, and Robert Weaver was appointed its secretary, the first Negro to serve in the cabinet. In 1966 the Department of Transportation was created and given cabinet rank.

In March 1967 Ramsey Clark of Dallas was appointed attorney general of the United States, an office his father, Supreme Court justice Tom Clark, had held under President Truman. Upon Justice Clark's retirement, his replacement, Thurgood Marshall, became the first Negro Supreme Court justice. Cyrus R. Smith, president of American Airlines and a native of Milam County, was appointed secretary of commerce in 1968. Marvin Watson, an executive of the Lone Star Steel Company in Daingerfield, was appointed postmaster general. In addition, numerous Texans went to Washington to serve on the executive staff.

Defeat. The Eighty-ninth Congress passed a great deal of domestic legislation designed to eliminate poverty and stimulate the economy, but tragedy was developing in foreign affairs. The war in Southeast Asia escalated. The United States had assisted the South Vietnamese since October 1954, when President Eisenhower promised aid in developing and maintaining a "strong, viable state, capable of resisting attempted subversion or aggression through military means," believing that collapse of South Vietnam would cause the fall of other Southeast Asian nations.

American assistance during the early years of conflict was

mainly nonmilitary, but American advisers helped train the South Vietnamese army. In the summer of 1964 when American destroyers in international waters were attacked by North Vietnamese vessels, President Johnson ordered retaliatory bombing strikes. Congress passed the Asiatic Peace Resolution, also known as the Tonkin Gulf Resolution, authorizing necessary measures to repel armed attack and to aid any nation covered by the Southeast Asia Treaty Organization which requested aid in the defense of its freedom.

By November 1965 some 165,000 Americans were in Vietnam. A year and a half later there were 460,000, and the United States was bombing North Vietnam. Students and others protested against the war. President Johnson offered to meet leaders of the Communist forces in any part of the world to work toward a ceasefire, but the Communist leaders failed to respond. In the summer of 1967 Israel and her neighbors went to war, and Russian premier Kosygin flew to New York to appear at the United Nations and conferred with President Johnson at Glassboro, New Jersey.

Times were good. There was full employment. But wartime expenditures were inflationary, and unrest was increasing. Civil disorders occurred in dozens of American cities during 1967. More disturbances followed after the assassination of Dr. Martin Luther King in April 1968.

Beset by troubles at home and abroad and harried by antiwar protests and critics, President Johnson announced in March 1968 that he would not seek another term. He hoped his action would demonstrate to the leaders of North Vietnam the sincerity of his desire to end the war. The president, in his 1965 State of the Union Message, was speaking of the Great Society when he said, "It will require of every American . . . both faith in the destination and the fortitude to make the journey." But those words were equally appropriate to the 1970s.

Discuss

1. What reasons might voters have for opposing annual legislative sessions?

410

2. Assess the election of John Tower as United States senator in light of political developments in Texas during the Shivers administration.

3. What major problems faced the Kennedy administration?

4. Why did Lyndon Johnson have more success in pushing civil rights legislation through Congress than did President Kennedy?

5. Compare the settlement of the Chamizal boundary dispute with the settlement of the 1846 Texas boundary dispute.

6. Summarize the domestic legislation passed by Congress during the Johnson administration.

7. Compare the three major areas of endeavor pursued during the Johnson administration: the Great Society, the space race, and the war in Vietnam. Which do you feel should have had the highest priority?

Identify

Henry B. Gonzalez	Civil Rights Act of 1964
John B. Connally	Chamizal dispute
John F. Kennedy	Economic Opportunity Act
PASO	Elementary and Secondary
Eligio de la Garza	Education Act
Joe J. Bernal	Medicare
George I. Sánchez	Ramsey Clark
Lee Harvey Oswald	Marvin Watson
the Great Society	Tonkin Gulf Resolution
Barry Goldwater	

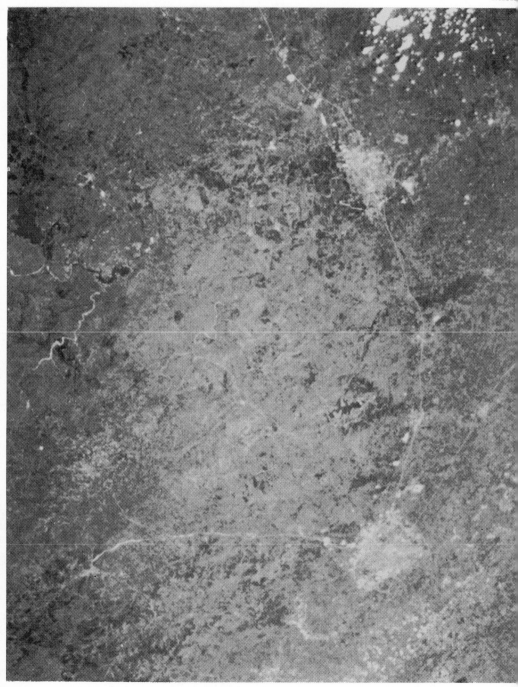

412

MAN SEES HIMSELF IN A NEW PERSPECTIVE FROM SPACE
SHOWN ARE SAN ANTONIO, AUSTIN, AND OTHER CEN-
TRAL TEXAS TOWNS.

CHAPTER 24

"Texas Reaches for Greatness"

The state to which Lyndon Johnson returned in January 1969 was vastly different from the Texas of his schoolteaching days in Cotulla and Houston. Many things had not changed. The Panhandle's northeast corner was still more than 800 miles from the southern tip of the state below Brownsville. And the easternmost point on the Sabine River was still 773 miles from the border west of El Paso. Guadalupe Peak remained the highest mountain. But Texas was no longer a remote province on the fringe of national life. Rich natural resources, location, leadership, and a diverse and able population had brought her to center stage in the affairs of the nation.

Texas in the Sixties

The Connally Administration. President Johnson returned to Texas as Governor John Connally was leaving office. Many changes in the state's economy and politics had taken place during the Connally years, 1963 to 1969. The changes reminded Texans that their constitution was drafted in an agricultural state by men recently abused by a reconstruction government. Some thought that revision of the constitution would help meet the needs of a progressive, urban state.

In his first inaugural address, on January 15, 1963, Governor Connally said, "We are all Americans. We are all Texans. Wearing these labels—and none other—let us be unified in our common purpose as we are united by our common heritage. . . . Let it be heard wherever there are men of purpose and good-will, that here, on this day, Texas reaches for greatness."

A native of Floresville and a graduate of The University of Texas, Connally had been a lieutenant commander in the navy during World War II. He was secretary to Lyndon Johnson in Washington and was secretary of the navy under President Kennedy before his election as governor of Texas in 1962. He returned to Washington in 1971 as secretary of the treasury.

During the Connally years the state's population increased by some 1 million. The state budget increased from $1.4 billion to $2.3 billion. Among the sources of state revenue, federal grants for highways, public health, welfare, and education accounted for almost 30 percent of state income in the fiscal year ending in August 1968. Production taxes on oil, gas, and sulfur brought in over 10 percent of the state's revenue, while the sales tax produced almost 12 percent. Motor fuel taxes were 11.5 percent, and cigarette, other tobacco, and alcoholic beverage taxes contributed 8 percent of state income. Motor vehicle sales tax and license fees produced almost 8 percent.

State expenditures for the same fiscal year reflect needs and priorities established by the people through their representatives. Of each state dollar, 43 cents went to education and 22 cents to highways. Eleemosynary and correctional institutions received almost 5 cents of each state dollar, and more than

414

16 cents were spent on public welfare. Less than 1 cent of the state's dollar was spent on the development and conservation of natural resources.

Higher Education. During the 1960s the number of Texans of college age nearly doubled. In addition, the demand for quality in higher education could no longer be ignored. Faculty salaries in public colleges and universities placed Texas forty-sixth among the states, a statistic suggesting inadequacy in facilities, equipment, and libraries also. Many young Texans left the state seeking a better education. Too few came back. Texas had lost potential industries because companies with highly motivated personnel demanded locations near first-class university and research resources.

In 1965 the Coordinating Board, Texas College and University System, replaced the more limited Commission on Higher Education. Its first task was an assessment of the state's educational resources. Then it would devise a master plan to minimize duplication of functions and maximize the utilization of educational facilities. The master plan developed by the board encompasses three systems: the junior colleges, the senior colleges, and the universities. Additional junior colleges and universities were recommended for various parts of the state.

At the same time enrollment was increasing, the cost of operating public institutions rose due to inflation, the raising of standards, and the greater number of students. Until the 1950s enrollment in private universities and colleges in Texas rivaled enrollment in state-supported schools. As tuition advanced at private institutions and as the number of college students grew, the emphasis began to shift. While there was an overall increase of 72 percent during the Connally years, public institutions grew by 95 percent while enrollment in private colleges and universities went up 15 percent. The number of students in private institutions declined from 29 percent to 19 percent of total college enrollment.

Vocational and Special Education. Like most states, Texas had not kept up with the need for vocational and technical training and education of the disadvantaged. The state, with substantial federal funds, set out to meet these needs.

Several groups had need of special instructional programs.

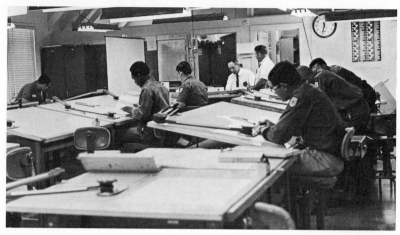

Drafting is one of thirty-four trades taught at the Gary Job Corps Center near San Marcos.

The children of migrant workers averaged going to school only six months of the year. For the rest of the year, they followed the crops with their parents. For many Texas children, English is a second language and Spanish is the language spoken in the home and community. Preschool instruction in English for Spanish-speaking children helps to bridge their entrance into the public schools. Adult basic education and programs for adult migrants were begun to help alleviate the problem of over a million functionally illiterate adults. In addition, programs for the education of the mentally retarded and for emotionally disturbed children were expanded.

The dependence of industry on skilled workers required a greater emphasis on technical training. By the Vocational Education Act of 1963, Congress provided funding for needed state programs. By 1968, more than half a million students were enrolled in vocational and technical programs. The Gary Job Corps Center in San Marcos opened in 1965. It trains some three thousand young men a year. The center provides instruction in thirty-four areas of knowledge and skill. In 1967 the McKinney Job Corps Center opened to extend technical and vocational training to women. James Connally Technical Institute, opened in 1965 at Waco, enrolled fourteen hundred students in 1968 to receive training in highly specialized skills. In 1969 it became the Texas State Technical Institute.

416

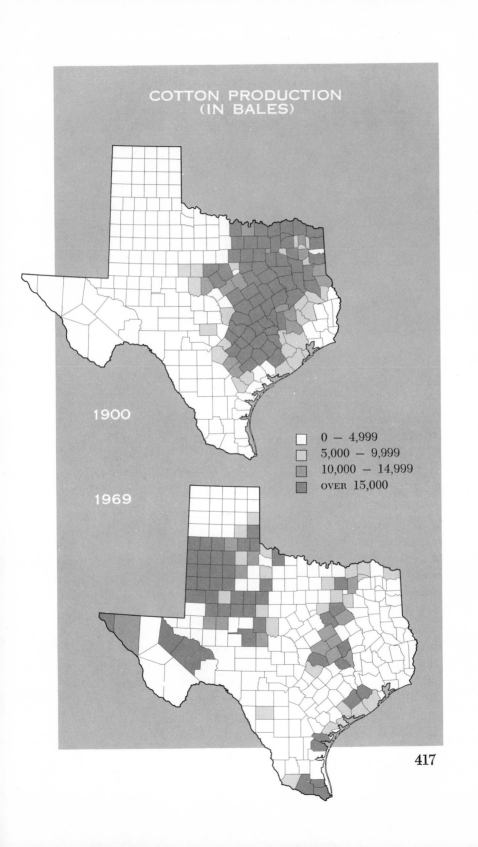

COTTON PRODUCTION
(IN BALES)

1900

1969

0 — 4,999
5,000 — 9,999
10,000 — 14,999
OVER 15,000

417

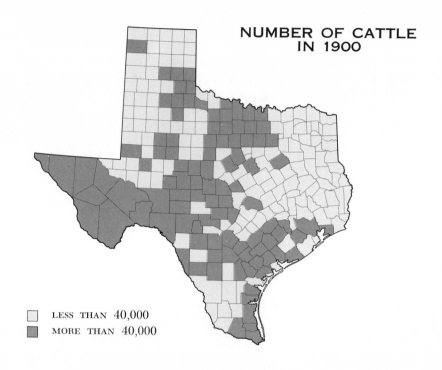

NUMBER OF CATTLE
IN 1900

LESS THAN 40,000
MORE THAN 40,000

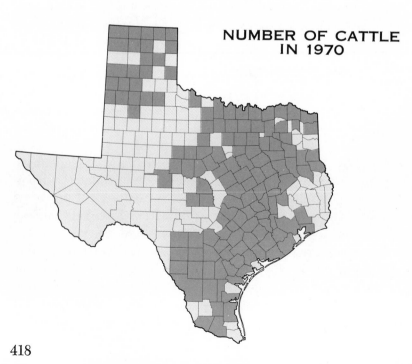

NUMBER OF CATTLE
IN 1970

Agriculture and Ranching. During the 1960s the number of Texas farmers diminished, but their productivity increased. Each agricultural worker produced food and fiber for some forty others. In 1968 Texas ranked third nationally in total crop and livestock cash receipts, remaining the chief producer of cattle, sheep, wool, goats, mohair, cotton, grain sorghums, rice, and grapefruit. Crops that accounted for the largest acreage were sorghums, cotton, wheat, hay, corn, oats, rice, peanuts, barley, and flaxseed. On the basis of crop value, cotton and cottonseed head the list, followed by sorghum grain and forage, wheat, rice, hay, corn, peanuts, oats, Irish potatoes, and sweet potatoes.

Farms increased in size and value, and many more crops were produced on irrigated land. All rice and citrus crops and more than half the grain sorghums, cotton, wheat, and vegetables were produced on irrigated land. Sixty-five percent of the irrigated land in Texas is located on the High Plains. Fayette County had the largest number of farms in 1968, with Hidalgo and Lavaca counties ranking close behind. El Paso County ranked first in livestock and livestock product sales, with Gonzales, Nacogdoches, and Shelby counties ranking next. Seven of the top ten counties in livestock and livestock product sales are in Central or East Texas, reflecting the shift in ranching from West Texas eastward.

Feedlot operations increased rapidly in the late 1960s, especially in the Panhandle. Whereas in the past Texas cattle had been shipped to other states for fattening, huge feedlot operations opened at Borger, Hereford, Dimmitt, Dumas, and elsewhere on the High Plains. In 1968 almost 2 million head of cattle were marketed from Texas feedlots. Packing plants have followed the establishment of the feedlots; adequate transportation facilities make these operations possible. Beef processed in Texas not only can be shipped to national markets but can be sent by air to markets all over the world.

Manufacturing. Texas's economy was as diversified as that of the nation in the 1960s. Texas was seventh among the manufacturing states, and in 1968 more than seven hundred thousand Texans were employed in factories. That year 321 new plants were built in the state, and 645 were expanded.

Petroleum and chemical products account for the bulk of Texas manufacturing in terms of product value, but in terms of wages paid to workers, the manufacture of transportation equipment ranked just behind the petrochemical industry in 1968. The manufacture of oil field machinery, electronic goods, food products, and metal and metal products are important industries. Wood-based manufacturing, long an important Texas industry, employed forty-nine thousand workers in 1968 in the production of lumber, furniture, paper, and pulp.

Many national concerns have Texas origins or Texas headquarters. Hilton Hotels, the world's largest chain, began with Conrad Hilton's Mobley Hotel in Cisco in 1919. Zales, the world's largest retail jewelry business, began in Dallas in 1924. Ling-Temco-Vought, Dr. Pepper, and Texas Instruments are known around the world. Southland Corporation of Dallas located its 7-Eleven Stores in other states and had $621 million in sales in 1968. Ling-Temco-Vought had sales of more than $2 billion in that year.

Aluminum Company of America

Natural gas reserves and water transportation were factors influencing the location of aluminum smelting and refining operations at Point Comfort.

420

Public Health. Since the end of World War II, Texas has developed important medical, hospital, and research centers at Dallas, Galveston, Temple, Houston, and elsewhere. The son of a Lebanese immigrant, Dr. Michael E. DeBakey, became the first surgeon to circulate blood by machine during heart surgery performed in 1963. Dusan Vlaco, a seventeen-year-old from Yugoslavia, traveled to Houston in 1968 to have Dr. DeBakey perform a heart transplant. Fifteen months later, Vlaco had recovered sufficiently to swim and dive. Dr. Denton Cooley of Houston was the first physician to implant an artificial heart in a patient's body.

In 1967 Texas had a total of 570 hospitals and 48 accredited schools of nursing. Many areas still experience a shortage of medical facilities and personnel. Heart disease and cancer continue to be the leading causes of death. Texas is fourth among the states in tuberculosis deaths and seventh in active cases. By 1969 some 1 million children annually were being vaccinated against smallpox, polio, diphtheria, and other diseases.

Public Welfare. Four major categories of citizens receive public welfare: the aged, dependent children, the blind, and the permanently and totally disabled. The State Board of Public Welfare administers the program. In 1968, 75 percent of the cost was absorbed by the federal government and 25 percent by the state, which has a constitutional limit of $80 million on the amount of state funds that may be spent for welfare in a year. In 1968 Texas was forty-first nationally in state aid to public welfare. The aged are the largest group receiving assistance, some 64 percent of welfare recipients. Dependent children constitute 30 percent of welfare recipients; the blind and the disabled account for the other 6 percent.

Public Safety. As urban populations increased and the crime rate grew, it was necessary that police departments, sheriffs' offices, and other enforcement agencies expand and modernize. Salaries were increased and educational standards raised. The Highway Patrol was increased by one-third, and the narcotics section was doubled in the Connally years. Emphasis was put on the education and training of officers. Junior colleges began offering courses in police administration. The Department of

421

Public Safety's Law Enforcement Academy at Austin was expanded to train law enforcement officers from all over the state. The Department of Public Safety established a Data Processing Division in 1966 and began putting records of 6.5 million drivers into the memory bank of a computer. Some 1.5 million criminal records were put on tape so that information would be available instantly to officers throughout the state. The computer knows the criminal by name and by method of operation. A crime can be described, and the computer will produce names of known criminals who operate in such a fashion.

The Texas prison population climbed to more than twelve thousand in 1969. In an effort to increase rehabilitation, new work areas were opened to prisoners. Goods produced by prisoners include automobile license plates, boxes, cheese, soap, clothing, bricks, mattresses, syrup, shoes, and much more. Rehabilitation and educational programs financed by the Texas Prison Rodeo, federal grants, and state funds are aimed at giving the convict a means of support on his release so that he will not get in trouble again. Some forty-five hundred prisoners were taking courses at the elementary and secondary level in 1969. In addition, several hundred inmates were taking college courses under a cooperative program with Alvin Junior College, Lee College, and Brazosport Junior College. The Texas Youth Council developed new programs for rehabilitation of juvenile offenders.

Transportation. The most important single factor in the development of Texas was transportation. Roads link urban areas and facilitate trade and travel. Even the farmer may live in town if he wishes. He travels over farm-to-market roads. Buses and roads did away with the one-room school. Texas has some sixty-nine thousand miles of highways.

The first jet airplane to land in Houston arrived in 1957, and almost immediately the state's airports had to expand and improve their facilities. The airplanes got larger, and air traffic grew. Houston's International Airport was completed in 1969, after seven years of construction and a cost of $100 million. Eighteen thousand acres of land have been set aside in the Dallas–Fort Worth area to build a billion-dollar facility. The number of airline passengers increased from one million to eight

One of the nation's best highway systems serves Texas motorists and has contributed to the development of the state.

million in the twenty years ending in 1968, and Texas ranked fourth in passengers and sixth in cargo.

The petroleum and refining industries along the Gulf Coast stimulated the development of ports from Brownsville to Orange. The Houston Ship Channel has enabled the Port of Houston to become the fifth largest exporter of goods in the nation. Over 190 million tons of goods were handled by Texas ports in 1965. The necessity for transferring goods from water to land transportation caused port cities to be business, banking, and industrial centers.

In 1968 Texas led the nation in railroad trackage, with about twenty thousand miles of usable tracks. Forty-seven railroads operate in the state, hauling freight and providing some passenger service. Passenger traffic declined from almost 26 million during 1944 to 1.3 million in 1967. The trucking industry has made heavy inroads on the railroads' freight business.

Changing Needs of Government. The state and counties, and cities to a lesser degree, have found themselves unable to take appropriate action many times because of the Constitution of 1876. When a solution does become possible, it is only after the delay and expense occasioned by amending the constitution. For example, Dallas County, desiring to issue road bonds which would create no obligation on the part of the state, had to wait until a regular session of the legislature and get a two-thirds vote in each house before the issue could be submitted to the voters. Then voters from Amarillo to Brownsville decided whether Dallas County should be permitted to issue road improvement bonds. By the slim margin of 941,575 to 916,727, voters in the general election approved the proposition, but had they not, Dallas County would have been thwarted in doing what its commissioners felt was best.

By constitutional provision, the state legislature still meets in biennial sessions whose length is constitutionally set at a maximum of 140 days. In recent years, as increased state spending and a fluctuating economy have made two-year budgeting more difficult, more special sessions have been needed to provide for unexpected fiscal emergencies. In 1967 and 1969 the legislature enacted one-year budgets, so that special sessions were required by design. Governor Preston Smith vetoed the 1969 bill.

The division of the executive power has made it impossible for the governor to govern except by persuasion. At the close of his service, Governor Connally warned of the need for immediate action, saying, "To continue to serve any useful purpose, to keep any authority and retain the treasure of states' rights—*the Texas Constitution must be revised.*"

Human Rights. In the 1960s Negro citizens worked for a greater voice in state government. Joseph Lockridge, a Dallas attorney, and Curtis Graves, a Houston public relations consultant, were elected to the Texas House of Representatives. Lockridge was chosen the outstanding freshman representative by fellow members. In 1971 Z.W. Holmes, Jr., of Dallas became the third black representative in this century. Barbara Jordan, a Houston lawyer, was the first Negro to serve in the state senate since 1882 and the first Negro woman to be elected senator in the history of the state. Senator Jordan sponsored Texas's first minimum wage law.

Support for the minimum wage came from the state AFL-CIO and from Mexican-American farm workers in the Rio Grande Valley. The president of the National Farm Workers, Cesar Chavez, helped rally workers in the Rio Grande Valley

424

in behalf of the $1.25 minimum wage bill. A march to Austin was organized. Governor Connally, Attorney General Waggoner Carr, and Speaker of the House Ben Barnes met the marchers at New Braunfels on August 31, 1966. The marchers reached Austin on Labor Day and held a rally at the capitol. Senator Yarborough and Congressman Gonzalez attended the rally at which Senator Jordan told the marchers, "What you really want to see is . . . a minimum wage bill. Take heart today, for no one is trying to give you anything but what you justly deserve."

Changing Politics. The year 1968 was one of significant change in state and national politics. Vice-President Humphrey and Senator Edmund Muskie won the Democratic nominations to oppose Richard M. Nixon and Spiro Agnew, the Republican nominees. Former Alabama governor George Wallace and General Curtis LeMay ran on the American party ticket. Nixon won the presidency with 43.4 percent of the popular vote to Humphrey's 42.7 percent. Wallace polled 13.5 percent of the vote. The Republicans had 290 electors, the Democrats 203, and the American party 45. Not since Woodrow Wilson's victory in 1912 had the winner's percentage of the electoral vote been so small. Texas gave her electoral votes to the loser for the first time since 1924.

In the state races the Republicans showed surprising strength. The Republican gubernatorial candidate, Paul Eggers, drew a record Republican vote of 1.25 million. Lieutenant Governor Preston Smith of Lubbock, who had defeated Democrat Don Yarborough of Houston in the primary, outpolled Eggers by some four hundred thousand votes. Ben Barnes polled 2 million votes to become lieutenant governor. Republicans won nine seats in the house and two in the senate. The Texas congressional delegation was composed of three Republicans and twenty Democrats, while Texas still had one Republican and one Democrat in the Senate.

Culture, Art, and Literature

San Antonio celebrated its two hundred fiftieth birthday in 1968. Some ninety-two acres of underdeveloped land were converted into a fairground at a cost of $156 million. Twenty-one nations exhibited at HemisFair '68, and millions of visitors came to San Antonio. The Institute of Texan Cultures, devoted to preserving Texas's cultural heritage, was continued on a permanent basis after HemisFair '68 closed. Other facilities were taken over by the city of San Antonio.

The sculptor of San José Mission's Rose Window, Pedro Huizar, began a tradition of artistic excellence that continues today. A native of Austin, Ishmael Soto, is a ceramicist and sculptor of international reputation. Porfirio Salinas from Bastrop has paintings of the Texas hill country in museums across the nation. The paintings of Manuel Acosta depicting Mexican Americans have been widely admired.

The works of Paul Hatgil, Michael Frary, DeForrest Judd, David Cargill, Cecil Lang Casebier, G. Harvey, and John Boynton hang in museums or stand in foyers across the nation. Heri Bert Bartscht came from Germany to Dallas to teach and sculpt. Abstract oils by Chinese-born Hsaio Hsai-Tsai, whose name means Morning of Glory, hang in locations as separated as India and Del Mar College in Corpus Christi. Rose Chin Wong paints still lifes and children's portraits in pastel and oil. Bonnie MacLeary, Charles Umlauf, and William McVey are outstanding sculptors. Tom Lea and E. M. ("Buck") Schiwetz illustrate the books they write. Lea's *The Brave Bulls* shows the influence of Mexican artists.

Texas architecture has evolved from simple dog-run houses and Mexican patio homes to sophisticated skyscrapers, yet beauty can be found in structures as different in style and purpose as the Governor's Mansion, designed by Abner Hugh Cook in 1855, and the Tower of the Americas, designed by O'Neil Ford for HemisFair '68. William Caudill and Hugo Neuhaus are also distinguished architects. Howard Wong studied with O'Neil Ford and twice won the Texas Society of Architects Honor Award for Excellence in Design.

Texans have made large contributions to music and entertainment. The symphony orchestras of Dallas, Houston, and San Antonio offer varied programs. Four cities have opera companies, and many offer ballet. Pat Boone had a local television show while attending North Texas State University.

Mexican Americans Trini Lopez and Vicki Carr began their careers in Texas—Lopez at Dallas's Crozier Tech and Miss Carr in El Paso.

Texans found places in radio, movies, the theater, and television. Walter Cronkite, a University of Texas student in the 1930s, was a war correspondent during World War II and became one of the most respected television news commentators. Dan Rather is another nationally known newsman from Texas. Fess Parker of Brownwood played first Davy Crockett and then Daniel Boone on television. Dan Blocker attended Sul Ross State College before leaving for Hollywood. Dorothy Malone, Rip Torn, Pat Hingle, Ginger Rogers, Joan Blondell, Zachary Scott, Martha Hyer, Ann Sheridan, Carolyn Jones, Cyd Charisse, Carol Burnett, and Jayne Mansfield all shared Texas backgrounds.

Margo Jones, the director of the Dallas Little Theater, played a significant role in the early career of playwright Tennessee Williams. Miss Jones co-directed *The Glass Menagerie* on Broadway and staged the first performance of *Summer and Smoke* at her Dallas theater in 1948. Outstanding theater groups across the state include Houston's Alley Theater, Dallas's Theater Center and Theater Three, and Fort Worth's Scott Theater. An unusual theatrical production is the pageant *Texas*, written by Paul Green and performed each summer at Pioneer Amphitheater in Palo Duro Canyon.

Tom Jones and Harvey Schmidt, graduates of The University of Texas, wrote the script and score for *The Fantastiks*. Directed by another University of Texas graduate, Word Baker, the musical comedy holds the record for the longest run of any off-Broadway production.

From the Spanish conquistadores to the present, Texas has called forth the best from writers. Mary Lasswell's nostalgic *I'll Take Texas* received critical acclaim. William Humphrey told of life in East Texas in *Home from the Hill* and *The Ordways*. Larry McMurtry dealt with West Texas in *Horseman Pass By*, *The Last Picture Show*, and *Moving On*. Bill Brammer and Larry L. King were concerned with the political life of the state in *The Gay Place* and *The One-Eyed Man*. King's nostalgic views of Texas life and political satires appeared in

Harper's magazine, edited by University of Texas graduate Willie Morris.

William A. Owens's novels *Walking on Borrowed Land* and *This Stubborn Soil* attracted a great deal of praise. Frances Mossiker of Dallas wrote prize-winning books of French historical romance, including *The Queen's Necklace* and *Napoleon and Josephine*. John Graves of Fort Worth wrote of a canoe trip down the Brazos River in his memorable *Goodbye to a River*.

The provincial who cultivates only his roots is in peril, potato-like, of becoming more root than plant. The man who cuts his roots away and denies that they were ever connected with him withers into half a man. . . .

It is not necessary to like being a Texan, or a Midwesterner, or a Jew, or an Andalusian, or a Negro, or a hybrid child of the international rich. It is, I think, necessary to know in that crystal chamber of the mind where one speaks straight to oneself that one is or was that thing, and for any understanding of the human condition it's probably necessary to know a little about what the thing consists of.[1]

A New Perspective

On July 20, 1969, Neil Armstrong and Edwin Aldrin stood beside the lunar lander *Eagle* on the Sea of Tranquillity and read to the world the plaque that they would leave behind. "Here men from the planet Earth first set foot upon the moon. July 1969, A.D. We came in peace for all mankind." But the first word spoken from the surface of the moon was the surname of the man who brought Texas into being. Neil Armstrong said, "Houston. Tranquillity Base here. The *Eagle* has landed."

The first native Texan on the moon was Alan Bean. On November 20, 1969, as Bean walked the moon, had he looked back toward Earth, and had human eyes power to span a quarter million miles and penetrate the earth's atmosphere, he would have beheld the land we call Texas. And it would

[1]John Graves, *Goodbye to a River* (New York: Alfred A. Knopf, 1960), 145.

have looked, from Bean's vantage, as untouched as it was in fact when Piñeda, four and a half centuries before, declared the country of the River of the Palms to be the fairest site he had seen for the location of a mighty civilization.

Discuss

1. Which area or areas of concern do you think should receive top priority in the 1970s?

2. What does a study of Texas's sources of income and areas of expenditures indicate?

3. What role does the federal government play in financing state government in Texas? Is this role likely to increase or decrease in the future?

4. What shifts in emphases in education took place during the 1960s? What caused these shifts?

5. The *Texas Almanac* is a source of information on state income and spending. Select two years and compare the sources of income and the items for which the money was spent. What conclusions can you draw?

6. What changes in the Texas economy are illustrated by the maps on pages 417 and 418?

7. Why is the Texas constitution in need of revision?

8. What progress has been made in representation of minority groups in Texas government in recent years?

9. How do you account for the growing strength of the Republican party in Texas?

10. Analyze the John Graves quotation on page 428.

Identify

Coordinating Board, Texas College and University System
Vocational Education Act
Dr. Michael E. DeBakey
biennial
Curtis Graves
Barbara Jordan
Paul Eggers
Preston Smith
HemisFair '68

Manuel Acosta
Tom Lea
Howard Wong
Trini Lopez
Walter Cronkite
Margo Jones
Larry McMurtry
John Graves
Alan Bean
Institute of Texan Cultures

430

Appendix

TEXAS AGRICULTURE

ITEM	1964	1940	1920	1900
Number of farms	205,109	418,002	436,033	352,190
Farms operated by:				
Owners	166,568	210,182	201,210	174,639
Managers	1,462	3,358	2,514	2,560
Tenants	37,080	204,462	232,309	174,991
Farm population	625,773	2,149,187	*	*
Average farm acreage	690.9	329.4	261.5	357.2
Farmland use (in acres):				
Harvested cropland	19,407,981	26,044,008	25,027,773	*
Fallow cropland	6,595,516	4,887,405	*	*
Pasture	111,568,590	*	*	*
Woodland	774,348	*	*	*
Irrigated land	6,389,703	894,638	*	40,952
Livestock on farms:				
Horses	*	638,406	991,362	1,393,863
Mules	*	537,801	845,932	526,651
Cattle	15,433,514	10,760,886	10,005,246	13,924,135
†Sheep	4,341,923	8,447,809	2,573,485	1,898,794
††Hogs	621,093	1,513,912	2,225,558	2,778,881
††Chickens	15,113,400	21,799,610	18,062,744	13,562,302
Selected crop harvests:				
Corn (bushels)	22,168,297	69,649,829	108,377,282	109,970,350
Wheat (bushels)	60,564,209	28,096,367	36,427,255	12,266,320
Rice (bushels)	43,832,131	10,352,456	5,306,369	159,708
Grain sorghum (bushels)	201,603,151	25,232,118	36,456,343	482,096
Cotton (bales)	3,914,681	2,724,442	2,971,752	2,506,212

*Data not available

†Before 1950, animals under six months old not counted

††Before 1950, animals and chickens under four months old not counted

EMPLOYMENT BY INDUSTRY
1940, 1969

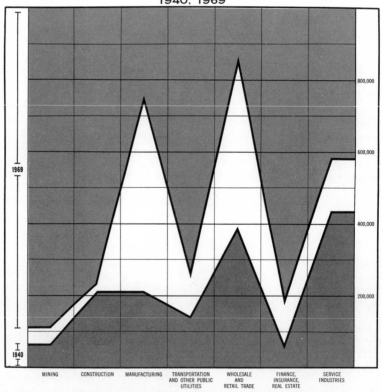

800,000

600,000

1969

400,000

200,000

1940

MINING CONSTRUCTION MANUFACTURING TRANSPORTATION WHOLESALE FINANCE, SERVICE
AND OTHER PUBLIC AND INSURANCE, INDUSTRIES
UTILITIES RETAIL TRADE REAL ESTATE

U. S. BUREAU OF THE CENSUS, STATISTICAL ABSTRACT OF THE UNITED STATES: 1940, 1970

432

STANDARD METROPOLITAN STATISTICAL AREAS

		POPULATION	
CITIES	COUNTIES	1960	1970
Abilene	Taylor, Jones	120,377	113,959
Amarillo	Potter, Randall	149,493	144,396
Austin	Travis	212,136	295,516
Beaumont-Port Arthur	Jefferson, Orange	306,016	315,943
Brownsville-Harlingen- San Benito	Cameron	151,098	140,368
Corpus Christi	Nueces, San Patricio	266,594	284,832
Dallas	Dallas, Collin, Denton, Ellis, Kaufman, Rockwall	1,119,420	1,555,950
El Paso	El Paso	314,070	359,291
Fort Worth	Tarrant, Johnson	573,215	762,086
Galveston-Texas City	Galveston	140,364	169,812
Houston	Harris, Brazoria, Fort Bend, Liberty, Montgomery	1,418,323	1,985,033
San Antonio	Bexar, Guadalupe	716,168	864,014
Texarkana	Bowie	59,971	67,813
Tyler	Smith	86,350	97,096
McAllen-Edinburg- Pharr	Hidalgo	180,904	181,535
Odessa	Ector	90,995	91,805
Laredo	Webb	64,791	72,859
San Angelo	Tom Green	64,630	71,047
Sherman-Denison	Grayson	73,043	83,225
Lubbock	Lubbock	156,271	179,295
Midland	Midland	67,717	65,433
Waco	McLennan	150,091	147,553
Wichita Falls	Archer, Wichita	129,287	127,972

POPULATION BY COUNTY, 1970

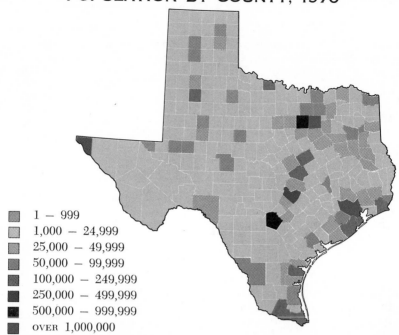

1 – 999
1,000 – 24,999
25,000 – 49,999
50,000 – 99,999
100,000 – 249,999
250,000 – 499,999
500,000 – 999,999
OVER 1,000,000

URBAN POPULATION, PERCENT OF COUNTY POPULATION, 1970

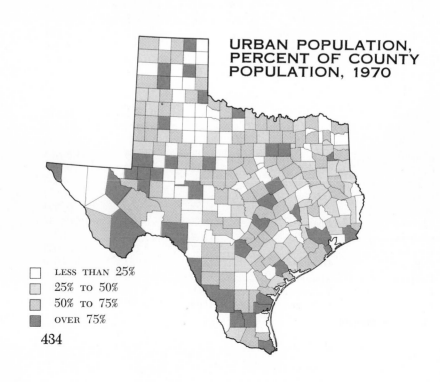

LESS THAN 25%
25% TO 50%
50% TO 75%
OVER 75%

434

TEXAS COUNTIES

NAME	COUNTY SEAT	ORGANIZED	POPULATION 1900	1970
Anderson	Palestine	1846	28,015	27,789
Andrews	Andrews	1910	87	10,372
Angelina	Lufkin	1846	13,481	49,349
Aransas	Rockport	1871	1,716	8,902
Archer	Archer City	1880	2,508	5,759
Armstrong	Claude	1890	1,205	1,895
Atascosa	Jourdanton	1856	7,143	18,696
Austin	Bellville	1837	20,676	13,831
Bailey	Muleshoe	1917	4	8,487
Bandera	Bandera	1856	5,332	4,747
Bastrop	Bastrop	1837	26,845	17,297
Baylor	Seymour	1879	3,052	5,221
Bee	Beeville	1858	7,720	22,737
Bell	Belton	1850	45,535	124,483
Bexar	San Antonio	1837	69,422	830,460
Blanco	Johnson City	1858	4,703	3,567
Borden	Gail	1891	776	888
Bosque	Meridian	1854	17,390	10,966
Bowie	Boston	1841	26,676	67,813
Brazoria	Angleton	1837	14,861	108,312
Brazos	Bryan	1843	18,859	57,978
Brewster	Alpine	1887	2,356	7,780
Briscoe	Silverton	1892	1,253	2,794
Brooks	Falfurrias	1912	*	8,005
Brown	Brownwood	1857	16,019	25,877
Burleson	Caldwell	1846	18,367	9,999
Burnet	Burnet	1854	10,528	11,420
Caldwell	Lockhart	1848	21,765	21,178
Calhoun	Port Lavaca	1846	2,395	17,831
Callahan	Baird	1858	8,768	8,205
Cameron	Brownsville	1848	16,095	140,368
Camp	Pittsburg	1874	9,146	8,005
Carson	Panhandle	1888	469	6,358
Cass	Linden	1846	22,841	24,133
Castro	Dimmitt	1891	400	10,394
Chambers	Anahuac	1858	3,046	12,187
Cherokee	Rusk	1846	25,154	32,008
Childress	Childress	1887	2,138	6,605
Clay	Henrietta	1873	9,231	8,079
Cochran	Morton	1924	25	5,326
Coke	Robert Lee	1889	3,430	3,087
Coleman	Coleman	1864	10,077	10,288

*Data not available

NAME	COUNTY SEAT	ORGANIZED	POPULATION	
			1900	1970
Collin	McKinney	1846	50,087	66,920
Collingsworth	Wellington	1890	1,233	4,755
Colorado	Columbus	1837	22,203	17,638
Comal	New Braunfels	1846	7,008	24,165
Comanche	Comanche	1856	23,009	11,898
Concho	Paint Rock	1876	1,427	2,937
Cooke	Gainesville	1849	27,494	23,471
Coryell	Gatesville	1854	21,308	35,311
Cottle	Paducah	1892	1,002	3,204
Crane	Crane	1927	51	4,172
Crockett	Ozona	1891	1,591	3,885
Crosby	Crosbyton	1886	788	9,085
Culberson	Van Horn	1912	*	3,429
Dallam	Dalhart	1891	146	6,012
Dallas	Dallas	1846	82,726	1,327,321
Dawson	Lamesa	1905	37	16,604
Deaf Smith	Hereford	1890	843	18,999
Delta	Cooper	1870	15,249	4,927
Denton	Denton	1846	28,318	75,633
De Witt	Cuero	1846	21,311	18,660
Dickens	Dickens	1891	1,151	3,737
Dimmit	Carrizo Springs	1880	1,106	9,039
Donley	Clarendon	1882	2,756	3,641
Duval	San Diego	1876	8,483	11,722
Eastland	Eastland	1873	17,971	18,092
Ector	Odessa	1891	381	91,805
Edwards	Rocksprings	1883	3,108	2,107
Ellis	Waxahachie	1850	50,059	46,638
El Paso	El Paso	1871	24,886	359,291
Erath	Stephenville	1856	29,966	18,141
Falls	Marlin	1850	33,342	17,300
Fannin	Bonham	1838	51,793	22,705
Fayette	La Grange	1838	36,542	17,650
Fisher	Roby	1886	3,708	6,344
Floyd	Floydada	1890	2,020	11,044
Foard	Crowell	1891	1,568	2,211
Fort Bend	Richmond	1838	16,538	52,314
Franklin	Mount Vernon	1875	8,674	5,291
Freestone	Fairfield	1851	18,910	11,116
Frio	Pearsall	1871	4,200	11,159
Gaines	Seminole	1905	55	11,593
Galveston	Galveston	1839	44,116	169,812

*Data not available

436

NAME	COUNTY SEAT	ORGANIZED	POPULATION 1900	POPULATION 1970
Garza	Post	1907	185	5,289
Gillespie	Fredericksburg	1848	8,229	10,553
Glasscock	Garden City	1887	286	1,155
Goliad	Goliad	1837	8,310	4,869
Gonzales	Gonzales	1837	28,882	16,375
Gray	Pampa	1902	480	26,949
Grayson	Sherman	1846	63,661	83,225
Gregg	Longview	1873	12,343	75,929
Grimes	Anderson	1846	26,106	11,855
Guadalupe	Seguin	1846	21,385	33,554
Hale	Plainview	1888	1,680	34,137
Hall	Memphis	1890	1,670	6,015
Hamilton	Hamilton	1858	13,520	7,198
Hansford	Spearman	1889	167	6,351
Hardeman	Quanah	1884	3,634	6,795
Hardin	Kountze	1858	5,049	29,996
Harris	Houston	1837	63,786	1,741,912
Harrison	Marshall	1842	31,876	44,841
Hartley	Channing	1891	377	2,782
Haskell	Haskell	1885	2,637	8,512
Hays	San Marcos	1848	14,142	27,642
Hemphill	Canadian	1887	815	3,084
Henderson	Athens	1846	19,970	26,466
Hidalgo	Edinburg	1852	6,837	181,535
Hill	Hillsboro	1853	41,355	22,596
Hockley	Levelland	1921	44	20,396
Hood	Granbury	1866	9,146	6,368
Hopkins	Sulphur Springs	1846	27,950	20,710
Houston	Crockett	1837	25,452	17,855
Howard	Big Spring	1882	2,528	37,796
Hudspeth	Sierra Blanca	1917	*	2,392
Hunt	Greenville	1846	47,295	47,948
Hutchinson	Stinnett	1901	303	24,443
Irion	Mertzon	1889	848	1,070
Jack	Jacksboro	1857	10,224	6,711
Jackson	Edna	1837	6,094	12,975
Jasper	Jasper	1837	7,138	24,692
Jeff Davis	Fort Davis	1887	1,150	1,527
Jefferson	Beaumont	1837	14,239	244,773
Jim Hogg	Hebbronville	1913	*	4,654
Jim Wells	Alice	1912	*	33,032
Johnson	Cleburne	1854	33,819	45,769
Jones	Anson	1881	7,053	16,106

*Data not available

437

NAME	COUNTY SEAT	ORGANIZED	POPULATION 1900	1970
Karnes	Karnes City	1854	8,681	13,462
Kaufman	Kaufman	1848	33,376	32,392
Kendall	Boerne	1862	4,103	6,964
Kenedy	Sarita	1921	*	678
Kent	Clairemont	1892	899	1,434
Kerr	Kerrville	1856	4,980	19,454
Kimble	Junction	1876	2,503	3,904
King	Guthrie	1891	490	464
Kinney	Brackettville	1874	2,447	2,006
Kleberg	Kingsville	1913	*	33,166
Knox	Benjamin	1886	2,322	5,972
Lamar	Paris	1841	48,627	36,062
Lamb	Littlefield	1908	31	17,770
Lampasas	Lampasas	1856	8,625	9,323
La Salle	Cotulla	1880	2,303	5,014
Lavaca	Hallettsville	1846	28,121	17,903
Lee	Giddings	1874	14,595	8,048
Leon	Centerville	1846	18,072	8,738
Liberty	Liberty	1837	8,102	33,014
Limestone	Groesbeck	1846	32,573	18,100
Lipscomb	Lipscomb	1887	790	3,486
Live Oak	George West	1856	2,268	6,697
Llano	Llano	1856	7,301	6,979
Loving	Mentone	1931	33	164
Lubbock	Lubbock	1891	293	179,295
Lynn	Tahoka	1903	17	9,107
McCulloch	Brady	1876	3,960	8,571
McLennan	Waco	1850	59,772	147,553
McMullen	Tilden	1877	1,024	1,095
Madison	Madisonville	1854	10,432	7,693
Marion	Jefferson	1860	10,754	8,517
Martin	Stanton	1876	332	4,774
Mason	Mason	1856	5,573	3,356
Matagorda	Bay City	1837	6,097	27,913
Maverick	Eagle Pass	1871	4,066	18,093
Medina	Hondo	1848	7,783	20,249
Menard	Menard	1871	2,011	2,646
Midland	Midland	1885	1,741	65,433
Milam	Cameron	1837	39,666	20,028
Mills	Goldthwaite	1887	7,851	4,212
Mitchell	Colorado City	1881	2,855	9,073
Montague	Montague	1858	24,800	15,326
Montgomery	Conroe	1837	17,067	49,479
Moore	Dumas	1892	209	14,060

*Data not available

			POPULATION	
NAME	COUNTY SEAT	ORGANIZED	1900	1970
Morris	Daingerfield	1875	8,220	12,310
Motley	Matador	1891	1,257	2,178
Nacogdoches	Nacogdoches	1837	24,663	36,362
Navarro	Corsicana	1846	43,874	31,150
Newton	Newton	1846	7,282	11,657
Nolan	Sweetwater	1881	2,611	16,220
Nueces	Corpus Christi	1846	10,439	237,544
Ochiltree	Perryton	1881	267	9,704
Oldham	Vega	1881	349	2,258
Orange	Orange	1852	5,905	71,170
Palo Pinto	Palo Pinto	1857	12,291	28,962
Panola	Carthage	1846	21,404	15,894
Parker	Weatherford	1856	25,823	33,888
Parmer	Farwell	1907	34	10,509
Pecos	Fort Stockton	1872	2,360	13,748
Polk	Livingston	1846	14,477	14,457
Potter	Amarillo	1887	1,820	90,511
Presidio	Marfa	1875	3,673	4,842
Rains	Emory	1870	6,127	3,752
Randall	Canyon	1889	963	53,885
Reagan	Big Lake	1903	*	3,239
Real	Leakey	1913	*	2,013
Red River	Clarksville	1837	29,893	14,298
Reeves	Pecos	1884	1,847	16,526
Refugio	Refugio	1837	1,641	9,494
Roberts	Miami	1889	620	967
Robertson	Franklin	1838	31,480	14,389
Rockwall	Rockwall	1873	8,531	7,046
Runnels	Ballinger	1880	5,379	12,108
Rusk	Henderson	1843	26,009	34,102
Sabine	Hemphill	1837	6,394	7,187
San Augustine	San Augustine	1837	8,434	7,858
San Jacinto	Coldspring	1870	10,277	6,702
San Patricio	Sinton	1837	2,372	47,288
San Saba	San Saba	1856	7,569	5,540
Schleicher	Eldorado	1901	515	2,277
Scurry	Snyder	1884	4,158	15,760
Shackelford	Albany	1874	2,461	3,323
Shelby	Center	1837	20,452	19,672
Sherman	Stratford	1889	104	3,657
Smith	Tyler	1846	37,370	97,096

*Data not available

NAME	COUNTY SEAT	ORGANIZED	POPULATION 1900	POPULATION 1970
Somervell	Glen Rose	1875	3,498	2,793
Starr	Rio Grande City	1848	11,469	17,707
Stephens	Breckenridge	1876	6,466	8,414
Sterling	Sterling City	1891	1,127	1,056
Stonewall	Aspermont	1888	2,183	2,397
Sutton	Sonora	1890	1,727	3,175
Swisher	Tulia	1890	1,227	10,373
Tarrant	Fort Worth	1850	52,376	716,317
Taylor	Abilene	1878	10,499	97,853
Terrell	Sanderson	1905	*	1,940
Terry	Brownfield	1904	48	14,118
Throckmorton	Throckmorton	1879	1,750	2,205
Titus	Mount Pleasant	1846	12,292	16,702
Tom Green	San Angelo	1875	6,804	71,047
Travis	Austin	1843	47,386	295,516
Trinity	Groveton	1850	10,976	7,628
Tyler	Woodville	1846	11,899	12,417
Upshur	Gilmer	1846	16,266	20,976
Upton	Rankin	1910	48	4,697
Uvalde	Uvalde	1856	4,647	17,348
Val Verde	Del Rio	1885	5,263	27,471
Van Zandt	Canton	1848	25,481	22,155
Victoria	Victoria	1837	13,678	53,766
Walker	Huntsville	1846	15,813	27,680
Waller	Hempstead	1873	14,246	14,285
Ward	Monahans	1892	1,451	13,019
Washington	Brenham	1837	32,931	18,842
Webb	Laredo	1848	21,851	72,859
Wharton	Wharton	1846	16,942	36,729
Wheeler	Wheeler	1879	636	6,434
Wichita	Wichita Falls	1882	5,806	121,862
Wilbarger	Vernon	1881	5,759	15,355
Willacy	Raymondville	1921	*	15,570
Williamson	Georgetown	1848	38,072	37,305
Wilson	Floresville	1860	13,961	13,041
Winkler	Kermit	1910	60	9,640
Wise	Decatur	1856	27,116	19,687
Wood	Quitman	1850	21,048	18,589
Yoakum	Plains	1907	26	7,344
Young	Graham	1874	6,540	15,400
Zapata	Zapata	1858	4,760	4,352
Zavala	Crystal City	1884	792	11,370

*Data not available

TEXAS DECLARATION OF INDEPENDENCE

The Unanimous Declaration of Independence Made by the Delegates of the People of Texas in General Convention at the Town of Washington on the 2nd Day of March, 1836.

When a government has ceased to protect the lives, liberty, and property of the people, from whom its legitimate powers are derived, and, for the advancement of whose happiness it was instituted; and so far from being a guarantee for the enjoyment of those inestimable and inalienable rights, becomes an instrument in the hands of evil rulers for their oppression: When the Federal Republican Constitution of their country, which they have sworn to support, no longer has a substantial existence, and the whole nature of their government has been forcibly changed, without their consent, from a restricted federative republic, composed of sovereign states, to a consolidated central military despotism, in which every interest is disregarded but that of the army and the priesthood—both the eternal enemies of civil liberty, the ever-ready minions of power, and the usual instruments of tyrants: When, long after the spirit of the constitution has departed, moderation is, at length, so far lost by those in power that even the semblance of freedom is removed, and the forms, themselves, of the constitution discontinued; and so far from their petitions and remonstrances being regarded, the agents who bear them are thrown into dungeons, and mercenary armies sent forth to force a new government upon them at the point of the bayonet: When, in consequence of such acts of malfeasance and abdication, on the part of the government, anarchy prevails, and civil society is dissolved into its original elements; in such a crisis, the first law of nature, the right of self-preservation, the inherent and inalienable right of the people to appeal to first principles and take their political affairs into their own hands in extreme cases, enjoins it as a right towards themselves and a sacred obligation to their posterity to abolish such government and create another in its stead, calculated to rescue them from impending dangers, and to secure their future welfare and happiness.

Nations, as well as individuals, are amenable for their acts to the public opinion of mankind. A statement of a part of our grievances is, therefore, submitted to an impartial world, in justification of the hazardous but unavoidable step now taken of severing our political connection with the Mexican people, and assuming an independent attitude among the nations of the earth.

The Mexican government, by its colonization laws, invited and induced the Anglo-American population of Texas to colonize its wilderness under the pledged faith of a written constitution, that they should continue to enjoy that constitutional liberty and republican government to which they had been habituated in the land of their birth, the United States of America. In this expectation they have been cruelly disappointed, inasmuch as the Mexican nation has acquiesced in the late changes made in the government by General Antonio López de Santa Anna, who, having overturned the constitution of his country, now offers us the cruel alternative either to abandon our homes, acquired by so many privations, or submit to the most intolerable of all tyranny, the combined despotism of the sword and the priesthood.

It has sacrificed our welfare to the state of Coahuila, by which our interests have been continually depressed through a jealous and partial course of legislation, carried on at a far distant seat of government, by a hostile majority, in an unknown tongue; and this, too, notwithstanding we have petitioned in the humblest terms for the establishment of a separate state government, and have, in accordance with the provisions of the national constitution, presented to the general congress a republican constitution which was, without just cause, contemptuously rejected.

It incarcerated in a dungeon, for a long time, one of our citizens, for no other cause but a zealous endeavor to procure the acceptance of our constitution and the establishment of a state government.

It has failed and refused to secure, on a firm basis, the right of trial by jury, that palladium of civil liberty, and only safe guarantee for the life, liberty, and property of the citizen.

It has failed to establish any public system of education, although possessed of almost boundless resources (the public domain) and, although it is an axiom, in political science, that unless a people are educated and enlightened, it is idle to expect the continuance of civil liberty or the capacity for self-government.

It has suffered the military commandants, stationed among us, to exercise arbitrary acts of oppression and tyranny; thus trampling upon the most sacred rights of the citizen and rendering the military superior to the civil power.

It has dissolved, by force of arms, the State Congress of Coahuila and Texas, and obliged our representatives to fly for their lives from the seat of government; thus depriving us of the fundamental political right of representation.

It has demanded the surrender of a number of our citizens, and ordered military detachments to seize and carry them into the Interior for trial; in contempt of the civil authorities, and in defiance of the laws and the constitution.

It has made piratical attacks upon our commerce, by commissioning foreign desperadoes and authorizing them to seize our vessels, and convey the property of our citizens to far distant ports for confiscation.

It denies us the right of worshiping the Almighty according to the dictates of our own conscience, by the support of a national religion, calculated to promote the temporal interests of its human functionaries, rather than the glory of the true and living God.

It has demanded us to deliver up our arms, which are essential to our defense, the rightful property of freemen, and formidable only to tyrannical governments.

It has invaded our country, both by sea and by land, with intent to lay waste our territory and drive us from our homes; and now has a large mercenary army advancing to carry on against us a war of extermination. It has, through its emissaries, incited the merciless savage, with the tomahawk and scalping knife, to massacre the inhabitants of our defenseless frontiers.

442

It hath been, during the whole time of our connection with it, the contemptible sport and victim of successive military revolutions, and hath continually exhibited every characteristic of a weak, corrupt, and tyrannical government.

These, and other grievances, were patiently borne by the people of Texas until they reached that point at which forbearance ceases to be a virtue. We then took up arms in defense of the national constitution. We appealed to our Mexican brethren for assistance. Our appeal has been made in vain. Though months have elapsed, no sympathetic response has yet been heard from the Interior. We are, therefore, forced to the melancholy conclusion that the Mexican people have acquiesced in the destruction of their liberty, and the substitution therefor of a military government—that they are unfit to be free and incapable of self-government.

The necessity of self-preservation, therefore, now decrees our eternal political separation.

We, therefore, the delegates, with plenary powers, of the people of Texas, in solemn convention assembled, appealing to a candid world for the necessities of our condition, do hereby resolve and declare that our political connection with the Mexican nation has forever ended; and that the people of Texas do now constitute a free, sovereign, and independent republic, and are fully invested with all the rights and attributes which properly belong to independent nations; and, conscious of the rectitude of our intentions, we fearlessly and confidently commit the issue to the decision of the Supreme Arbiter of the destinies of nations.

RICHARD ELLIS, *President*

CHARLES B. STEWART	THOS. J. GAZLEY	EDWIN O. LEGRAND
THOS. BARNETT	R. M. COLEMAN	STEPHEN W. BLOUNT
JOHN S. D. BYROM	STERLING C. ROBERTSON	JAS. GAINES
FRANCISCO RUÍZ	JAS. COLLINSWORTH	WM. CLARK, JR.
JOSÉ ANTONIO NAVARRO	EDWIN WALLER	SYDNEY O. PENNINGTON
JESSE B. BADGETT	GEO. C. CHILDRESS	WM. CARROL CRAWFORD
WM. D. LACEY	BAILEY HARDEMAN	JNO. TURNER
WILLIAM MENEFEE	ROB. POTTER	BENJ. BRIGGS GOODRICH
JNO. FISHER	THOMAS JEFFERSON RUSK	G. W. BARNETT
MATHEW CALDWELL	CHAS. S. TAYLOR	JAMES G. SWISHER
WILLIAM MOTTLEY	JOHN S. ROBERTS	JESSE GRIMES
LORENZO DE ZAVALA	ROBERT HAMILTON	S. RHOADS FISHER
STEPHEN H. EVERITT	COLLIN MCKINNEY	JOHN W. MOORE
GEORGE W. SMYTH	ALBERT H. LATIMER	JOHN W. BOWER
ELIJAH STAPP	JAMES POWER	SAM A. MAVERICK
CLAIBORNE WEST	SAM HOUSTON	SAM P. CARSON
WM. B. SCATES	DAVID THOMAS	A. BRISCOE
M. B. MENARD	EDW. CONRAD	J. B. WOODS
A. B. HARDIN	MARTIN PARMER	ASA BRIGHAM
J. W. BUNTON		

443

TEXAS GOVERNORS, 1691-1972

GOVERNORS OF TEXAS

1691-1692	Domingo Terán de los Ríos
1693-1716	Texas unoccupied but included in Coahuila
1716-1719	Martín de Alarcón, appointed governor of Texas on December 7, 1716 (On August 5, 1716, he had been appointed governor of Coahuila.)
1719-1722	The Marqués de San Miguel de Aguayo, governor of Coahuila and Texas
1722-1726	Fernando Pérez de Almazán
1727-1730	Melchor de Mediavilla y Ascona
1730	Juan Antonio Bustillo y Zevallos
1734	Manuel de Sandoval
1736-1737	Carlos Benités Franquís de Lugo
1737	Fernández de Jáuregui y Urrutia, governor of Nuevo León, governor extraordinary and *visitador*
1737-1740	Prudencio de Orobio y Basterra (governor *ad interim*)
1741-1743	Tomás Felipe Wintuisen
1743-1744	Justo Boneo y Morales
1744-1748	Francisco García Larios (governor *ad interim*)
1748-1750	Pedro del Barrio Junco y Espriella
1751-1759	Jacinto de Barrios y Jáuregui. Appointed governor of Coahuila in 1757, but retained in Texas until 1759 to complete a task.
1759-1766	Angel de Martos y Navarrete
1767-1770	Hugo Oconór (governor *ad interim*)
1770-1778	The Barón de Ripperdá
1778-1786	Domingo Cabello
1786	Bernardo Donavia, appointed July 8; apparently did not serve
1787-1790	Rafael Martínez Pachecho, appointed February 27, 1787; removal approved October 18, 1790
1788	The office of governor was ordered suppressed and the province put under a presidial captain.
1790-1799(?)	Manuel Muñoz
1798(?)	Josef Irigoyen, apparently appointed but did not serve
1800(?)-1805	Juan Bautista de Elguezábal
1805-1810	Antonio Cordero y Bustamante
1810-1813	Manuel de Salcedo
1811	Juan Bautista de las Casas (revolutionary governor, January 22-March 2)
1814-1818	Cristóbal Domínguez
1817	Ignacio Pérez and Manuel Pardo (governors *ad interim*)
1817-1822	Antonio Martínez
1822-1823	José Felix Trespalacios
1823(?)-1824	Luciano García

GOVERNORS OF COAHUILA AND TEXAS

1824-1826	Rafael Gonzales
1826-1827	Victor Blanco
1827-1831	José María Viesca
1831-1832	José María Letona
1832-1833	Juan Martín de Beramendi (Veramendi)
1834-1835	Juan José Elguezábal
1835	Agustín Viesca
1835	Ramón Eca y Músquiz

November 14, 1835–March 1, 1836   Henry Smith
January 11, 1836–March 1, 1836   James W. Robinson

PRESIDENTS OF THE REPUBLIC OF TEXAS

March 17, 1836–October 22, 1836   David G. Burnet (president *ad interim*)

October 22, 1836–December 10, 1838   Sam Houston
December 10, 1838–December 13, 1841   Mirabeau B. Lamar
December 13, 1841–December 9, 1844   Sam Houston
December 9, 1844–February 19, 1846   Anson Jones

GOVERNORS SINCE ANNEXATION

February 19, 1846–December 21, 1847   J. Pinckney Henderson
December 21, 1847–December 21, 1849   George T. Wood
December 21, 1849–November 23, 1853   P. Hansborough Bell
November 23, 1853–December 21, 1853   J. W. Henderson
December 21, 1853–December 21, 1857   Elisha M. Pease
December 21, 1857–December 21, 1859   Hardin R. Runnels
December 21, 1859–March 16, 1861   Sam Houston
March 16, 1861–November 7, 1861   Edward Clark
November 7, 1861–November 5, 1863   Francis R. Lubbock
November 5, 1863–June 17, 1865   Pendleton Murrah
July 21, 1865–August 9, 1866   Andrew J. Hamilton (provisional)

August 9, 1866–August 8, 1867   James W. Throckmorton
August 8, 1867–September 30, 1869   Elisha M. Pease
January 8, 1870–January 15, 1874   Edmund J. Davis
January 15, 1874–December 1, 1876   Richard Coke
December 1, 1876–January 21, 1879   Richard B. Hubbard
January 21, 1879–January 16, 1883   Oran M. Roberts
January 16, 1883–January 18, 1887   John Ireland
January 18, 1887–January 20, 1891   Lawrence Sullivan Ross
January 20, 1891–January 15, 1895   James S. Hogg
January 15, 1895–January 17, 1899   Charles A. Culberson
January 17, 1899–January 20, 1903   Joseph D. Sayers
January 20, 1903–January 15, 1907   S. W. T. Lanham
January 15, 1907–January 19, 1911   Thomas M. Campbell
January 19, 1911–January 19, 1915   Oscar Branch Colquitt
January 19, 1915–August 25, 1917   James E. Ferguson
August 25, 1917–January 18, 1921   William P. Hobby
January 18, 1921–January 20, 1925   Pat M. Neff
January 20, 1925–January 17, 1927   Miriam A. Ferguson
January 17, 1927–January 20, 1931   Dan Moody
January 20, 1931–January 17, 1933   Ross S. Sterling
January 17, 1933–January 15, 1935   Miriam A. Ferguson
January 15, 1935–January 17, 1939   James V. Allred
January 17, 1939–August 4, 1941   W. Lee O'Daniel
August 4, 1941–January 21, 1947   Coke R. Stevenson
January 21, 1947–July 11, 1949   Beauford H. Jester (died)
July 11, 1949–January 15, 1957   Allan Shivers
January 15, 1957–January 15, 1963   Price Daniel
January 15, 1963–January 21, 1969   John B. Connally
January 21, 1969–   Preston Smith

445

Bibliography

GENERAL

ACUÑA, RUDOLPH. *The Story of the Mexican Americans: The Men and the Land.* New York: American Book Company, 1969.

ADAMS, ANDY. *The Log of a Cowboy.* 1927. Reprint. Lincoln: University of Nebraska Press, 1964.

ALTSHELER, JOSEPH A. *The Horsemen of the Plains.* New York: Macmillan, 1967.

ARBINGAST, STANLEY A.; KENNAMER, LORRIN G.; and BONINE, MICHAEL E. *Atlas of Texas.* Austin: Bureau of Business Research, The University of Texas, 1967.

BARKER, EUGENE C. *Mexico and Texas, 1821-1835.* 1928. Reprint. New York: Russell and Russell, 1965.

BARTLEY, ERNEST R. *The Tidelands Oil Controversy.* Austin: University of Texas Press, 1953.

BEDICHEK, ROY. *Adventures with a Texas Naturalist.* 1947. Reprint. Austin: University of Texas Press, 1961.

BENTON, WILBOURN E. *Texas: Its Government and Politics.* 2d ed. Englewood Cliffs: Prentice-Hall, 1966.

BILLINGTON, RAY. "How the Frontier Shaped American Character." *American Heritage,* April 1958, p. 4.

BLEGEN, THEODORE C. *Norwegian Migration to America, 1825-60.* 2 vols. New York: Haskell, 1969.

BURMA, JOHN H. *Spanish-speaking Groups in the United States.* Durham: Duke University Press, 1954.

BURTON, H. T. *History of the JA Ranch.* 1927. Reprint. Ann Arbor: University Microfilms, 1966.

CASTEL, ALBERT. "Sam Houston's Last Fight." *American Heritage,* December 1965, p. 80.

CATTON, BRUCE. "The Restless Decade." *American Heritage,* August 1965, p. 5.

CISNEROS, JOSÉ. *Los Chicanos, an Awakening People.* El Paso: Texas Western Press, 1970.

CLARK, JAMES A., and HALBOUTY, MICHEL T. *Spindletop.* New York: Random House, 1952.

CONNOR, SEYMOUR. *Adventure in Glory.* The Saga of Texas, edited by Seymour V. Connor, vol. 3. Austin: Steck-Vaughn Co., 1965.

DANIELS, JOSEPHUS. *The Wilson Era.* 2 vols. Chapel Hill: University of North Carolina, 1944, 1946.

DANIELS, WALTER M., ed. *American Indians.* New York: Wilson and Co., 1957.

DEGLER, CARL. "There Was Another South." *American Heritage,* August 1960, p. 52.

DOBIE, J. FRANK. *A Vaquero of the Brush Country.* Rev. ed. Boston: Little, Brown, 1960.

DUVAL, JOHN C. *Early Times in Texas.* 1892. Facsimile ed. Austin: Steck-Vaughn Co., 1935.

EATON, CLEMENT. "Everybody Liked Henry Clay." *American Heritage,* October 1956, p. 26.

EGGENHOFER, NICK. *Wagons, Mules and Men.* New York: Hastings, 1961.

FAULK, ODIE B. *A Successful Failure.* The Saga of Texas, edited by Seymour V. Connor, vol. 1. Austin: Steck-Vaughn Co., 1965.

FIERMAN, FLOYD S. *Some Early Jewish Settlers on the Southwestern Frontier.* El Paso: Texas Western Press, 1960.

FLEMING, THOMAS. "Goodbye to Everything." *American Heritage,* August 1965, p. 89.

GALLAGHER, ROBERT S. "Me for Ma—and I Ain't Got a Dern Thing Against Pa." *American Heritage,* October 1966, p. 46.

GARD, WAYNE. "How They Killed the Buffalo." *American Heritage,* August 1956, p. 34.

GEUE, CHESTER W., ed. *A New Land Beckoned: German Immigration to Texas, 1844-1847.* Waco: Texian Press, 1966.

GIBSON, CHARLES. *Spain in America.* New York: Harper and Row, 1966.

GRAVES, JOHN. *Goodbye to a River.* New York: Knopf, 1961.

GRAYSON, GARY T. "The Colonel's Folly and the President's Distress." *American Heritage,* October 1964, p. 4.

HAINES, FRANCIS. "How the Indian Got the Horse." *American Heritage,* February 1964, p. 16.

HALEY, J. EVETTS. *The XIT Ranch of Texas.* 1953. Reprint. Norman: University of Oklahoma Press, 1967.

HELLER, CELIA S. *Mexican American Youth: Forgotten Youth at the Crossroads.* New York: Random House, 1966.

HOGAN, WILLIAM R. *The Texas Republic: A Social and Economic History.* 1946. Rev. ed. Austin: University of Texas Press, 1969.

HORGAN, PAUL. *Great River: The Rio Grande in North American History.* Rev. ed. New York: Holt, Rinehart and Winston, 1960.

THE INSTITUTE OF TEXAN CULTURES has begun publication of *The Texians and the Texans,* a series of twenty soft-cover booklets telling the stories of the racial, national, and cultural groups who have contributed to the development of Texas. Titles already published include:
> *The German Texans*
> *The Indian Texans*
> *The Mexican Texans*
> *The Norwegian Texans*

Future publications will include the following groups: Spanish, Polish, Negro, Anglo-American, French, Lebanese, Greek, Danish, Dutch, Belgian, Japanese, Italian, Czech, Jewish, Swedish, Irish, Scottish, English, Wendish, Swiss, and Chinese.

INTER-AMERICAN INSTITUTE. *The Role of the Mexican American in the History of the Southwest.* Edinburg: Pan-American College, 1970.

JONES, BILLY MAC. *The Search for Maturity.* The Saga of Texas, edited by Seymour V. Connor, vol. 5. Austin: Steck-Vaughn Co., 1965.

JORDAN, TERRY G. *German Seed in Texas Soil: Immigrant Farmers in Nineteenth Century Texas.* Austin: University of Texas Press, 1966.

JOSEPHY, ALVIN. "These Lands Are Ours." *American Heritage,* August 1961, p. 14.

LEA, TOM. *The King Ranch*. 2 vols. Boston: Little, Brown, 1957.

LECKIE, WILLIAM H. *The Buffalo Soldiers: A Narrative of the Negro Cavalry in the West*. Norman: University of Oklahoma Press, 1967.

LORD, WALTER. *A Time To Stand*. New York: Harper and Row, 1961.

McCLESKY, CLIFTON. *The Government and Politics of Texas*. Boston: Little, Brown, 1966.

MacCORKLE, STUART A., and SMITH, DICK. *Texas Government*. 4th ed. New York: McGraw-Hill, 1960.

McKAY, SETH S., and FAULK, ODIE B. *Texas After Spindletop*. The Saga of Texas, edited by Seymour V. Connor, vol. 6. Austin: Steck-Vaughn Co., 1965.

MARTIN, ROSCOE C. *The People's Party in Texas*. Austin: University of Texas Press, 1970.

NAVA, JULIAN. *Mexican Americans: Past, Present, and Future*. New York: American Book Company, 1969.

NEWCOMB, W. W., JR. *The Indians of Texas*. Austin: University of Texas Press, 1969.

OWENS, WILLIAM. "Gusher at Spindletop." *American Heritage*, June 1958, p. 34.

PINCKNEY, PAULINE A. *Painting in Texas, The Nineteenth Century*. Austin: University of Texas Press, 1967.

PUSEY, MERLO. "FDR vs. the Supreme Court." *American Heritage*, April 1958, p. 24.

RAMSDELL, CHARLES. *Reconstruction in Texas*. Austin: University of Texas Press, 1970.

———. "The Storming of the Alamo." *American Heritage*, February 1961, p. 30.

RICHARDSON, RUPERT N. *Texas: the Lone Star State*. 3d ed. Englewood Cliffs: Prentice-Hall, 1969.

RIFKIND, ROBERT S. "The Colonel's Dream of Power." *American Heritage*, February 1959, p. 62.

SAUDEK, ROBERT. "Program Coming in Fine." *American Heritage*, August 1965, p. 24.

SCHLESINGER, ARTHUR M., JR. *A Thousand Days: John F. Kennedy in the White House*. Boston: Houghton Mifflin, 1965.

SIEGEL, STANLEY, ed. *Selected Readings in Texas History*. Berkeley: McCutchan, 1970.

SMITHWICK, NOAH. *The Evolution of a State, or Recollections of Old Texas Days*. 1900. Reprint. Austin: Steck-Vaughn Co., 1936.

SPRATT, JOHN. *The Road to Spindletop*. Austin: University of Texas Press, 1970.

STEEN, RALPH W. *The Texas News*. Austin: Steck-Vaughn Co., 1955.

———. *Twentieth Century Texas: An Economic and Social History*. Austin: Steck-Vaughn Co., 1942.

THE TEXAS STATE HISTORICAL ASSOCIATION is involved with the publication of several items:

> *The Handbook of Texas*, ed. Webb, Walter P., and Carroll, H. Bailey. 2 vols., 1952. Vol. 3 in preparation.
> *The Southwestern Historical Quarterly*
> *The Texas Historian* (formerly *The Junior Historian*)

TUNIS, EDWIN. *Frontier Living.* New York: World Publishing Co., 1961.

VIGNESS, DAVID. *The Revolutionary Decades.* The Saga of Texas, edited by Seymour V. Connor, vol. 2. Austin: Steck-Vaughn Co., 1965.

WALLACE, ERNEST. *Texas in Turmoil.* The Saga of Texas, edited by Seymour V. Connor, vol. 4. Austin: Steck-Vaughn Co., 1965.

WALLACE, ERNEST, and VIGNESS, DAVID, eds. *Documents of Texas History.* Austin: Steck-Vaughn Co., 1963.

WEAVER, JOHN. "Bonus March." *American Heritage,* June 1963, p. 18.

WEBB, WALTER PRESCOTT. *The Great Plains.* Waltham: Ginn, 1959.

————. *The Texas Rangers.* Rev. ed. Austin: University of Texas Press, 1965.

WOLFF, LEON. "Black Jack's Mexican Goose Chase." *American Heritage,* June 1962, p. 22.

WOODWARD, C. VANN. "The Birth of Jim Crow." *American Heritage,* April 1964, p. 52.

YOAKUM, HENDERSON. *History of Texas.* 2 vols. 1855. Reprint (2 vols. in 1). Austin: Steck-Vaughn Co., 1953.

ZAMORA, JULIAN. *La Raza: Forgotten Americans.* Notre Dame: University of Notre Dame Press, 1966.

BIOGRAPHICAL

BARKER, EUGENE C. *The Life of Stephen F. Austin.* 1925. Reprint. Austin: University of Texas Press, 1969.

BRANCH, HETTYE W. *The Story of "80 John."* New York: Greenwich Book Publishers, 1960.

BREWER, J. MASON. *Negro Legislators of Texas.* Rev. ed. Austin: Pemberton Press, 1970.

CLARK, JAMES A., and HART, WELDON. *The Tactful Texan: A Biography of Governor Will Hobby.* New York: Random House, 1958.

COTNER, ROBERT C. *James Stephen Hogg.* Austin: University of Texas Press, 1959.

CRAWFORD, ANN FEARS. *The Eagle.* Austin: Pemberton Press, 1966.

DAWSON, JOSEPH MARTIN. *José Antonio Navarro, Co-Creator of Texas.* Waco: Baylor University Press, 1969.

DOBIE, J. FRANK. *John C. Duval: First Texas Man of Letters.* 2d ed. Dallas: Southern Methodist University Press, 1965.

DUGGER, RONNIE, ed. *Three Men in Texas: Bedichek, Webb, and Dobie.* Austin: University of Texas Press, 1967.

DURHAM, PHILIP, and JONES, EVERETT L. *The Adventures of the Negro Cowboys.* New York: Dodd, Mead, 1966.

FARROW, MARION HUMPHREYS. *The Texas Democrats.* San Antonio: Naylor, 1944.

FISHEL, LESLIE H., JR., and QUARLES, BENJAMIN, eds. *The Black American: A Documentary History.* Rev. ed. New York: Morrow, 1970.

FRIEND, LLERENA B. *Sam Houston: The Great Designer.* Austin: University of Texas Press, 1969.

HALEY, J. EVETTS. *Charles Goodnight.* 1949. Reprint. Norman: University of Oklahoma Press, 1968.

————. *George W. Littlefield.* Norman: University of Oklahoma Press, 1943.

HARE, MAUDE C. *Norris Wright Cuney.* 1913. Facsimile ed. Austin: Steck-Vaughn Co., 1968.

HARRITY, RICHARD, and MARTIN, RALPH G. *The Human Side of F.D.R.* New York: Duell, 1960.

HENDERSON, RICHARD B. *Maury Maverick: A Political Biography.* Austin: University of Texas Press, 1970.

JAMES, MARQUIS. *The Raven.* Dunwoody: Berg, 1968.

KING, IRENE M. *John O. Meusebach, German Colonizer in Texas.* Austin: University of Texas Press, 1967.

LAY, BEIRNIE, JR. *Someone Has To Make It Happen.* Englewood Cliffs: Prentice-Hall, 1969.

LOMAX, JOHN. *Will Hogg, Texan.* Austin: University of Texas Press, 1956.

PHILLIPS, CABELL. *The Truman Presidency.* New York: Macmillan, 1966.

PREECE, HAROLD. *Lone Star Man.* New York: Hastings, 1960.

RICHARDSON, RUPERT N. et al. *Heroes of Texas.* Waco: Texian Press, 1964.

SHUFFLER, R. HENDERSON. *The Houstons at Independence.* Waco: Texian Press, 1966.

SORENSON, THEODORE. *Kennedy.* New York: Harper and Row, 1965.

TUMULTY, JOSEPH. *Woodrow Wilson as I Know Him.* New York: Doubleday, 1921.

WHITE, WILLIAM S. *The Professional: Lyndon B. Johnson.* Boston: Houghton Mifflin, 1964.

Index

In this Index, *m* indicates a reference to a map;
p indicates a reference to a picture.

451

452

454

East Texas Field, *m* 200, 204, 205, 296

East Texas Normal College, 258

Eberly, Mrs. Angelina, 79, 82

Economic Opportunity Act, 406

Economy, 299-301, 304, 309, 312-14, 318, 327; changes in, 1900-1929, 285-86; chapter on, 1850-1920, 211-23; during depression, 293-96; during World War II, 349-50; following World War II, 353-54; impact of space race on, 390-92; of nation during 1960s, 410; of Texas during 1950s, 377-79; of Texas during 1960s, 419-20

Education, 182-83, 242; adult, 416; federal aid to, 401, 409; higher, 89, 179-83, 415; impact of Servicemen's Readjustment Act on, 354-55; influence of space race on, 390-91; law enforcement, 421-22; modernization of, 370-74; Negro, 128, 181-82, 184-85, 369-70; professional, 183-85; in the Republic, 76; rural schools, *p* 273; sources of revenue, 373, 374; special, 415-16; state aid to, 257, 268, 273, 371-74; technical, 416; vocational, 415-16

Edwards, Benjamin, 55, 56

Edwards, Haden, 55, 56

Edwards Plateau, *m* 13, 14, 271

Eggers, Paul, 425

Eighteenth Amendment, 237, 322, 336

Eisenhower, Dwight D., 300, 310, 351, 369, 382, 383, 384, 390, 398, 409

El Campo, *p* 160, 165

Election: of 1836, 72; of 1844, 95; of 1857, 116-17; of 1859, 117; of 1869, 129; of 1873, 130; of 1906, 233; of 1910, 235; of 1912, 244-45; of 1914, 256-57; of 1916, 255, 259; of 1918, 268; of 1920, 272; of 1924, 277-79; of 1926, 281-82; of 1928, 291-93; of 1930, 295; of 1932, 298-99; of 1934, 315; of 1936, 314; of 1938, 331-33; of 1940, 334-35, 360; special, of 1941, 336-37; of 1942, 337; of 1944, 360-61; of 1946, 362; of 1948, 363-66; of 1952, 382; of 1954, 386-87; of 1956, 387, 398; special, of 1957, 398; of 1958, 398; of 1960, 399, 401; special, of 1961, 399; of 1964, 408; of 1968, 425

Electra Field, *m* 200, 201

Elementary and Secondary Education Act of 1965, 409

El Paso, 107, 136, 152, 163, 220, 221, 249, 250, 251, 264, 348, 403, 407, 413, 427

Emancipation Proclamation, 125

Eng, Mary, 312

Erath, George B., 52

Ernst, Frederick, 4, 80

Ervendberg, Louis, 89

Esteban, 3, 24, 25

Ethnic groups: Anglo-American, 38, 41-44, 50, 51, 52, 62-63, 145-46; Austrian, 5, 52, 198; Belgian, 6; Chinese, 6, 164, 251-52, 310, 426; Czech, 5, 108, 120, 183, 264, 265; Danish, 5, 165, 221; Dutch, 4-5, 82, 189; English, 3, 50, 82, 83, 146-47, 155; French, 26-27, 40, 50, 81, 84, 103-5, 120, 148, 156, 188, 264-65; German, 4, 37, 50, 52, 80-81, 84, 89, 104-7, 120, 155, 156, 187, 347, 426; Greek, 6, 163-64, 310, 348; Irish, 3, 37, 44, 50, 82, 84, 147-48, 154-55, 189; Italian, 6, 50, 189-90, 221, 312; Japanese, 6, 349; Jewish, 213, 220-21, 251, 287, 310; Lebanese, 6, 310-11; Mexican, 7-8, 43-44, 50, 58-59, 62, 84-85, 144, 152, 185-86; Mexican-American, 9, 123, 152, 190-91, 290-91, 347-48, 355-56, 398, 401-3, 424-25, 426, 427; Negro, 2-3, 37, 50, 53-54, 60, 64, 121, 125, 128-29, 137, 140, 144-45, 181-82, 184-85, 219-20, 250-51, 265, 287, 305-6, 307-8, 310, 311-12, 346, 368-70, 424; Norwegian, 5, 108-9, 289; Polish, 5, 50, 108, 120, 265; Scottish, 3-4, 50, 81, 228; Spanish, 2, 22-26, 31-37, 426; Swedish, 5, 81, 109, 148-49, 183, 203, 349; Swiss, 5-6, 81, 109, 149

Evans, Hiram Wesley, 275, 277

Expenditures, state, in 1968, 414-15

Eyth, Louis, 189

Fandango, 86, *p* 87

Fannin, James W., 3, 53, 63, 65

Farmers: organizations of, 168-73 (*See also* individual entries); problems of, 167-68; tenant, 167, 256, 314

Farmers' Alliance, 161, 170, 173, 225, 313

457

459

461

Peter, Joseph, Jr., 108
Petri, Friedrich Richard, 105
Petrolia Field, m 200, 201
Pierce, Abel H. ("Shanghai"), 146
Piñeda, Alonso Alvarez de, 24, 429
Pine Woods, 12-13, m 13, 213-15
Plainview, 308, 326
Pliska, John, 264
Plum Creek, Battle of, 76
Poage, W. R., 388
Political Association of Spanish-speaking Organizations (PASO), 401-2
Polk, James K., 95, 96, 98, 99, 100, 103
Poll tax, 231, 299, 332
Pollution Control Act, 389
Population: in 1834, 80; in 1845, 109; in 1860, 109; shift 1940-1950, 350; shift 1950-1960, 1960-1970, m 394; in 1960s, 393, 414; by county, 1970, m 434; urban population, m 434
Populist party, 170-72, 225, 226, 242, 313
Port Arthur, 27, 200, 347, 350
Porter, Katherine Anne, 305
Porter, William Sidney, 154, 192
Power, James, 44
Prairie View University, 181, 182, 251
Primary election: established, 232; importance, 232-33; white, 368-69
Prison system, 234, 242, 385, 422
Progressive party, 242, 244
Progressivism, 225-27, 233-38, 255
Prohibition, 233, 235-37, 259, 267, 268, 269, 273, 279, 292, 316, 322
Prohibitionist platform, 236
Prohibition party, 257
Provisional government, 61, 62
Public utilities, 215-16
Public Works Administration (PWA), 309
Punitive expedition, 250, 251, 265

Quakers, 150
Qualia, Frank, 221
Quivira, 1, 2, 10, 25

Radical Republicans, 126, 127
Railroads: abuses, 168; construction, 161-63; early, p 165, 165; effect on industry, 214; importance of, 216; in 1960s, 423

Rainey, Homer P., 362
Ranger Field, m 200, 202
Rayburn, Sam, 247, 298, 330, 360, 361, p 366, 366, 377, 388, 390, p 400, 400, 405
Reagan, John H., 125, 173, 174, 229
Reconstruction, 125-32, 241, 245, 399; congressional, 127-30; presidential, 126-27
Reconstruction Finance Corporation, 295
Redistricting, legislative, 385
Red River, 12, 18, 33, 37, 38, 76, 81, 143
Refugio, 44, 78
Reiersen, Johan Reinert, 108
Republican Army of the North, 39
Republican National Convention of 1952, 383
Republican party, strength of, in 1968, 425
Republic of Texas: agriculture, 83; architecture, 85; chapter on, 71-91; clothing, 85; Congress, 180, 381; culture, 86-88; education, 88-89; finances, 73-77, 78; food, 84; immigration, 79-83; life in, 83-89; problems of, 72, 77-78; trade and commerce, 52
Resaca de la Palma, Battle of, 99
Revenue Act of 1964, 406
Revenue, state, sources of in 1968, 414
Reverchon, Julien, 104
Revolution of 1848, 105, 108
Rice farming, 12; Japanese influence on, 6
Rice University, 288, 391, 392
Rickard, George L. ("Tex"), 287, 293
Right-to-work law, 363
Rio Grande, 12, 14, 15, 24, 32, 34, 37, 68, 78, 98, 99, 100, 102, 104, 152, 242, 249, 407, 408
Rio Grande Valley, 290, 424
Risien, E. E., 147
Rivera, Diego, 305
Roads, early, 218
Roaring Twenties, the, 272-77
Roberts, Meshack, 125
Robertson, Felix O., 277
Robertson Insurance Law, 234
Robertson, Sterling C., 43
Roberts, Oran M., 119, 127, 174-75, 180, 187-88
Robinson, Joseph, 292

464

465

Utopian colonies, 104. *See also* individual entries
Uvalde, 247, 263, 297, 308, 335, 404, p 412

Valencia, F., 291
Vale, Robert L., 402
Van Buren, Martin, 63, 94, 95
Vandricourt, A. de, 156
Vehlein, Joseph, 44, 52
Versailles Peace Conference, 246, 266
Veterans Land Board scandal, 387
Viana, Francisco, 39
Victoria, 8, 44, 65, 76, 220, 371
Victoria, Guadalupe, 44, 55
Victor, Prince of Leiningen, 80
Viesca, Agustín, 58
Vietnam, war in, 393, 406, 409, 410
Villa, Francisco ("Pancho"), p 249, 249-50, 252
Vince's Bridge, 67
Vinson, Robert, 261
Viva Kennedy clubs, 401
Vocational Education Act of 1963, 416
Volstead Act, 292, 299
Volunteers in Service to America (VISTA), 406
Von Behr, Ottomar, 107
Von Roemer, Ferdinand, 4, 86
Voting Rights Act of 1965, 407

Waco, 52, 143, 162, 212, 216, 219, 247, 264, 272, 307, 308, 311, 346, 388, 416
Waco Indians, 136
Waggoner, W. T., 201
Wagner, Robert F., 309
Wallace, Daniel Webster, 3, 144-45
Wallace, George, 425
Wallace, Henry, 335, 359
Wallace, W. A. A. ("Big Foot"), 99
Ward, Thomas William, 82
Warehouse Act, 248
War of 1812, 41
War on poverty, 406
Warren, Earl, 370
Wars. *See* individual entries
Washington, Booker T., 219
Washington-on-the-Brazos, 61, 65
Waskow, Henry, 347
Water management, need for, 388-90

Watershed Protection and Flood Prevention Act of 1954, 388
Waters-Pierce Oil Company, 224, 230, 231, 234, 235, 246
Weaver, James B., 171
Weaver, Robert, 409
Webb, Walter Prescott, 150, 306, 307, 397
Webster, Daniel, p 112, 115, 118
Weinert, R. A., 333
Welfare, public, in 1960s, 421
Western Trail, m 142, 143
Western Union Telegraph Company, 215
West Texas Agricultural and Mechanical College, 260
West Texas, settlement of, 166-67
West Texas State Normal School, 259
Wharton, John Austin, 121
Wharton, William H., 61, 65
White, Josh, 308
White, William Allen, 172
Wichita Falls, 201, 370, 399
Wichita Indians, 13, p 19, 20, 33
Wiess, Simon, 5
Wigfall, Louis T., 114
Wilbarger, J. W., 191
Wiley College, 125, 182
Wilkins, Roy, 401
Willard, Jess, 287
Williams, Benjamin Franklin, 128
Williamson, Robert McAlpin, 53
Williams, Samuel May, 52
Willkie, Wendell L., 335, 360
Wilmot Proviso, 114
Wilson, Woodrow, 82, 221, 222, p 240, 241, 243-48, p 245, 249, 250, 255, 257, 259, 262, 263, 266, 297, 303
Wister, Owen, 154
Woll, Adrian, 74, 78
Wolters, Jacob, 205, 243, 266, 274
Womack, O. T., 182
Woman's Army Corps, 346
Women's suffrage, 259, 267, 268
Wong, Howard, 426
Woodrow Wilson State Democratic League of Texas, 243
Works Projects Administration (WPA), 305
World's Columbian Exposition, 187
World War I, 237, 243, 251; airplanes in, 264; America in, 262-66; beginning of, 255-56; effects on Texas, 267; Negro troops in, 265; reaction to, in 1920s, 272

466

DATE DUE
